T5-ALR-747

Canadian Real Estate

Books by Richard Steacy

CANADIAN REAL ESTATE

LAND TITLES REGISTRATION IN CANADA AND THE USA

YOU CAN BEAT INFLATION WITH REAL ESTATE

STEACY'S PRACTICAL CANADIAN MORTGAGE GUIDE

LISTING AND SELLING REAL ESTATE IN CANADA

A PRACTICAL CANADIAN MORTGAGE GUIDE

Canadian Real Estate

EIGHTH EDITION

RICHARD STEACY
REVISED BY WALTER SARAFYN

First published by Real Estate Press in 1973

Eighth edition published in 1992 by
Stoddart Publishing Co. Limited
34 Lesmill Road
Toronto, Canada
M3B 2T6

No publication can keep up with the mortgage rates — the rates used in this book are a guide and an example only.

Canadian Cataloguing in Publication Data

Steacy, Richard, 1919-
Canadian real estate

8th ed.
ISBN 0-7737-2567-9

1. Real estate business — Canada. 2. Real estate investment — Canada. 3. Mortgages — Canada. I. Sarafyn, Walter. II. Title.

HD316.S74 1992 333.33′0971
C92-093264-9

Cover design: Brant Cowie/ArtPlus
Typesetting: Tony Gordon Ltd.

Printed in Canada

To my sons
Charles Richard Graham Steacy
William Harold Denham Steacy
and their mother, Mary,
my wife

Contents

Part Three: Buying

Part Four: Selling

Part Five: Leasing

Part Six: Last Words

Acknowledgments

The author sincerely thanks the following, and acknowledges their generous time and patience in helping with research:

Lorne S. Speck, staff director, membership services, Canadian Real Estate Association, for his preparation of the chapter "Metric Real Estate."

Mr. R. Ryan of the Mortgage Insurance Company of Canada, for preparing the chapter "The High-Ratio Mortgage."

The State Farm Insurance Companies for its permission to use the material in the chapter "A Comparative Guide for Househunters," which is an excerpt from its publication "Finding the Right Home for You."

Mr. John Marsh, a leading hotel broker in Toronto, for his help preparing the chapter "Buying a Hotel."

Robert Yeanma, a leading Canadian mathematician, who was a great help on the subject of interest and mortgage schedules.

Mr. Robert Lajoie, Canada Mortgage and Housing Corporation, for carefully reviewing CMHC writing.

The Insurance Institute of Ontario for the advice in the chapter "Property Insurance."

The advice contained in the chapter "Condominium Ownership" is taken from extracts from "Home Ownership through Condominium" published by Canada Mortgage and Housing Corporation, Ottawa.

Preface

The United States purchased one million square miles of very prime land from France for about two-and-a-half cents an acre. What a deal! Of course, the Louisiana purchase was made in 1803, but it still sounds cheap to me.

Then, in 1867, the US purchased 570,000 square miles of real property from Russia for about two cents an acre. The Alaska Purchase was another hot deal for Uncle Sam; today's oil reserves up there are worth billions. If Britain had made that deal with Russia, all that vast area would now be a part of Canada.

But, alas, Russia and Britain had been shooting at each other in the Crimean Peninsula and Russia wasn't ready for such overtures.

In 1953, the City of New York bought a 3 1/2 acre parcel of land near the southwest corner of Central Park for $2 million, US. Three decades later, this same land was sold for US$456 million, an increase of 22,700%.

From $13 to $3,000 per square foot!

I remember renting a nice six-room brick home for less than $50 a month in 1952. And I rented rooms in Toronto for $10 a week during the sixties.

The rent you pay today for a six-room house is the rent you will pay for a single room 35 years from now.

A good detached brick home could be purchased in the sixties for much less than $20,000.

Know why I'm telling you all this? The late Will Rogers said it all when he advised one and all, "Buy land — they're not making any more of it."

I would like everyone who can afford it, to take some money out of the bank and buy some real estate. If you already own some, buy some more!

To the majority of single persons, apartment living is the way to do it. I don't agree. Singles who have lived in an apartment for the last few years would be much much better off financially if they had purchased a home. Look at the roaring increase in the cost of housing during those years — but it is not too late! There is absolutely no point in looking back and saying, "If I had only . . . " Look ahead.

When I read about couples who say they just can't afford a home, despite the fact that they have substantial incomes, it is enough to make me shudder. What they are really saying is that they don't want the responsibility of owning a home and the debt structure that goes with it.

What do they do with the money? Purchase fancy cars, exotic holidays, jazzy clothes? Sure, we would all like a touch of that, but homeowners have their feet on the ground — their ground.

If a person under forty doesn't own a home, where is he or she going to live at 65 or 70? In the poorhouse? They have fancier words for such places now, but it is still the poorhouse.

In many cases it is the poor taxpayer who is footing the bills because old so-and-so liked the good life and he ran out of money and steam at the end of the line, with nowhere to hang his hat.

Don't let that happen to you. If you don't own a house, *buy one*. Go right out and do it. If you can afford a new car, you can afford to buy a house.

You won't have to live in it if you don't want to. Rent it. The rental income from today's house can be about 8% of its value. A house worth $190,000 can rent for about $1,267 a month — 8% of its value.

The costs in mortgage differential and taxes will be offset and overcome by the increasing value of the house. I don't have to remind you about the staggering increase in house prices during the past few years.

If you buy and sell a house without living in it, the net profit of the sale will be taxed at capital gain rates and not at income tax rates. The financial gain during the period of your own occupancy will be tax free.

The mortgage debt even protects against inflation. One borrows healthy dollars this year, and repays the debt with cheaper, depreciated dollars later. The mortgage repayment will be cheaper and cheaper as time goes by; today's dollar would be worth 61 cents in ten years with a 5% annual inflation rate . . . Buy a house and ten years from now you'll be well on the road to financial independence when you are one of our "senior citizens."

There are tens of thousands of retired couples living in small houses they paid for over a period of about 25 years. All paid for now, so they don't have to go begging for a place to live. The provincial and federal allowances keep bread on the table, the taxes paid, the house heated and something for self respect. Where would these old couples be today without their homes? Why, we wouldn't be able to keep up with the demand for subsidized housing. It is not only good economics, it is good citizenship.

So you be independent. Get out there and do yourself a favor — buy a house. If you already own your own home, then buy some land. Even an acre or two in the country.

How could Grampa know, when he planted that black walnut tree 50 years ago, that a tree buyer would offer the present owner $20,000 for it? *Twenty thousand dollars* for one tree!

There are about 80,000 real estate agents in Canada. In buying, selling, leasing and mortgaging, these agents should be able to take care of themselves. But what about the 25,000,000 Canadians who are not real estate agents?

A good method of providing yourself with additional real estate ammunition is to read about it. This book will provide you with helpful information in one volume that would take weeks of research to find (if you knew where to look). It will describe short cuts, things you never thought about, pitfalls to avoid, hints on making money, saving money, and using it wisely, and ideas for establishing a firm foothold in the greatest money-making business in the world — *Real Estate.*

When you lend money to a bank or trust company, with a modest return to you in the form of interest, the borrower uses your money to lend it to somebody else at a higher rate of interest, and that somebody else uses your money to make more money.

A great deal of this money is used to finance real estate, so instead of lending your money to A to lend it to B to use it to make *his* pile in real estate, eliminate the middleman and *get a piece of the action yourself.*

Richard Steacy

PART ONE

LAND AND MONEY

1

IN THE BEGINNING

The first man known to plant a flag on what is now North American land was an Italian from Venice, popularly known as John Cabot, in the year 1497. He was sponsored by King Henry VII of Great Britain, so the land claims Cabot made were on behalf of the British.

Before 1600 there was no set way of spelling proper names, and one may find in contemporary documents several variant spellings of the same name. It is therefore difficult to state what was the correct, original spelling of Cabot. The librarian of the British House of Lords gives us Cabote, Cabotto, Shabot and Cabot, but however we spell the man's name, he was the one who did it.

The land Cabot discovered didn't look very inviting: too many rocks and trees, but the fishing was something else. Cod fish by the millions; just dip down a basket and scoop them in. When word got back to England about the excellent fishing off North America, commercial fishermen got onto a good thing, traffic started, and business boomed.

So we can thank an Italian and the cod fish for generating the initial rush of interest in this land of ours.

Thirty-seven years later (1534) the King of France got into the act and he sent Jacques Cartier over, who made his own claims for France.

In establishing the British and French colonies, settlers were recruited and land holdings in North America began. The French gave large tracts of land to seigneurs, who in turn broke it in parcels and granted rights to individuals, who in turn paid the seigneurs farm produce, or money, for this favor. The British land grants were outright grants, and the grantees owned them, whether they obtained them by paying for them or not.

For more than two hundred years there was a great amount of territory being captured, recaptured and ceded between the British and the French, who finally ended it with the Treaty of Paris in 1763, which ended the Seven Years' War.

Under the terms of this Treaty, France agreed to cede Canada on condition that Britain guaranteed the inhabitants the right to practice the Catholic religion according to the Roman rite. King George III agreed to this insofar as the laws of Great Britain allowed, and the one chapter in twenty-five of the Treaty of Paris that dealt exclusively with Canada saw Louis XV cede to Britain all French territory as far as the western plains.

The inhabitants could choose to leave the country within 18 months, during which time they could sell their property to British subjects, or they could stay, becoming subjects of Great Britain.

The King issued a Proclamation, imposing English criminal and civil law on the inhabitants of New France.

The inhabitants, accustomed to French law, were most unhappy about this, and after much representation to George III, the *Quebec Act* (1774) established the Province of Quebec, an area that included part of what is now Ontario, and provided for a Governor and Legislative Council with rights to make ordinances.

The *Quebec Act* revoked the Proclamation of 1763, insofar as it concerned civil rights and property, and re-established the French law as it existed before the proclamation. It provided for the continuance of the criminal law of England, as introduced by the Proclamation.

When war broke out between Britain and her American colonies, a large number of British subjects emigrated to the Province of Quebec. They settled chiefly in the western part of the province, along the banks of the St. Lawrence River and around lakes Erie and Ontario. Serious complaints were made by the new British settlers about the state of affairs in the province of Quebec, and a demand was made for a new constitution.

The result was the *Constitutional Act* (1791) which separated the Province of Quebec into Upper Canada and Lower Canada, each having its own Governor, Legislative Council and Assembly.

English common law was introduced in Upper Canada in 1792, by its first statute, the *Property and Civil Rights Act*, which stated that the area had been settled principally by British subjects, who were unaccustomed to French law, and repealed the provisions of the

Quebec Act regarding civil rights and property, replacing them with English law.

Under the *Constitutional Act,* Lower Canada retained its French law of real property, except that grantees would be entitled to grants in free tenure if they wished. (Feudal rights and duties were abolished in 1851.)

Conflict ensued between the English and the French. Rebellion broke out in 1837 and the Constitution of Lower Canada was suspended. A High Commissioner was appointed to adjust the relations and government of the two provinces.

The result of this was the *Union Act* (1840) which united Upper Canada and Lower Canada into the single Province of Canada.

French civil law continued in the area of the former Lower Canada and English common law continued in the area of the former Upper Canada. English criminal law was in force over all.

The British North America Act of 1867 was an act to unite the provinces of Canada, Nova Scotia and New Brunswick. Three provinces went into the BNA Act and four came out of it: the Province of Canada became two provinces — Ontario and Quebec.

The newly formed Dominion of Canada's motto was "From Sea to Sea," which wasn't fulfilled until British Columbia joined in 1871, after being promised a railway, which it got. So from sea to sea, our great country began.

Canada is the second-largest country in the world, with an area of nearly ten million square kilometres. About 7% of the land is economically viable for farming, which means that on paper we have 700,000 square kilometres of workable land for 25,000,000 people, or about 36 square kilometres each. Which sounds great until we see the population crowded into urban centers. Do you know that we have inhabitants who have never seen a *cow*?

So we have a land of vast population contrasts. Some people have so much land they need a telescope or an airplane to give it the once-over, while others are so crowded they can't stand the proximity of their neighbors.

The prime objective of this book is to get you involved in some of this land of ours, to own some of it. If I can accomplish this, my writing has been worthwhile.

Don't let me down.

2

LAND TENANCY

Land is considered to be permanent. Real. So we have an estate that is real. Real Estate.

Real estate is landed property, and landed property is land. So "real estate" only refers to land.

Put a building on the land, and we have real property, which includes the land *and* the building.

Terminate *real property* and we have *realty*.

Land, generally speaking, is held by the Crown-in-Right of the Provinces in Canada. Reference to this will be found in Section 109 of the *British North America Act* of 1867. When we hold land, we do so subject to the rights of the Crown, and this is why expressions such as the following include the word "tenant."

Tenant in Fee Simple: Fee — from the feudal term fief (tenure of land subject to feudal obligations). The feudal system was in effect in Europe during the Middle Ages, based on the holding of land in return for services to a lord by a vassal. Simple — unaffected. Therefore, this is real estate in its most untrammelled sense. It is an estate granted absolutely to a person and his heirs, forever.

Joint Tenancy: There are four unities here:

a) Unity of Possession: Each entitled to undivided possession of the whole of the property, and none holds any part separately to the exclusion of the others.
b) Unity of Time: The interest of each joint tenant must vest at the same time.
c) Unity of Title: Each person must obtain title under the same instrument.
d) Unity of Interest: The interest of each is identical. Joint tenancy is land ownership by two or more persons. If one person dies, his

interest in the estate passes to the survivors(s). Joint tenancy can be severed and turned into a tenancy in common.

Tenancy in Common: There is just one unity here, and that is the unity of possession. It is ownership by two or more persons, but if one of them dies, his share passes to his *estate*, and *not* to the survivor(s) of the tenancy.

Historically, all land was owned by the King, who in turn granted it to his nobles. The land owner kept the proof of ownership in his own possession, from the time of the original grant from the King, or patent from the Crown. When he sold or mortgaged, he handed over all the documents.

In the early 1700s, registry offices were set up in counties in Britain. The documents themselves were not registered, but a note or memorandum was registered. These were registered alphabetically under the owner's or mortgagee's name, a system which was found to be most unwieldy.

Canadian land registry offices were established under authority of Upper Canada Statute 35, George III, Chapter 5, passed August 10, 1795, and entitled "An Act for the public registering of deeds, conveyances, wills and other incumbrances which shall be made, or may affect, any lands, testaments or hereditaments within this Province."

The alphabetical system was changed in most parts of Canada before Confederation, when abstract books were set up as we know them today, and documents themselves were registered against lots and plans.

Registration of a deed in a registry office does not necessarily imply absolute ownership. Competent persons can examine documents registered, or "search title," and give an opinion as to status of title. Although the opinion may be considered reliable, it may be quite impossible to state definitely that the title is clear.

Recognizing this, a government guaranteed system of registration was introduced in parts of Canada in 1885, known as "Land Titles," or the "Torrens System," a history which is covered in the next chapter.

Real estate in the province of Quebec is handled a little differently from the rest of Canada. All lands in Quebec, generally speaking, are held under free tenures. The owner of land holds it as absolutely as it is possible for anyone to hold it, and can dispose of it freely.

The owner may be an individual, or a group of individuals owning in equal or unequal shares, or a legal entity such as a corporation.

In all of Canada, with the exception of Quebec, a real estate purchase and sale, and conveyancing, will be handled for you by a lawyer.

In Quebec, it will be handled by a legal practitioner known as a Notary, whose chief duty is to draw up and execute deeds and contracts. A Barrister or Solicitor in Quebec is not allowed to do this, just the Notary. Which makes it easy to find a good real estate lawyer!

An interesting way to spend an afternoon is to do a bit of "title searching" in a registry office or land titles office. Trace the history of your own property, and all the ownership and encumbrances before you came along. It is most enlightening.

NOTE: In British Columbia a notary is also authorized to do real property conveyancing.

3

LAND TITLES REGISTRATION

Land registration systems are very ancient, and probably go back to Babylonian days. They were common in medieval Europe, but before the middle of the last century there was no system of land registration anywhere in the world which included all the desirable features of the "Torrens" or Land Titles system of registration.

If property is registered under the Land Titles system, the title is guaranteed by the provincial government, and in Canada, what better guarantee could there be?

All property ownership in Alberta and Saskatchewan is registered under Land Titles, and in most of British Columbia and Manitoba. In Ontario, land titles were made available as far back as 1885 in the County of York, and later all the northern districts and many other countries were added. The remainder of our provinces do not use the system.

Compared with registry office systems, land titles transfers have no complicated covenants as in deeds. The whole title, and everything to which it is subject, is contained in a single page. Long descriptions are not required. The system saves a great deal of time in "searching title," because everything is on one page and the search can be done in a few minutes.

There can be no adverse possession (squatter's rights) under land titles, which does happen in the registry system.

The Land Titles system originated with Sir Robert Richard Torrens, former Premier of South Australia, Collector of Customs, and Registrar-General of Deeds.

One of the most controversial figures in South Australian history, Torrens was elected as one of the members for Adelaide, and became Treasurer. In 1857 he formed a Cabinet himself, but was Premier for only a month.

So much property was passing so quickly to so many new settlers in the early days of South Australia that the old English conveyancing laws could not cope with the situation. Bitter agitation among the settlers led to the formation of an active committee, in an endeavor to evolve a more simple, secure, and less costly method of obtaining title to property.

Torrens conceived the idea of applying the simple method of registration of shipping to the registration of land, and thereby setting up a simple straightforward method of procedure in dealing with land. He was the author of the *Real Property Act*, an act to simplify the laws relating to the transfer and encumbrance of freehold and other interest in land. It was assented to on January 27, 1858, and took effect on July 1st of the same year.

Torrens became the first Registrar-General under the Act, and was promptly vilified by the press and legal profession who opposed the measure. The lawyers adopted every device possible to render the Act ineffective and advised their clients not to deal in any land which was under the Act.

Lawyers objected to the Act because it was too simple — and apparently would cost them dearly in lost legal fees.

Even the Bench showed a very critical attitude towards the Act years after Torrens had won the battle. In 1874 Mr. Justice Gwynne said of certain sections: "I would countenance this simple system (if anything so crude, so ill-conceived, clumsily executed, and unscientific can be called a system) and accept it with all its sins against the science of jurisprudence, contenting ourselves with the reflection that it is cheap and simple and sufficient for the general purpose of the colonists. . . . In my opinion the *Real Property Act*, as it stands at present, is a scandal on the legislation of the Colony."

Despite the objections of the legal fraternity, within 16 years the principles of the *South Australian Act* were being used by all the Australian states and New Zealand. Later, it spread to many parts of the world (about 60 countries) and to many States in the US. The "Torrens system" has been described as South Australia's greatest export.

The system removes all risk from defective deeds by stipulating that the ownership of the person whose name shows in the register book shall be paramount. Registration makes his ownership conclusive. It cannot be forfeited. A person deprived of land through the operation of the system does not suffer loss, and, if he is the victim of fraud, he can recover possession of his land.

If an innocent third party has become registered as proprietor, the victim can proceed against the wrongdoer, not for the land, but for pecuniary damages, as the third party's title will be indefeasible. If that action fails, the victim can recover compensation from the provincial government.

The original Act was extensive, containing no less than 50 pages, and because of a man named Torrens, millions of people the world over sleep just a little more soundly.

Before Torrens departed for England in 1862, he was given an address signed by 10,000 citizens of Adelaide, and in 1864 petitions were made to both Houses of Parliament, signed by 14,000 people, praying that his services be recognized.

He was elected to the House of Commons for Cambridge in 1865, and received the KCMG in 1872. He was advanced to the GCMG in 1884, the year of his death.

LAND TITLES IN CANADA

The Yukon Territory:	The *Canada Land Titles Act* (Revised Statues of Canada 1970, Chapter L-4) applies to the Yukon Territory, and it is a Torrens system.
The Northwest Territories:	The Northwest Territories land registration system is purely Torrens.
British Columbia:	With the exception of certain Crown lands, and a very small percentage of complicated titles, all lands are under the Torrens system.
Alberta:	The province of Alberta was part of the North West Territories and became subject to the *Territories Real Property Act 1886*, Statutes of Canada, Chapter 26. This Act appears to be

the oldest Torrens Act in Canada. It was followed by the *Land Titles Act 1894,* Statutes of Canada, Chapter 28.

When the Province of Alberta was formed by the *Alberta Act* 1905, Statutes of Canada, Chapter 3, it took over the Torrens offices created by the *Territories Real Property Act 1886*, and the two Torrens Land Titles offices in Calgary and Edmonton.

Alberta passed its own *Land Titles Act* by 1906, the Statutes of Alberta, Chapter 24.

Any land conveyed or granted prior to 1886 has been completely brought under the Torrens system. At the present time 100% of the land in Alberta is under the Torrens system.

Saskatchewan:

All land in Saskatchewan is based on the Torrens system. This does not mean that all land in Saskatchewan has been brought under the Land Titles Act so there is a certificate of title for all Saskatchewan land, but means that if any land in Saskatchewan is ever dealt with, it will be brought under the Act upon the registration of any transfer or grant from the Crown, etc.

About one-half of the land in Saskatchewan has been brought under the *Land Titles Act*, and approximately one-half is still owned by Her Majesty the Queen in the Right of Saskatchewan.

Manitoba:

No accurate survey of all of the Land Titles Offices in Manitoba has ever been made to determine the proportions of land area of land holdings as divided between the two registration systems. The estimate is that over 85% of the settled land area in the province and perhaps 95% of individual land holdings are under the Torrens system.

Ontario: The Land Titles Act governs all land granted in the North after 1887.

In the South, the introduction of the Land Titles System into specific areas has been left throughout most of the past to the initiative of local authorities — the councils of counties, towns and cities. This power to take the initiative has been shifted to the provincial government. Once the system is introduced into an area, an owner may apply to have his land so registered.

The Ontario Law Reform Commission recorded a reasonable estimate has been made that there are about 2,200,000 parcels of land in Ontario, of which 15% are governed by the Land Titles system.

Quebec: No reference.

New Brunswick, Nova Scotia, Prince Edward Island: The Land Registry and Information Service, a project created by the Council of Maritime Premiers, is presently at work on a land survey and primary work leading to a Land Titles system. This project is jointly funded by the federal and provincial governments, and is scheduled to accomplish a Land Titles registration in the three provinces by 1997.

Newfoundland: Studies are being conducted into a federal-provincial program which may be available to Newfoundland. If implemented, it will probably result in the establishment of a satisfactory Land Titles system.

4

PROPERTY RIGHTS

Just what is this business of "property rights" that concerns so many of us?

In 1215, King John signed the *Great Charter*, and in it a most important chapter stated, among other things, that no free man shall be "disseized." That meant that no man shall have his property taken from him except by the lawful judgment of his peers and by the law of the land.

Sounds reasonable, but as you read English history you will see that monarchs for the next few hundred years had their own ideas about how to administer that new deal. It was not until parliament invited William of Orange to start a revolution that we began to get this matter of who's who straightened out.

In 1689, at the end of the Glorious Revolution in England (so named because it was bloodless), the balance of power between king and parliament tipped in favor of the latter. No king or queen since has ever tried to rule in defiance of parliament.

John Locke's classic *Treatise on Government* was then effectively adopted by parliament as its second Bible. In it, Locke proposed two principles: That men set up government to preserve their property, and that they may change it if and when it fails to do so.

Now we come over here. When Sir John A. Macdonald and the boys drafted the *British North America Act* of 1867, here is how this was interpreted: The Act said that all of Canada is held by the Crown in "right of the provinces," which meant that any time the government wants our land, it gets it. How much we get for it is something else.

This means that we all effectively are tenants of the Crown. That's why we find the word in the way we hold our land, viz: "tenants in common" and "tenant in fee simple," etc.

I like the idea of "allodial" landholding, but it's a pipe dream. The word "allodial" means real estate held in absolute independence, without acknowledgment to a superior. Of course, this would be impossible, because although we elect our government, it remains our superior — like it or not.

If we don't like the government, we can change it. But if we do, the next one will retain the right to grab our land, and I cannot argue with that very much.

It would not make much sense to hold land in defiance of the needs of government. We certainly wouldn't have many highways if farmers could say that they won't allow roads to go through their properties, would we? It is not the taking of our land for the public good that bothers people so much; it is the way governments go about it that is so upsetting, and the price land owners receive for their property.

So let's call a spade a spade. It is that last bit, the price, that really concerns us. Give us a handsome price for our land, and take it. With very few exceptions, I have found this to be true.

Oh, I know, there are some who just absolutely won't move until hell freezes over — and not even then; they have their own reasons, and good luck to them. But the majority of us will take the big price and laugh all the way to the bank.

There are other things that annoy us, such as lowering the value of land with greenbelts, and rezoning, which can annoy neighbors who find themselves next to odors and buildings they don't like. But most of these problems can be solved with compensation — which means money.

Is this what property rights boils down to — dollars and cents? It certain looks like it to me.

The ownership of property has many benefits. It provides security and independence, builds equity, maintains a hedge against inflation, and even provides enjoyment. For these and other reasons Canadians have always strived for property ownership. Our Common Law as it is administered by the provinces generally presumes a right to ownership of property, although this right is not written into law. The Civil Code of Quebec, on the other hand, takes the view that in order for one to have a right that right must be written into law, and limits to that right must also be written.

In 1982 both the Canadian and the Ontario Real Estate Associations began lobbying the government to have the right of Canadians to own property recognized and written into the Constitution and have the civil law define the limits to those rights.

5

EXPROPRIATION (As Practiced in Ontario)

Expropriation is the taking of land without the consent of the owner. It can be done by hundreds of bodies called "expropriating authorities," such as federal and provincial governments, municipalities, school boards, universities and hospitals.

It is done under something called "eminent domain" — the right to seize land and/or control its use.

When we are going to get the boot, we will be advised of the imminent action. We are informed personally and by advertising once a week for three straight weeks in a newspaper with general circulation in the landowner's area.

If we don't like the idea, we can ask for a hearing. This request must be made by registered mail, or personally, within 30 days of receiving notice of expropriation. An enquiry officer will then be appointed who will set a time and place.

At least five days before the date fixed for the hearing, we shall be served with a notice indicating the reasons for losing our land. We may then examine documents, including maps and plans, that our foe intends to use at the hearing.

One thing to be clear about is that at this hearing the price offered for our land will not be discussed. It is just to discuss the merits, for and against, the land grab. The hearing will not be bound by technical or legal rules of evidence.

The enquiry officer may recommend that a party to the hearing be paid costs not to exceed $200. The enquiry officer's report will be considered by the Ministry or other final approving authority. The expropriation will be approved, not approved, or approved with modification.

The approving authority shall give written reasons for its decision to all parties within 90 days of receiving the enquiry officer's report.

Now get this: Where a proposed expropriation has been approved, we may as well kiss our land goodbye. Within three months of approval, the expropriating authority registers a plan of our seized land, which it then owns. It doesn't matter if our great-grandparents cleared the land we enjoyed so much; never mind the memories.

We are legally bound to get lost. All we have left is the question of compensation.

How much? Just what does the land grabber think a fair price will be?

Governments say compensation is based on the market value of the property estimated by a Ministry appraiser based on what the land might realize on the open market.

It also says there is a provision for payment of other reasonable allowances such as legal and survey costs, relocation costs and inconvenience. Owner's appraisal costs are also considered.

After the appraisal, a property agent presents an offer of compensation based on the appraisal report.

We hope, says the government, that an agreement can be reached. How nice!

Governments can squander staggering sums of money on hare-brained schemes, but give them a chance to be fair to a citizen under these circumstances and they become the original Scrooge.

Here is what would be fair to all:

Have the property appraised for its fair market value by at least two independent, fully qualified appraisers.

Then double it.

Once expropriation has been approved, a plan of the seized land will normally be registered within three months, thereby depriving an owner of his land.

But the rights of Ontario Hydro under the *Power Corporation Act* are something else. The utility can register a "preliminary plan" against one's land, with or without local description.

The landowner may not know anything about this. He could innocently sell his land, make plans to move by buying another property and get bashed on the head when the buyer's lawyer discovers the preliminary plan upon searching title.

This preliminary plan has the same legal effect as a properly registered plan by an expropriating authority — thereby confirming the seizure — and no agreement about payment has been made. Here is what happens:

The expropriating authority may serve the landowner, within 30 days after the date of registration, with a notice of expropriation. You will note the law says the notice *may* be served, which means failure to serve it does not invalidate the expropriation. How's that for stacking a deck?

Now get this little gem. The owner who has lost his land has 30 days to serve notice on the expropriating authority that he does not agree with the price offered for his land. If this is not done, the owner shall be deemed to have agreed with the price.

Talk about living on a one-way street! The land grabber can ignore its 30-day requirement and blithely do it later, but not the landowner. If he doesn't comply within 30 days, he has had it.

Here is the basis of compensation, payable to one having land expropriated:

- The market value of the land;
- The damages attributable to disturbance;
- Damages for injurious affection;
- Any special difficulties in relocation.

The market value is the amount the land might be expected to realize if sold in the open market by a willing seller to a willing buyer.

The land grabber is a willing buyer all right, but a landowner under expropriation certainly cannot be said to be a willing seller. See how we get shafted?

In determining market value, no account shall be taken of any special use to which the expropriating authority will put the land. Now, this is downright insulting and most unfair. Consider this scenario:

A block of homeowners has been expropriated — kicked off their land. What if the expropriating authority erects a fine big building, thereby vastly increasing the value of the grabbed land?

The ones who lost the land will not get a sniff of the added value to the land. Why not, pray tell?

A homeowner losing his land will be paid an allowance of 5% of the market value of the lost land to compensate for inconvenience and the cost of finding another residence. There's also compensation for moving, legal and survey costs incurred in acquiring other premises.

A tenant occupying expropriated land can realize as much of the foregoing costs as is appropriate having regard to the length of the lease, the portion of term remaining and any rights to renew the tenancy, or even reasonable prospects of renewal.

Plus, of course, the extent of a tenant's investment in the land.

When a business is located on expropriated land, compensation will be paid for business losses resulting from the relocation of the business.

Unless the business owner and the expropriating authority otherwise agree, the business loss will not be determined until the business has moved and been in operation for six months, or until a three-year period has elapsed, whichever occurs first.

Payment for injurious affection includes the reduction in value of land remaining where only part of an owner's land is expropriated and possibly personal and business damages resulting from expropriation.

Claims for injurious affection must be made by the person suffering the damage or loss, in writing, within one year after damage was sustained, or after it became known to him.

If this isn't done, the right to compensation is forever barred.

Where no agreement for compensation has been made with an owner, the expropriating authority shall, within three months of registering a plan on title against the owner, and before taking possession of the land:

- Serve upon the registered owner an offer of an amount in full compensation for his interest;
- Provide a statement of the total compensation being offered for all interests in the land. This would exclude payment for business loss;
- Offer the owner immediate payment of 100% of the amount of the

market value of the owner's land as estimated by the expropriating authority.

Where there is no agreement about money, the statutory authority or the owner may serve notice of negotiation upon each other, stating that compensation is required to be negotiated.

When negotiation proceedings produce no satisfactory results, the whole matter will go to arbitration.

This means the end is in sight and both parties haul out their big guns with all the help they can get. If horns remained locked, with no winner, an appeal lies to the Divisional Court.

It is said we can be sure of death and taxes.

Add expropriation, because landowners can be sure of being kicked off their land — like it or not.

6

PROVIDING PROOF OF OWNERSHIP

Here is a summary of five basic means available to a property owner to reassure him of his rights to property.

1. If the property is registered in a land titles office, the title documents are guaranteed by the provincial government, and the office will provide the rightful owner with a certificate of title. This certificate is conclusive proof of ownership and is indefeasible.

   If an innocent third party has become registered as owner, the victim can proceed against the wrongdoer; not for land, but for pecuniary damages. If that action fails, the victim can recover compensation from the government.
2. If the property is registered in a registry office, in many areas the property owner can apply to the land titles office for a certificate of title, despite the fact that the property is not registered in the land titles office.

   For a prescribed fee, the director of titles will authorize a title search in the registry office, and, after a thorough investigation, if satisfied that the applicant does indeed own the property, will issue a certificate of title. This has the same protection and guarantee as though the property were registered in Land Titles, but with a time limitation.

   When one is "searching title" on this property in the future, it would be necessary only to go back in time until the date of the certificate of title. Everything registered after that would be subject to the same rules in registry; the strength of the registered documents standing on their own merits and not being guaranteed by the government.

3. In buying real estate, the purchaser's interest will be protected by a lawyer in the change of ownership.

   Although registration of documents in a registry office has no guarantee of validity as in a land titles office, a lawyer, upon completing his search and satisfying himself that there is a sound indication of title, will state this in writing to the purchaser on completion of the conveyance of title.

   Provincial statutes require this registry office search to be made through a number of years past: In Ontario, for example, a 40-year search will suffice.

   If registration is under Land Titles, the new owner will, of course, be provided with a certificate of title.
4. Commercial title insurance may be available to all property owners, mortgagees, and tenants.

   It is protection against financial loss through such defects as those arising from fraud, forgery, conveyances by minors or persons of unsound mind, demands of missing heirs, rights of divorced persons, errors in registration, etc.

   Under the terms of a title policy, if the title is attacked, the insurance company will defend it in court at its own expense and, if a loss is suffered, the insured will be protected. There are three types of policies available:

   Owner's Policy: Insures estates of ownership, occupancy and possession and remains in force as long as the insured or his heirs have any interest in the policy.

   Mortgagee Policy: Insures interests held by lenders as security for the payment of a debt. Liability is reduced as mortgage payments are made, and ends with the final payment of the debt.

   Leaseholder Policy: Protects a tenant against loss or damage sustained by reason of eviction or curtailment of his leasehold interest through title difficulties.
5. Adverse possession is something that probably would seldom occur to property owners in establishing rights to ownership.

   In Ontario, for example, the statute of limitation here is ten years — which means that simply occupying your own home continually and unopposed for ten years can be ample proof of your right to ownership.

This can also apply to an unbroken chain of ownership. For example, if you purchased a house from one who had occupied it continuously for seven years, and you, as the new owner, continued the unbroken chain of occupancy for three years, this would constitute your ten years' right of ownership, providing you had irrevocable proof of the former owner's occupancy, which could probably be established by obtaining a signed affidavit to this effect from the former owner.

7

UNDERSTANDING INTEREST

Hundreds of years ago loans were regarded as forms of help that one owed his neighbor in distress. To profit from the distress was considered to be evil and unjust.

The noun *usury* is from the Latin *usura*, meaning the "use" of something; borrowed capital for example. Usury was once defined as "where more is asked than is given," and was prohibited by the Church and State. It was considered to be a form of robbery. Collecting interest today is not considered to be robbery, but if the interest is excessive, it is considered to be usury.

It was gradually accepted that a loss could occur through lending — the Latin verb *intereo* means "to be lost" — interest was a loss, and the word interest gradually came to mean the compensation due to a creditor because of a loss incurred through lending. This loss was considered to be the difference between a lender's current position and that in which he would have stood if he had not made the loan.

In early times, loans were interest free, but incurred the penalty of interest if not repaid promptly. Lenders then saw the light and adopted the practice of charging interest from the beginning of the loan.

Today we have two types of interest: (a) simple, or fixed interest, and (b) compound interest.

If one borrows money and agrees to repay it plus 10% interest when the loan is repaid, the principal amount of the loan would be repaid plus the 10%, regardless of the repayment date. This is simple interest — interest on principal (the amount borrowed).

However, if one agreed to repay the loan at 10% interest *per annum* a loan is immediately created with compound interest, because if the loan is not repaid at the end of the year, the 10% interest due will be added to the indebtedness, and when the loan is repaid at a later date, interest will be paid on the new outstanding balance of the loan, which requires interest to be paid on interest.

Always remember that the more frequent the compounding, the greater the yield to the *lender.*

If the interest were compounded twice-yearly, or semi-annually, here is how it would look on $1,000 at 10%.

$$\begin{array}{lll} \text{1st period (6 months)} & \frac{10\%}{2} \times 1{,}000 = & \$\ 50.00 \\ \text{2nd period (6 months)} & \frac{10\%}{2} \times 1{,}050 = & \underline{52.50} \\ & & \$102.50 \end{array}$$

So the lender, receiving his interest at the end of the year, receives a return of 10.25 % on the 10% loan.

If the loan interest were compounded quarter-yearly, here is the result:

$$\begin{array}{lll} \text{1st period (3 months)} & \frac{10\%}{4} \times 1{,}000.00 = & \$\ 25.00 \\ \text{2nd period (3 months)} & \frac{10\%}{4} \times 1{,}025.00 = & 25.62 \\ \text{3rd period (3 months)} & \frac{10\%}{4} \times 1{,}050.62 = & 26.26 \\ \text{4th period (3 months)} & \frac{10\%}{4} \times 1{,}076.89 = & \underline{26.92} \\ & & \$103.80 \end{array}$$

The lender receives 10.38% on the 10% loan.

The foregoing illustrations of actual return only apply if the loan interest is repaid once a year.

If the interest were paid at the end of each period, and the lender simply put the money in his pocket, the money in his pocket draws no interest so he would be getting 10% a year regardless of the compounding. For example, if the lender received the interest in two periods, the borrower would pay $50 interest at the end of each six months. The first $50 would not be added to the loan and therefore interest would not e paid on the $50 as in compounding.

On the other hand, if the borrower paid the periodic interest out of a pile he kept in a shoe box, he wouldn't *pay* any more than 10%, because money in a shoe box earns no interest.

This is basically why compound interest is said to produce an "effective yield."

The lender, to receive his 10.25% on the 10% loan would either (1) receive the interest at the end of the year, or (2) *immediately* re-invest the periodic payment of interest on the same terms as the loan on which he received the interest. Only then would he get his 10.25%, and make the compounding effective.

Interest rates (or factors as they are sometimes called) are easy to establish, providing the payments are to be made *with the same frequency.* To establish the periodic interest rate on a loan in which the interest is compounded monthly, simply divide the annual rate of interest by twelve. If the interest were compounded quarter-yearly, divide the annual rate by four, and so on.

Calculate: ↑ (synonymous) ↓	from the Latin *calculus* which means pebble or stone used in counting. *Calculus* from the Latin calx, which means small pebble. *Calculate* means *compute.*
Compute:	from the Latin *com* which means together, and Latin *putto* which means reckon.
Reckon:	from Old English, Swedish, Danish, etc., which means *count.*
Compound:	from *compounen* (to put together). Composed of two or more parts; not simple. *Synonymous* with Amalgamation, combination, mixture.
Simple Interest:	That interest which arises from the principal sum only.
Compound Interest:	That interest which arises from the principal with the interest added at stated times, as yearly, twice-yearly, etc. *Interest on interest.*

8

OUR CEILING ON INTEREST RATES

Remember the federal *Small Loans Act*? That's the one that drove lenders up the wall with restrictions on loans of $1,500 and less.

Two percent a month on the first $300, 1% a month on the next $700, and 1/2% on a balance of up to $1,500.

Away back in 1971, I wanted to know how the Act affected mortgage loans and my inquiry to the Department of Insurance provided some revealing facts.

Real estate and mortgage brokers probably never knew it, but they were considered moneylenders under the *Small Loans Act*. This brought them into restrictions in lending $1,500 or less — and, remember, not so many years ago there was a lot of small-mortgage lending going on.

The government took the view that the licensed lending rates under the Act should not be applied in the case of mortgage loans, but it also said such loans were to be limited to a rate of 1% per month on balances outstanding.

One percent a month is 12% a year, but it is compounding the interest monthly.

The *Federal Interest Act* (not the *Small Loans Act*) says a blended-payment mortgage must show the annual rate of interest calculated annually or semi-annually.

So 12% compounded monthly would have to read 12.682503% in the mortgage to comply with the Act, which would look silly, wouldn't it?

So I kept my mouth shut.

I was surprised to hear on radio a business commentator remark that there are no government restrictions on usury, or words to that effect. This caused me to get out my copy of something called *Bill C-44*, an Act to amend the Small Loans Act and to amend the Criminal Code. It received royal assent on December 7, 1980. The Act repealed the *Small Loans Act*, so the latter doesn't exist any more.

Mortgage lenders can relax.

In amending the Criminal Code, the Act placed restrictions on what anyone can charge for lending money. Section 305.1 of the Criminal Code says everyone who:

(a) enters into an agreement or arrangement to receive interest at a criminal rate, or (b) receives a payment or partial payment of interest at a criminal rate, is guilty of: (1) An indictable offence and is liable to imprisonment for five years, or (2) an offence punishable on summary conviction and is liable to a fine of not more than $25,000 or to imprisonment for six months, or to both.

The Act defines "criminal rate" as being "an effective annual rate of interest that exceeds 60% on the credit advanced."

This 60% means the aggregate of all charges and expenses, whether in the form of a fee, fine, penalty, commission or other similar charge or expense.

Regardless of how exorbitant the 60% may be, there are severe penalties for usury in Canada.

Don't believe everything you hear on the radio.

9

CAPITAL GAINS TAX RULES

Determining whether the sale of property is considered income or capital gain is a question of fact to be answered by the circumstances of each individual case. The difference in cost to a taxpayer could be substantial.

You sell a piece of land this year, one you have owned for a couple of years and realize a net profit on the deal of $20,000. If Revenue Canada agrees this is a capital gain, you are home free.

But if the net profit is income, the result of an "adventure in the nature of a trade," as the government describes it, the entire $20,000 will be taxable.

In deciding if the profit resulting from a real estate deal is income or capital gain, the courts have looked at a number of guidelines:

a) The period of ownership. Normally, property held only a short time will be considered to have been purchased for the purpose of resale and the profit will be treated as income, while property that has been held a long time is more likely to be considered an investment, producing a capital gain on eventual sale;
b) The frequency of similar transactions. A taxpayer's history of extensive buying and selling of similar properties, or of quick turnovers, may be taken as evidence that the taxpayer is carrying on a business of dealing in real estate.
c) Improvement and development work. When an organized effort is made to put property into a better marketable condition, such as laying sewers, building roads or preparing a plan of subdivision, it certainly indicates a business of selling properties.

Currently, if you earn a capital gain, 75% of that gain is taxable and 25% is tax exempt subject to the following limitations:

(a) If you realize a capital gain from your principal residence, then this capital gain is not taxable. Prior to 1982 a husband could own a principal residence and the wife could own a different principal residence. After 1982 only one principal residence could be declared.

(b) Since 1984 capital gains from the sale of farmland or the sale of shares of a Canadian controlled private publication which meets the condition as a qualified small business corporation have been exempt from tax up to a maximum lifetime capital gain of $500,000.

(c) Properties other than principal residences, and any other capital gains — from the stock market, for example — have had a lifetime exemption limit of $100,000. These exemptions, however, could not be earned all at once but in graduated stages. A $10,000 exemption could be earned in 1985, an accumulated total $25,000 in 1986, $50,000 in 1987, $100,000 in 1988. Since February 1992 the government has proposed that real estate properties are no longer exempt; 75% of the capital gain is taxable.

Taxpayers are required to keep track of their net gains and compute the cumulative deductions available to them. If you earn a capital gain above these lifetime limits, then 75% of that additional gain is taxed at your marginal tax rate. The use of any capital gains deduction may be restricted by a taxpayer's Cumulative Net Investment less amount.

10

PUTTING THE BITE ON THE BANK

One dictionary definition of a bank is that it is a "pile," and the way today's Canadian banking institutions are piling up profits, it appears to be a very *apropos* description.

Never lose sight of the fact that a bank is in business to make money, and nobody but nobody knows how to do it better than a bank. Everything it does is geared to making money, and with the net assets of Canadian banks increasing at more than 20% a year, it would appear that they are the all-time champions in the art of piling it up. The 20% is a *net* increase; compound it for four years and the banks double in size.

Manufacturers and insurance companies have been forced by the government to return a part of their immoderate profits to the consumer, and corporate presidents may be forgiven for wondering why they should be singled out and not the banks.

Aside from such little gems as charging you $3.00 for a phone call to say that your account is overdrawn, banks basically amass their profits by lending money. But to get some of that money requires step-by-step methodical planning.

Banks may provide similar services, but individual branches are as different as night and day because some managers have rapport with customers, while others don't seem to know the meaning of the word. Managers who allow customers to leave without establishing rapport with them are making a serious banking error. Some managers make their customers feel good, whether the answer is yes or no to a loan request, while others seem to think they're doing their customers a favor by actually allowing them to cross the threshold of their offices.

There are several things one can do to ensure getting a bank loan, but before setting your plan in motion, "case" the bank, watching the personnel carefully. Change a bill and see if the clerks go about their business happily. Their attitude is generally affected by the personality of the manager, so watch for him and see how he conducts himself. If he appears to be a sourpuss, his clerks won't be doing much smiling, so think twice about doing your business there. Unless of course you are a sourpuss yourself. Then you just might hit it off.

When you decide on a branch, open a current account. Banks love to have customers with current accounts because banks pay no interest on the money piling up in such accounts. And keep the account active. Make deposits and withdrawals every other day. Banks like to see an active account because they charge for every movement in the account.

To establish a credit rating at a bank, you should borrow money when you don't need it. This is the best time to approach the bank, because you will be relaxed and secure in the knowledge that if you don't get it, you are not going to worry about it. And if you don't get it, switch banks fast — if you can't get money when you don't need it, what chance would you have if you *did* need it?

When you get the loan, simply pay it back on time, and your good record of prompt payment will go on your loan record. The interest you pay on the loan will be your nominal cost of establishing a credit rating.

The most important part of your plan is to ensure that the manager knows you. Clerks are nice to banter with, but the manager is the important one who says you get it or you don't. A clerk can't authorize a loan, and even the chief accountant is restricted in what he can do. So channel your charm and rapport to the manager.

The first time I used this system, it worked like a dream. I found a bank with a big, cigar-chomping manager who was all over the place keeping everybody happy, and I noticed that when he approached his clerks they actually seemed to be glad to see him.

So I put my plan into effect, and after three or four weeks of keeping my current account busy and passing the time of day with the big man, I walked into his office one day, sat on the edge of his desk and told him I would like to put the bite on him for a couple of thousand.

He just reached for the magic drawer where managers keep their demand notes, and I knew I had it made.

Over the next two years, I built up my credit rating with the branch to $15,000, which was the manager's personal loan limit. Bank managers are given authority to lend up to a certain amount on their own authority, and the amount depends on the size of the branch. Any loan over this limit must be referred to a higher authority, so don't pick on the smallest branch in town if you can avoid it.

Well, while all this was going on, I was astute enough to establish a current account at another bank, in case of contingency, and had good rapport with its manager. This was fortunate thinking, because one day my manager at bank No. 1 was promoted, and a new man was sent in to take charge.

My brother Charles, the Air Force colonel, once showed me the instrument panel of a zippy fighter aircraft. Staring at the pilot, with stark reality, is a large button stamped with the word PANIC. Push this button and there is no turning back. Out you go, parachute and all, and what you leave behind comes crashing down.

After decades of experience in doing business with Canadian banks, I am rapidly reaching the conclusion that newly appointed and caretaker bank managers are supplied with these buttons as part of their rations in the kit of new management.

Many of you reading this will recall with horror your own experience with a new manager: demand loans were recalled, overdrafts were cancelled, cheques bounced, and with it you suffered temporary frustration and anger. But you survived.

My notes were being honored, the overdraft wasn't causing the giant corporation any pain, my cheques were being cashed, and everything was at peace in my small banking world. Then *bang*. The new guy pushed the panic button which shot me out of the front door and everything I had built up inside came crashing down. But I had my parachute which worked beautifully.

It was my custom to drop into the bank on a Friday to pick up a couple of hundred for my wife's weekend shopping and pocket money for the following week. Consider then, my frustration on black Friday when I walked in for my weekly ration and was advised that my overdraft was too high so, ha ha, no money today.

The annoying part of this was that I had just made a deposit!

However, with my parachute I landed gently in the manager's office at bank No. 2, put the bite on him for a few hundred with ridiculous ease and survived. Bank No. 1 was later paid off with gusty glee.

I still have a reserve bank in the wings in case the head office decides to promote my man and install one of those guys with a panic button.

Don't think for one minute that a bank feels it owes you any loyalty. Business is business, and if a bank suspects that you are coming on to hard times it will drop you like a hot brick. And then what do you do?

Why, you just trot along and see your pal at bank No. 2.

If you are falling on hard times, however, be careful not to misjudge your ability to repay. When you borrow from bank No. 1 to pay bank No. 2 and then borrow from bank No. 3 because you can't pay bank No. 1, you can very quickly be buried with no way out. Be prepared with alternate sources of funds but do it wisely.

11

CERTIFIED CHEQUES

In the old days, it was said to be the practice of real estate agents to get cheques certified by crafty means.

When a buyer left a deposit cheque with an agent and had second thoughts about the deal, he would head for his bank the next morning to stop payment on the cheque.

When he arrived, he would be surprised to see the agent standing outside the bank. The agent would engage him in idle conversation while, unknown to the buyer, a pal was inside getting the cheque certified.

I suppose it has happened, but I would take such stories with a grain of salt.

However, what can a buyer do about stopping payment on a certified cheque if he senses there may be something wrong or fishy about a deal? Like being talked into buying land sight unseen?

It is an interesting question, and here are the answers:

A cheque is certified "before delivery" or "after delivery." "Before delivery" means that the payer will go to his own bank and certify his own cheque before giving it to the payee. What the payer is doing, in fact, is asking the bank to certify that funds are in the account at the time of certification, thereby giving credence to the payer. It is not an absolute guarantee of payment.

The bank will certify the cheque and immediately remove the funds from the account to a holding account, keeping the money there until the payee presents the cheque for payment.

The bank's attitude is that the payer obviously had every intention of having the cheque honored, and it simply wants to ensure the money is still there when it is presented for payment.

However, the *Bills of Exchange Act* quite specifically says that the payer may countermand (stop) payment on a cheque before it is presented to the bank for payment by issuing such instructions in writing to the bank.

If the bank received such instructions from the payer, it would have to put a "stop payment" order on the account.

"After delivery" is a different story. When a payer gives his cheque to the payee, and the payee presents it to the bank for certification, the payee is effectively saying to the bank: "Look, I want you to cash this cheque, but I don't want the money now. I want you to promise to pay me later."

So the bank obliges, certifies the cheque, removes the money from the account, and holds the money to honor its commitment to the payee.

The payer cannot stop payment on this cheque because it has been presented for payment, and the bank has honored it. The cheque therefore becomes a charge on the bank, which it must honor. It has effectively paid the cheque, but is holding the money until the payee comes back for it.

If you are getting involved in a deal you may be wary of, think twice — and get professional advice.

Once you hand over that cheque and the payee certifies it, you may have trouble getting your money back, regardless of how sour or crooked you may think the deal is.

Believe me.

12

CAPITALIZATION

To capitalize something is to convert it to capital, *capital value.* It is essential to understand it clearly before venturing into any type of real estate investments.

If you pay one thousand dollars for a bond or other security, and receive one hundred dollars interest once a year, it is obvious that the investment has a return of 10% per annum.

But what happens to the value of the bond if you, the holder, wish to sell it?

If a buyer can be found who will be satisfied with a 10% return, the bond could be sold for its original purchase price, one thousand dollars.

But what happens if a buyer can't be found at 10% return, one who is not satisfied with 10%? What is the bond worth if the ultimate buyer receives 12%? That is, what should the selling price of the bond be if the $100 annual return is to represent 12%, and not the original 10%?

Take a look . . .

$$\frac{\$100}{.12} = \$833.33$$

And if the market pendulum is swinging the other way, and a buyer can be found who is satisfied with a return of 8%, then what? Take another look . . .

$$\frac{\$100}{.08} = \$1,250.00$$

In this case, the constant $100 annual return represents 8% of the bond's new price. Get the idea?

Now, the same principle applies when we look at the "cash flow" of an investment in real estate, such as a small apartment building.

Cash flow is what is left after municipal taxes and all operating expenses related to the property have been paid, including the mortgage payments.

To illustrate:

Annual gross return (rental)	$ 50,000
Less taxes and operating expenses	18,000
	32,000
Less annual payments on $200,000 mortgage, interest and principal:	25,000
CASH FLOW	$ 7,000

Now then, if a buyer for this property can be found who will be satisfied with a return of 8% on his invested cash, what will its approximate selling price be, cash to mortgage?

Here we are . . .

$$\frac{\$7,000}{.08} = \$87,500.00 \text{ cash}$$

To which we add the principal balance of the mortgage ($200,000) and the price is $287,500.

If an 8% buyer cannot be found, and we can only come up with a 10% buyer, then we have:

$$\frac{\$7,000}{.10} = \$70,000.00 \text{ cash}$$

To which we add the principal balance of the mortgage ($200,000) and the price is $270,000.

See how it works? When looking for a real estate investment, a first consideration will be the return required on the cash invested.

When selling, or acquiring any investment, the purchase price must at least produce a return that will reflect current market rates at the time of the transaction.

Periodically we hear about those "perpetual" bonds sold by the federal government many years ago which produce about 3% interest. The present owners are stuck with them, and if such bonds were offered for sale, the buyer would wish to acquire them at current rates of return.

If current rates are 9%, here is what one might expect to receive for $1,000 worth — the $1,000 being what the original buyer paid. Remember now, the $1,000 bond pays 3%, or $30 per year.

$$\frac{\$30,000}{.09} = \$333.33$$

That's all the bond would be worth today, $333.33.

Consider some of your own securities. If they yield 6%, what are they worth to a buyer today if the current rates available on similar securities are 8% or 9%? Now that you understand capitalization, figure it out quickly with one of those marvellous little calculators we can buy today for less than ten bucks.

13

LEVERAGE

Leverage is the act of lifting an object with as little exertion as possible. In the area of money, it is the act of making as much as possible with as little as possible.

The most prominent and profitable leverage in real estate is in buying property with a view to selling it shortly after the purchase. The less one invests in such a venture, the more one makes!

Buy property for $50,000 cash and turn it over quickly for $55,000 cash. Profit: 10%.

Buy property for $50,000 with $5,000 down, turn it over quickly for $55,000 and the profit is 100%.

See how it works? The profit here is based on the amount of cash invested; not what the property cost.

Take the $50,000 purchase, resold quickly at $55,000 with different down payments. Here is your profit on the investment.

Cash Invested	*Profit*
$ 5,000	100.0%
7,000	71.4%
10,000	50.0%
12,000	41.6%
15,000	33.3%
20,000	25.0%
25,000	20.0%
30,000	16.6%

See, the less one invests, the more one makes.

The foregoing are round figures. There will be acquisition costs (principally legal fees) and in selling, more legal fees — and possibly a real estate agent's selling fee.

So the cash invested will have to include the acquisition costs, and the net return will have to be what is left after selling costs.

Then you will have to consider the capital gains tax on what you made.

Take the purchase with $5,000 down for example. Say the acquisition costs total $500. Now we have invested $5,500.

Assuming the property is resold quickly for $55,000 and we are lucky enough to make a private deal without paying anyone a selling commission, we will still have to pay our legals — say $500.

We sell for $55,000 cash to the mortgages totalling $45,000. We knock off $500 for legals, leaving us with $9,500 cash.

Cash realized in selling	$ 9,500
Less cash invested	5,500
Gain:	4,000
Return on cash invested:	72.7%

If we had to pay a selling commission of 5% of the $55,000 ($2,750) we would show a net gain of $1,250 resulting in a return of 22.7%.

Even after we pay our taxes, that's still a very nice return on the money invested.

Well, you say, how does one buy property at a price that will justify a sudden increase in its market value? Why, do it the way others do it — make offers, plenty of them.

Review chapter 81, "Speculation," and chapter 9 on capital gains tax rules.

PART TWO

MORTGAGES

14

THE MORTGAGE DEED

Where would we be without the mortgage? Living in cramped shacks, no doubt.

Who would have believed during the fifties or sixties that a laborer could today live in such luxurious surroundings, complete with broadloom?

Don't curse the mortgage lender. Bless him. He makes it all possible, and at a much cheaper rate than the loans on cars and a few thousand other items.

When we sign a mortgage deed, we borrow money. The rate of interest on this money is lower than money borrowed for other necessities (and luxuries) in life.

Who pays cash for a house? Usually someone who has just sold a house that was all paid for over a number of years. And how was this possible? By a mortgage or two, or course.

To you who have built up your large equity in your home, remember that it was a mortgage lender who made it possible.

And to you who have yet to own a home, and want one, grit your teeth and prepare to sacrifice a bit like the rest of us. It will be worth it.

Who's Who?

Mortgagee and mortgagor. You will find them throughout this book, also referred to as lender and borrower.

When you are a tenant in a building, you are a lessee.

When you receive a gift, you are a donee.

When you purchase goods, you are a vendee.

Notice that each one of the foregoing is one upon whom a right is conferred. The right to occupy a building, the right to own the gift and the right to the goods purchased. Everyone on the receiving end is the one with the EE on the end of the name.

When one lends money to a real property owner, the property owner signs a mortgage deed and gives it to the lender. This is the lender's proof of security. The lender, receiving the mortgage from the borrower, is therefore the one to whom the right to the security is conferred. The mortgagee. The one with the EE on the end of his name.

Perhaps an easier way to remember who's who is to remember that the one with the OR on the end of the name is the one who has title to something.

The lessor owns the building which the lessee occupies.

The donor owns the gift he is giving the donee.

The vendor owns the goods he is selling the vendee.

And so it is with the borrower in a mortgage deed. He owns some real estate which he is using as security for a loan, and is therefore the one who has title to something, the property.

The mortgagor. The one with the OR at the end of the name.

MORTGAGOR: Borrower

MORTGAGEE: Lender

Defining a Mortgage

We all know what a mortgage is. Right? Wrong.

The noun mortgage comes from two French words, "mort" (dead) and "gage" (pledge). The pledge becomes dead when the loan is paid off, or, as some say, the real estate pledged becomes dead (lost) due to failure to pay. Take your pick.

A mortgage is contained in a document called a deed. A mortgage deed is what we have.

A deed is a document that contains a contract, or agreement, that is signed, sealed, contains proof of its delivery, and is effective on the date of delivery (to the lender).

It is signed by the borrower in English Common Law. In Quebec by borrower and lender.

It is often signed under seal. The seal is old hat — it signifies that the borrower was conscious of what he was doing when he signed the deed. So he signs it and sticks a seal on it.

The one signing places the seal with his signature. If one signed a deed and weren't conscious of the seal — in other words if the seal were placed on the deed after he signed and left the room — it wouldn't mean a thing. He must know about the seal at the time of signing.

You will find deeds in a registry office with seals and without seals. As a matter of fact some court judgments on the subject have said seals are unnecessary *period*, so if your lawyer tells you you don't need a seal, don't ask me to argue with him. But we must admit at least a seal does make a deed look better.

Proof of delivery. Signing a deed in the presence of one's solicitor and giving the deed to the solicitor is considered to be proof of delivery, because solicitors act in trust. So the one signing is trusting the solicitor to deliver the deed to the rightful party, and that's good enough.

It is effective on the date of delivery — which would be the date the signature goes on because that is done in the presence of a solicitor who is accepting delivery of it on that day for the lender.

There is a difference between Quebec and the rest of Canada in the handling of a mortgage deed and what it means.

In English Common Law (all of Canada except Quebec) there is, strictly speaking, only one legal mortgage. This may sound a bit confusing, but it is really very simple.

English Common Law says that the legal mortgagee is *entitled* to the *title* deed.

There could be only one person *entitled* to the *title* deed in this statement, so he would be obviously the mortgagee who is the one who received the *first* mortgage deed signed by a borrower using the *title* deed as security. Once this mortgagee is entitled to the title deed by law, no one else could be entitled to it.

So a legal mortgage in English Common Law is a first mortgage — but only a first mortgage registered against property in a *land registry office*. This requires a bit of further explanation.

There are two basic systems of land registration — the registry and land titles offices.

In land titles registration, the mortgage is a *charge* against the property, and therefore the legal mortgagee is not entitled to the title deed; he can't get it, because the mortgage is a charge on the property. Only in the registry office is he entitled to it.

Okay. So a legal mortgage in English Common Law is a mortgage of first priority in a land registry office. Well, what about all the other mortgages? Aren't they legal? Sure, but they are not called legal mortgages.

When one signs a first mortgage to be registered in a registry office, he is left with what is known as an equity of redemption.

He has the right to redeem his property by paying off the mortgage.

When one borrows additional funds, and signs another mortgage deed, he is borrowing against his equity in the property, and so this mortgage is called an equitable mortgage. So are a third and a fourth mortgage.

So a first mortgagee in a land registry office holds the (strictly speaking) legal mortgage, and the junior mortgagees in a land registry office hold equitable mortgages. But they are all legal. If it sounds like a lot of hocus pocus, it is not intended to be, because apparently that is the way it is.

The legal mortgage is where we get the definition of a mortgage in that it is a conveyance of real property as security for a debt, and when the debt is repaid the property is returned, or reconveyed to the borrower. But not always.

You see, if there happens to be a second (equitable) mortgage registered against the property, the minute the first (legal) mortgage is paid off and discharged, the second mortgage automatically becomes the first (legal) mortgage.

Well what about Quebec?

Now, here is a province that really knows how to define a mortgage. In Quebec a mortgage is called a deed of loan with hypothèque. And get this — the Quebec Civil Code goes on to define hypothèque as being a *lien on an immoveable* (which really is a first-class definition of a mortgage without all the gobbledygook of English Common Law.)

In Quebec no mortgagee is entitled to a title deed because all mortgages are a charge (lien) against property.

There we are. A mortgage is one of three things — (a) implied conveyance of property to the lender, or (b) an equitable lien (or charge) on property in favor of the lender, or (c) in Quebec, a lien on an immoveable.

I like the last definition. Because that's really what a mortgage is all about.

What's in a Mortgage?

The essential element in a mortgage deed is a covenant to repay the debt, plus interest.

Most basic. The lender puts up the money for one purpose and one purpose only — to obtain a financial return on the investment satisfactory to the lender. An exception to this may be Aunt Sally helping out Cousin Joe, but generally speaking, the name of the game is money. As much as possible, as safely as possible, as securely as possible.

The borrower wants to get the money as cheaply as possible, but mortgage markets being what they are, he hasn't got much choice in the public sector. The private sector is the one where a borrower can pay less for the use of borrowed money, and also where he can get a real hosing and pay the most.

So the mortgagor and the mortgagee reach an agreement as to the size of the loan and its terms, and then get formal about it by proceeding with the business of preparing a deed and entering into a legal contract.

A mortgage deed may start right off at the top calling itself an indenture. It is an interesting word, which simply means an agreement between two or more parties, but its history of terminology is interesting.

Many years ago, before carbon paper and all of today's common means of copying, such an agreement would be penned in duplicate (two original copies) and then the copies would be placed evenly, one on top of the other, and a wavy line, or indentation, would be cut along a side of the copies. Each party would receive one, and of course the idea was that when the two were placed together, the wavy cutting would match and this was supposed to establish authenticity.

Don't tell me. Already you are thinking what fun a slick forger with a pair of shears could have. Anyhow, that's where the word "indenture" came from.

A mortgage to be registered in a land titles office will have the word *charge* on it, so it will be easily identifiable as to its registry.

The names of the borrower(s) and lender(s) will be in it, that's for sure, and a legal description of the property secured as collateral for the loan.

It will clearly state the principal amount of the money *owed* by the mortgagor. You will notice that I did not say the principal amount of the money *borrowed*. One can borrow, say, $9,000 and have a bonus of $1,000 tacked onto it, producing a $10,000 debt, although the borrower never sees the $1,000 bonus until he hands it over to the lender at a later date.

Watch the bonus deals, they can be especially expensive. The borrower not only owes the bonus he never saw, but he pays interest on money that doesn't exist for the duration of the loan.

The mortgage will clearly state the rate of interest charged on the loan, but it is here that perhaps the biggest bones of contention exist because of the various means lenders decide to take in extracting the interest. Ensure that your mortgage, if you are the borrower, *clearly* states that the interest will be compounded either annually or semi-annually, not in advance, and with no more frequency than that. Many lenders, especially private lenders, will extract interest compounded monthly, which is more expensive.

The term will be there. This is the length of time the borrower has the use of the money (subject, of course, to default in the loan).

The repayment amount will be shown as monthly, quarter-yearly, half-yearly or annually. It can take many routes, the most common of which are:

a) A payment covering the interest only.
b) A fixed payment covering the interest and a portion of the principal amount of the loan.
c) A fixed principal payment, plus interest.

If a mortgage contains a stated fixed amount at regular intervals to cover "interest and principal" be sure it is large enough to at least cover the interest. Believe it or not, mortgages *are* sometimes thoughtlessly written and when a calculator goes to work on it, it is discovered that the payment actually is a little short of covering the interest!

A court judgment ruled, so I have been told, that in one such mortgage held by the vendor of a property, the vendor's lawyer obtained a court order to have the sale cancelled because, apparently, the effect of the payment not covering the interest was that the vendor had not actually sold the property, but had given the purchaser an option to buy it. Before the purchaser exercised the option, I suppose by rectifying the error, the vendor cancelled the purchaser's right to the option and got the property back. Read this again, and remember it.

The responsibilities of the borrower will be spelled out, and basically they are to maintain the payments, keep the property insured, keep the property in a good state of repair, and not misuse it.

The borrower's rights will be shown, such as to have quiet enjoyment of the property and to be free of the lender's rights when the debt is finally paid.

The lender's rights will be shown, and they are quite lengthy. For example, the rights to possession of the property on default by the borrower, and legal recourse to seize the property. These are the most serious. There are many others, such as what happens if the borrower is lazy about paying municipal taxes. The lender can pay them and add the amount to the mortgage debt, plus interest. Ditto for insurance.

One could go on and on and on about the contents of a mortgage, but the foregoing are the basics. I suggest you obtain a blank copy of a mortgage deed and study it. The document will be a long-winded legal affair, but it is necessary to be legal in detail about such a contract; after all, there is a sizeable amount of money involved.

The mortgage will be signed and witnessed, and everybody is in business hoping nothing goes wrong.

How a Mortgage Is Registered

There are two basic systems of registering real property and mortgages in Canada. I say two *basic* systems, because the province of Quebec has a system that embraces a part of each of two systems used in the rest of Canada.

It was in Upper Canada (later Ontario) that the first land registry office was established in Canada: August 10, 1795 to be exact.

Early registry offices used an alphabetical system to register title and mortgage deeds, but it became a bit cumbersome so was changed to a system using abstract (history of ownership) books where the documents were registered against lots and plans.

The registry office system with abstract books is a lulu. If it is in your area, and your property is registered there, do a title search sometime and learn what frustration really is. You will hop from page to page and book to book all over the place, and drive yourself up the wall going to the root of title to your property.

In registry offices nothing is guaranteed. For example, when property changes hands the legal practitioner acting for the purchaser will say in his closing letter that he is of the *opinion* that the title is good and marketable, but can't guarantee it.

It is in this registry system that we find the legal mortgages referred to earlier.

Mortgage deeds are registered against title and stamped for time and date. As a matter of fact the first mortgage recorded in Canada had the time on it — 11 a.m., April 13, 1796.

In the registry office the senior mortgage is the legal mortgage, as we have discussed. All junior mortgages are equitable mortgages — the seniority being established by the time and date of registration.

In the land titles office the mortgage is registered as a charge against title.

In Quebec, a registry office system is used which in one respect is similar to land titles — the mortgage is a lien (charge) against title, although no title registration is guaranteed by the province of Quebec as in land titles registration.

When you pay off a mortgage, get a discharge certificate from the lender, and ensure that the discharge of the debt is recorded on title. Otherwise the mortgage registration will just stay there.

It is the lender who registers the mortgage on title, but it is up to the borrower to remove it.

15

AMORTIZATION

To amortize means to deaden.

To amortize a loan is to extinguish it by means of a sinking fund; in other words, an allowance of payments over a period of time will be made to reduce the debt to zero.

The most common method of amortizing a mortgage is to have the repayment schedule computerized to ensure that all monthly payments are identical, with each payment containing the amortized principal amount, plus interest on the outstanding balance of the loan.

To illustrate this, the following table shows the first year's repayment schedule for a 20-year, $20,000 loan at 10%, compounded semi-annually, each line representing one month's payment, and each payment being exactly $190.34.

Payment Number	Interest Payment	Principal Payment	Balance of Loan
1	163.30	27.04	19972.96
2	163.08	27.26	19945.70
3	162.85	27.49	19918.21
4	162.63	27.71	19890.50
5	162.40	27.94	19862.56
6	162.17	28.17	19834.39
7	161.94	28.40	19805.99
8	161.71	28.63	19777.36
9	161.48	28.86	19748.50
10	161.24	29.10	19719.40
11	161.01	29.33	19690.07
12	160.77	29.57	19660.50

In the beginning, each payment is practically all interest. As the loan progresses, each payment contains less interest, and more principal. Each monthly payment still remains the same, with a minor adjustment on the last payment (to take care of the fractions).

Note the allowances for principal payments during the final year of this loan.

Payment Number	Interest Payment	Payment Principal	Balance of Loan
229	17.66	172.68	1989.91
230	16.25	174.09	1815.82
231	14.83	175.51	1640.31
232	13.39	176.95	1463.36
233	11.95	178.39	1284.97
234	10.49	179.85	1105.12
235	9.02	181.32	923.80
236	7.54	182.80	741.00
237	6.05	184.29	556.71
238	4.55	185.79	370.92
239	3.03	187.31	183.61
240	1.50	183.61	.00

One thing to be quite clear about is that regardless of the differences of principal and interest in each payment, the borrower only pays interest on the outstanding principal balance of the loan at the time of each payment. As the loan progresses the borrower is making larger principal payments, because there is less principal on which to pay interest.

If this loan were amortized with equal principal payments, plus interest, this is how the monthly payments would vary:

1st month:	$ 83.33 principal plus $163.29 interest ($246.62)
120th month:	$ 83.33 principal plus $ 81.64 interest ($164.97)
240th month:	$ 83.33 principal plus $ .68 interest ($84.01)

The obvious disadvantage with this method is that the highest payments are in the beginning, when the homeowner probably needs all the available money to support his family.

With rising interest rates, the only possible way to keep monthly mortgage payments down is to lengthen the amortization of the loan.

The following illustrates the repayment of 15-, 20-, and 25-year amortized mortgages of $50,000, 12% interest compounded twice-yearly.

The table presumes that the mortgage structures will remain constant throughout the loan, which they probably won't, but are used to illustrate the total amount of interest debt possible.

	15 years	20 years	25 years
Monthly payment	$ 590.81	$ 540.49	$ 515.95
Yearly Cost	7,089.72	6,485.88	6,191.40
Total cost	106,345.80	129,717.60	154,785.00
Total interest paid	56,345.80	79,717.60	104,785.00

By adding $74.86 to the monthly payment on the 25-year amortization, bringing it down to 15 years, a total of $48,439.20 can be saved.

And by reducing the 25-year deal to 20 years by adding $24.54 to each monthly payment, a very respectable $25,067.40 can be saved.

Further savings can be made by *weekly* mortgage payments, which are now available from several big lenders.

Do not confuse the *amortization* of a loan with its *term*. If one is told that a mortgage is amortized for 25 years, it must not be assumed that the loan has a 25-year term. The following chapter will explain.

16

THE MORTGAGE TERM

The term of mortgage is the period of time a borrower has before the lender can demand the principal balance owing on the loan, subject to mortgage default by the borrower.

It is very important to understand this clearly.

Years ago, it was a common practice of lenders to make loans for long periods of time, such as 25 years, at a fixed rate of interest for the entire term. But with the shrinking value of our dollar, this ended.

Canada Mortgage and Housing Corporation considered that if it amended the long-term, fixed interest mortgage to one that would allow an adjustment of interest to periods of from one to five years, it would attract more mortgage money.

The amendment was made and other lenders fell in line. With the exception of banks and other large lenders doing business with favored customers, and some private lending, mortgages with a term of more than five years became scarce. Recently, however, seven-year and ten-year terms have surfaced.

There are other reasons for the five-year term.

Trust and mortgage loan companies are offering a prime rate of interest to the public for investing in five-year certificates and debentures. The trust and mortgage loan firms use the money for mortgage investments at about 2% increase to the mortgagor. The term of such loans must obviously match the term of the certificates — five years.

If you were the borrower with a repayment schedule amortizing a loan over a period of 20 years, and the mortgage had a five-year term, it would mean that despite the 20-year amortization, you would have to repay the outstanding principal balance of the loan at the end of the five years.

This can be dynamite to your pocketbook.

Take a look at the following table in a $20,000 loan, 9 1/2%, compounded semi-annually, amortized over 20 years.

Principal balance owing at end of:

Year 1	$19,640	Year 11	$13,420
Year 2	19,240	Year 12	12,420
Year 3	18,820	Year 13	11,320
Year 4	18,340	Year 14	10,120
Year 5	17,820	Year 15	8,800
Year 6	17,240	Year 16	7,360
Year 7	16,620	Year 17	5,760
Year 8	15,920	Year 18	4,020
Year 9	15,160	Year 19	2,100
Year 10	14,340	Year 20	0

You will notice that in 20 years the loan will be extinguished, but here is where the five-year term will grab you.

At the end of the five years, the lender wants his money, namely $17,820. To repay the loan, you probably will have to commit yourself to another mortgage, and borrow the rounded balance of $17,800. If you commit yourself for a further five-year period (same amortization and rate) this is what your outstanding balance will be over the next five years in round figures:

Year 1	$17,479
Year 2	17,123
Year 3	16,749
Year 4	16,322
Year 5	15,859

At the end of this five-year period, when you have to repay the loan, you may repeat the process. We'll do this just twice more, to take us to the end of four five-year terms.

Third five years:		Fourth five years:	
($15,800 loan)		($14,000 loan)	
Year 1	$15,515	Year 1	$13,748
Year 2	15,199	Year 2	13,468
Year 3	14,867	Year 3	13,174
Year 4	14,488	Year 4	12,838
Year 5	14,077	Year 5	12,474

Each new five-year term will result in smaller monthly payments because the principal amount of each succeeding term will be less.

If one keeps up the pattern of the five-year terms by starting each new term with the outstanding principal balance of the previous one, and amortizing the loan over 20 years, it will never reach zero.

Whereas if the term of the mortgage had been 20 years, it would have been reduced to zero in that time, although the monthly payments would have remained constant (and larger) than under each renewed five-year term.

If the 20-year mortgage is to be retired, or paid in full in 20 years, then each time the mortgage is renewed, the principal balance owing must be amortized for no longer than a period than the remaining number of years in the original amortization.

Examine the chart and remember it.

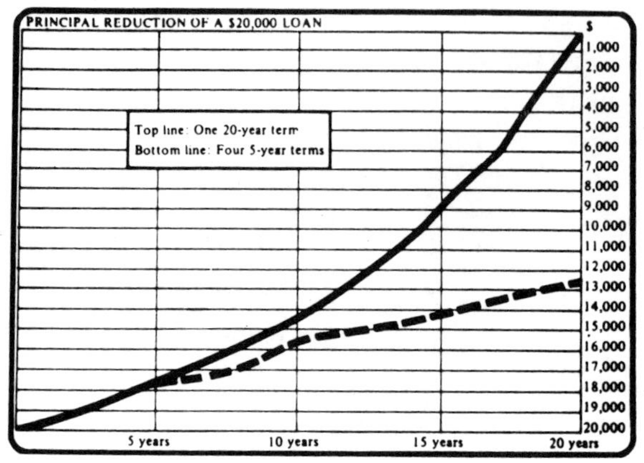

17

COSTS OF ARRANGING A MORTGAGE

The two most misunderstood charges to a real estate buyer are the legal fees in obtaining a mortgage loan, and the insurance fee added to many mortgages.

A lawyer is entitled to reasonable compensation for his services, and considering the work involved in acting for a purchaser, the generally accepted tariff appears to be fair.

In acting for a purchaser, there is one necessary aspect of the lawyer's work that surely must drive some of them "up the wall." That is when a property is registered in a registry office.

In a land titles office (not used east of Ontario) all title documents registered are guaranteed by the provincial government, but not so in the registry office. Hours and hours of patient sifting through abstract books can be required, going from page to page and book to book, the lawyer all the time being acutely aware that there just might be something wrong in the chain of title that will interfere with the client's enjoyment of the property at a later date.

The legal fees in acting for a purchaser can amount to about 1 1/4% of the cost of the average home. This is for the lawyer's services, and in addition to this, there will be adjustments to the date of closing made on such things as the municipal property taxes, hydro and water charges, insurance, and if oil heated, the cost for a full tank.

Then there will be a charge for a land transfer tax, which the provincial government gets.

There will be a charge made by the registry offices for every document registered. If the property covers parts of more than one lot, it costs more.

Some mortgage lenders will deduct a portion of future municipal taxes from the mortgage principal, which can be annoying to one's pocketbook, resulting in more cash to be coughed up by the buyer. Also, many mortgage lenders require an up-to-date survey, and if one is not available, this can cost hundreds of dollars.

Then there will be a final check made with the sheriff's office to see if any last minute liens or charges have been made against the property, for which there will be a nominal charge.

The average buyer, after paying for much of the foregoing, can be forgiven if he finds himself in a state of shock upon being presented with an additional bill for third party mortgage charges. The following are the three basic areas of financial escalation in mortgaging costs for the borrower, and will clearly indicate just how you can save money in mortgaging.

A common method of mortgaging in buying real estate is for the purchaser to "assume" an existing mortgage, one already registered against the property. The one assuming the mortgage is agreeing to basically maintain the payments and be jointly responsible for the debt with the one who originally signed the mortgage deed.

Assuming a mortgage when buying real estate normally incurs no extra financial charges to the buyer — it is already there.

Another method is for the seller to agree to "take back" a mortgage from the purchaser for part of the purchase price. This is another cheap way to get a mortgage.

Such a mortgage has several advantages. It requires no credit check of the borrower, no appraisal fees to be paid by the borrower, smaller legal fees than other mortgaging, instant knowledge that the "mortgage application" has been approved, and in many cases can be secured at a lower rate than third party mortgages, with longer terms. Furthermore, they usually have "open" repayment privileges.

The most expensive method of mortgaging is for a purchaser to arrange a mortgage from a third party, such as a bank, insurance or trust company.

An inspection or appraisal fee of about $150 does not seem unreasonable, but the financial crunch comes when a lawyer presents his bill for legal fees and disbursements.

Legal tariffs in mortgaging can be just as much proportionately as they are for services in closing the purchase. The reason for this is that many of the services performed in mortgaging are identical to services in closing. For the lender's protection, the title must be searched in the same manner, right down to a last-minute visit to the sheriff's office.

Lending institutions usually prefer to retain the services of their own approved lawyers, which is understandable. This results in a complete job being done in the title search, etc., in addition to the one done by the purchaser's lawyer for closing purposes. Result — the additional fee.

If a purchaser is fortunate enough to have his own lawyer do the legal work in the third-party mortgage, the combined fee for mortgaging and closing will undoubtedly be much less than the separate fees of two lawyers. It therefore follows that it can be advisable for a purchaser to determine what lawyer will be acting for the mortgage lender, and retain him also to close the purchase.

Or better still, have one's own lawyer arrange for the funds through a lender who will allow him to act in the mortgage.

One thing to keep in mind is that the mortgagee (lender) pays for absolutely nothing, with the exception of a small charge for registering the mortgage. The borrower pays all costs, the simple reason being that if the lender paid for any part of it, his investment would be "watered down." When a lender advances money at 10%, he wants 10%, and he *gets* 10%.

The second puzzling charge confronting a borrower is the mortgage insurance fee. This charge is found in two types of mortgages, *National Housing Act* loans and loans insured by the Mortgage Insurance Company of Canada.

When a mortgage is obtained that amounts to no more than 75% of the value of the property, it is generally accepted that there is sufficient equity in the property to require no monetary insurance.

But when the loan amounts to as much as 90% of the purchase price, it is understandable for the lender to consider that the borrower who has a 10% equity in the property is a risk that requires additional assurance that the loan will be secure. This assurance is realized by having the loan completely insured, and the borrower pays the premium.

The insurance premium is not normally paid for directly out of the borrower's pocket. It is added to the principal amount of the loan and the total will be registered principal sum in the mortgage deed, although MICC will accept a direct payment. The lender then sends a cheque matching the premium to the insurer, Canada Mortgage and Housing Corporation or the Mortgage Insurance Company of Canada.

If the loan is repaid before the mortgage term expires there is no provision for any rebate of the insurance premium.

Regardless of the source of mortgage funds, the lender will require the borrower to have the security adequately covered by property insurance. It is mandatory, written into the mortgage deed, and paid for by the borrower.

Summary: Consider the following:

a) Property where there is a mortgage already registered at current rates or lower. If you can't come up with the cash to the mortgage, see if the vendor will hold a second at a reasonable rate of interest.

b) Property where the vendor will take back a mortgage for a large part of the purchase price.

c) If you must go to a third party for a mortgage, retain the mortgagee's lawyer to close your purchase, or have your lawyer act for the mortgagee (lender) if possible.

d) Be wary of short-term mortgages that have to be replaced. It can be expensive.

18

MORTGAGE REPAYMENT SCHEDULES

There are more than *one million* new and refinanced mortgage transactions each year in Canada.

Conventional mortgagees such as banks, insurance, and trust companies provide the borrower with a computerized repayment schedule showing the interest and principal parts of each payment, and the principal balance owing on each payment date. This ensures that both the borrower and the lender know exactly where they stand, right to the penny.

However, in many areas of mortgaging, and especially secondary financing, millions of dollars are undoubtedly being lost annually by borrowers simply because the mortgage repayment is not computerized.

The following is an example which illustrates why under normal circumstances, it is incorrect to compute an interest payment on a level balance over six months.

Calculated vs. Compounded

The statement of interest in most mortgages may read, for example, "6% per annum calculated half-yearly, not in advance."

Note: It is the *interest rate* which is calculated half-yearly, *not the interest payment.*

In most cases, the interest payment is due monthly with the principal. The word "calculated" does not imply that the interest payments are computed on a level balance over six months. In fact, the following shows it is quite incorrect to compute interest payments in this way.

Interest Paid Monthly for Six Months vs.
Interest Paid on a Level Balance over Six Months

Suppose, for example, a mortgage of $10,000 with interest at 6% per annum calculated half-yearly, is to be paid off in equal installments of $100, interest and principal included. The 6% per annum interest rate calculated semi-annually is equivalent to a monthly interest rate of 0.4938622%. The first six rows of schedule will read as follows:

Payment Number	Interest Portion	Principal Portion	Total Payment	Balance of Loan After Payment
1	$ 49.39	$ 50.61	$100.00	$9949.39
2	49.14	50.86	100.00	9898.53
3	48.88	51.12	100.00	9847.41
4	48.63	51.37	100.00	9796.04
5	48.38	51.62	100.00	9744.42
6	49.12	51.88	100.00	9692.54
Total	$292.54	$307.46	$600.00	$9692.54

On examining the schedule, you will note that the sum of the interest on the first six payments is $292.54 whereas the interest on $10,000 for half a year at 3% is $300. The difference arises because the principal is being reduced by a portion of the monthly instalments as the amount of interest decreases within the six-month period.

It would be improper under the *Interest Act* for the lender to compute the balance due after the sixth payment by simply adding $300 interest and subtracting $600 in total payments to obtain a balance of $9,700. In fact, if $300 were actually collected, the interest rate would not be 6% compounded semi-annually but approximately 6.22% compounded semi-annually. This would then contravene the mortgage agreement.

Simple vs. Compound Interest

Question: On a $10,000 loan at 7% compounded semi-annually and payable in monthly payments of $100, principal plus interest, I calculate the interest of the first payment to be $58.33. Your figure is $57.50. Please explain the difference.

Answer: When you calculated the interest payment, you probably used a simple interest calculation. If you did this, you are assuming, incorrectly, that interest is compounded monthly. The computation schedules are based on the assumption that interest is compounded as stated, that is, semi-annually. Examine the schedules below.

Loan $10,000/Rate 7% Compounded Monthly/ Payments $100 Payable Monthly

Simple Interest

Payment Number	Interest Payment	Principal Payment	Balance of Loan
1	$58.33	$41.67	$9958.33
2	58.09	41.91	9916.42
3	57.85	42.15	9874.27
4	57.60	42.40	9831.87

Loan $10,000/Rate 7% Compounded Semi-annually/ Payment $100 Payable Monthly

Compound Interest

Payment Number	Interest Payment	Principal Payment	Balance of Loan
1	$57.50	$42.50	$9957.50
2	57.26	42.74	9914.76
3	57.01	42.99	9871.77
4	56.76	43.24	9828.53

Examine your schedule carefully. It should correspond to the lender's figures. Make certain he has a copy of the schedule (an example is shown at the end of this chapter).

Note that:

1. The basic amounts should correspond exactly to your mortgage terms.

2. Compounding should be identical to the statement of interest in your mortgage: e.g. 9% per annum calculated (compounded) *semi-annually*, not in advance.
3. The first payment is recorded and made on the proper date.
4. If the compounding is semi-annual, the amount of interest on the first payment is *less than* one-twelfth of $25,000 times the annual interest rate. The lender and borrower should both be aware of this: $184.08 is less than $25,000 × 9% ÷ 12 = $187.50.
5. Each payment and exact current balance can be easily kept track of by checking off each date as the payment is made.
6. The interest portion plus the principal portion will add up to the total payment amount.
7. The interest on each subsequent payment is slightly less than the interest on the previous payment. Verify that this occurs not just once each half year, but for every payment.
8. The interest accumulated over a calendar year is mandatory information for lenders who must declare interest as income. Send the schedule (copy) in with your income tax return as a supporting document.
9. Verify that the mortgage pays out in 25 years.

Obtaining the Schedule

Here is how to fill in a schedule order form. State the:

1. Loan amount.
2. Annual interest rate and compounding.
3. Blended payments (interest and principal included in one payment) *or* fixed principal payments only, with interest in addition (non-blended).
4. Date that interest is to be calculated from (usually the mortgage closing date).
5. Date the first payment is due.
6. Date control; *periodic* means that payments are made on a regular day each month.
7. Number of payments until the mortgage is paid off.
8. The amount of each payment.

Other Computerized Schedule Services

There are many variations of the mortgage repayment schedule. Some examples and their uses are:

1. The Variable Payment Schedule can be used for many other situations. It will handle payments that change, extra lump-sum payments, tax payments (as minus amounts), investment situations, missed payments, payments made on different dates and payments that are not large enough to cover the interest. The payment amount and payment date can be listed for each individual transaction.
2. The regular Mortgage Repayment Schedule is similar to the above except that it does not include dates or any variations.
3. The Level-Balance Schedule calculates interest on a fixed balance over six months. The interest amount decreases only once every six months. It has the effect of not crediting the principal portion of each payment until six months have elapsed.
4. The Wraparound Schedule is used by a borrower to secure additional funds. The borrower gives a third party a mortgage blanketing an existing mortgage. The new lender covenants to be responsible to maintain the existing mortgage payments, lends the borrower the additional funds (secured by a mortgage) and the borrower then makes his mortgage payment to the new mortgagee.
5. Yield Calculations: lenders buy and sell mortgages among themselves just as goods are bought and sold. The purchaser will often want to discount the mortgage so as to yield a higher rate of interest.
6. Interest Calculations: A series of 16 special calculations are available. Want to find an effective interest rate? Convert an *add-on advance* rate to *not-in-advance*? Calculate a present worth on a loan amount? Evaluate a fund accumulation?
7. Table Services: A number of tables are available for the finance business. Examples are small loans consumer tables for instalment financing and conversion tables for metric, mensuration, payroll, and tax conversions.

The Computer Tells You

Some of the things that these schedules and calculations will show you are very interesting. For example, if you had arranged a $25,000 mortgage, 25-year, at 9% compounded twice-yearly with a blended payment of $207 per month, you could:

1. Increase your monthly payment:
   (i) $5 more to $212 saves $ 3,500 in interest.
   (ii) $10 more to $217 saves $ 6,300 in interest.
   (iii) $20 more to $227 saves $10,500 in interest.
   (iv) $50 more to $257 saves $17,900 in interest.
2. Prepay with borrowed money: Make extra anniversary payments with borrowed money at a higher rate, say 10%. Pay this loan back over a year.
   (i) $500 borrowed each year at 10% saves $15,300.
   (ii) $1,000 borrowed each year at 10% saves $20,900.
3. Pay fixed principal interest: Divide the $25,000 into equal principal amounts of $83.33 per month over 25 years. You pay more on the first payments and less thereafter. You save $9,300.
4. Avoid paying "simple interest." Dividing by twelve means total interest repaid is $40,444 rather than $37,093 (if the rate is compounded semi-annually). You save $3,300.
5. Avoid the "level-balance" technique: The borrower pays $41,649 rather than $37,093. You save $4,500.
6. Avoid extending the amortization period. A 1% interest rate rise to 10% after five years with the payment remaining at $207 per month means you pay $14,000 more than the original $37,093 in interest.
7. Did you know that $85 per month invested at 1% per month for 40 years makes you a millionaire?

All calculations above are illustrations only. Specific calculations are to be interpreted in accordance with the terms of the particular mortgage document. The calculations do not include adjustments for taxes, inflation and/or interest earned on alternative investments.

*The Computerized Schedule
(Courtesy CSC, P.O. Box 400, Willowdale, Ont.)

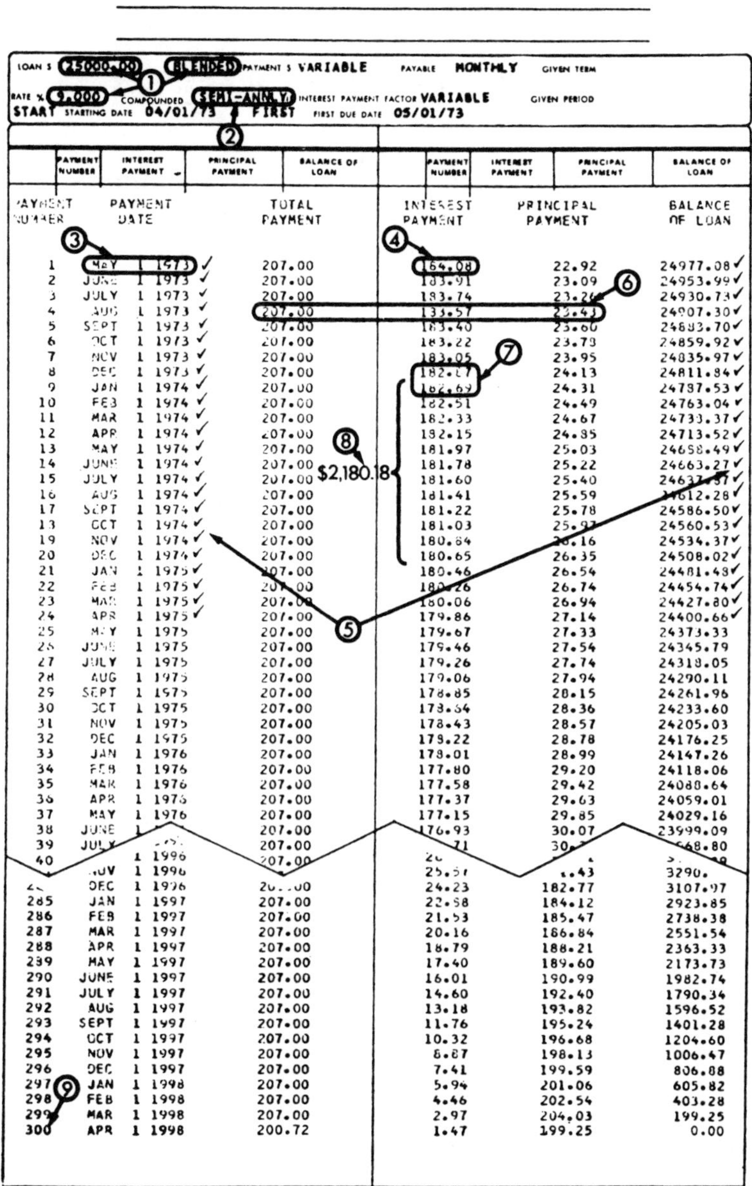

LOAN $ 25000.00 BLENDED PAYMENT $ VARIABLE PAYABLE MONTHLY GIVEN TERM
RATE % 9.000 COMPOUNDED SEMI-ANNLY INTEREST PAYMENT FACTOR VARIABLE GIVEN PERIOD
START STARTING DATE 04/01/73 FIRST FIRST DUE DATE 05/01/73

PAYMENT NUMBER	PAYMENT DATE	TOTAL PAYMENT	INTEREST PAYMENT	PRINCIPAL PAYMENT	BALANCE OF LOAN
1	MAY 1 1973	207.00	184.08	22.92	24977.08
2	JUNE 1 1973	207.00	183.91	23.09	24953.99
3	JULY 1 1973	207.00	183.74	23.26	24930.73
4	AUG 1 1973	207.00	183.57	23.43	24907.30
5	SEPT 1 1973	207.00	183.40	23.60	24883.70
6	OCT 1 1973	207.00	183.22	23.78	24859.92
7	NOV 1 1973	207.00	183.05	23.95	24835.97
8	DEC 1 1973	207.00	182.87	24.13	24811.84
9	JAN 1 1974	207.00	182.69	24.31	24787.53
10	FEB 1 1974	207.00	182.51	24.49	24763.04
11	MAR 1 1974	207.00	182.33	24.67	24738.37
12	APR 1 1974	207.00	182.15	24.85	24713.52
13	MAY 1 1974	207.00	181.97	25.03	24688.49
14	JUNE 1 1974	207.00	181.78	25.22	24663.27
15	JULY 1 1974	207.00	181.60	25.40	24637.87
16	AUG 1 1974	207.00	181.41	25.59	24612.28
17	SEPT 1 1974	207.00	181.22	25.78	24586.50
18	OCT 1 1974	207.00	181.03	25.97	24560.53
19	NOV 1 1974	207.00	180.84	26.16	24534.37
20	DEC 1 1974	207.00	180.65	26.35	24508.02
21	JAN 1 1975	207.00	180.46	26.54	24481.48
22	FEB 1 1975	207.00	180.26	26.74	24454.74
23	MAR 1 1975	207.00	180.06	26.94	24427.80
24	APR 1 1975	207.00	179.86	27.14	24400.66
25	MAY 1 1975	207.00	179.67	27.33	24373.33
26	JUNE 1 1975	207.00	179.46	27.54	24345.79
27	JULY 1 1975	207.00	179.26	27.74	24318.05
28	AUG 1 1975	207.00	179.06	27.94	24290.11
29	SEPT 1 1975	207.00	178.85	28.15	24261.96
30	OCT 1 1975	207.00	178.64	28.36	24233.60
31	NOV 1 1975	207.00	178.43	28.57	24205.03
32	DEC 1 1975	207.00	178.22	28.78	24176.25
33	JAN 1 1976	207.00	178.01	28.99	24147.26
34	FEB 1 1976	207.00	177.80	29.20	24118.06
35	MAR 1 1976	207.00	177.58	29.42	24088.64
36	APR 1 1976	207.00	177.37	29.63	24059.01
37	MAY 1 1976	207.00	177.15	29.85	24029.16
38	JUNE 1 [illegible]	207.00	176.93	30.07	23999.09
39	JULY [illegible]	207.00	[illegible]	[illegible]	[illegible]68.80
40	[illegible] 1 1996	207.00	[illegible]	[illegible]	[illegible]
[illegible]	NOV 1 1996	[illegible]	25.57	[illegible].43	3290.[illegible]
[illegible]	DEC 1 1996	[illegible]	24.23	182.77	3107.97
285	JAN 1 1997	207.00	22.88	184.12	2923.85
286	FEB 1 1997	207.00	21.53	185.47	2738.38
287	MAR 1 1997	207.00	20.16	186.84	2551.54
288	APR 1 1997	207.00	18.79	188.21	2363.33
289	MAY 1 1997	207.00	17.40	189.60	2173.73
290	JUNE 1 1997	207.00	16.01	190.99	1982.74
291	JULY 1 1997	207.00	14.60	192.40	1790.34
292	AUG 1 1997	207.00	13.18	193.82	1596.52
293	SEPT 1 1997	207.00	11.76	195.24	1401.28
294	OCT 1 1997	207.00	10.32	196.68	1204.60
295	NOV 1 1997	207.00	8.87	198.13	1006.47
296	DEC 1 1997	207.00	7.41	199.59	806.88
297	JAN 1 1998	207.00	5.94	201.06	605.82
298	FEB 1 1998	207.00	4.46	202.54	403.28
299	MAR 1 1998	207.00	2.97	204.03	199.25
300	APR 1 1998	200.72	1.47	199.25	0.00

* Most financial institutions will supply a computerized schedule on request for free but some will require a fee. Financial software is also available for your personal computer.

19

AVERAGING THE INTEREST RATE

If you wish to know what your annual rate of interest is on a combination of mortgages, here is how to do it:

Take the per cent of each mortgage to the total debt (of 100%) and multiply by its rate of interest, viz:

Example		*Principal Amount*
1st mortgage:	8%	\$16,000
2nd mortgage:	14%	4,000
Total mortgage debt:		\$20,000

$$\frac{16{,}000}{20{,}000} \times \frac{100}{1} = 80\% \times 8\% = 6.4\%$$

$$\frac{4{,}000}{20{,}000} \times \frac{100}{1} = 20\% \times 14\% = 2.8\%$$

Total: *100%* 9.2% (average)

Example:		*Principal Amount*
1st mortgage	8.25%	\$12,544
2nd mortgage:	10.50%	3,724
3rd mortgage:	13.00%	3,332
Total mortgage debt:		\$19,600

$$\frac{12{,}544}{19{,}600} \times \frac{100}{1} = 64\% \times 8.25\% = 5.280\%$$

$$\frac{3{,}724}{19{,}600} \times \frac{100}{1} = 19\% \times 10.50\% = 1.995\%$$

$$\frac{3{,}332}{19{,}600} \times \frac{100}{1} = 17\% \times 13.00\% = 2.210\%$$

Total: *100%* 9.485% (average)

(Sometimes you're not as bad off as you think you are . . .)

Here is another way to do it. Follow the figures I have given you in the second example, and round out the interest on an annual basis:

	Principal		*Interest*
1st mortgage:	$12,544.	@ 8.25%	$1,034.88
2nd mortgage:	3,724.	@ 10.50%	391.12
3rd mortgage:	3,332.	@ 13.00%	433.16
	$19,600.		$1,859.16

Now, just divide the interest by the principal and multiply by one hundred:

$$\frac{1{,}859.16}{19{,}600.00} \times \frac{100}{1} = 9.485\%$$

Same thing, see?

20

A COSTLY ERROR IN PRIVATE MORTGAGING

In mortgaging done by conventional lenders such as banks and trust companies, the mortgage deed will contain a statement showing that the interest is compounded twice-yearly. This automatically complies with the federal *Interest Act*, which states:

> Whenever any principal money or interest secured by mortgage of real estate is, by the mortgage, made payable on the sinking fund plan, or on any plan under which the payments of principal money and interest are blended, or on any plan that involves an allowance of interest on stipulated repayments, no interest whatever shall be chargeable, payable or recoverable, on any part of the principal money advanced, unless the mortgage contains a statement showing the amount of such principal money and the rate of interest chargeable thereon, calculated yearly or half-yearly, not in advance.

I would not think that the foregoing reference to a "statement" means that it must be shown in total in one paragraph in the mortgage deed. A statement means "something stated," and I would assume that providing the information required is *somewhere* in the mortgage deed, it would qualify as being stated. So the conventional lenders ensure that their deeds comply by having it printed as a part of their forms.

In private mortgaging, it is quite common to find that although the mortgage deeds naturally state the annual rate of interest in the loan, no mention is made of any frequency of compounding, or calculating the interest. Most of these private mortgages require monthly payments, and this is where a costly error may be found.

To arrive at the interest to be paid for the period (month) the lender quite often simply divides the annual rate of interest by twelve. Which isn't right, if the mortgage is to comply with the *Interest Act.* After all, dividing the annual rate by twelve means that the interest is being compounded monthly. A mortgage showing an annual rate of 12% would not comply with the Act if the interest were compounded monthly, producing a rate of 1% per month.

This error arises in mortgages that require the payment to be blended — as $200 per month, including principal and interest, for example.

Take a $12,000 12% mortgage, payments $200 each month. I @ P.

If the lender divides by twelve to arrive at the interest to be paid for the first month, here is what we see:

$$\frac{12\%}{12} = 1\% \text{ of } \$12{,}000 = \$120 \text{ interest}$$

The payment will therefore be $120 interest and the balance, $80, credited to principal.

The second month will show that the principal balance owing is $12,000 less $80, or $11,920. Here is the second month's breakdown:

$$\frac{12\%}{12} = 1\% \text{ of } \$11{,}920 = \$119.20 \text{ interest}$$

The payment will therefore be $119.20 interest and the balance, $80.80, credited to principal.

Still with me? Now, if this mortgage interest were compounded yearly, here is what the first month would show, breaking down the $200 payment:

$12,000 × 0.948879 = $113.86 interest, and the balance of the payment ($86.14) would be credited to principal.

The borrower, in the foregoing example of compounding monthly, pays $61.4, or 5.39% more than he should, in one payment alone!

The interest factor of 0.948879 was obtained from the tables in this book, which can come in quite handy.

Examine your mortgage deeds carefully. As a borrower, you just might save a bundle, and as a lender, you just might save yourself a headache.

21

MORTGAGE ACCELERATION SAVINGS

Mortgage payments acceleration is one of the greatest means available to force oneself to save money.

The example used is a repayment schedule of the first twelve months of a 40-year 10% mortgage loan of $25,250, each monthly payment being $210.41.

Payment Number	Interest Payment	Principal Payment	Balance Owing
1	$206.16	$4.25	$25,245.75
2	206.13	4.28	25,241.47
3	206.09	4.32	25,237.15
4	206.06	4.42	25,232.80
5	206.02	4.39	25,228.41
6	205.99	4.42	25,223.99
7	205.95	4.46	25,219.53
8	205.91	4.50	25,215.03
9	205.88	4.53	25,210.50
10	205.84	4.57	25,205.93
11	205.80	4.61	25,201.32
12	205.76	4.65	25,196.67

When a mortgagor reaches the twelfth payment of this loan, he has the privilege of paying an additional amount of principal, not in excess of 10% of the original amount of the mortgage.

The additional payment made under this privilege is not made in a round figure such as exactly $100. It is a payment that will reach a future balance of the loan. For example, the principal balance owing at payment No. 32 is $25,095.36.

The difference between the balance owing at the twelfth payment and the balance owing at the thirty-second payment is $101.31. By paying the lender this amount, 20 payments of $210.41 each are eliminated. This amounts to $4,208.20.

The chart illustrates the savings that can be effected by making various additional mortgage principal payments at the end of the first year.

Additional Payment	No. of Payments Eliminated	Payment Dollars Eliminated	Balance Owing	Time Left on Mortgage
$101.31	20	$ 4,208.20	$25,095.36	37 yrs., 4 mos.
201.38	37	7,785.17	24,995.29	35 yrs., 11 mos.
301.91	52	10,941.32	24,894.76	34 yrs., 8 mos.
407.48	66	13,887.06	24,789.19	33 yrs., 6 mos.
508.04	78	16,411.98	24,688.63	32 yrs., 6 mos.

22

DEDUCTIBLE MORTGAGE INTEREST

Aside from deducting mortgage interest on investment properties, how about deducting the interest on the mortgage you have on your own home, your principal dwelling? In the United States it is easy. Just do it, because that's the way it is for the lucky American homeowner. And what a difference it makes in the income tax one pays.

Take a US mortgage of 9% for example. When one knocks the interest off the annual tax bite, it is no longer 9%. Here is what it *really* is.

Tax Bracket	Real Mortgage Rate
25%	6.75%
30%	6.30%
35%	5.85%
40%	5.40%
50%	4.50%

That's right. If one is in a 40% tax bracket in the United States, the 9% mortgage will cost less than 6%.

We pay our mortgage interest in after-tax dollars. Here is what we really pay on a 10 1/2% mortgage using the same formula:

Tax Bracket	Comparable Rate
25%	14.00%
30%	15.00%
35%	16.15%
40%	17.50%
50%	21.00%

What this means is that, for example, the Canadian borrower in the 40% tax bracket would be paying 17 1/2% interest on his mortgage if he had the privilege of deducting it from his income tax, to bring it down to the 10 1/2% after deduction.

However gloomy the foregoing, there is one way to deduct the interest paid on your principal dwelling mortgage. Our *Income Tax Act* allows one's principal dwelling to be used as security to obtain a loan for the purpose of acquiring investments that will produce income. Of course, you can really use anything for security that a lender will accept to get the money, but many of us overlook the good old homestead.

This doesn't mean that you can suddenly purchase an interest-bearing security with your spare cash and then start deducting the interest on your mortgage. The money must be specifically borrowed for a specific investment purpose, which means that you would take out a new mortgage on your home, and invest the entire proceeds in the investment venture. You will have to prove this to the income tax people. Then you may deduct the mortgage interest from your income tax.

There are variations, of course. If one borrowed $40,000 by a mortgage and only used $30,000 of it for investment, then only the interest on the $30,000 portion could be deducted, and not the interest on the entire loan. Again, you will have to prove it.

However, before you rush out and borrow a pile for investment purposes, examine it. There would be no point in borrowing money at 10 1/2% and lending it at 9%. That would obviously be a losing proposition, so you must ensure that your investment will show a profit over the net costs of borrowing the money, regardless of its nature.

Also, check with your bank manager regarding the latest rules about registered retirement savings plans. You may be in for a pleasant surprise in the way you may engineer an interest-deductible loan using your home as security for investing in your RRSP.

23

PAYING OFF THE MORTGAGE

There are four basic types of repayment privileges in mortgage deeds — your mortgage will conform to one of them.

Corporate Borrowers

The *Interest Act* precludes any prepayment privileges in a mortgage where the borrower is a joint stock company or other corporation, and in any debenture issued by any such company or corporation.

If the mortgage is one with a 20-year term, the mortgagor is bound to its deed for 20 years. However, if the lender wishes to allow the borrower to repay the loan before its maturity, it is his privilege to do so. This can be written into the deed, or otherwise negotiated.

If the prevailing interest rates at the time of a request to discharge such a mortgage are much higher than the rate in the mortgage, this will probably create no problem. The lender will obviously be glad to have his money returned in order to reinvest it at a higher rate of interest.

Conventional Loans

Here I refer to loans made by such corporations as insurance and trust companies, banks, and other large lenders.

Again, the *Interest Act* applies. Whenever any mortgage is not payable until a time of more than five years after the date of a mortgage (a mortgage with a term of more than five years), the borrower is entitled to repay the principal balance owing at any time after the first five years.

With this prepayment, an additional interest charge equal to three months' interest of the mortgage balance is to be made.

The *Interest Act* states that the balance may be paid in such circumstances "together with three months' further interest *in lieu of notice*."

One might assume that if a borrower gave the lender three months' notice of his intention to repay the loan, no additional interest would be required. But with no guarantee that the borrower will in fact repay the mortgage in three months, such notice is not acceptable by lenders, and the additional interest must be paid.

National Housing Act Loans

Direct funding from CMHC is presently in very short supply, but there is plenty of money available from its approved lenders.

If the mortgage loan is not in default, the borrower has the privilege of paying an additional amount of principal, not in excess of 10% of the original amount of the mortgage, on the first anniversary of the date for adjustment of interest (when the mortgage is one year old).

A similar amount may be paid on the second anniversary date. In each case, three months' interest must be paid on the amount of any such additional payment. These two repayment privileges are not cumulative.

When the mortgage is three years old, and on any instalment date thereafter, the borrower may repay the whole amount owing, or any part of it, together with three months' additional interest on any such additional payment.

"Open" Mortgages

It is quite common for a property owner to accept a mortgage as part of the purchase price of the property he is selling.

The majority of the "purchase mortgages" will contain a clause allowing the mortgagor to pay any part (or all) of the mortgage at any time, or on any payment date, without requiring the borrower to pay any interest penalty.

The obvious reason is that the lender will be delighted to get his money.

In addition to the above, of course, conventional and private lenders can (and often do) insert additional repayment clauses in deeds.

24

WHY PAY OFF A MORTGAGE?

This question often comes up. A mortgagor has about $20,000 principal balance owing on a mortgage which has not reached the end of its term. A repayment privilege is that it can be repaid at any time without notice or bonus. Now, the mortgagor finds himself with a financial windfall and wonders if he should leave the mortgage alone or pay it off.

That answer is a matter of simple arithmetic. Let us assume that:

a) The rate of interest in the $20,000 mortgage is 9%.
b) The mortgagor could safely invest his money at 10%.

Investing $20,000 at 10% produces a round $2,000 annually. If one is in a 40% tax bracket, the government will take $800 of this, which will leave net income of $1,200 on the investment. Twelve hundred dollars is 6% of $20,000.

So, in this example, one would receive a net return of 6%, and pay the mortgage at 9%, which would cost money. If the mortgage were paid off with the $20,000 there would obviously be a saving.

Take the same example with a $50,000 mortgage, at 9%, and a $50,000 investment at 10%.

Return @ 10%	$5,000
Taxable: $5,000 @ 40%	2,000
Net return on $50,000 investment	$3,000

Now, the picture is a little bleaker. The net sum of $3,000 represents a return of 6%, on the $50,000 investment. The money comes in at about 6% and goes out at 9%. Obviously, this is going to cost about

$1,500 a year right out of the mortgagor's pocket, so the mortgage should certainly be paid off.

The principal consideration here should be: What would you do with the money if you didn't pay off the mortgage? Could it be used to better advantage, possibly to buy some realty or an old masterpiece?

The choice is yours, but if it is a matter of weighing invested capital to produce a fixed return, use the foregoing examples to fit your own particular circumstances, and the answer to the original question will be quite clear to you.

25

THE DISCHARGE CERTIFICATE

How would you like to have the sale of your house held up because of a debt you paid five years ago?

When a creditor obtains a judgment against a debtor, the judgment is registered with the sheriff's office.

When property is conveyed from one person to another, the last thing checked by the purchaser's solicitor before registration of the deed is the sheriff's records. He wants to be sure there are no outstanding judgments registered against the seller. If there are, they must be cleared off and paid before the property can change hands.

When a judgment is registered with the sheriff, there are two ways to pay it off. Pay the sheriff or pay the judgment creditor.

Paying the sheriff will ensure the judgment is removed — not so paying the creditor.

The creditor registers the judgment but there's no law that says he has to cancel it in the sheriff's office.

If you pay the creditor, ask him to advise the sheriff the debt has been paid. Ask for a copy of his letter to the sheriff. Then check with the sheriff to ensure the debt has been removed. Keep after it.

Why?

Well, suppose you're the debtor. You paid the bill and the creditor didn't advise the sheriff.

Two years later, the creditor goes to heaven. Then his solicitor has a heart attack. Then the purchaser's solicitor finds the judgment registered with the sheriff.

Now, if you've lost the proof of payment, why should the sheriff remove it? You have a problem!

And so it is with the mortgage. When it's paid off, the mortgagee or the lender certainly isn't going to see that the deed is removed from the title records. The borrower must do that.

The only costs required of a mortgage lender are the nominal charges for registering the mortgage, and sometimes the borrower even pays for that.

So, when you pay off your mortgage, get a mortgage discharge certificate from the lender. Give it to your lawyer and, for a nominal fee, it will be removed from registration against your property.

If this isn't done, it could cause problems years after paying off the mortgage — when you're selling your property.

For example, the lender might have died — or moved. You'll have difficulty convincing a lawyer the debt has been paid. All the buyer knows is that the mortgage is still registered.

Say you have some work done on your house and later have a financial dispute with the tradesman. You could find a mechanic's lien registered against the title to your property.

Clouds on a title can be downright annoying. Give a man a short option to buy your land and what can happen? Why, he could assign his rights to the option to another, who could register the assignment. Now try and get that one removed years later without a few headaches.

For your own peace of mind, check government records on your own property periodically — just to ensure that everything is A-O.K.

Your property will be registered in one of two ways: in a registry or a land titles office.

Searching title in a land titles office is comparatively simple. Everything pertaining to your own property will be registered in a book in one place.

But not so with the registry office. That's where the frustration begins. You may find yourself jumping from page to page, skipping some and then going into another book. And another.

Take your copy of the title deed to the county records office (in Toronto, at City Hall). They'll tell you where and how to check your own property.

26

RENEWING THE MORTGAGE

For years the mortgagor has been doing his best to keep up the payments on the loan, and now the mortgage is nearing the end of its term. This is when a mortgage must be paid off, replaced, or renewed.

Well, most of us can't pay it off, so that's out. Replacing it with a new mortgage from a different lender can be costly and usually means a new set of fees all around. So we logically look to the lender in our present mortgage deed.

If one has a record of making payments on time, or reasonably on time, there will be no problem with large institutional lenders. However, many borrowers have been late with a payment or two or more, and some may have even gone through the traumatic experience of a court action, or something approaching it. Such factors may make one feel that the lender will be reluctant to renew the loan, but this is not necessarily true.

One of the advantages of doing business with a larger lender, such as a bank, is that this lender likes to keep a high profile in its public image, plus the fact that it is in business to make money, and therefore it will be reasonable in assessing renewal.

I know of one borrower who had a record of being consistently late in making mortgage payments to a bank, although the payments were always brought up-to-date eventually. The borrower began wondering about the chances of renewal when, one day, about six weeks before the term expiry, an offer from the lender to renew the loan was received in the mail. Right out of the blue and most welcome. Here is how it was handled.

The lender, in assessing the loan, naturally knew of all the late payments, but it also knew that they were brought up-to-date. So it offered to renew the mortgage loan at a rate of 1/4 of 1% *above* the rate it would have charged if the borrower had made his payments on time.

The renewal had a face value of about $38,000 which meant, in round figures, that the 1/4% increase carried an additional cost of close to $100 a year. The total cost over a five-year term would be just about what the cost of *replacing* the mortgage would be, so the borrower accepted it. The only other additional cost was a reasonable $75 administrative charge.

If the borrower had had a first-class record of payments, the cost of renewing his mortgage loan would have been just $75, and interest would be at the prevailing rate at the time of renewal. Stick with your present lender if you can — you will probably save money.

With offers of renewal from large lenders, there are options available, such as reduction in the amount of renewal or possibly an increased amount.

An agreement for a penalty-free mortgage may be obtained by agreeing to pay a higher rate than that offered in the renewal agreement. This means that during the life of the term (usually five years) the borrower can make additional lump-sum payments to reduce the debt, without being charged an interest penalty. This is worth considering and is simply a matter of arithmetic. The savings could be substantial if one wished to pay off the entire loan before maturity, which normally could be very costly.

If one wished to have a reduced term on the loan, such as three years, it would probably be available at *less* than one with a five-year term.

Also, mortgage debt insurance is usually instantly available covering the life of the mortgagor, reasonably, and without a medical. The insurance payment is made with the monthly loan payment.

The foregoing is what one can expect from large corporate lenders, but what about those "private" mortgages? That's where you take your chances on renewal, unless it is written into the mortgage deed.

One thing to remember about the renewal: Ensure that the *amortization* of the loan does not exceed the remaining number of years in the original loan. Otherwise, you'll never get it paid off.

Here is something for mortgagees and mortgagors to remember:

A common expression of a right to renew a mortgage is "Mortgagor shall have the privilege of renewing this mortgage for a further term of five years upon the same terms and conditions save any further right to renewal." The term, of course, could be for any agreed length of time.

It is often restricted to a condition that the borrower proves to be one of the good ones by never missing a payment. But not always . . .

How does a borrower renew the loan? Is notice required to be sent to the lender before the first term expires? Is it automatically renewed? Is it done by mailing some post-dated cheques to the lender?

Borrowers and lenders will be surprised to hear what the Ontario Court of Appeal had to say about one option to renew a mortgage:

> Where a mortgage drawn for five years contains a mortgagor's optional right of renewal for one further five-year term unrestricted by any stipulation as to the time in which the option may be exercised and not expressly conditioned upon the mortgagor not being in default, it may be validly exercised by a mortgagor three months after the maturity of the original term.

That decision came, "even though he (the borrower) had been frequently late in making instalment payments and was in default under the mortgage as well as in arrear in his covenanted payments of municipal taxes at maturity."

In a very recent case, a lender received no notice before or at the end of a mortgage term saying the borrower was exercising its option to renew the mortgage. So the lender fired off a letter to the borrower saying that in view of receiving no renewal notice, the principal sum, plus accruing interest, was "now due and payable."

This mortgage had a clause simply giving the borrower the right to renew, the only restriction being for one further term in the agreement.

The borrower, on the day after receiving the demand for payment, advised the lender it was exercising its right of renewal. The whole thing ended up in the Supreme Court, and the judge agreed with the borrower.

The judgment stated that where "no action had been taken by the lender to enforce payment of the mortgage, the right to renew had not been lost."

"Enforcing payment" would presumably be a court action, which was not done.

The judge noted that, "It will be observed that the agreement as to renewal is unrestricted as to the time within which the privilege may be exercised and not expressly conditioned otherwise."

It therefore would be in a lender's best interest to be most explicit about when and how a mortgage term may be extended.

This is not to suggest to a borrower that if there is a similar unrestricted renewal clause in a mortgage, the borrower can just relax and renew it any old time.

Remember the rights of the lender. The day after a borrower is late in a mortgage payment, the lender can fire off a writ of foreclosure, which is not only damned costly to the borrower, but it certainly interferes with any renewal rights that were not exercised — to say the least!

In a power of sale, the lender has to wait 15 days after default before taking legal action.

So the safest route to take with unrestricted (or any) renewal clauses is for the borrower to have his lawyer advise the lender (in plenty of time) that the option to renew is being exercised.

The lawyer should specialize in real property law.

PLEASE NOTE: The foregoing time limits for an action of foreclosure and power of sale are examples from Ontario Statute law.

27

THE POSTPONEMENT CLAUSE

This short chapter can save many headaches.

Remember, mortgage seniority is established by the time and date of registration in a land registry office or land titles office.

If one becomes a borrower in a second mortgage, and the term of the second mortgage has a longer period of time to run than the existing mortgage on the property, what happens when the first mortgage becomes due?

When such a situation occurs, the first mortgage cannot be renewed or replaced without the express permission of the one holding the second mortgage.

This can mean trouble.

If there are two mortgages on a property, it is unlikely that the mortgagor has the funds to pay off the larger first mortgage and allow the second to take its place.

There is only one solution.

The second mortgage must contain a postponement clause, which will automatically allow the mortgagor to renew or replace the first mortgage when it becomes due.

This does not mean that a $10,000 first mortgage can be increased to $15,000 with the borrower putting the $5,000 in his pocket.

Any increase in the principal amount of a first mortgage being renewed or replaced under these circumstances is paid to the second mortgagee to reduce his mortgage.

Know the mortgage expiration date and remember the postponement clause.

28

BUYING A MORTGAGE

The most common mortgages bought and sold are the "second" mortgages. There is no mystery about them and they are, if properly purchased, a sound and profitable investment.

Before you buy one, however, a few guidelines will not only help you decide which one to buy but also ensure that the price is right.

The four prime areas that require scrutiny are (1) the real estate used as a security; (2) the equity in the property; (3) the covenant, or the ability of the mortgagor (borrower) to repay the loan; and (4) the details of the mortgage terms.

Whenever a mortgagee (lender) is asked to loan money, the property involved will be inspected and appraised to ensure that there is sufficient tangible security for the loan. The mortgagor pays for the inspection.

When considering the purchase of second mortgages one cannot very well have an appraisal done on all the real estate involved. This would require a fee to be paid for each mortgage considered.

The alternative is for the mortgage purchaser to inspect the property himself. In this inspection, it is wise not only to check carefully the condition of the building, but also to note how the title holder (owner) is maintaining it.

Regardless of any documents produced to show what the current market value of the property is, the mortgage purchaser should, if possible, inspect properties for sale in the same area that are of a similar plan and size to the one secured by the mortgage and make comparisons.

Also, check with the hydro authority, municipal buildings department and registry office to see if there are any outstanding work orders issued against the property. If there are, the work will have to be done, and the cost of repairs or renovations must be considered in the value.

Mortgage seniority is established by the time and date of registering the mortgage deed. A second mortgage ranks second, so that the mortgagee of the first priority has first claim to the dollar value of the security.

Other, but junior, mortgages may be registered against the property, but the second mortgage will take precedence over these.

The equity in a property is its market value, less the total amount of all mortgages and other financial charges registered against the property. It is therefore important to know something about the mortgagor and his ability to repay the loan, because his only stake in the property is this equity.

If there is very little equity, it does not necessarily mean that the mortgagor will be any more lax in his payments than one with a larger equity, but regardless of the tangible security, a mortgagee likes to have some reasonable assurance that the debt is going to be paid, and paid according to contract.

The decision to purchase a second mortgage must be based on two prime factors: (1) the rate of interest; and (2) the terms of the loan.

Second mortgages, having a secondary position, normally require a higher rate of return than first mortgages. If the current rate of interest, for example, is 14% on secondary financing, then the rate in the mortgage considered must be adjusted accordingly.

The hard-headed mortgage buyer will demand it. A rule of thumb method of rapid calculation is as follows: Assuming the rate of interest on an existing second mortgage is 9%, and one wishes to have it produce 14%, the 5% difference is multiplied by the number of years remaining in the term of the mortgage, or to its maturity, when the principal balance is due and payable.

The result is the discount at which the buyer can purchase the mortgage. Some examples are shown in the chart.

By the purchase of a mortgage in this manner, two obvious bonuses are secured: (1) the additional interest extracted from the mortgage is obtained in advance; and (2) this additional interest is based on the present outstanding principal balance of the mortgage, and not on a reducing balance which occurs as the loan payments progress:

Examples of One Method Mortgage Buyers Use in Discounting Second Mortgages

Mortgage Principal	Rate of Interest	Interest Required	Difference	Mortgage Term	Discount
$2,000	10%	14%	4%	3 years	12% ($ 240)
3,000	9%	15%	6%	4 years	24% ($ 720)
4,000	8%	13%	5%	5 years	25% ($1000)
5,000	10%	14%	4%	2 years	8% ($ 400)

To know the *exact* price one should pay for a mortgage to produce a specific yield, write to Consumers Computer Limited, Box 400, Willowdale, Ontario. An analysis will be tailor-made for you for a few dollars. If you are *selling* a mortgage, it is also important to obtain an accurate market evaluation of the mortgage. Don't sell it for less than you have to. The foregoing illustrations are not precisely accurate, and are used only as a rough guide to illustrate discounting.

REMEMBER THIS: If you are going to be a mortgagee in a purchase mortgage with the intention of selling it, keep the interest rate as close as possible to current market rates, and the term down to three years if possible.

29

PROTECTING ONE'S FAMILY

A wise and loving parent will have term life insurance to at least match the outstanding principal amount of the mortgages on the family home.

This will ensure that in the event of his or her death, the survivors will be left with a debt-free roof over their heads. A comforting thought!

Could your husband maintain your present mortgage payments? Would your wife be forced to sell the home you shared and fend for herself and your children? Think about it. We are a nation of procrastinators.

Unfortunately, not everyone can get term life insurance at the drop of a hat. It requires a medical examination, which not all can pass. Then what?

If one wished to borrow $20,000 would it be better getting it from a mortgage lender at 11%, or from a bank at 14%?

In many instances, it would be wiser for the borrower to take the 14% bank loan. Banks offer consumers two loan features that are well worth examining:

- The loan is insured at a small cost to the borrower, which means, of course, that if the borrower should expire, the loan will be automatically paid off and the debt cancelled.
- The loan is "open"; that is, it can be paid off at any time without penalty to the borrower.

The automatic debt-insured bank loan is an excellent feature. It forces one into an act of responsibility at no cost, in that it provides the borrower with needed coverage that may not be otherwise available.

There is no medical examination required to obtain this debt insurance, which is effective the minute one signs on the dotted line. Drop dead three feet from the bank and you're covered.

And the bank's open repayment privilege is a big bonus. Ask a mortgage lender what it would cost to pay off a loan before its maturity, and you'll see what I mean.

There are many things to consider when you are shopping for a loan, two absolute musts being life insurance to cover the debt, and the costs of payment before maturity.

The difference between the foregoing examples in the cost of borrowing is 3%. Simple interest on the $20,000 is $600 per year. The bank loan will therefore cost $50 per month more, but consider this: If the borrower could get term insurance to cover the debt, what would it cost? It depends on the borrower's age, so call an insurance agent and do your own arithmetic.

Subtract the answer you get from the bank costs.

Then ask a mortgage lender what it would cost to pay off the loan before maturity.

With the answers to these two points, the $50 a month extra payment to the bank could very well turn into a credit.

Always remember that when one commits oneself to a mortgage debt, there is the possibility that before the debt matures an opportunity may present itself to sell the property at a handsome profit — to say nothing of an opportune time.

It the buyer wants the property free of debt, the mortgage lender might turn out to be a monster in his legal demands for repayment. Someone has to pay the bonus, which certainly affects the selling price.

So read the mortgage deed carefully before signing it.

And don't forget, if one *can't* get term insurance, and pops off, the bank costs will be peanuts to the estate when reaching the bottom line.

30

CANADA'S NATIONAL HOUSING ACT

Canada's federal government has been involved in housing development since the Depression of the 1930s.

In 1935, the *Dominion Housing Act* was passed, principally as a means of providing jobs, but also to help improve the quality of Canadian housing and to establish building standards.

Under the *Dominion Housing Act*, the federal government provided one-quarter of the money for high-ratio mortgages with private lenders providing the balance. The objective was to make it easier for people to build and buy houses by supplying bigger mortgages — and make possible smaller down payments than would be available from private lenders.

Between 1935 and 1938, about 5,000 new houses were put up with financing provided in part under the *Dominion Housing Act*. Then, in 1938, the first act was replaced with the *National Housing Act*, which provided more mortgage money and which, for the first time, offered loan assistance for the construction of housing for low-income families.

But the federal government really didn't come into its own in the housing field until after World War II. Housing starts fell off during the war, so when hostilities ended, there was an enormous backlog of demand. To help meet this demand, a new *National Housing Act* was passed in 1945.

Central Mortgage and Housing Corporation, a Crown Corporation, put up 17,000 new houses for veterans and took over ownership of all other wartime housing so that, by 1949, the government agency owned 41,000 houses. Most of these wartime houses have since been sold to former tenants.

Under the *National Housing Act* (1945), postwar housing construction entered a real boom period. In the early years, lots of private money also was available for mortgage financing. Canada's output rose from 64,400 new houses in 1946 to 92,350 in 1950, when almost half of the year's total production was financed under NHA.

By the early fifties, however, private mortgage money sources began to dry up; the boom had been so explosive that most "conventional" money was fully committed. So in 1954 the *National Housing Act* was again overhauled, this time establishing a system of insurance of NHA mortgages so that these mortgages became an attractive alternative to bonds as long-term investments. Under this system, the full amount of the mortgage was provided by a private lender and the government guaranteed, first 98%, and finally the full loan amount (the borrower paid the insurance fee that provided this guarantee). In this way the government for a while stopped actually lending money — except as a last resort — for housing, and simply made it 100% safe for private lenders to provide funds.

At around the same time, the *Bank Act* was changed so that, for the first time, the chartered banks were allowed to make long-term mortgage loans. This increased available funds for home building tremendously.

By 1958 the number of housing starts in Canada had risen to the unprecedented total of 164,000.

Since then things have become more difficult for builders and buyers alike. Land costs, wages, and cost of materials have all risen, driving up the price of new houses, to say nothing of rising interest rates.

Because the banks were limited by law to charging 6% interest, they virtually stopped putting money into NHA mortgages in 1959 when interest rates started rising. The other lenders — life insurance, trust, and loan companies — still had money to put into mortgages, but they put more and more into higher-paying private mortgages, and less into the low-paying NHA variety.

So, although housing starts reached an all-time record of 166,565 in 1965, the supply of private money for mortgages began to dwindle away.

To keep the industry going and to put roofs over Canadians' heads, the government changed the *Bank Act* again to allow the bank to lend mortgage money at interest rates higher than 6%. Even more significantly, the government has pumped vast amounts of public money directly into housing as private funds started staying away. By 1967, the federal government was holding, through CMHC, about three *billion* dollars worth of mortgages.

During the past few years, further amendments were made to the Act, and today the help provided by CMHC is varied and extensive. Here are the current provisions for home ownership loans.

The down payment must be within your financial means and the monthly payments on your mortgage plus municipal taxes and other continuing charges such as heat, electricity, maintenance costs (and condominium costs, where applicable) should be covered comfortably by your housing budget. Whether you build or buy your new or existing home, the financing terms and conditions will be the same.

NHA Loans

National Housing Act loans are available for the purchase of a newly built home or the purchase and improvement (if required) of an existing dwelling.

The type of dwelling that may be bought or improved includes a single detached house, a unit of row housing, a duplex, a unit in a condominium, or one or both units of a semi-detached dwelling. Cooperative housing associations wishing to purchase new or existing housing projects may also obtain NHA loans.

Loans may also be made to builders for the construction of houses for sale or for financing houses acquired as "trade-ins" which are to be resold to a buyer who intends to occupy the dwelling. The buyer makes a down payment to the builder and assumes responsibility for repayment of the mortgage.

Types of NHA Loans

Approved Lender Loans: The *National Housing Act* provides for loans by approved lenders. These are private companies such as chartered banks, life insurance companies, and trust and loan companies authorized by the federal government to lend under the terms of the act. A list of these companies is available from any Canada Mortgage and Housing Corporation office.

Direct Loans: Direct Loans from CMHC are available only in those areas not normally serviced by approved lenders. For information regarding your particular locality, you should discuss your requirements with the nearest office of CMHC.

In 1992 a new program was introduced for first-time buyers in addition to the existing program for buyers with minimal down payments. This new program will be evaluated over a period of two years; in 1994 a decision will be made whether it should continue. These two programs vary in their requirements and criteria.

CRITERIA	PROGRAM 1 (Existing Program)	PROGRAM 2 (New Program)
Eligibility	everyone	first-time buyer or one who has not owned property within the past five years
Price Ceiling	no maximum value	value cannot exceed: • $250,000 (Toronto census area) • $250,000 (Vancouver census area) • $175,000 (major centers) • $125,000 (rest of Canada)
GDS*	32%	35%
TDS**	42%	42%
Maximum Loan	blended formula based on appraised value and not on sale price.	

	95% maximum 90% of 1st $180,000 plus 80% of balance of appraised value.	
Down Payment	Price minus the loan amount to minimum of 10% Down payment cannot be borrowed; it must be the buyer's own funds or a gift (usually from family)	
Term of Loan	No restriction	Minimum 5-year term.

*GDS = gross debt service ratio: cost of principal and interest of the loan, municipal taxes, heating cost and 50% of the maintenance fee if applicable, expressed as a percentage of gross income.

**TDS = total debt service ratio: same as GDS but includes all monthly payments of other debt or lease obligations (e.g. car loan, car lease.)

Interest Rate

The interest rate for loans made by approved lenders is negotiable between borrower and lender, but must be within current market ranges.

Taxes

Under NHA arrangements, your monthly payment to the lender includes an amount equal to one-twelfth of the estimated annual taxes on your home.

When you receive your tax bill from the municipality, you forward it to your lender for payment. Some lenders arrange with the municipality to have tax bills sent directly to them for payment and then mail the receipted bill to the homeowner.

The monthly amounts collected are based on an estimate of your taxes for the year ahead. Where taxes prove to be higher or lower than the estimated amount, the lender adjusts the tax portion of your monthly payment accordingly.

Repayment of Loan

Most NHA loans are made on a one- to five-year basis, with repayment amortized over a period of 25 years.

The interest rate and related monthly mortgage payments are constant for one to five years, after which the borrower must renegotiate the interest rate with the lender. Monthly payments are then adjusted to reflect the new interest rate.

Prepayment of Loan

Various lenders have different policies regarding prepayment of all or part of the balance owing on your loan. An annual prepayment of 10% to 15% of the loan amount without penalty is quite common. However, prepaying more than is specified in the stated policy of the lender or prepaying the entire amount would likely carry a penalty of three months' interest or a penalty based on the interest rate differential, whichever is greater. See chapter 37, "The Conventional Mortgage," for a comprehensive discussion of mortgage products available.

Application for Loan

Formerly, a loan application could not be approved if work had gone beyond the first floor joist (including subfloor) stage of construction for one- and two-unit houses.

Now, applications can be approved if work has gone beyond the first floor joist when units are registered to New Home Warranty programs and NHA standards, or equivalent, are enforced by the municipality.

There is an application fee.

Mortgage Insurance Fees

All NHA approved lenders are insured against loss on the loans they make through the operation of a Mortgage Insurance Fund established under authority of the act. A table of current charges follows:

LOAN SIZE (as a percentage of property value)	PREMIUM
up to 65%	.50%
more than 65% up to 75%	.75%
more than 75% up to 80%	1.25%
more than 80% up to 85%	2.0 %
more than 85% up to 95%	2.5 %

Insurance of this type must not be confused with mortgage life insurance, which provides for payment of the outstanding balance in case of death of the borrower. Mortgage life insurance may be obtained from insurance agents and, quite commonly, from large lending institutions.

Other Charges

In addition to the application fee and mortgage insurance fee, the approved lender may deduct from your loan, or bill you, for costs involved in obtaining a surveyor's certificate or its equivalent showing the location of your house on the lot, and for legal work performed for the lender. You also are required to pay the accumulated interest on mortgage advances made during construction.

Start of Construction

It is a condition of loans under NHA that a construction stage inspection be requested within six months of approval of the loan.

Loan Advances

Construction of your house may be started when your loan has been approved. The loan will be disbursed to you in progress advances as work proceeds, or in a single advance on completion as requested by the lender.

The amount of each advance is based on the percentage of work completed.

Inspections

While your house is being built, a number of construction inspections are made by CMHC. These are not full architectural or engineering inspections; they are made to protect the investment of the lender by ensuring that the house is built in reasonable conformity with the plans and specifications, and housing standards prescribed by CMHC.

They may also serve to check the construction progress of loan advances.

31

THE HIGH-RATIO MORTGAGE

Prior to 1964, a Canadian buying a house with a conventional mortgage had to come up with either one-third of the value of the house and lot in cash or put down less cash and assume, or obtain, a second mortgage. This second usually carried a fairly high rate of interest and involved additional legal costs.

Consequently, many were unable to realize their dream of owning their own home. In 1964, conventional high-ratio mortgages, jointly funded by a regulated lending institution (i.e., an insurance company, trust company or loan company) and a nonregulated mortgage investment company, and insured by The Mortgage Insurance Company of Canada (the first private sector mortgage insurance company in Canada), became available and the picture changed dramatically. Initially, first mortgages were available up to 83 1/3% of value and subsequently to 87 1/2%. For six years, until 1970, variations and refinements made the high-ratio mortgage an important part of the housing scene.

In March of 1970, amendments to the *Canadian and British Insurance Companies Act,* the *Foreign Insurance Companies Act*, the *Trust Companies Act*, and the *Loan Companies Act* were passed by the Parliament of Canada. Under these amendments, lending institutions operated under these Acts, as well as the chartered banks, were authorized to make mortgage loans over 75% of value (using all of their own funds) provided the excess was insured by a policy of mortgage insurance, issued either by a federal or provincial government or agency thereof, or an insurance company registered under the *Canadian and British Insurance Companies Act.*

In 1973, the private mortgage insurance industry expanded with the creation of two other companies, the Sovereign Mortgage Insurance Company and Insmor Mortgage Insurance Company. These companies merged in 1977 and Insmor carried on in the business.

Late in 1981, Insmor and MICC merged, leaving the Mortgage Insurance Company of Canada as the only private mortgage insurer in Canada.

Since 1964, one in three families have bought their own home, using the MICC insured high-ratio mortgage plan. Under this plan, the mortgage lender is provided with substantial protection against loss in the event the borrower does not make his mortgage payments, and the homeowner is able to purchase a home with a modest down payment.

Using an MICC high-ratio mortgage, a house may be purchased with as little as 10% down to one 90% mortgage. The loan amount obtainable is based on a formula as follows:

90% of the first $180,000 of value
plus
80% of value in excess of $180,000

If you meet the criteria for first-time buyers as set out in chapter 30, "Canada's National Housing Act," you may purchase a house with as little as 5% down to a mortgage of 95%, up to a ceiling price depending on your geographic area.

A mortgage insurance premium is payable by the borrower. It does not have to be paid in cash, but may be added to the mortgage. The premium varies with the loan amount, the loan-to-value ratio and the term of the policy. Following is the premium structure for a high-ratio mortgage on an existing house for the type of coverage usually required by lenders:

Loan to Value Ratio	*Policy Term*	*Premium*
75–80%	20 years	1 1/4% of loan amount
80–85%	20 years	2% of loan amount
85%	20 years	2 1/2% of loan amount
	First-time buyers:	
90–95%	20 years	2 1/2% of loan amount

MICC also offers a range of other coverages to lenders at varying premium rates.

The following example illustrates the loan amount available, the down payment required, and the mortgage insurance premium payable for a typical case:

Home Value (existing property)	$180,000
Basic loan amount available =	
90% × $180,000 =	$162,000
Down payment required	$ 18,000
Mortgage insurance premium =	
2 1/2% × $162,000 =	$ 4,050
Total mortgage	
(unless premium paid in cash)	
Basic mortgage	$162,000
Mortgage Insurance premium	4,050
TOTAL MORTGAGE	$166,050

MICC high-ratio mortgages are available to finance the purchase of a new or existing home, to finance the construction of a new home for sale or occupancy, and to refinance an existing mortgage to obtain cash, consolidate debts, or carry out home improvements.

Eligible properties include detached houses, semi-detached properties, duplexes, triplexes and units in condominium projects. There is no minimum market value or maximum age limit for a house to qualify. Homes built prior to 1950 will be expected to be substantially modernized: e.g., new heating system, renovated bathroom and kitchen, improved insulation, etc. New houses must conform to the National Building Code and the Residential Standards Canada or the applicable municipal or provincial building codes. All new housing for sale must be covered by the applicable provincial or regional New Home Warranty Program.

High-ratio mortgages are available in all of Canada's major cities and communities constituting part of their market territory. Further information regarding communities where the MICC insured program is available may be obtained from the Mortgage Insurance Company of Canada.

The interest rate on an MICC insured high-ratio mortgage today, all across Canada, is generally the going rate of interest on conventional mortgage loans.

The borrower makes application to the mortgage lender in the usual way, and there is a complete lack of red tape and no special procedures involved. The low down payment makes buying easier. The larger mortgage amount also makes selling easier, should the homeowner decide to move.

The advent of the insured high-ratio mortgage has opened up the housing market to a large number of Canadians who have difficulty saving a large down payment or who are unwilling, or unable, to pay the high interest rates demanded on most second mortgages. Thousands of homeowners would undoubtedly be still paying rent, unable to enjoy the pride of ownership of their homes, if it were not for this facility.

High house prices and high interest rates make it difficult for some, and impossible for others, to buy. Land costs, labor costs, interest rates, and house prices will no more return to levels of the past than will the costs of autos, hamburgers, or golf balls. However, we can hope that items making up the end price of housing will stabilize, perhaps even ease somewhat. We can hope that items such as mortgage interest rates, which affect the carrying costs of housing, moderate as inflation eases.

Most mortgage lenders follow the general rule that borrowers should not commit themselves to pay more than 27% to 30% of gross salary for mortgage payments and taxes. (If a borrower has no other debts a higher ratio may be accepted.) This ratio is called the Gross Debt Service Ratio (GDS ratio).

A portion of the spouse's income may be used, depending on his or her age and the stability of his or her employment.

Example

Gross monthly income = $1,750.00
27% = $ 472.50
30% = $ 525.00

Therefore, a person with an income of $1,750 a month (before deductions) should normally not pay more than \$472.50 to \$525.00 per month on a mortgage, including taxes.

The lender also looks at the borrower's other debts, credit rating, and so on when reviewing a mortgage application. The general rule is that borrowers should not commit themselves to pay more than 37% to 40% of their monthly gross income to their mortgage payment (including taxes) and the monthly amount to be paid on other bank loans, finance company loans, etc. This ratio is referred to as the Total Debt Service Ratio — TDS ratio.

In order to determine the amount of mortgage that a borrower can afford, the amount of his or her income that can be committed to a monthly mortgage payment must be established using the GDS and TDS guidelines above. Assume that the amount available for the mortgage and taxes payment is \$500 and taxes are \$75 per month; the amount then available to cover mortgage principal and interest is \$425 per month. What amount of mortgage will a payment of \$425 per month repay?

A schedule of monthly payment factors is now required to assist in determining the mortgage amount. This schedule indicates the monthly payment required to pay off, or amortize, a mortgage of \$1,000 at various rates of interest over varying numbers of years. Assume that you can obtain a mortgage at 11 1/2% on a 25-year repayment plan. The monthly payment factor is \$9.97 per month per \$1,000 borrowed. Then \$425 per month would handle a mortgage of:

$$\frac{\$425}{9.97} \times \$1{,}000 - \$42{,}627$$

Application for a high-ratio mortgage loan is made to any MICC approved lender (i.e., banks, trust companies, credit unions, life insurance companies, savings and loan companies, caisses populaires.)

In addition to insuring high-ratio mortgages on homes, MICC also insures mortgages on income-producing properties such as apartment buildings, shopping centers, office buildings, etc. Details are available from MICC on request.

For a complete list of approved lenders, and detailed information on this service to home buyers, write to:

THE MORTGAGE INSURANCE COMPANY
OF CANADA
1 Dundas Street West, Suite 1600
Toronto, Ontario
M5G 1Z3

32

THE EXISTING MORTGAGE

This mortgage is already there, registered against the property. Without reference to interest rates, it is the cheapest way to get a mortgage.

When property is purchased that already has a mortgage registered against it, which the buyer would like to use in financing the purchase, a part of the purchase agreement would say something like "the purchaser agrees to assume an existing first mortgage now registered against the property" — with the details of the mortgage following this statement.

Well, what is the buyer really saying when he "agrees to assume" the mortgage?

All he is really saying to the vendor is that he will maintain the mortgage payments without the permission of the mortgagee!

The vendor (or a previous owner) is the one who signed the mortgage deed and has the covenant and responsibility to repay the debt. The covenantor is not released of his obligation simply because he transfers his property equity to someone else.

So the buyer assumes the mortgage, takes possession of the property and continues making the payments required by the mortgage. As long as the payments are received in time, the mortgagee is happy and not the slightest bit concerned about the new guy.

When one buys a property and assumes the existing mortgage(s) consider the financial and other advantages:

a) no mortgage application
b) no credit check (very seldom)
c) no waiting
d) no mortgage appraisal fee
e) no "arranging" fees
f) no legal fees

It can save a buyer hundreds of dollars, and, when the term expires, the buyer who has been paying the mortgagee on time will have an excellent chance of obtaining an immediate renewal of the loan, providing it was originally obtained from a conventional source. Private lenders often do not wish to renew mortgage loans.

A buyer, especially one who is in no particular hurry, would be well advised to restrict his house hunting to properties that have mortgages already registered against them that would suit him.

If one finds a property with an acceptable mortgage against it, but it falls short of loan requirements, study the availability of secondary financing and then average the interest rate in the total mortgage package. But if this route is taken, ensure that the *total* costs of the secondary financing are clearly understood.

The best and cheapest way to obtain secondary financing is covered in the following chapter, where the vendor lends a helping hand.

A point to remember here is to read the actual mortgage deed if you intend to assume a mortgage. Some deeds have a non-transfer clause in them, which means that if the secured property is sold, the mortgage must be paid off. Also, many lenders stipulate that anyone assuming an existing mortgage must be approved by the lender.

33

THE PURCHASE MORTGAGE

Who says it is hard to borrow money?

A man with a horrible credit record would have difficulty floating a loan at his bank for a few hundred dollars, but the same man can borrow as much as *fifty thousand dollars* or more quite easily when buying a home.

How? Why, he simply borrows it from the one selling him the home.

No credit check (or at least very seldom), no waiting for results of a mortgage application, instant approval of the loan, no problems. How about that?

It is the purchase mortgage. The mortgage held by the one selling the property. If one is looking for a top deal in a mortgage, here is where it is really possible.

When looking through the listing files or a real estate broker, this financing will be indicated on the listing by the notation "VTB" (Vendor Take Back) usually followed by "at current rates,) which, of course, refers to the current market interest rates.

What usually happens, though, is that the buyer makes his offer to the vendor with the interest rate lower than market rates, and often gets the deal.

There are two basic reasons for a vendor to agree to lend the buyer the money secured by the mortgage:

1. It is considered to be a good investment. A mortgage on property that is security familiar to the vendor, which produces a higher yield than other usual investments.
2. It makes the property very saleable because of the financing available to the buyer.

The purchase mortgage does not necessarily have to be one first mortgage. The majority of purchase mortgages are second mortgages, which are created after the buyer assumes an existing first mortgage or the buyer arranges a new first mortgage. Or a vendor might agree to hold two mortgages, the larger the first mortgage and the smaller the second, the reasons being:

1. Two separate mortgage deeds create two separate securities.
2. The vendor, holding the two mortgages, could perhaps give one to a relative, or use them as security in borrowing money on two separate occasions. Some people follow the old adage "don't put all your eggs in one basket."

Any way one looks at it, a property offered with the vendor helping with the financing can be a sweet deal.

In taking advantage of this financing, ensure that there is an "open" privilege clause inserted in the mortgage deed which will enable the borrower to repay any part or all of the outstanding principal balance at any time (or on any payment date) without notice or bonus.

34

PROS AND CONS OF THE PURCHASE MORTGAGE

Would you lend a stranger $50,000 cash?

It is done every day by people selling their homes and accepting a mortgage from a buyer as part of the purchase price. Here are some advantages and disadvantages to this, and sensible guidelines to follow.

The advantages are:

- The security for the loan is land, which is permanent. It won't go away. Anytime you need reassurance that your loan is secure, just go and take a look. The land is still there.
- Furthermore, it is security that is familiar to you: your own home. If the borrower goes into serious default, you could end up with the security back in your own hands through foreclosure. Not a nice thought, but, after all, it is your money.
- The interest you will receive on the loan will be more than you can get from current bank interest. Mortgages pay more than a bank can afford to pay you.

When lending the money, you can make the loan renewable on an annual basis if you wish, and adjust the interest rate to current market rates. That way you can keep ahead of what banks will pay.

However, remember that trying to predict future rates is a futile exercise. If rates go down, you lose. If they go up, you win. If you accept a fixed rate for a number of years, at least you can budget with a known income.

- Offering to accept a mortgage makes the purchase attractive for a buyer, because he knows where he can get instant financing and save all the legal and other charges of arranging a third-party mortgage. This can also mean a higher selling price for your home.

The disadvantages are:

- Your money is tied up in a security that, although very sound, will probably have to be sold at a discount if you need the cash.

  If you wish to keep the mortgage, you will not necessarily be able to borrow the full face value of it if such a need arises.
- The borrower, being an individual, is naturally a poorer risk for the loan than a bank would be. There is always the danger of not receiving payments on time, or worse, not receiving them at all. You can get your money back all right, but with such problems it takes times.

My sensible guidelines are:

- Before lending a stranger a large sum of money you should run a credit check on him, and also see if there are any judgment executions registered against him.

  He might seem like the greatest guy in the world to you, but if he has a severe debt load it could create problems for you. Also, it would be a good idea to check his employment record and obtain references.
- The amount of the loan is most important. If you sell your property for about 10% down, I certainly would not recommend holding a mortgage for the balance of the purchase price.

  With the vagaries of a housing market, the 10% equity in the property could be eroded, leaving you with a mortgage of the entire market value of the property. If problems arose in repayment, it would be unlikely that you would recover your entire loan.

  A safe limit in lending would be to ensure that your loan does not exceed 75% of the selling price. And if the buyer obtains first mortgage financing and asks you for secondary financing, ensure that the total of the first mortgage and the second mortgage does not exceed the 75%.

Of course, the buyer would be free to obtain further financing secured by other mortgages, but they would not affect the safety of your own mortgage seniority.

I shall never cease to be amazed at the almost casual way a seller will agree to hold a mortgage when accepting an offer. Take your time and think about it.

The Dangers of Low Down Payments

You think that because a first mortgage has a priority, there is nothing to worry about? Think again.

Years ago a small house in a rural community sold for $26,000. One first mortgage of $21,000 was taken back by the seller. The agreement said the balance of the purchase price would be paid by certified cheque.

Seems reasonable, but what happened was a disaster for the seller.

The accepted offer called for a deposit of $500 and here is where all the trouble really began.

Unknown to the seller, the buyer arranged to borrow $4,500 from a private source, which was secured by a second mortgage.

The seller was paid the $5,000 and received a first mortgage to secure the balance of the selling price. Of course, a real estate commission and legal fees came out of this, which left the seller with about $3,000 cash.

The buyer didn't move into the house. It was immediately rented, with the rent going right into his pocket.

Not one payment was made on the seller's first mortgage or to the owner of the second mortgage.

Now, what have we got? A real mess, that's what.

The buyer disappeared, apparently turning up once a month to pick up the rent.

Oh, I know, there are all kinds of legal courses open to the lenders in those mortgage deeds, but who needs all that flak?

Both lenders handed their money over in good faith and all they can look forward to now are legal bills for straightening out the mess.

In any legal action to recover money in a mortgage, the borrower has the responsibility of paying the bills.

But if he hasn't got any money and is hard to find, kiss your own money goodbye.

The foregoing gives a seller and a lender several warning signs. Here are two of the better ones:

- Accepting a modest payment such a $500 as a deposit with an offer to buy your property could be a serious mistake. It could mean the buyer is short of money.

  Some agents, when confronted by this thought, will tell the seller that the buyer has money "tied up" in stocks or bonds and it will take a few days to cash them. Not to worry.

  Oh yeah? If you hear this, tell your agent to remind the buyer money can be quickly raised by borrowing against the securities. Demand more money a a deposit, or at least more solid evidence of where it is coming from.

  Of course, there is nothing to prevent the buyer from eventually raising the money by secondary financing.

  In the example I have cited, the buyer never had any more than $500, so a demand for more money would have cancelled the deal — and prevented a lot of grief.
- If you are asked to lend money through secondary mortgaging, take a good look at the arithmetic.

  If there is going to be an owner's cash equity of just $500 after adding up the mortgage totals, forget it. Look at the problems that confronted the second mortgage lender in this deal!

  The second mortgagee bought the first mortgage at a $3,000 discount.

  The seller lost and the second mortgagee became first mortgagee.

35

CAVEAT FOR MORTGAGE LENDERS

An elderly couple asked me for some advice on where they should invest about $60,000 in second mortgages.

I asked why they wanted second mortgages, and the response was that in addition to receiving a higher rate of interest, they wouldn't have to pay income tax on the interest.

When I pointed out that, regardless of where earned income comes from, it must be reported, they replied: "Everybody does it."

This sort of thinking can get one in a mess of trouble. Agents from the income tax department make a practice of periodically surveying registry offices to identify private mortgage loans. And the reason is very basic.

When one receives interest income from conventional borrowers like banks and trust companies, the one paying the interest provides the lender with T5 information slips. One copy is sent to the government, and two to the lender. The lender knows the government is aware of the money received, so naturally includes the information when preparing the annual income tax return.

But borrowers of private mortgage funds by the thousands never bother to fill out these forms and pass a copy along to the government. They don't do it basically because it is of no benefit to them; they are the borrowers in household mortgages and the interest is not deductible in any way. They are just glad to be able to pay the interest and couldn't care less what the lender does about income tax.

If the government allowed such borrowers a small deduction on their income taxes, say 2 1/2% of such payments, provided they filled out and mailed the T5 slips, the government's income would dramatically increase.

On a $20,000 mortgage at 12%, the interest paid annually is about $2,400. Allow the borrower to deduct $60 from income tax and you can be sure that T5 slip will go in the mail. The lender will then realize he or she is hooked, and will cough up.

Well, what happens to lenders who don't receive the T5 slips and don't bother to report the income? If one has been getting away with it for years and it finally caught, the mortgage itself might have to be sold to settle everything. Or even the old homestead. Phew!

First of all, tax returns for the years involved are reassessed. Then, in most cases, a penalty is charged equal to 25% of the additional tax assessed. On top of this goes interest on the assessed tax; and the total of tax, penalty and interest can be substantial.

Where significant amounts of mortgage interest income have not been reported, the taxpayer's affairs will be investigated and one may end up being prosecuted for tax evasion. That can mean criminal fines and jail sentences.

Conviction can be humiliating

Conviction means details of one's sticky fingers reported in the press. How would you like to have your friends and neighbors read about something like that? And what about the cruel taunts thrown at your kids in school?

However, do not despair. There is a voluntary disclosure policy available which enables taxpayers to report hidden income without the headaches of prosecution. It won't mean freedom from financial penalties, but it will mean a good night's sleep.

This voluntary disclosure, however, is subject to verification, and if it is shown that the taxpayer disclosed only those amounts which he or she thought the government would become aware of, it will not be considered as voluntary, but rather as an attempt to further deceive the government.

And here's a horrible thought: When one expires, the government takes a good look at all the assets in the estate. When it comes across mortgages, it naturally wants to see some evidence of tax payments made on the income.

Sooner or later, the government is going to get it.

36

THE FEDERAL INTEREST ACT

Now that he long-term mortgage is here with us again, let's not forget the *open* privileges in a *closed* mortgage.

Section 10(1) of the *Interest Act* is a bit long-winded, but well worth reading in its entirety:

> Whenever any principal money or interest secured by mortgage of real estate is not, under the terms of the mortgage, payable until a time more than five years after the date of the mortgage, then, if at any time after the expiration of such five years, any person liable to pay or entitled to redeem the mortgage tenders or pays, to the person entitled to receive the money, the amount due for principal money and interest to the time of payment, as calculated under sections 6 to 9, together with three months further interest in lieu of notice, no further interest shall be chargeable, payable or recoverable at any time thereafter on the principal money or interest due under the mortgage.

If a borrower signs a mortgage deed with a 10-year term, for example, Section 10(1) says he can repay the entire balance owing at any time after five years have expired.

It says the borrower can repay this, but must also pay three months' interest in *lieu of notice*. What does this mean?

Reading it, one would logically assume that if, any time after five years, the borrower gave notice to the lender that in (say) three months' time the outstanding balance would be paid, no three months' interest would also have to be paid.

The only cited case to challenge this exact reasoning was in a district court in Alberta, in 1959, and the borrower was shot down in flames.

The judgment noted that "the lender is held entitled to three months' additional interest to set off against the probable loss of interest suffered during the period required to reinvest the fund."

With all the mortgage money available today, this could be a fact, and not just "probable," but the main thrust of the ruling was in the grammatical phrasing of the act, which was held to disallow such a choice for a borrower.

Now read what section 10(2) says:

> Nothing in this section applies to any mortgage upon real estate given by a joint stock company or other corporation, nor to any debenture issued by any such company or corporation, for the payment of which security has been given by way of mortgage on real estate.

If one buys a parcel of real estate and assumes payments on a long-term mortgage in which a corporation signed the deed, the five-year break for a borrower does not apply. Why? Because the corporation signing the deed places itself under covenant and is responsible for the debt until the bitter end, regardless of who makes the payments.

I am very familiar with Section 10 of the federal *Interest Act.* I have written about it, lectured on it, and referred many people to it. It is seared in my brain.

But after all these years, one little item that stands out in Section 10 went right past me. I never caught it. And I'll bet thousands of real estate and mortgage brokers never caught it either.

Laws concerning interest charges go back a lot of years. The first one was a 1777 ordinance in Quebec, which said the maximum will be 6% per annum. This rate was carried into the *Upper Canada Act* of 1811.

Then the government got generous and the *English Act* of 1854 repealed the usury statutes and generally left interest rates up to the borrower and lender.

Section 10(1) of today's interest act is the same as it was in 1925 when a Saskatchewan Court of Appeal made an interesting observation on it.

Briefly, the section says that when a mortgage has a term of more than five years, the person liable to redeem the mortgage may pay to the lender the amount due for principal and interest at any time after the expiration of five years.

With this payment, the borrower must pay three months' further interest. Then it says no further interest shall be chargeable, payable or recoverable at any time thereafter (on the mortgage).

We have long-term mortgages available now, so this statute, in favor of the borrower, sounds pretty good. Pay off the mortgage after five years with a reasonable bonus and that's the end of the matter.

Not so.

Sixty-five years ago, the honorable court said: "This Section does not give a mortgagor entitled to redeem the right to discharge on tender of the mortgage monies, or interest, after the expiration of five years from the date of the mortgage.

"There is nothing in the Section which says he should be entitled to have the mortgage discharged. Ordinarily, if a mortgagee cannot obtain any further interest, he will take his money and execute a discharge of the mortgage. But the section does not say he must do so."

If you think I am digging up ancient history, forget it. This 65-year old precedent was affirmed in 1983 in the B.C. Supreme Court, which said: "It is difficult to understand what use a mortgagee can make of an instrument where payment is made in full. Nonetheless, if he wishes, it seems he may refuse to discharge the mortgage until the date of its maturity."

All the foregoing suggests that a borrower in a long-term mortgage may be well advised to be polite to the lender. If rates take a dive from a high-rate mortgage, the borrower can certainly take advantage of Section 10. But it doesn't guarantee the lender will discharge the mortgage.

Which could be damned annoying if a cash buyer came along for the property: he would want a nice, clean title. If the lender won't hand it over, what is the borrower going to do?

Despite the law, the lender did lose a lot of high-rate interest when that mortgage was paid off before maturity, and he's pretty sore about it. Are we going to find borrowers paying hefty bonuses to get that discharge under such circumstances?

And why wasn't the act amended to take care of this annoying matter? Sixty years is too long to leave some crummy wording on the books!

37

THE CONVENTIONAL MORTGAGE

This mortgage is called conventional because it is the customary, prevalent and most commonly used method of obtaining a mortgage loan. It usually implies a first mortgage, and that the purchaser has at least 25% of the purchase price as a down payment.

When an agreement to buy a house is made, a conditional clause is often inserted in the agreement, giving the buyer about ten days to arrange a new mortgage.

Immediately on acceptance of the purchase agreement by buyer and seller, the buyer makes application (usually through the suggestions of the real estate broker who made the sale) to a mortgage lender such as a bank, insurance or trust company.

It is a sound move to follow the suggestion of a real estate broker in making the application, because the broker should know not only where the best flow of money is, but where he can get the fastest action on the application.

If the buyer is a person of means with an excellent credit rating, he could buy the property without the conditional clause simply because he would have no difficulty in obtaining financing. Vendors are more willing to sell without conditional clauses in the sales agreements.

Most lenders have a clause to allow you to prepay 10% of the value of the loan once a year on the anniversary date, without penalty. In some cases they allow up to 15% annually.

Another variation is to allow you to increase your monthly payment by 10% or 15% as the case may be. One lender I know allows you to double your monthly payment any month or every month if you wish, again without penalty.

Some lenders offer both options. You can increase your monthly payment by 10% as well as prepay an additional 10% lump sum annually. In all cases any increase over your regular monthly payment is credited against the principal balance.

For an additional monthly cost lenders offer life insurance to cover the mortgage amount in the event of death, or even insurance to cover job loss. They offer weekly, biweekly, semi-monthly or monthly payment plans. The more frequent the payment the more you save in interest cost over the life of the mortgage.

Some lenders accept extra payments and then if you fall on hard times and miss a payment or two later, those extra payments are credited as regular payments and you are not considered in default.

If you sell your home some lenders will waive the penalty for paying off the mortgage in full, while others will allow you to transfer your mortgage to another property, increase the mortgage, blend the rate and take it with you to the new home that you purchased.

These are some of the ways to avoid paying the penalty. Because of these alternatives it is becoming hard to find a property for sale where the vendor requires you to assume a mortgage. Usually the lender requires that the purchaser who wishes to assume an existing mortgage be qualified and approved by the lender.

If you must prepay your mortgage over and above the stipulated limits or pay off the mortgage in full, penalties are usually three months' interest or based on the interest rate differential, whichever is greater. For example, your principal balance remaining is \$100,000. The current interest rate in the marketplace is 9% per annum but your interest rate is 10% per annum and two more years remain in the term. If you pay \$100,000 in full, three months' interest is \$2500. The interest rate differential would be:

$$(10\% - 9\%) \times \$100{,}000 \times 2 \text{ yr.}$$
$$= 1\% \times \$100{,}000 \times 2 \text{ yr.}$$
$$= \$2000.$$

Since the three months' penalty is greater, your cost to prepay this amount would be \$2500.

Lenders are so competitive that they are willing to pay legal fees and application cost if you transfer your mortgage from another lender to them, so shop around.

38

THE BLANKET MORTGAGE

The original concept of blanket mortgage probably began with a house builder.

The builder obtains an agreement with a lending institution to cover (blanket) it financially in the construction of a multiple housing project.

The original mortgage deed signed by the builder will cover the entire project, and as the construction of houses progresses, the borrower will be given loan advances to pay the bills.

Finally, when the houses reach the selling stage, a buyer for house number one will appear and sign an agreement to buy the first house from the builder, subject to credit approval.

The builder then marches the buyer down to the blanket mortgagee's office where a mortgage application is processed. If approved, the one house sold is taken off the covenant in the builder's blanket mortgage and a single mortgage for the house buyer's signature is prepared.

The builder and his lender proceed in this fashion until all the houses are sold, and the original blanket mortgage which covered the entire project is reduced to zero and discharged.

This is a very favourable method for large lenders to place funds, because they can do it in large chunks initially, which will be reduced and spread over hundreds of individuals eventually. It makes for easier and faster accounting of the lenders' budgets because of the size of the initial mortgages.

39

THE UMBRELLA MORTGAGE

When a borrower wishes to float a loan secured by a mortgage, the equity in the proposed realty to be used for security sometimes is not large enough to satisfy the lender.

If the borrower owned more than one parcel of realty, he could borrow against each parcel but this would normally require separate mortgage deeds.

So, sometimes the borrower will put up more than one parcel to secure the loan, and sign just one mortgage deed to cover all the parcels used for security.

The mortgage will be registered on title against each parcel so secured.

One mortgage. One payment. Voilà, the umbrella mortgage, which shelters more than one parcel.

A clause would probably be in the mortgage deed covering the eventuality that the borrower may wish to sell one or more of the secured parcels of property. This clause would stipulate the principal reduction and possible penalty required if carried out.

40

THE PIGGYBACK MORTGAGE

Here's an example:

A homeowner has a first mortgage registered against his property. He wants to borrow some money so gets it from a private source and signs a mortgage deed that is registered as a second mortgage.

In this deed, there will be a clause requiring the mortgagor to do one of the following:

a) Provide the mortgagee in the second mortgage with monthly payments made payable to the first mortgagee, which the second mortgagee will post immediately to the first mortgagee.
b) Provide the mortgagee in the second mortgage with proof positive that the monthly payment on the first mortgage has been made. It will require that the proof be supplied within a specified period of time.

In other words, the second mortgagee is constantly on the borrower's back to ensure that the senior mortgage is always in good standing.

Piggyback!

41

THE VARIABLE RATE MORTGAGE

To simplify this, no principal payments will be made in the example — just interest. The mortgage limit will be 70% of the mortgage appraisal of the property. A real estate agent may say your property has a reasonable market value of $150,000, but the appraiser working for the mortgage lender may not agree.

If the mortgage appraiser says $140,000, then the borrowing limit will be 70% of that, or 98,000.

Conventional lenders usually go as high as 75% without resorting to mortgage insurance, which would bring the lending limit on this property to $105,000. The reason for the lower ratio will become apparent as you read on.

- The term can be as long as five years.
- The rate of interest in the mortgage will be the bank's prime lending rate, which is lower than market mortgage rates.
- The interest will be compounded monthly, and payable monthly. This simply means that if the prime rate in the mortgage is 12% a year, the borrower pays 1% a month. Just divide the contracted annual rate by 12.
- The mortgage can be paid off any time with a reasonable penalty. Now it gets interesting . . .

The bank prime rate will be adjusted once a month in the mortgage deed. If it goes up 1% in a monthly adjustment, a 12% loan becomes 13%. However, the payment remains the same.

How's that again? If the interest rate goes up, how can the monthly payment remain the same? Here's how it works:

Take the above figures. The borrower makes a monthly payment of 1% of the $98,000 ($980). When the rate goes to 13%, it would normally mean paying 1/12 of 13% of the $98,000 — or $1,061.66 but the payment stays at $980, leaving a shortage of $81.66.

This $81.66 is added to the mortgage debt, and now it is $98,081.66. In month two, the payment stays at $980 — and if the prime rate is still 13%, there will be another shortage. This time the payment will be short by $82.55, which is added to the debt.

Now, if the prime rate stays above the original contracted prime rate, the debt becomes larger each month. If it should get as high as 75% of the property value, then everybody takes another look at the loan, and one of two things will happen.

The property will be appraised again. If the appraisal indicates a higher figure, everybody just carries on, because the new appraisal will bring the loan ratio down to less than 75% of value.

But if the appraisal remains the same, the difference in each monthly payment — instead of being added to the loan principal — will be paid each month by the borrower, and there will be no more increase in the loan amount.

Okay, so what happens if the prime rate goes below the original contracted rate? Well, the borrower makes the same $980 monthly payment, but now will have credit in his mortgage account.

He doesn't knock this off his payment or get a cash refund. It is taken off the outstanding principal amount of the loan — which means he will get a bigger credit each month the prime rate stays below his contracted rate.

Rates go down, you win; rates go up, you lose.

And if the borrower isn't happy with the way things are going, he can convert to a fixed rate. But once this is done, then that's it — no turning back.

42

THE LEASEHOLD MORTGAGE

Not all building owners own the land on which the building stands.

The owners of some very large buildings in Canada lease the land under the buildings, which is called leasehold property. Leasehold property creates a leasehold mortgage.

Before a builder signs a ground lease, he will have an irrevocable mortgage commitment for his building. The mortgage requires an assignment of the ground lease, or sub-lease, and the terms of the ground lease will be satisfactory to the mortgagee, or there is no lease.

The principal sum of a leasehold mortgage is understandably less than it would be if the mortgagor owned the land.

If the mortgagee takes his mortgage under assignment of the lease, a situation is established between the lessor and mortgagee whereby the mortgagee becomes responsible for the terms of the lease, including that of paying the ground rent. The mortgagee would be liable for all breaches of covenant that might occur.

Under a sub-lease arrangement, the requirement would be that the mortgagor would hold the last day of the term of the lease in trust for the mortgagee, in order to allow the mortgagee to control the last day and thereby control the renewable term. This is necessary, because although the mortgage term is usually of shorter duration than that of the lease, it could be possible for the mortgagee to have not received his final payments by the end of the term.

A leasehold mortgagee will most certainly protect himself fully to ensure that there is no termination of the ground lease, and will therefore have an agreement with the lessor to allow the mortgagee time to remedy any default on the part of the lessee.

The mortgage will contain a clause stipulating that a default by the mortgagor under the terms of the ground lease will automatically become a default under the mortgage.

The leasehold mortgage will require that the lessee pays the ground rent to the mortgagee, who in turn will pay it to the lessor, or require the lessee/mortgagor to produce receipts promptly.

This will answer the question "Which has priority — the ground rent, or the mortgage payment?"

Remember:			
	lessor	—	owner
	lessee	—	tenant
	mortgagor	—	borrower
	mortgagee	—	lender

43

SHAFTING THE MORTGAGEE

There is a new game in town played by the mortgagor and mortgagee. The expert in the game is obviously a graduate of Shaft University (Shaft U for short).

The Shaft U graduate is the borrower in, say, a $60,000 mortgage deed with a five-year term at 11%. The mortgage is two years old.

The mortgagor wants to pay off the mortgage because he is selling and the buyer doesn't want a mortgage, or he came into a financial windfall and doesn't want the debt, or any one of a dozen other reasons.

He discovers that the mortgagee is willing to accept a payoff and provide a discharge certificate, but wants six months' interest for the privilege, which could cost the borrower more than three thousand dollars. The mortgage term, having another three years to go, could cost the borrower a lot more, but in this case the lender is being reasonable. But three thousand dollars is three thousand dollars, and the borrower decides that he could make better use of the money than handing it over to the lender.

So the mortgagor starts his game. He does a bit of play acting and lets the lender know that he is sorry, but he can't make the next payment, which, of course, is a lot of hogwash. The lender is a bit disturbed by this, and the borrower merrily goes on ignoring the lender.

Finally, the borrower receives a warning letter from the lender's lawyer, which he promptly tosses in the garbage. Another letter, ditto.

And then, *Whoopee*, a sheriff's officer arrives at the mortgagor's door and serves him with a writ of foreclosure. *Hooray.* This is just what the borrower was waiting for!

You see, in the writ the lender can just claim arrears of interest, plus principal, but *not* the six months' penalty he wanted to pay off the mortgage. So the borrower pays off the writ, plus a few hundred to the lawyer, and he has just saved himself a bundle.

Well, one can imagine what this sort of behavior would cost and save if the mortgage were a big one like maybe a couple of hundred thousand.

However, some lenders are catching on to the game, especially the ones holding the big mortgages, and if they suspect the borrower is playing this little game, they will sue him for the *arrears* owing and *not* for foreclosure. This keeps the affluent borrower on the hook and if he now wants to pay off the mortgage it might cost a bit more than the six months' interest.

If the mortgagor played this game to pay off the mortgage, and there was a junior mortgage registered behind the big one, he would obviously have to move quickly in paying off the writ. The junior mortgagee could march in and bring the arrears of the first mortgage up to date and charge the amount to its mortgage, plus a legal fee, which would put the mortgagor back in square one.

However, don't quote me. Better you should *check with your lawyer* first!

44

FORECLOSURE

Years ago, it was the accepted practice for lenders to recover loans by way of a writ of foreclosure.

Here were the basic rules in Ontario:

The lender's lawyer, having a good sense of propriety, sent a letter to the borrower advising him if late payments were not brought up to date forthwith, further legal action would be necessary, and costly.

If the borrower did nothing about it, a writ of foreclosure was served by a sheriff's officer, which made the matter very serious business. Some lawyers, of course — and I suspect through nothing else but greed — didn't bother with a warning letter.

They just charged ahead with the writ, tacking hundreds of dollars onto it for their trouble.

If the borrower did not seek legal advice, and ignored the writ, the lender could proceed to gain title to the property and the matter would be at an end.

Of course, all subsequent encumbrances would be also served, having the opportunity to pay off the plaintiff mortgagee and own the mortgage.

When the lender obtained a final order of foreclosure, the borrower forfeited all equity he had in the property. This was the sad part. However, if the lender later sold the property, and didn't get enough to cover his mortgage loan, it was too bad for him.

There were three basic things a borrower could do about a writ of foreclosure:

- He could bring arrears up to date within the time specified by the writ, pay the lender's legal fees, and carry on making payments under the mortgage.
- He could pay into court $150 and ask that the property be sold by

the sheriff's office. After the sale — and after paying for its cost, the mortgage debt, and everybody having liens against the property — the borrower would be paid any money left over.

This could prevent him from losing his equity in the property. But if there was a shortage in the mortgage account, he could be sued.

- He could file a request to redeem the mortgaged property. This would give him a period of six months, after taking of the account of the amount due the lender, in which to get the money to settle the matter.

Sometimes the legal business of figuring out precisely how much was owing (taking of the account) could delay matters for a couple of months, which meant the borrower had eight months on his side.

Despite the advantage of an occasional property gain by foreclosure, the long, drawn-out business was a drag for most lenders, especially financial institutions which just wanted the debt repaid. So it became more popular and quicker to proceed by notice under a power of sale.

This cleans the matter up in a matter of weeks, instead of months. After the sale, any money left after paying everybody off is given to the borrower, the one who lost the property.

But if the sale doesn't produce enough to pay off the lender and his lawyer, the borrower will be sued for the balance.

Now — and read this carefully — the period of time allowed to redeem property in a foreclosure action has been reduced from six months to *60 days*.

I believe some private lenders will view this as an invitation to return to foreclosures and the opportunity of getting something for nothing; the borrower's equity.

If you are a borrower on shaky ground, don't lose your lawyer's phone number.

And another thing, the ante for a borrower asking for a judicial sale is now $250.

45

THE POWER OF SALE

In Ontario, nothing can cause a homeowner more grief than receiving a notice from his mortgagee that it is exercising its right under the "power of sale" provision in the mortgage deed.

There is a lot of this going on, and with massive unemployment it will get worse. Aside from shyster lenders and others who have no patience with delinquent borrowers, here is what you may expect from conventional mortgagees such as banks and trust companies when your mortgage is in arrears.

You will receive one or two letters from your lender demanding that arrears be brought up to date. If you ignore them, you will receive an initial letter from the lender's solicitor, reminding you about your overdue payments, along with a demand for payment plus a fee for his services in writing the letter.

Ignore this and you get another letter from the same solicitor demanding more money for his services, plus mortgage arrears, and a warning about the lender selling your home to satisfy the debt.

Ignore this and you will receive a notice under a power of sale, which will say that the entire amount of the mortgage principal plus interest arrears, plus a whopping legal fee must be paid by a date a couple of days beyond 35 days of receipt of the registered notice.

You will receive it, and so will your spouse and any party holding judgment executions against you. It won't do any good to refuse the registered notice, because the law says that when it was placed in the hands of the post office it was "delivered," whether you accepted it or not.

Your initial reaction will be that if you can't pay the arrears, how do they expect you to pay the whole thing? What the notice doesn't say is that if the mortgage term has not reached an end, usually you don't have to.

But you must make the late payments, and pay the lawyer's charges, which will be added to your mortgage debt.

When you receive the notice, do not delay or procrastinate in doing something about it. If you ignore it, and the time limit expires, you will receive a notice to vacate your home within a few days; if you ignore this, you will be evicted by the sheriff. And your home will be sold.

It will not be given away as distress merchandise, but on the other hand your mortgagee will be under no obligation to wait for a top market price.

Such short notices will provide extreme hardships because, even if you have a chance to immediately rent a house, you will have to put up the first and last month's rent which will probably be at least two thousand dollars. Even an apartment means laying out about one thousand.

Then you will have moving expenses to pay, plus all the disruptions of moving on short notice. And it will be short, because the lender is not in any mood to do you any favors at this stage of the game.

If you make part payment to a bank branch thinking that this will delay the fatal day by causing the lender to go around again, don't count on it. You will receive a letter acknowledging the payment, but subject to the lender's rights under the power of sale.

Other than raising money for your arrears, the only recourse you have is to sell your home. And this is where you especially need the broad shoulders of good lawyer to intercede on your behalf.

Your home could be put on the market and sold before the power of sale notice is received, but have your lawyer call the lender and let it know what you are doing. This will show a bit of good faith, and you will probably receive a sympathetic hearing at this point.

If it is sold during the term of the sale notice, you will still have to bring the arrears up to date within the time limit. If the sale is a good, solid one with no conditions, your lawyer is a good man to look to for interim financing. He'll get the advanced money back out of the proceeds of the sale.

I cannot stress too strongly the importance of good legal counsel early in your misfortune.

Don't allow your family to be thrown out on the street.

The Lender's Responsibilities

The lender (or mortgagee) who has paved the way to sell a house under his power of sale has certain responsibilities which should not be taken lightly.

He properly serves the borrower (or mortgagor) with his notice, which the borrower does nothing about. Then the lender has the homeowner evicted, leaving the lender with an empty house on his hands.

At this point, some lenders undoubtedly are of the opinion they can then sell the property for any price as long as it covers the mortgage debt and legal fees.

Fortunately, we have courts that take a dim view of such behavior and have gone so far as to render sales null and void made under such circumstances.

Large conventional lenders normally take the safe route and do it properly, ensuring that the borrower who is losing his property at least gets a fair shake out of his misfortune. But not always, it seems.

One bank, as lender and mortgagee, had a sale criticized and was penalized by a court because the property was sold too cheaply. Whether this was the active fault of the bank is not for me to say, but here is what happened:

The bank sold a property under power of sale for $45,000. The court found the value of the property was about $65,000 and decided it had been sold too cheaply.

The bank was held responsible for selling in a negligent and careless fashion and had to compensate the former owner of the property for this.

It was observed that the bank didn't put forth enough effort in the sale and that the property should have received wide exposure by being placed on multiple-listing, a service provided by a real estate board.

While judges have on more than one occasion said a lender is not a trustee in the power of sale, and can give preference to its own interests, they have also said the lender must act in good faith and take reasonable precaution in obtaining the true market value of the property at the time it wishes to sell it.

One court stated that the prime duty of such a lender is to act *bona fide* in exercising the power of sale. It went on to list further duties of the lender:

- To try to realize the fair value of the property.
- To deduct only reasonable expenses of sale from the proceeds.
- To consider the interests of the borrower as well as the lender's own interests.
- Not to conduct the sale in bad faith.

It would therefore be prudent for a lender to first have the property properly appraised. The cost of this, of course, would come off the top in the accounting to the borrower.

Next, have the property listed on a multiple-listing service, to give it wide exposure.

These two basic steps would show good faith to all and the lender could not be criticized for attempting to take advantage of a hapless borrower by sacrificing the property in order to gain his own ends quickly.

The broker listing the property should certainly have his For Sale sign on the front lawn, and the lender should ensure the broker earns his money by doing a bit of advertising also.

A major problem in obtaining a reasonable market price is that many people think power of sale means nothing but bargains, and they make lowball offers.

A responsible lender will not be impressed by such people, and with reasonable effort on the part of his broker, a decent market price will be realized.

The one who lost the property receives what's left after everything is paid off, so it would be in his own best interests to ask his lawyer to do what he can to ensure that he is getting treated fairly.

PART THREE

BUYING

46

THE LOCAL REAL ESTATE BOARD

Before the age of organized real estate it was hard to find a buyer ready and willing to pay your price for a piece of property. Then brokers turned this frustration into an opportunity. They would find a buyer for your property and deal with all the attendant frustration for a fee. Owners were happy to seek out brokers who made it their business to have contacts, buyers and a wealth of pricing knowledge.

Our present system evolved over a period of time, beginning with an open system where a vendor would invite any number of brokers to find a buyer for a fee. A broker would spend much effort and money to find buyers yet make no profit because the property was sold by some other broker.

Soon, therefore, exclusive listings became popular. The broker would enter into an agency contract with the vendor allowing the broker to be the only one to market the property and find a buyer. Brokers operated in isolation. Each had a selection of properties and a number of buyers, but properties did not always match the needs of the buyer. While driving down the street to view a house the buyer would ask his broker about the house across the street that was listed by another broker. If he was interested in the house, he had to deal with the other broker. Suddenly his original broker had lost the buyer and the commission. Since a broker could sell only his own listings, buyers jumped from broker to broker looking for the ideal property.

Gradually a buddy system developed. Brokers would exchange information with other brokers. One had a suitable buyer while the other had a suitable property. They would then make a deal and share the fee. The more buddies you had the luckier and more prosperous you were. It was better to earn 50% of something than 100% of nothing. Buyers also found that they had more choices available.

But if one's broker was not particularly well connected, vendors discovered it was harder to sell their property and buyers experienced difficulty finding something suitable. Brokers found it awkward to compile information and to distribute it among their various networks, and so an association was formed that was the basis for our present-day concept of the local real estate board.

A real estate board is formed for the benefit of its members. Brokerage firms and the salespeople that work for them form the membership base. It is generally accepted that the primary responsibility of the board is to the brokerage firms and to a lesser extent the salespeople attached to the firms. The members elect a board of directors to oversee the affairs and operations of the local real estate board. Members pay a fee that covers the cost of operations and services. The primary function of the board is to act as a central depot or clearinghouse for information. It also arbitrates disputes between members, disciplines its members for unethical behavior and acts as a lobby group or a political voice for the concerns of its members.

Organized real estate in North America is highly developed and sophisticated. The Toronto Real Estate Board is reputed to be one of the largest real estate boards in the world with more than 25,000 members. Organizations from all over the world come to Toronto and other Canadian centers to study our system.

Real estate agents often assume that their clients are familiar with the MLS (multiple listing service) system. However, lack of understanding has led to serious misconceptions that reduce the agents' effectiveness in serving the needs of the client. Let's look at how the MLS system functions and then look at a few misconceptions. We will use the sale of a home as a basic example, although the process applies to any type of property.

Once a broker has a signed contract with a client to sell the house, this contract, a description and all pertinent information regarding the house is sent to the local board via the mail, courier, computer, fax, personal delivery or any other means acceptable by the board. It can take as little time as it takes to get to a computer or as long as a few days to get the information to the board.

This information is assembled and printed. One common form of print is a postcard-size format with a picture on one side and information on the other with several postcard descriptions on a page. This format is usually distributed daily. However, it can also be assembled into a book format and distributed on a regular basis — for example, weekly. The board provides a distribution service that delivers this information to each broker and/or sales agent. Although distribution through printed form is very popular and still widely subscribed to, access to information through computers is far more effective.

What can computers do? Most real estate boards have computers to manage the information they gather. Not only are listings of property information stored but also each board may choose to supplement information from other sources. Municipal tax rolls, government registry information, map references, historical sales information, digitized pictures, zoning information, and other useful information can be gathered.

The user, on the other hand, can sort and search the database in several ways to find just the right property for the client. The agent may search by street address, property type, price range, or by district or neighborhood. Each board will have different search criteria. The possibilities are endless.

How can buyers or vendors work more effectively with their agents? First you must remember that once you have selected an agent you are partners trying to achieve the same goal — to find a property to buy, or to sell the one you already have. The greater the loyalty between agent and client the greater the commitment and service you can expect from your agent. Today agents have office phones, phones at home, pagers, car phones and portable phones. There is no reason why you would not be able to get in touch with an agent quickly. He or she may not take your call if with another client or on vacation or at the dinner table. But with all the beepers and gadgetry you can be sure that you will be called back at the first convenient opportunity. Here are some common misconceptions clients have about real estate agents.

- "I didn't call you because I thought that you could only sell your own company's listings, and the property I wanted to see was listed with XYZ Realty."

That may have been true when our grandparents bought their first houses, but not anymore. By listing a property on the multiple listing service of the local board an agent automatically invites all members to show their clients a property. When an agent sells another company's listing, the brokers share the fee.

- "I didn't call you because the listing was someone else's exclusive listing."

In most such cases you should still call your agent. It will reinforce in the agent's mind that you are loyal; he or she will be appreciative and will make that extra effort to get you a good deal. The concept of an exclusive listing is usually obsolete. The vendor may have thought it would be a little cheaper to list exclusively. For a lower fee the vendor gets much less exposure and the property is much harder to sell. The listing agent is often so desperate to get an interested client that he or she is more than willing to share the commission with another agent and will often pay a bonus to encourage an offer. Your agent will, however, be required to call the listing agent and confirm in writing that he is willing to share the commission and on what basis. Only the most greedy of listing agents would refuse to share. Most real estate boards consider it unethical behavior for the listing agent to refuse to allow your agent to inspect the property with you, even though it would not be unethical to refuse sharing the commission.

In such a case, remain loyal to your agent. Make your offer through your agent and pay him or her a commission yourself; make it known on the offer that you have paid a commission and that the offered price reflects that fact. Greediness is rarely rewarded.

- "I didn't list my house with Uncle Joe because the other broker promised me buyers from Hong Kong."

"Hong Kong buyers" are buzzwords that you will often hear, and usually reflect an agent's attempt to exploit your lack of understanding of the MLS system. A vendor ready to list property should not fall for this kind of slick talk. If the agent has not even seen your house yet, the clients have not see the house either, so how can he say that he has someone waiting to buy it? Have those buyers seen all the properties listed on MLS and now yours is the only house in Canada left for them to see? If your house was listed on MLS with Uncle Joe, and the slick agent had a buyer from Hong Kong, would he not show your home and earn a handsome commission? Every agent with property listed on the MLS system has Hong Kong buyers, not to mention German buyers, Ukrainian buyers, Italian buyers, French buyers and so on. If there are buyers out there, agents will bring them to see your property if it is listed on MLS at a realistic price.

If an agent comes to your door and truly has a client ready to buy, you have an opportunity to save a bundle of money. Offer the agent an open listing. That is to say, any agent who has a buyer can bring an offer. If the offer is acceptable you agree to pay a selling commission but the listing commission is your extra profit. If you suggest such an arrangement to a slick but insincere agent, you will discover that suddenly all those Hong Kong buyers decided to go back to Hong Kong without buying. Strange, isn't it? Put those agents to the test.

Let the MLS system do its job. All you need to do is find an an agent that you trust and feel comfortable with. Give the agent your loyalty and he or she will work hard to sell your property.

- "I work with five agents, so I'm five times as likely to find the right house."

Again, loyalty to your agent will produce better results. Here is an example of a situation that I was faced with. I had an appointment to pick up a couple at their home at 7:00 p.m. As I pulled into the driveway another agent pulled in beside me. The husband got into my car and the wife into the other. As I drove to my first property, the other car followed. We both arrived at the same house at the same time. The other agent and I looked at each other suspiciously and then went inside. After the showing the two agents stood in the driveway and discussed the situation. We both finally shrugged our shoulders, got in our own cars and drove off, leaving the husband and wife standing in the driveway. These clients got the service they deserved, and I'm sure that eventually they bought the house they deserved.

Remember, all members of the real estate board get the same MLS information. If you ask five agents to find you a three-bedroom bungalow on a particular street, you can expect to get five calls when a bungalow becomes available. Once the agents discover that you are like an unfaithful spouse, they will either stop working with you altogether or they will call you from time to time when business is slow and they have nothing better to do. Or they may pressure you to buy the first shack that comes along, whether it suits your needs or not.

It's better to stick with one agent you like. You will end up with good service, a house you like, and probably a new lifetime friend.

47

WHAT IS A REALTOR?

Thousands of signs all over Canada have the word "Realtor" on them. Here is what it means:

We must first start by defining real estate, which is landed property. And landed property is just land. Nothing else.

When something is built on land, it is then called real property, which is land and houses, barns, fences, etc. Combine the words "real" and "property" and you get: "Realty."

Now we go to the "ee" which designates the receiver of whatever is being given; a mortgagee, for example, receives the mortgage from the borrower. The "or" designates the giver, such as a donor, vendor, grantor and so on.

So a realtor could logically be defined as one who is giving, or providing, a service in realty, or real property. True, but with some variation.

The word "realtor" was first used in 1916 in the U.S. and registered by the U.S. Patent Office after World War II by the National Association of Real Estate Boards. The Association exercises legitimate control over the use of the word for the "brokerage of real estate, industrial brokerage, farm brokerage, mortgage brokerage, in the appraisal of real estate, management of real estate, in the building of structures on real estate, in the subdivision of real estate properties, and for consultative and advisory services in community planning for the development of raw land and slum clearance areas."

In 1958 the Canadian Association of Real Estate Boards filed an application for registration of the world "realtor" as a certification mark and used similar examples of services in its application. The Canadian government examiner of this application referred to a dictionary which defined realtor as "a real estate broker who is an active member of a local board having membership in the National

Association of Real Estate Boards, an organization incorporated in 1908 for the advancement of the interests of real estate brokers and the protection of the public from unprincipled agents or brokers."

This prompted the examiner to decide that the word "realtor" did not appear to be registrable in Canada. The objection was overcome by pointing out that the entry in the dictionary did not suggest that the word was part of the common language. It was further noted that the definition restricted the use of the word to a real estate broker who is an active member of a local board having membership in the National Association of Real Estate Boards.

Furthermore, the dictionary was published in the U.S., and it was relevantly noted that the trade mark Realtor had been registered in the U.S. Patent Office (and not in Canada).

In 1960, Canadian Trade Mark Registration No. 117,275, "Realtor," was granted to the Canadian Association of Real Estate Boards (now the Canadian Real Estate Association). The mark has actually been in use in Canada since 1921.

A stringent requirement for ownership of a certification mark is that it may be adopted and registered only by one who is not engaged in the performance of service such as those in association with which the certification mark is used. However, the owner of the mark may license others to use it in association with these services.

Therefore, in Canada, "realtor" is not a person or corporation. Realtor refers to a standard of service provided by members of the Canadian Real Estate Association, and the dictionary definition put it succinctly when it said "for the protection of the public from unprincipled agents or brokers."

This is not to say that brokers who are not members of the Canadian Real Estate Association are unprincipled; what it does say is God help any members who are.

It has a very strict code of ethics.

48

CAVEAT EMPTOR (Let the Buyer Beware)

Most real estate is bought, sold and leased through licensed real estate salesmen working under the direction of real estate brokers, who effectively operate clearinghouses for the salesmen.

All brokers, large and small, from the giant trust companies to the small one-man brokerage offices, operate under a provincial license. All are subject to the same rules of conduct.

When one is in the market as a buyer, the salesman's initial job is to introduce the potential buyer to property. Don't be offended by a few pointed questions that may be asked of you by a salesman. He is just doing his job by "screening," paving the way to a better working relationship. This screening is most important, because it will enable the salesman to better fit you and properties together, principally in the area of finance, which will save you both a lot of time.

However, regardless of whether you inspected property privately or through an agent, it is a good idea to have a checklist of points to remember *before* considering an offer to purchase the real estate. Read the following carefully — it may save a few headaches.

Zoning: What is the approved municipal zoning? On the property, on the street, in the neighborhood? Look at the zoning map, then study the by-laws.

The fact that a house is being used as a rooming or boarding house does not necessarily mean that one could buy it and continue to use it as such. It may be used this way by the present owner under legal nonconforming use, which means that it was used as a rooming or boarding house *before* the area zoning was changed. There is an assumption that if a property is under "legal nonconforming" a buyer can continue the use providing there is no time break between the seller and buyer in the nonconforming use. But don't count on it. Get it in writing from the municipality.

Municipal zoning by-laws could be very important to you. Some neighborhoods allow multiple roomers in houses, but perhaps you don't want this, with the possibility of a lot of transients in your neighborhood. There are areas in cities that forbid a property owner to rent even one room — the houses must be occupied by the owner and his family and no one else.

A nice house could be on the fringe of industrial zoning, which isn't the best location. One might inspect such a property on a weekend when the plants are closed down, and smell nothing but the flowers. Then, to the dismay of the buyer, after he has committed himself to a contract he might find that the smell of operational industrial plants is not coming up roses.

A house might have a basement apartment leased to someone — be very careful about this one. You might find to your dismay that the apartment is not there legally, with the result that you would be deprived of its use as a source of income if the municipality decided to inspect the house.

Look carefully at all factors in zoning. Do not assume anything about what you see in the property. Be sure that it conforms with all municipal by-laws, and especially your intended use. If you don't, you could be one very sad buyer.

Condition of Property: Don't let a can of paint or a piece of wallpaper fool you. Check the condition of the structure itself, the heating plant and equipment, the plumbing, the wiring, and the roof.

Ureaformaldehyde foam insulation (UFFI) has been banned from use in Canada. If you are unsure, or suspect that the property is insulated with this material, you can have it inspected by professionals. UFFI can be very costly to remove. Your offer should include a clause that the current owner warrants that this material was not used to insulate the property.

If you are buying an industrial site or are a lender and using an industrial site as collateral, an environmental audit of the site could save you a lot of headaches in the future. Site restoration could cost more than the site itself.

If you are unsure about something, get professional help and advice. It will be worth it. Review the chapter "Selecting Your House."

Work Orders: Ensure that the property will stand rigid inspection by the fire department, and that no part of the land or any building or other erection on the land has been confiscated, taken or expropriated by any provincial, municipal or other authority with this right. Check to see that no alteration, repair, improvement, or other work has been ordered or directed to be done or performed to or in respect of the land or any building thereon. If this has happened, it will naturally affect your thinking about the offer.

Value: Perhaps you are one of the lucky ones, and have found the ideal property. Perhaps it is worth more to you than the listed price. Perhaps less. If you find *your* property, act quickly, but not hastily.

Most real estate that has been listed with a real estate broker has been listed realistically. Confirmation of the market value of a property you are interested in can be made by (1) viewing other comparable listings, and more important, (2) seeing a list of comparable *recent* sales in the area, which can be provided by the agent.

"Hot buys" are hard to find, basically because alert real estate salesmen are watching for them every day, and when one appears on the market it will be pounced on quickly by one of the agent's buyers.

Read chapter 67, "Don't Be Afraid to Make an Offer," for some guidance in price.

If you feel that a property you have found is just the last word as far as you are concerned, consider blanketing the opposition by offering *more* for the property than the listing price. The extra money could be peanuts spread over the years if you have found just what you want.

Remember that whatever your offer is, the agent *must* bring it to the attention of the vendor.

Terms: If you intend to pay cash for property, the seller will have to consider discharging any financial encumbrances against it that other buyers might agree to assume. If recent mortgaging has taken place, getting the mortgagee to agree to discharge the mortgage could run into a sizeable sum. This will have a bearing on the price.

If you agree to assume the existing mortgage(s), ensure that you have all the facts. There could be an open or prepayment privilege not noted on the listing. The term could be shorter than you realize, which may not be brought to your attention until your lawyer checks it. Real estate brokers usually have all the mortgage details available, but just be sure.

If you are going to ask the seller to help with your purchase by holding a mortgage or two, always go for an "open" clause. Even if you won't want to discharge it at a later date without penalty, perhaps some future buyer may wish to do so. You might also include a clause in your purchase mortgage (one to the vendor) to the effect that if the mortgagee wishes to sell it, you are to have first refusal in its sale. If such a mortgage is sold, it is usually sold at a discount, and if you are in funds at the time, you could save some money.

It is very important to have no misunderstanding about what chattels go with the purchase price. Do not assume, for example, that a chandelier in the living room goes with the property because you saw it there. The owner might have other ideas without telling you and replace it with a light bulb. Then what will you do? Put it all in the agreement.

Be clear about any possible tenancy. Make it a part of your offer. The present tenant in that little flat on the third floor may look all right today, but is the seller going to tell you he gets drunk and noisy three nights of the week? He might even be the second mortgagee.

Don't expect to call for the production of any title deed, abstract, survey or other evidence of title except such as in the possession of the vendor.

Allow yourself (your lawyer) as much time as possible to examine title. This will be at the buyer's expense. If within this time any valid objection to title is made in writing to the vendor, which the vendor is unable or unwilling to remove, and which you will not waive, the agreement will, not withstanding any intermediate acts or negotiations in respect of such objections, be null and void and you will have your deposit returned without deductions.

When your offer has been accepted, all buildings and equipment on the property will remain at the risk of the vendor until closing.

Pending completion of the sale, the vendor will hold all insurance policies and the proceeds thereof in trust for the parties as their interest may appear, and in the event of damage to the premises, the buyer may either have the proceeds of the insurance and complete the purchase, or alternatively, require the vendor to use the proceeds to repair the damage so that on closing the buyer will acquire the property in its condition at the time of acceptance of the offer. It is possible that under these circumstances, the premises may be so damaged that the contract may be voidable.

The deed or transfer is prepared at the expense of the vendor.

The mortgages are prepared at the buyer's expense.

If the vendor is a trustee, the deed or transfer will contain trustee covenants only.

In the estimates of purchase costs, do not forget the costs that will be incurred by the services of your lawyer, and costs that will be incurred in the adjustments of insurance, rentals, mortgages, taxes, water, fuel and local improvements.

Do not commit yourself to something you cannot handle. Remember that, in addition to the mortgage payments and municipal taxes, the place will have to be heated, lighted, maintained in good repair, and insured.

When making out the deposit cheque to go with the offer, make it out in trust to the *listing broker* — not to the owner of the property if it can be avoided. The broker holds your cheque in trust for the seller, but if something on the seller's part makes it impossible for him to convey title to you, it is sometimes difficult to have your money returned if the seller has it in his bank account — he may have left on a three months' holiday. Your broker is always there.

49

REAL ESTATE SHORTHAND

What do you suppose "Brft. rm. Ens. to M.B. Gar. C/Air" means?

Apparently it is part of the new real estate advertising language. But what grabs me about it is the value of the properties being so advertised.

If I were having to pay a real estate commission of tens of thousands of dollars, I would a least expect to have my property advertised so buyers could read the offer without trying to figure out a broker's shorthand.

The opening shorthand here may seem to say there is a breakfast room ensuite to a master bedroom with a garage and central air conditioning.

Not really. There is a breakfast room. There is a bathroom ensuite with the master bedroom. There is a garage, and the home is air conditioned.

In an advertisement for a house priced at close to $1 million we see: "lge 3rd flr master suite." Paying about a $50,000 commission would surely rate the words "large" and "floor" being spelled out.

Or how about a "fam rm" in a $700,000 job? Why take the two "o's" from room? And where did the "ily" go from family?

The best reading in real estate advertising has always been *The Times* of London. When an agent had a rundown house to sell, it would be advertised as a real dog. *Buyer Beware.*

Sell the sizzle, not the steak, said the famous guru Elmer Wheeler.

Look at a page of real estate advertisements and what do we see? Plenty of sizzle, but not much steak. All the homes advertised are really something special, and I suppose that's the way it should be. Why promote doom and gloom?

Criticizing a broker for using shorthand may prompt an indignant response, saying that advertising costs are causing it all. Baloney.

When I see an expensive home being advertised with a two-line advertisement saying it has a "main fl. library," I choke.

Get a listing at a fair price and the agent can look forward to a fast trip to his bank with a deposit that will tickle the bank manager.

So why say the floor is a "fl." when the owner is going to hand over a hefty commission for a few days' work?

If you are looking for a home, you may require a real estate shorthand dictionary.

Here are some translations:

ACS	Acres	LGE	Large
ADJ	Adjacent (Not adjutant)	LG	Same as large
BDRMS	Bedrooms	PKRG	Parking
BSMT	Basement	RENO	Renovated
DBL GAR	Double Garage	SEP D.R.	Separate dining room
FAM RM	Family room	FIN	Finished
SITRM	Sitting room	FL	Floor
STE	Suite	FPL	Fireplace
STY	Story (or storey)	FURN	Furnished

All the foregoing are quoted from recent advertisements. The market is hot, so why bother spending more than is necessary to get the message across?

Ah, well, maybe I'm taking the run out of it by all this carping. After all, where else can we find a house with a "w/o to lge gdn open on the wknd?"

And I have never been able to figure out what an "executive" home is. A "senior executive" home is advertised at double the price of a "junior executive" home.

I know a barber who lives in a home worth more than these executive homes. How should it be advertised? A good agent will think of something to catch your eye; whether these agents realize it or not, they are following Elmer Wheeler's advice to "sell the sizzle" and not the steak.

No agent worth his salt would call a small den a small den. It is a "cosy" den. This conjures up visions of intimacy, doing whatever one's imagination wishes to do in it.

The optimist says a bottle is half full, and the pessimist says it is half empty. A home is five years new, not five years old.

A "full basement" is one that is a cemented hole in the ground under the full perimeter of the house. Thousands of homes have been built with a half-basement, but I have never seen one advertised that way. If it's only half, shut up about it.

"Must be seen" is a common piece of advice in real estate. Why? What's so special about it that it must be seen, especially if the price isn't mentioned? If the asking price of a house isn't mentioned in the ad, there is a reason for it. Phone calls, prospects.

When an expensive house is on the market, how many calls do you suppose an agent gets if the price is listed? Not many, unless it is advertised in a hot area.

So the ad goes in without the price. Callers ask about it, and if the price turns them off at least the agent can suggest other cheaper houses.

"Steps to public transit." This one makes me think I walk out the front door and, after a very short walk, I'm at the bus stop. I paced one of these and it was three city blocks. How many steps to a block?

"Owner leaving town" and "owner has bought" suggest that a real bargain is waiting for some lucky buyer. Well, pay attention to these because maybe there is a good deal here.

When a seller has already bought another home with no conditions he has a closing date to meet and he certainly doesn't want to carry two houses. Even if he has bought a home with a condition that he sells his present digs, he still wants to get cracking.

"Can be carried for $500 a month." This is probably quite true, but it only refers to the mortgage debt. Some buyers may get the idea that this is great, just a few thousand dollars down and we move in. Maybe 80% down?

"Open for offers." Of course they are; 99% of them. Most houses sell for less than the listed price.

"Must sell." Don't overlook these. Why must they sell? If the house really interests you, and the agent says he is under a power of sale or some such thing, ask him to prove it.

Maybe you really can get a good deal here. Tough for the owner but a buyer would probably be doing him a big favor. It would save him from being kicked out of his home to say nothing of those hefty legal charges.

AIDA is the acronym used by real estate agents for decades. Attention. Interest. Desire. Action.

The idea is first, get your attention; then arouse your interest and create desire; and the action occurs when the offer is asked for and signed.

50

WHO CAN YOU TRUST?

A cousin of mine sold a small island on a lake near Gananoque. When I asked him to show me the agreement, I was astounded. It was in pencil, written on a small piece of paper torn out of a school exercise book, with words to this effect:

"I, John E. Steacy, agree to sell to Mr. R. Barfoot of Massena, N.Y., my island in Charleston Lake for $5,000. Five hundred down and the rest when the summer starts and he owns it." Dated and signed by both parties.

The deal went through like a dose of salts, and everybody was happy. Barfoot got his island and cousin John got his money.

Cousin John was a farmer from the day he was born until the day he died, after a horse kicked him. More than sixty years doing business mostly on a handshake or verbal agreement. I think this had a lot to do with that deal, because I never met a farmer I couldn't trust.

Farmers are different from city slickers. A farmer working a mixed farm has to be the hardest working man in Canada. He gets up at 4:30 a.m. and heads for the barn to do a couple of hours' work before breakfast. Then he works his butt off for the rest of the day. No 9-to-5 sinecure for him. He is too busy working to bother figuring out how to cheat anybody.

The sophistication of the city slicker necessitates an awareness of mistrust in his fellow man, and so we have carefully worded legal agreements to protect us when buying real estate.

This, of course, is as it should be because committing oneself to a large debt load is not to be taken lightly. But reading some of the advice available to a purchaser is enough to make one just forget about the whole thing.

One lawyer outlined the legal aspects of buying real estate with about 20 pages of very sound advice. The guy really knew his business, but if a purchaser were to wade through it, he might never get around to signing anything because of the ifs, ands, and buts facing him.

The safest plan is to have your lawyer read the agreement after the salesman has prepared it. If this is not possible and you are pressed for time in having the offer presented, ask the salesman to have his manager go over it and give it his stamp of approval.

When the sales manager is approached in this manner, he will know that he is being asked to give his professional opinion of the prepared offer and he will not take this lightly. There just might be something the salesman or you happen to forget. It's just a little insurance for you.

I remember one buyer who turned on his tape recorder and started asking questions. Every answer from the agent was recorded, and I distinctly remember the agent being very careful about what he said.

He told me he was a bit nervous because what he said might come back to haunt him six months down the road in a lawsuit, and there are court judgments that would agree with him. When people hold themselves out as professionals, the courts expect them to be just that.

One well-known judgment held an agent liable for damages when he provided incorrect information about the size of a lot. The purchaser discovered this when he started building and ended up on someone else's property.

Ask all the questions you can think of before you sign the offer. Your agent will do his best to be careful in giving you factual answers, but he is no mind reader.

51

HOW SAFE IS A TRUST ACCOUNT?

Real estate brokers are required by law to have a trust account, which is used to hold money in trust for others.

For example, the money could be rents collected on behalf of property owners who have retained the broker to manage property, or deposits on real estate transactions. Government inspectors keep a watchful eye on the movement of money in and out of the accounts, and woe to the broker who misuses the trust.

But what does a trust account mean to a bank?

It is simply another bank account — which leads one to ask just how secure the money really is in the account. Can a judgment creditor seize the money in a trust account?

A broker will have three accounts in a bank. One for his personal use, one for his general business use, and one for money held in trust. If a sheriff's officer arrived at the bank and produced a notice of seizure to the bank manager to seize the broker's money on behalf of a judgment creditor, what would the bank manager do?

Is your money safe in the trust account?

The bank manager, in his wisdom (and they are pretty smart cookies) would know that the trust account is there to hold money in trust for others, so here is what his response to the sheriff's officer would be:

Money from the broker's personal account and his general business account (if it is not a limited company) would be surrendered up to the amount of the seizure. If the broker's personal and general account were depleted by the seizure, what happens to the third account, the trust account?

The trust account is a different matter. The banker would accept the seizure, but would *not* surrender any money from the trust account. He would, however, put a "hold" on the account.

Whenever the broker wished to write a cheque on the trust account, he would have to satisfy the banker that the cheque really was, in fact, someone else's money that had to be paid according to the terms of the trust. Once this was established, the bank would honor the cheque and release the funds.

If the broker, for example, held a deposit on a real estate transaction for $5,000, and the broker's commission were $4,000, when the sale is completed the broker could write a cheque for $1,000 to be paid to the vendor, but he could not write a cheque for the $4,000 commission to be transferred to his general account. This portion could be seized by a judgment creditor because when the sale closed it belonged to the broker.

You must remember that not all of that $4,000 really belongs to the listing broker. Technically the money belongs to the broker and normally he would disperse half of it to the selling broker and a portion of the remainder to the listing agent. Upon its seizure the selling broker and the listing agent would get nothing of that hard-earned commission.

In 1992, in an effort to protect the salesperson and other brokers, real estate associations recommended that upon closing, the trust account disperse funds first to the vendor if a surplus was held over and above the amount of the commission. The balance would then be transferred to a commission trust. Out of this trust account other brokers and salespeople would be paid, and the amount owing to the listing broker would be transferred to the general accounts and then it could be seized. This practice has been widely accepted within the industry to protect not only the public but also the salespersons who deserve their hard-earned commissions.

So you see, your money held in trust by a real estate broker should be quite safe from seizure.

52

BUY OR RENT?

For some families, ownership of a home is like a love affair. They find exactly the right place in the right location. Home ownership has always been their goal. It will make them independent and respected.

For others, ownership has an economic value. A house is an inflation-resistant investment and a tangible incentive to save.

Others are less enchanted by ownership. They have neither time nor inclination to manage the upkeep of a house. They may find available rental properties best suited to their needs. They fear hidden or unexpected expenses sometimes connected with ownership, and possible shrinkage of capital of property as values go down.

Others do not have and may never have the capital to buy a house. Renting makes adapting to changing family needs easier than owning. Because real estate transactions take so much time, the mobile family wants no house to lessen its bargaining power for a new position or to lose mobility for other than occupational reasons. This, of course, can sometimes be contingent upon the lease.

The decision to own or rent is related to stages in the life cycle that begins at marriage and extends some time after the dissolution of the family. A typical sequence of changes upgrades shelter as assets, age, and family needs increase. Net worth is normally highest after 35. Home ownership is greatest after that, and does not begin extensively before age 25.

The residential cycle may begin in a small rented apartment, perhaps after a couple has lived for a time with the parents of one. The next step may be a larger apartment, or the purchase of a small new or used house with equity. The owners may sell this after about age 35 in favor of a larger, newer house.

Later, demands of children call for expansion by remodelling or even buying another house. If finances permit, a custom-planned house may be built at this stage.

It may be the last house until old age and retirement indicate a smaller house, a cooperative or rental apartment. After the death of one spouse, the owner may remain awhile, but later may seek accommodation with children or other relatives, or in homes or projects for the aged.

Families move through the life cycle at varying rates, and with varying numbers of moves. When changed residential status is not the result of a promotion or desire to upgrade, turning points usually come during the expanding and contracting phases. Changes in residence, rented or owned, entail changes, often abrupt and substantial, in allocation of family resources. Whether as rent, mortgage installments, taxes or repairs, the residence claim is regular, and it is inexorable.

Home ownership is most often achieved with the help of mortgages. The average time required to pay off a mortgage on a house is about 25 years, which is about the same time it takes to rear a child from infancy to maturity and slightly longer than the couple has together after the children have left. If a family moves several times during this period, the feat of owning a home free and clear of debt is accomplished by enlarging the equity in succeeding houses.

A young family buying its first home often has little money, but if the buyers can carry a stipulated debt load, homes may be purchased with as little as 5% down (or less) through the availability of mortgaging that is default-insured by the buyer for the benefit of the lender.

Another avenue open to those with modest down payments is to get the seller to help with the financing by holding a mortgage or two as part of the purchase price.

Besides the down payment, buyers need money for closing costs — legal fees, mortgagee's service charges, and adjustments necessitated in balancing taxes, insurance, fuel etc, to the date of closing. These are items not to be overlooked.

There are pros and cons for both buying and renting.

Some morning when you are shovelling snow in front of your house wondering whether it is worth the effort, and you see your neighbor leaving his apartment building whistling cheerfully, you may think he has the answer. On the other hand, when the apartment building neighbor is feeling a bit cramped in July, and sees you entertaining friends with a nice outdoor barbecue in the garden, he may think you have the answer.

Here is an examination from both sides — renting and ownership.

Owning as Opposed to Renting

Pride of Ownership: This is ours. Our house. We can make a beautiful home out of it, or live in a shambles. We can keep up, or down, with the Joneses. As long as we comply with the by-laws of our municipality, we can live just the way we want to live.

Apartment: We are restricted. We have to watch the noise; no loud parties after midnight. Turn down the television. No smelly cooking, it might offend the neighbors. Can't be ourselves. Somebody's always complaining.

Children: A really big reason. One or a dozen, no matter. Pack them all in the house. Double bunks if necessary, but we'll get them in.

Apartment: No children allowed in many places, or none under a certain age, or you have to live on children-only floors.

Roominess: Lots of room to stretch, get out of each other's hair. A yard for barbecues and gardening. Very private parking.

Apartment: Cramped. Get on each other's nerves.

Pets: Just got a cute little pup that's going to be as big as a baby horse in a year? So what? If you can afford to feed it, keep it.

Apartment: What? If you are going to have a dog, lady, make it a small one. Or none at all.

Credit: Property ownership definitely is an asset when you want to put the bite on a bank or loan company. If you paid ten thousand dollars down for the house, who is to say that the equity now isn't worth twenty?

Apartment: Renting may go on the debit side of a credit application, unless you have been in the building for a few years.

Stability: Real solid citizen. That's Mr. Smith, he owns 512 up the street.

Apartment: Oh, we live in an apartment.

Income Potential: Couple of extra rooms? Perhaps you can rent them, if the by-laws allow it. It will pay the taxes. Two rooms at $50 a week each amounts to $5,200 a year. Probably enough left over to redecorate the house and pay the hydro.

Apartment: Nothing extra here. If you rent an extra room, it will probably only cover your rent on the extra room.

Possible Appreciation: Property values do go up, and how. For every dollar you credit yourself in paying off the principal on your mortgage, you could be adding another dollar in increased value.

Apartment: Nothing goes up but the rent.

Better Furnishings: When you have settled into a house, you feel that this is it, and you can safely spend more money on furniture and decorations because you will be there long enough to get the long-range economic enjoyment out of it.

Apartment: Too many factors can cause you to move, so why spend a bundle on decorating the temporary premises with anything permanent?

Peace of Mind: Usually a responsible homeowner will carry term insurance to cover the principal balance of the mortgage to ensure that the family will be left with a debt-free roof over its head if the breadwinner is gone.

Apartment: What's going to happen to my family?

Permanence: It's nice to make friends out of compatible neighbors, people you know who have roots like your own. It is a nice feeling to open your front door and welcome friends into *your* home.

Apartment: Too many come and go.

Responsibility: A properly run household is like running your own small business. It takes planning, foresight and decisive action.

Apartment: Something wrong? The superintendent may be too busy to fix it.

Civic Mindedness: Everything your municipality discusses concerning your local neighborhood concerns you. Join a ratepayers association, and your local homeowners association. They are stimulating and interesting.

Apartment: Oh, I don't know. So what if they are going to rip down those houses up the street or build something next door. I probably won't be here long enough to let it bother me anyhow.

Economy: You think about money when you own your own home. You don't splash it around. Too many things you could use the money for on the house. Your principal payments on the mortgage force you to save, to gain equity.

Apartment: Let's have a party. I got a bonus today.

Renting as Opposed to Owning

Freedom: Ah, this is it. When I leave my apartment, I can just close the door and walk away knowing the superintendent is on the job. I can move into a new building as soon as my lease expires. Try something different with new surroundings.

House: Can't stay away too long. If I go on holidays, I have to notify all services and police that I shall be away for a while, and put the bite on a neighbor to keep an eye on the place. Bit concerning. Stuck in same neighborhood.

No Capital Tied Up: I can do what I want with my bank balance. It's really flexible; there when I want it. I can invest it in anything I like, and readily.

House: Down payment tied up, and increasing equity in house.

Debt Free: Chunky mortgage commitments don't worry me, or maintenance or other service bills. All I do is pay the monthly rent, hydro (sometimes not even that) and telephone, with no extensions all over the place.

House: Always concerned about major disaster. New furnace? stove? fridge? roof? Other necessary expenses. Always something.

Freedom-Loving Neighbors: I live in a building with some gorgeous chicks and nice neighbors. We really enjoy that pool. Carefree types with happy outlook on life. Company readily available.

House: Sourpuss neighbor next door. And the other one can't communicate. I like to mix a bit.

No Children: Haven't any of my own. Can't stand them as a steady diet. Always under your feet. Noisy. They are on children-only floors.

House: Well, they are my own little darlings, but some of those kids they bring home from school. Phew!

Less Housekeeping: Small area to look after. Easy, once over lightly.

House: It takes a lot of work to make a house a home.

No Pets: Boy, do I hate the sound of a yappy dog at 1 a.m. Especially when it's not mine! Not bothered with that. They're all on the pets-only floor.

House: The first thing the kids want when they learn to talk is a shaggy dog. I have to look after it and feed it, and pay the vet's bills. I can't tell them there is no room for it.

Save Money on Furnishings: I just have to provide modest furnishings. The owner supplied the stove and fridge, my living room was broadloomed when I moved in, and the drapes were in place.

House: At least five rooms plus stove and fridge. Wow.

Dollars and Cents

Compare the carrying costs of a modest, detached house with an apartment that will provide about the same room. Consider the basement a freebee, because there won't be one in the apartment.

Now, regardless of what the down payment and closing costs are on the house, the interest that we could have earned on this money, say 8%, will have to be shown as an expense under the house. Also, the mortgage principal, as it is paid, will be added to this.

Housing costs in your area won't be the same as mine, so you copy the following guide and fill in your own figures for comparison.

	House	*Apartment*
Rent	$	$
Insurance		
Water/Hydro		
Heat		
House Maintenance		
Grounds Maintenance		
Municipal Taxes		
Interest on Mortgages		
Interest on down payment and closing costs	_______	_______
	$	$

From this you can draw your own conclusions. There are fringe benefits in both cases.

The apartment has a nice swimming pool and other amenities. The freedom of movement is there. The cash is in the bank.

The house has a nice garden and barbecue area for entertaining. It provides forced savings, roominess and roots. A big plus here of course, is the possibility of strong property appreciation.

The decision is yours.

53

HOW TO GET SERVICE FROM A SALESMAN

There is an old saying in real estate — "all buyers are liars." It is not meant literally, but many people who go looking for a home or other real estate really don't know what they want.

Two-story buyers buy bungalows, new-house buyers buy resales, detached-house buyers buy duplexes or doubles, downtown buyers buy in the suburbs, and so it goes.

The new salesperson can't understand it. The buyer did say he wanted to be near the subway, and now he has bought in the country.

This can be disconcerting to a salesperson who has patiently done his homework for days to find the "right" house, but it can be delightful for the salesperson who suddenly made a quick sale. The latter got the buyer at the end of the search, when the buyer was fed up with house hunting and simply bought one, or suddenly found the ideal one.

Everyone who is setting out to buy a house should accept the fact that perhaps he too might buy a house that he really didn't want.

Here are some suggestions on how to find a real estate salesperson and how to get the best possible service from him, or her, so that in the end you wind up with the house you really want.

Once you have settled on an area in which you feel you would like to live, visit the offices of real estate brokers in the immediate vicinity, preferably ones who are members of a local real estate board, because they have access to all the properties listed for sale through a multiple-listing service. This system not only provides the details of each property, but also a photograph.

Do not restrict yourself to one broker. Visit as many as possible, because brokers will have their own exclusive listings, which other brokers may not know about, and one of these listings could mean the end of your search. However, do restrict yourself to one salesperson in each broker's office. He has access to all the listings in his office, and if he feels that you are his "exclusive" buyer, he will work harder for you.

When you have half a dozen salesmen from various offices assisting you, you might lean toward one over all the others for any of several reasons, such as his knowledge of the market, enthusiasm, deportment, etc. You have found your agent.

If you notice an advertisement in the newspaper, or a "for sale" sign on a house that looks good, regardless of the area or the broker's name, ask your salesperson to get all the information for you, and introduce you to the property through the cooperation of the listing broker.

Your salesperson knows what you are looking for, and this can relieve you of the pressure of a new man trying to make a sale. This saves confusion.

When you cooperate with one salesman, he will feel he has a red-hot buyer who is really sticking with him, and will knock himself out to get the results that will please you.

54

PRIVATE "FOR SALE" SIGNS

An approach to buying a home (or other real estate) that could be financially very dangerous is to knock on the door behind a private "for sale" sign.

The obvious reason for selling privately is so that the seller can obtain as much money as possible from the sale and avoid paying a real estate sales commission, therefore saving the buyer some money.

This can be dynamite to an unsuspecting buyer's pocketbook, especially to one who is of the opinion that he too is being clever in avoiding a real estate agent.

There is certainly nothing illegal or wrong in selling one's own property privately, but if you are considering such a buy, ensure that it is done properly.

The most vulnerable buyer is one who is searching for a house in an unfamiliar area. Values are not consistent from province to province, and certainly not from city to town.

A standard six-room brick bungalow in an urban fringe town with a market value of $160,000 could very well command as much as $40,000 more in the city and, not only that, the city property would probably be on a smaller lot.

A buyer, after searching in the city and becoming discouraged with its inflated market, could reasonably look to the suburbs and surrounding towns. Coming across a private "for sale" sign in a town on a comparable $100,000 city property could be an expensive experience. If he found that the vendor was asking $75,000 for the property, it might seem like a bargain, when in reality the market price locally might dictate a value of $60,000.

I am not suggesting that a buyer should ignore a private sign, because the home might be very suitable for his particular needs.

What I do strongly suggest is that a true and reasonable local value be determined.

This can be done by employing an established local real estate broker to do one of the following:

a) Appraise the property. This will cost about $150.
b) Act as a counsellor for the purchase, for a prescribed fee.

A vendor who is not actively engaged in real estate is not really qualified to appraise his own home — the basic reason being that he has a built-in inflated idea of what his own property is worth.

As a matter of fact, real estate brokers often enlist the aid of other brokers in valuing their own homes.

So an appraisal must be done to establish what the value is. If the private seller is doing a good job, he will have an appraisal done to justify the selling price. If the seller objects to having an appraisal done, the purchaser should become cautious.

The appraisal will come into the picture when a purchaser has found a property he is genuinely interested in buying, and when one reaches this stage, it is better to be out $150 rather than three or four thousand, which could happen. If the appraisal should justify the private seller's price, then it would certainly be worth $150 to know that one at least did not pay more than the market value of the property.

Retaining a broker on a fee basis means that the broker would have to represent the buyer in negotiating the purchase, and this would cost more than an appraisal. If one did not wish a broker to go this far, at least the broker could draw up a proper offer, possibly with advice that could save the buyer money.

The local broker would know, through experience, what the market value of the property really is, and his advice in negotiating would be invaluable.

When you are the buyer, get a little help to ensure the price is right.

55

SELECTING YOUR HOUSE

The Choice Is Yours: Most of us will own a number of houses in our lifetime. We increase our incomes; we move. We are transferred by our company; we move. We enlarge the family; we move. We decrease the family; we move. Just count the number of moving vans the next time you are on the highway. When are *you* going to move?

Let the choice be a good one or at least a thoughtful one, for even if you stay in a place only a short time it can influence you and your family's well-being, sometimes even your identity and happiness. A mistake, if you make one, can be corrected, but a mistake almost always leaves some kind of mark.

The Community: Before you make your choice, compare the costs in money, time and fatigue of commuting with the advantages and disadvantages of space, privacy, and quiet for you and your family.

Do not overlook differences in public amenities and municipal services, and in taxes and the cost of insurance and utilities. Choose, if you can, to live within the jurisdiction of a municipal government that has a master zoning and development plan, and legislation to support it. During this period of increases in population and fast-growing cities, it is hard to foresee the future of a community or to influence its development. Without a plan, growth is chaotic and unpredictable.

Many families have built houses in the country only to find the city at their doorsteps sooner than they had expected. Many others have built or rented in city neighborhoods whose residential character becomes eroded by conversion to incompatible uses. Do not buy or build a house on land that has a potential for industrial, commercial, or multiple-housing development except as a calculated investment. Seek a site protected by zoning.

You will find other advantages in legislation for planning. Visual quality — beauty and order — depends on the goodwill and sensibility of each property owner and the competence of the architect, but laws can control some of the influences that have contributed to the deterioration of the landscape — signs, billboards, and utility structures. Some communities limit the location of billboards, the size of signs, and require that wires and pipes of utilities be put underground. Choose a community like this one and one that is alert to the possibilities of such improvements.

Local government and public education are financed largely by taxes on real property. Tax rates and assessment practices vary among communities, but do not assume that communities with low taxes are necessarily more efficient. They quite often provide fewer or inferior services. The property tax has inevitable shortcomings, because it penalizes quality by rewarding shoddy property with low assessments.

Nothing is more important than good schools. They are not easy to develop. They are built by the efforts of dedicated people over long periods. Your school age children get no benefit from long-range improvements. They need good schools now. Good schools are expensive. Usually they co-exist with higher real property taxes, but differences in tax rates in communities with good schools and those with poor schools are seldom great enough to influence one's choice and are never worth the savings.

Communities with good schools usually are stimulating in other ways. So when you are looking for a place to live, look into opportunities for intellectual activity: libraries, museums, theaters, concerts, or perhaps even an amateur symphony or little-theater groups. Mutual interests foster friendships more than geography does.

Look also for a beautiful place, or at least one that is not ugly. Visual quality, like a good school system, is not achieved quickly. It depends on long traditions of pride and long-continued programs of responsible public works. Street trees take years to mature. Established visual elegance in a residential community is literally priceless.

Consider also convenience to work, shopping, and schools in terms of distance and methods of transportation, for a house for most families today is a center from which to commute to work. Children travel to school; parents to shops. Anticipate travelling costs in your estimate of housing costs.

The place you live often determines whether you need one or two automobiles or none. Sometimes it will be found to be cheaper to hire cabs while travelling within the community and rent cars on weekends when you want to get away, rather than tying your cash up in the cost of owning an automobile or two.

The European lives in his city at large. Public and neighborhood gathering places — piazzas, parks, sidewalk cafes, coffeehouses — serve as extensions of his house into which some social parts of life are projected. We have fences along our property lines, but we are experiencing a revival of interest in public amenities; especially in cities. Consider then the relationship between the kind of urban situation in which you live and the kind of housing facilities you may need or that are available.

Sometimes, a neighborhood is so attractive that it determines one's choice of community, but usually the community is selected first. Transportation may influence the second decision as well as the first. So, inevitably, will the housing situation. If you are interested in a particular kind of house or lot, or one at a certain price, you may find it only in a limited number of places. But, assuming there are alternatives, how to proceed?

Sometimes, when moving into a community, there is an advantage in renting for a while. Many qualities, especially the intangibles that have to do with sociability, common interests and even climate, cannot be understood without experience. Renting in an unfamiliar community will give you a clearer idea of the kind of house you want and the neighborhood in which you would like to live.

Look for visual character. It is even more important in the neighborhood than in the community, because the neighborhood is closer to home.

Established neighborhoods have at least two advantages. You can examine the houses and the landscape has had time to mature. Some of our best houses are very old, but middle-aged houses and neighborhoods tend to deteriorate.

Judge the viability of an established neighborhood before placing a new house there. If you don't trust your own evaluation, seek professional advice. New developments still under construction are harder to visualize, but plans can give some indication of their eventual completed appearance.

Houses for sale or rent, and remaining lots in stable residential neighborhoods, command higher prices. So does property in thoughtfully planned and sensitively designed new residential areas that can reasonably be expected to develop admirably.

Your choice is difficult. Whether to accept an area that is not attractive and probably will not be developed attractively, or place a larger percentage of your investment in land and improvements to take advantage of a superior location, remembering that you will be able to do little to change the aspect of the neighborhood.

Look for a location where you can walk to stores and shops, schools and a park. That may be difficult because much zoning legislation has produced antiseptic neighborhoods, which, by being unvaried, are also lacking in services. Communities vary a great deal in the availability of facilities and programs for recreation. Do not overlook the importance of these for children.

Select a location that is free from unpleasant sources of noise, fumes and dirt and not near a main traffic artery, railroad, airport or objectionable industry. Noise travels surprising distances on quiet nights. So do fumes and dust on breezy days.

Consider the views. If the terrain is hilly, the views are more extensive, but construction costs will probably be higher.

What does the street look like? Smaller streets are relatively quiet and safe. Subtly curved streets usually are more attractive than straight ones, but excessively curved ones are puzzling to strangers and casual visitors.

What do the neighborhood houses look like? Is there fencing? Landscaping? What is the orientation of the lot? Can you take advantage of winter sunshine, yet keep out excessive summer sun? What is the direction of the prevailing winds? Are cooling summer breezes accessible? Is the lot readily drained? What is the character of the soil? Is it subject to movement, settling, slides?

Check the zoning regulations. Find out what you can and cannot do there; the restrictions on the house itself, and the kinds of room rental regulations in the area. Can you practice a part-time profession or occupation, or build a swimming pool?

Ask whether there has been a recent flood in the neighborhood. If not, and if it has survived a severe rainy season, its drainage facilities are adequate unless subsequently overloaded by new developments.

Inquire about provisions for collecting trash and garbage.

Is there a periodic water shortage, or is the supply adequate for house and garden?

Attractive and compatible developments, such as a new college campus, golf course or public park, exert stabilizing influences on residential properties.

If you follow these criteria and acquire a well-designed and soundly-constructed house, property values probably will be sustained. A house that is no more expensive than the average in the neighborhood, and perhaps a little less so, is a conservative investment.

The House: When we acquire a house, we are inclined to think of the enterprise as an investment. A house can be ostentatiously out of place in its neighborhood or too expensive for a given market to support, especially in small communities without diversified demands.

Experience does not support the commonly held assumption that when a minority group moves into a neighborhood, property values automatically decline. Sometimes they increase.

Of course, all the economic factors involved in the venture should be considered: the relative advantages of renting and owning; indirect costs, such as transportation; and the direct costs — the land and improvements, building, landscaping, furnishing, and operation (maintenance, taxes, insurance and what about the mortgage?).

Land costs are lowest in the country and highest in the central city, and vary with the desirability of the location and the extent of its improvement.

Do not overlook the costs of site improvements. As a prospective owner, determine your liability to the municipality for current or future work. All things considered, it is better to live in a community that requires first-class utilities, drainage, street construction and lighting.

At the other end of the process, think of landscaping and furnishing costs. Families often find themselves with inadequate funds for these items simply because they follow site and structure in the sequence of acquisition.

Insurance costs vary with the quality and proximity of fire and police protection, but differences in premium do not measure the advantages of adequate protection.

The building itself represents the largest single expenditure. Many variables influence its cost. For some families, cost will be critical and the alternatives severely limited, while for others, several choices will be available.

At this point, turn to considerations other than price. How important to you is an unspoiled stretch of wilderness, or the sound of music, or the company of friends?

Existing houses, new or old, can be examined before the purchase. Building a new house, on the other hand, presents the opportunity to achieve a uniquely personal environment, given competent professional design — at least an architect, and preferably also a landscape architect.

Many houses could have been put up more economically had an architect designed them, but good professional service entails costs and so does custom building. Select your architect carefully on the basis of his work — one who is interested and experienced in house design. Select the builder carefully, too. Most people assume that competitive bidding is the only way to solicit a reasonable price. Sometimes it is, but limit the bidders to good contractors. The best procedure, if you can manage it, and if your community is fortunate enough to have such people, is to select the best builder just as you selected the best architect. Builders who take a professional interest in their work usually quote the same price whether bidding competitively or simply invited to bid.

If your house is being designed for you, its form has limitless possibilities. Take advantage of the opportunities to make it truly original, but avoid exotic excesses, which disrupt visual harmony in the neighborhood and can make it difficult to sell in the future.

In the final analysis, the value of a house, regardless of its location, can be judged only in terms of its success as a personal environment for each member of the family in an emotional as well as a functional sense.

A Well-Built House: How can you tell whether a house you are thinking of buying is well built?

First, get a copy of the plans and specifications. Compare what you can see of the house with what is shown on the plan. Sometimes plans are revised during construction, for better or for worse, unless the builder has registered his plans for mortgaging.

Some general features are not structural, but still may be important to you. Among them are: Which way does the house face? Is the arrangement and size of rooms good? How about natural light and cross ventilation? Do the rooms provide enough wallspace or storage space? Does the plan permit some flexibility of living arrangements? These are partly matters of personal taste. Do they satisfy your family's needs or preferences?

Then inspect the structural part of the house — the foundation, walls, floors, ceilings and roof. Start from the outside. Walk around the house.

Look at the foundation walls, which should extend well above the finish ground level. Watch for vertical cracks, which may indicate the structure has settled. Hairline cracks in the concrete are due to volume changes and have no great significance.

If the concrete is uneven or honeycombed, or has broken corners, it probably did not have enough cement or was carelessly placed in the forms — a sign of poor workmanship.

In block or stone walls observe the character of the joints. Use a pocketknife to pick at the mortar and see if it crumbles easily. If it does, it is a sign that too much sand or a poor quality cement was used. A nail driven in the joint will indicate if the mortar is skimpy there. If you wish to check the wall thickness, measure the thickness of the casement of a basement window.

The slope from the foundation at the grade line should be enough for rain to run off.

Basement window wells must drain readily. Water from the roof should be carried away by adequate eavestroughs and downspouts of noncorrosive material. If downspouts are not connected at a storm sewer or other suitable outlets, splash blocks at the outlet will divert the water.

Check basement window jambs and trim to see if they fit snugly against masonry wall. The sills of all windows should have sufficient pitch to drain water outward. Here is a place where decay may have occurred — probing with a small screwdriver will soon tell you.

After a final look at the foundation walls to make sure the corners are even and walls are vertical, we can inspect the framed sidewalls. They may be covered with wood or composition siding, shingles, brick, stucco, stone, or other types of enclosing materials. All are good if used properly.

If the siding has been painted, examine the condition of the paint. See if the paint film is dense and opaque, or if the wood is showing through. Check for any gloss on the surface. Painted surfaces that are dull and chalky indicate that repainting is necessary.

The horizontal lap siding should be laid evenly, with correct overlap and tight butt joints. At the corners, the siding may be mitered or fitted snugly against vertical corner boards. An end of the siding board should not be exposed to the weather because it will soak up moisture.

Make sure the nails are of the noncorrosive type and that the space between the nailhead and the face of the siding has been filled in before painting. Simply scratch to find out.

Windows and doors should have a protective flashing of noncorrosive metal above them. They should be checked for weatherstripping. Check the sills for sufficient pitch for good drainage. A drip groove under the sill will permit the water to drop clear of the siding.

You have now had an opportunity to form an opinion on the quality of workmanship that has gone into the outside walls. Neat foundation walls, good metal eavestroughs and downspouts, snug-fitting woodwork, and provision for surface drainage all indicate the builder has made a conscientious effort to erect a house that will endure.

Signs that the builder has skimped are chipped or honeycombed concrete, loose mortar in the brickwork, large cracks between the ends of the siding and window or other trim, rust stains from an inferior grade of outside hardware, and thin or flaked-off paint in a nearly new house.

Now go inside the house. In the basement, look more carefully at the foundation walls, posts, and girders, and at the floor joists if they are not concealed by the ceiling material. The basement floor should be dry.

The basement floor should slope to the floor drain to permit quick runoff. A concrete floor should have a hard smooth surface without spilling, cracking, or dusting.

The joists that support the floor above rest on the foundation walls and are supported by wood or steel girders. These girders in turn are supported by posts or division walls. If wood posts are used, they should be set on a concrete base block above the finish floor level.

When wood girders are built up by nailing several members side by side, make sure the members are well nailed together and that joints are over a post or a division wall.

Check to see that the ends of wood joists are not embedded in masonry or the concrete wall, as this practice may invite rot unless there is an air space at the sides and end of the beam.

The wood joists should be spaced evenly. Examine them for sagging, warping, or cross-breaks. Look carefully at any joists that have been cut for heating ducts or piping. Notches or holes on the bottom edge or near mid-span have the greatest weakening effects.

Check the area between the foundation wall and sill. Any opening should be filled with a cement mixture or a caulking compound. The filling will lower the heat loss and prevent the entry of insects or mice into the basement.

Most construction in the living area will be hidden by various wall and ceiling finishes, but you can check the interior finish and such items as flooring, windows, doors and other trim. Examine the trim for any open joints, hammer marks, warped pieces or rough nailing.

Over the door where the side casings meet the horizontal, the joint is often mitered. If this joint is tight, as all joints should be, you have a pretty good sign of careful workmanship.

Note, too, if the baseboard fits snugly against the flooring and wall at all points.

Interior finishes are commonly of plaster, or of such a drywall construction as wood or composition material. You seldom see plaster cracks in a newly built home, because they develop slowly. In a house a year or more old, the absence of cracks indicates a well-built house. Of course, cracks can be concealed temporarily by wallpaper or a coat of paint. Cracks extending diagonally from the corners of windows or doors may be signs of poor framing or that the house has settled.

As you walk over the floors, notice if they squeak or seem too springy. If the floor joists are big enough and the sub-floor has been laid correctly, neither fault should occur. If you wish to check to see if the floors are level, stretch a string across them.

If the flooring is exposed, hardwood flooring or the harder species of softwood are usually preferred. If carpeting is used wall to wall, the underlay may be of any material that presents a smooth and firm surface.

Look carefully for signs of nailing. Flooring of a standard thickness is tongued and grooved and is blind nailed along the tongue so that the nailing does not show. Small nailheads on the face or top of the flooring mean that a very thin flooring has been used. Wood strip flooring normally becomes dry and cracks open between the strips in the winter. These cracks, if they are not too wide, will close up in warmer weather.

Do not condemn floors in an old house simply because they are scratched and marred. Perhaps all they need is refinishing. If so, take this extra cost into account.

Perhaps the kitchen and the bathroom have tilework on the floor, on the wall, or wainscot. The tile floor should be smooth, without raised tile or depressed areas. Wall tiles should fit snugly around all windows, door trim and around the fixtures. Joists should be caulked tightly to keep water out.

Check the doors to see if they swing freely and close tightly without sticking. Is there a threshold under the exterior door to keep out snow and cold winds? Some of these doors may have metal weather-stripping. Are the interior doors hung so as to clear your rugs? Do they interfere with other doors? Do they latch readily and stay latched? Check all doors to see that they are not excessively warped.

Open and shut all windows to be sure they work properly. The weather-stripping should not interfere with the ease of operation.

Don't forget to raise the window shades to check for cracked windowpanes.

Check window woodwork and plaster for water stains and signs of decay. Note the kind of glass in the window. Is it clear and flawless, or does it create distortion? Also, see that the putty that holds the glass in is in good condition and is painted.

It is well to check the attic for the thickness of insulation between the ceiling joists and to see if there is a moisture barrier on the room side of the insulation.

Ureaformaldehyde foam insulation has been banned from use since the late 1970s. Newer homes are unlikely to contain this material; however it was a popular insulating material in older homes because it could be injected into the cavities in between the walls. Since this material gives off a formaldehyde gas, special equipment is required for its detection.

Question the owner and the agent regarding a warranty that this material has not been used, or if it has been used that it has been successfully removed. If you have any fears or doubts you can call for an inspector to test the house for a fee.

Check the attic ventilators. They should be open summer and winter. In summer, ventilation helps to lower the attic temperature. In winter, ventilation removes moisture that may work through the ceiling and condense in the attic space.

Frost on the ends of nails in winter indicates insufficient ventilation and excess moisture.

Check the roof rafters or trusses to see that they are unbroken and that framing joints are tight. Can you see any daylight under the eaves? Water staining on the rafters or roof sheathing is a sign of a roof leak.

Questions that are more complex, or that cannot be answered by comparison with standards, may require the services of a qualified inspector or architect. The cost of this service may be small compared to the troubles that can arise from a serious defect.

56

A COMPARATIVE GUIDE FOR HOUSEHUNTERS

This chapter lists the many physical aspects to check when inspecting properties. By comparing the results, the househunter will be able to decide which house is the right one.

Exterior Setting

Street Front: Check general appearance of neighborhood. Other homes should be of like or better quality.

- ☐ Unpaved street, or lack of sidewalks, storm and sanitary sewers, may mean future assessments for improvements.
- ☐ If builder says he'll pave streets in new development, get it in writing.
- ☐ Check location of street lights, fire hydrants, if any.

Grounds: Determine lot's boundaries. Ask about easements.

- ☐ Note general quality of landscaping. Good lawn, plenty of shrubs, trees can be worth thousands. Lack of them will cost you money, work. If new house, get in writing what builder will provide. Check for dead or dying trees. Their removal can be costly.
- ☐ Note condition of driveway, walks. Their length, grade, are important factors in wintry climes.
- ☐ Adequate outdoor lighting is convenient, also deters prowlers.
- ☐ Visualize water runoff, drainage. Of special concern with low-lying houses. If in doubt, check grounds after heavy rain.
- ☐ Check for above-ground seepage if there's a septic tank. Correcting condition is expensive. Leaving it is a health hazard.

House Exterior: Be systematic. From ground, inspect all sides, top to bottom.

- ☐ Chimney: Note bricks, cap, flashing.
- ☐ Roof: Shingles should lie flat in even rows. Wide roof overhangs offer both practical, aesthetic advantages.
- ☐ Gutters, leaders (downspouts) should be solidly attached, without signs of deterioration, clogging.
- ☐ Check general condition of exterior walls, paint.
- ☐ Look for rot on windows, doors. Check whether storms, screens are installed.
- ☐ Foundation: Look for cracks, settling, low spots that collect water.
- ☐ Check number, location of hose connections.
- ☐ Waterproof, grounded electrical outlets are handy, especially near patio, sundeck, porch.

Living Areas

General: Layout should provide free traffic flow.

- ☐ Keep family's living style in mind. Anticipate problem areas.
- ☐ Ideally, kitchen and living room should have southern exposure to get plenty of sunlight.
- ☐ Empty rooms can appear deceptively large. Get measurements, note placement of windows, doors, etc. to make sure your furniture will fit.
- ☐ If home has wallpaper you don't like, remember it can be a chore for you to remove, expensive to have it done. Painting over is usually less than a satisfactory solution.

Kitchen: Probably the most important room. Also most costly on square foot basis if it needs remodeling.

- ☐ Check layout, placement of stove, refrigerator, sink, counters for efficiency.
- ☐ Ask what appliances come with the house, how old they are. See that they're in good working order. Frost-free refrigerator, self-cleaning oven are a plus.
- ☐ If your present appliances are to be installed, make sure they'll fit available space.

- ☐ Adequate cabinet, counter space with plenty of work area are critical. Measure, compare with what you now have.
- ☐ Ample electrical outlets are also important.
- ☐ Kitchen close to garage, laundry room, family room, patio, can save steps.
- ☐ Ventilation over range a plus. Combination hood and exhaust fan most practical.

Living Room: Size most important factor, followed by layout, location.

- ☐ Measure, sketch rough layout to see if furniture will fit.
- ☐ Foyer preferable to door opening directly into room. Reduces drafts, provides privacy.
- ☐ In older house especially, fireplace may not be in working order. Check.
- ☐ Coat closet should be handy.
- ☐ Check number, location of electrical outlets, wall switches.

Dining Room/Area: Measure, make sure it's big enough for your needs, furniture. Size of dining areas, in particular, are often deceptive. Should be sufficient room for guests to circulate around the table without crowding.

- ☐ Seclusion important. Screen, divider, even plants can achieve it in dining area.
- ☐ Consider convenience to kitchen, whether kitchen is visible to guests.
- ☐ Check number, location of electrical outlets, wall switches, adequacy of lighting. Dimmer switch is a real convenience.

Bathrooms: Size, number of bathrooms important, especially for growing families. Quality of fixtures important too.

- ☐ Generally figure one bathroom for every 2-3 people, or two bedrooms per bathroom.
- ☐ Powder room near main living area is a great convenience.
- ☐ Look for leaks under basin, behind toilet, etc.
- ☐ Test water pressure adequacy by turning on all taps and flushing toilet. Drop in pressure can indicate problem. If so, have plumber check.
- ☐ Note condition of grout in tile walls.

- ☐ Check size of medicine cabinet.
- ☐ Lighting should be adequate.
- ☐ Electrical outlet for razor, hair dryer a convenience.
- ☐ Exhaust fan essential in windowless bathrooms. Frequently required by building code.
- ☐ Linen closet should be handy.
- ☐ Make sure door locks can be easily opened from exterior in case of emergency.

Bedrooms: Preferably isolated from main living area to minimize disturbing sounds.

- ☐ Size, closet space, ventilation important.
- ☐ Small windows high on wall dangerous in case of fire, especially for the very young or very old.
- ☐ In children's' rooms, think twice about windows far from the ground, especially if there's nothing below to break fall.
- ☐ Check number, location of electrical outlets, wall switches.
- ☐ Ceiling fixtures are useful, but many bedrooms don't have them.
- ☐ Bedrooms with roofs immediately above (as in Cape Cods and finished attics) may be hot in summer, cold in winter.
- ☐ If doors lock, make sure they can be opened from outside in emergency.

Basic Household Services

Electrical System: Check service panel, or entrance box. 100-ampere, 200-volt system absolute minimum today; 150-200 amperes, 220 volts may be needed if household's electrical demand is high because of ranges, dryers, air conditioners, etc.

- ☐ Circuits from box serve various parts of house. Should be minimum of 6, preferably 8-10, in average house. Spare capacity valuable.
- ☐ Inadequate system is not only hazardous, but affects appliance lifespan, performance. Old wiring is especially dangerous.
- ☐ Modernizing can be expensive.

Heating System: Heating is major household expense; ask to see bills from previous winter.

- ☐ Check age of unit.

- ☐ Both gas, oil have advantages, disadvantages. Electric heat is too costly in most parts of country; A-1 insulation a must.
- ☐ *Forced Air Heat* — Furnace should have blower, preferably belt-driven, easily removable filter. Humidifier a plus. Turn furnace on-off, listen for noisy ducts. Advantages to system: it warms house fast, can be adapted for central air conditioning. Continuous blower system advantageous.
- ☐ *Hot Water/Steam Heat* — Furnace pipes usually take up less space. Furnace also may be used to heat water for faucets. But initial cost is high, responds slowly to heating needs, lacks humidifier and may have unattractive radiators. Cast-iron boiler, baseboard radiators best. Radiant heat in slab floor has many drawbacks.
- ☐ *Hot Water Heater* — Check name plate for capacity, recovery rate. Both important. 40-gallon capacity adequate for average family; 30 gallons should be minimum. Unit should be able to heat at least 30 gallons 100 degrees in hour.
- ☐ Check age of unit.
- ☐ Also check inside of burner compartment, floor beneath heater for signs of leakage.
- ☐ Gas heaters are usually cheaper to install, operate than electric.

Plumbing: Inspect pipes in basement, under kitchen sink, in bathrooms. Copper, brass, bronze preferable. Some plastic pipes now being used, but not permitted in many areas.

- ☐ Grease trap is especially important in homes with septic tank.
- ☐ Inadequate water pressure may indicate serious problem.
- ☐ Wells can be tricky. Purity, adequacy of water supply are vitally important.
- ☐ Plumbing repairs are expensive; system replacement even more so.

Air-Conditioning System: Turn on to test cooling power, noise level.

- ☐ Look for name of manufacturer. Some off-brands lack quality, adequate dealer servicing.
- ☐ Sizes required depend on area cooled, climate, insulation, etc. Generally one ton (or 12,000 BTU's per hour) needed for every 500-600 square feet. Insufficient capacity can be a problem.

- ☐ Water-cooled units can be costly to operate.
- ☐ Central system preferable to several individual units. Besides providing comfort, it's cheaper in long run, adds to home's resale value. Zone control thermostats also a plus.

Basement: Should be watertight. Look for wet spots, water stains, warped floor tiles. Musty smell can also be tipoff.

- ☐ Consider storage possibilities.
- ☐ Check floor for signs of heaving, cracking.
- ☐ Check joists for sagging. Inspect for rotted wood at point where joists rest on foundation. Also check for termites, but, remember, only an expert can really tell.
- ☐ Outside door great convenience.
- ☐ Heated basement a plus in cold-weather areas, a necessity if basement's finished.
- ☐ 220-volt grounded outlet useful for power tools, etc.

Laundry: Location near living, sleeping areas saves lugging clothes up and down steps.

- ☐ Consider size, lighting of work area. Also placement of washer, dryer, etc. for efficiency.
- ☐ Find out whether laundry appliances come with house. If not, make sure yours will fit available space.
- ☐ Make sure dryer is properly vented.
- ☐ Electric dryers are considerably more costly to operate than gas in most areas. Should have 220-volt grounded outlet.
- ☐ Shelves, counter space are helpful. Ditto stationary tub, which many newer homes don't have.

Garage: Two-car garage a plus even for one-car families, who'll get extra storage space for lawn mower, bikes, etc.

- ☐ Convenience to kitchen great help in carrying in groceries.
- ☐ Put car(s) into garage, see how they fit. Garages in older homes may be a tight squeeze.
- ☐ 220-volt grounded outlet convenient for power tools, etc.
- ☐ Adding garage space can be expensive. Carport is less costly, but still not cheap.

Attic: Consider accessibility, storage potential, possibility of finishing at later date.

- ☐ Louvres provide necessary ventilation, help cool home in summer, prevent condensation.
- ☐ Attic fan an asset in home without air conditioning.
- ☐ Wet spots, stains indicate leaky roof, expensive repair job, maybe new roof. Especially note area where chimney meets roof.
- ☐ Poor insulation or none at all, guarantees costly heating, cooling bills, plus likely discomfort.

Miscellaneous

Good insulation cuts cost of heating, cooling house considerably. Check normal requirements for your region. Weather stripping, storm doors, storm windows also money-savers. Double-glazed (even triple-glazed) windows especially important in extra cold climates.

- ☐ Nobody ever has enough closet, storage space. Total up what you now have, compare with house you're considering purchasing.
- ☐ Although not a critical item, you'll probably want to check on TV reception, especially in fringe areas.
- ☐ Increasingly popular are such accessories as intercom, central vacuum, burglar, fire alarm.

57

WHAT'S THE HOUSE WORTH?

When viewing houses, you naturally wonder about value. Especially if you are moving from province to province, one city or town to another. Within cities there are also substantial differences in neighborhood value.

Many househunters, after selling a home in smaller towns or rural areas, are shocked when faced with large-city prices. The first reaction is annoyance, and possibly anger, which is sometimes vented on the real estate salesman showing the moving householder around his new locale.

The most obvious way to establish value is to inspect as many comparable properties as possible. This will familiarize you with local *asking* prices, which will provide an overview, but ask the agent to show you recent *selling* prices.

The majority of real estate brokers maintain up-to-date files on sales, especially sales in their own territory. Also, many have access to a commercial service that can rattle off recent sales on a given street in a matter of minutes. The information will also provide details of how each sale was financed.

Many real estate boards publish periodic volumes of sales for the benefit of members so they can provide better service to the public. So you see, the recent-sale information is readily available. All one has to do is ask.

Although recent-sale figures are a great help in determining market value, if one is looking at six-room bungalows, the recent sales of two-story homes would not be of much help. The recent-sale figures for comparable six-room bungalows must be obtained, and if there are none, or few, or no sales recorded during the last year or two, then other approaches must be made.

Averaging is one. Brokers have records of the average monthly sales figures of *all* properties. If it can be seen that the average rise, for example, of *all* housing for the past year was 4% in the area, then this could be helpful. If the most recent sales of six-room comparable bungalows were a year old, then the 4% increase could be used as one guide in updating the figures.

Sales figures on half a dozen comparable properties may be closely related. Driving past these properties will allow you to compare the physical characteristics of each, but you won't be able to inspect the interiors. This is where averaging can help.

If the one you are interested in seems to be in average condition, fine, but if it is run-down and needs extensive work, or, conversely, is in beautiful condition, these will be plus and minus facts for you.

All the foregoing, of course, is assuming that the properties are reasonably standard. If the house in question is very dissimilar to the others, it will be difficult to assess the value. Perhaps the original cost of the house, if it is not too old, could be used as a basis for averaging over the years.

One thing is sure, though, and that is that the selling price on a house cannot be established until an offer to buy the place has been accepted by the vendor.

Some homes will be difficult to appraise. An area of fine old homes would be an example of this. The homes would all be individually designed by architects, each with its own characteristic charm. Appraising such homes presents a challenge not found in an area of predominantly six-room bungalows.

There are several approaches to appraising a large, well-built, vintage home. And, many years ago, they certainly were well built!

It can be said that the truest appraisal would require the property to be placed on the open market, to see just what buyers would be prepared to pay. Market value is generally defined as being: "the highest price estimated in terms of money which a property will bring, if exposed for sale in the open market, allowing a reasonable time to find a purchaser who buys with knowledge of all the uses to which it may be put, and for which it is capable to being used."

Testing the market to establish property value is done by listing the property at a price higher than prudent brokers would recommend. "Let's see the offers, then we'll know." However this direct market approach to appraising property can backfire and prove to be an expensive experience.

The overpriced property just might suit someone perfectly, one who would offer the full listed price. Then what would happen? If the offer was for the full price, but the terms in the offer did not *exactly* match the agent's listing agreement, the seller could reject it.

For example, a house is listed for $250,000 "cash to an existing mortgage." If a buyer offered $250,000 cash for the property, it would not be terms to which the seller agreed in the listing and the offer could be rejected. With no problem and the seller would have a great appraisal.

But if a buyer should come along and sign an offer to exactly match the listing, then what?

The seller would not have to accept the offer, but would probably be stuck with the dismal obligation to pay his agent the agreed selling commission. And it would damn well serve him right.

58

BUYING BEFORE SELLING

Should you sell before buying, or buy before selling? Most homeowners don't give this much thought until faced with the decision to move. Here are the most common situations when the decision to sell is made:

- in a hurry to sell
- to sell and move by a specific date
- in no hurry to sell
- to sell before buying another property.

If the move is a hurry-up affair, it means listing the property with a real estate board member on its multiple listing service (MLS). This exposes the listing to all members of the board, who are provided with the details and a photograph.

It is important to ensure that the price is right. Unfortunately, for the seller in a hurry the top price is not always obtainable.

If the property is listed too high, there will be a noticeable lack of interest in it, which you certainly wouldn't want. Too low and you will think you're at an auction sale with several offers in your lap within a day or two. It is difficult to place a "right" price on a house today.

So do it by averaging. Which means that you will have to get the opinion of about three local brokers, average their prices, select the one who impressed you the most and let him get on with the job of moving the property.

Ensure your MLS agent holds an "open house" for inspection by other agents. This is most important. If the property has been priced right, you could have it sold quickly.

To wish to sell and move by a specific date can be a problem.

If an acceptable offer comes along, but the moving date doesn't suit you, think twice before turning it down. Remember that, in selling, it is always best to make it easier for the buyer, so have your agent discuss this point over the telephone with the buyer.

This is important, because if you change the date or anything else on the offer, it is dead unless the buyer agrees to your change.

If the buyer won't budge on the moving date, you may be faced with interim financing, which is annoying and costly. If the buyer's closing date is later than your own moving date, ensure that there is a substantial sum of money placed in trust on the sale — at least enough to compensate you for the headache of having an empty house on your hands if the buyer doesn't go through with the deal. Oh, yes, it has happened.

Being in no hurry means you can ask more for the property. List it higher and see what kind of action you get. It is easier to come down than go up with the price.

Every coin has two sides. And so it is with whether to sell first before buying or to buy first before selling.

When prices are rapidly rising 1% or 2% from one month to the next the market is buoyant, the economy is good, and unemployment is low, there are plenty of buyers, and serious thought must be given to buying first with a longer closing. Once you have bought it, you can sit back and watch the value of your new house rise. Before long you realize that if you had waited a few months to buy it, the price would have gone beyond your reach. A further bonus is that while you're waiting for your old house to sell, its value is also rising. When after a few months you sell it, you discover you got more money from your home than you expected. You paid less for the new house and got more for the old one.

The danger is in waiting too long. If your old house remains unsold and you need the money to close the new home, you could be stuck with the heavy burden of carrying both. To protect yourself you could make your offer conditional on being able to sell your house. In a strong buoyant market, however, conditional offers have no advantage for the vendor because there are plenty of buyers ready to pay a higher price and make it a firm offer.

A common blunder in buying first is to overestimate the value of your present home. All homeowners believe that their house is the best in the neighborhood and artificially inflate its value. Even when an agent gives them a realistic estimate they don't accept it. Then they buy a house based on the inflated perception of value and overprice the house they want to sell. When they put their house on the market they find that it can't be sold for the expected sum, yet they cannot reduce the price because they would not have enough down payment for the new house. If you sell first, you know exactly to the penny what down payment you have and you can buy the new home knowing your financial position. If you dilly-dally in a hot market, prices could increase faster than you expect and again you would face financial pressure.

In a dead market when buyers are scarce and economic conditions are less than ideal, selling first makes a lot of sense. With your house sold and money in hand you can find another home easily. There is lots of selection and prices are low and very competitive. In a dead market buying first should only be considered if an offer conditional on the sale of your home can be successfully negotiated.

My first choice would be to sell first, most of the time. My second choice would be to buy first conditionally on selling my home. Only in exceptional situations, when the market is hot and when I believe it will continue that way for several months, would I consider buying first unconditionally.

59

CHECK THE ZONING!

So you found a nice little bungalow with a basement apartment. The price is a little more than you figured on spending, but it'll be okay because the rent from the apartment will help with the mortgage.

Issat so? Who says you can rent that apartment?

Every municipality has zoning by-laws which tell us what we can and can't do with our lands and buildings.

The fact that a present owner is renting an apartment does not necessarily mean that he is doing it with the blessing of his municipality. It may be quite illegal, and if discovered by a zoning inspector the tenant may find himself on the street and the owner will be deprived of his much needed income.

Years ago I was surprised to find an abattoir in a residential area in Toronto. Cattle were driven to the place along a lane behind some houses and they came out of there in pieces ready for the butcher. The reason this was allowed to continue was that it was operating under something called legal nonconforming use, which means that the abattoir was there and in operation before restrictive by-laws came into use, so it wasn't stopped.

I sold a large rooming house in a top residential area operating under similar circumstances. The buyer was allowed to continue business because the building's use did not change from the seller to the buyer. It was continuous and uninterrupted.

But such legal nonconforming use being passed from one owner to another is not guaranteed. I wouldn't want to make a bet allowing the abattoir to continue with another new owner.

I came across a lady sitting on a curb crying her eyes out, so I stopped and asked her if there was something I could do to help. She was sitting in front of a large bungalow, and told me she had purchased the property to operate a child day-care center.

The area was zoned for the operation all right, but she discovered too late that the by-law stipulated that it was allowed only if the building was specifically constructed for such use.

You would be reasonable in assuming you could rent a couple of rooms to help with the overhead in your home, but don't count on it. I can show you areas where it is strictly forbidden.

The probable reason that many zoning violations go on for years is that it is done quietly, and the neighbors don't complain.

Basement apartments are common and many owners aren't unduly concerned about it because they know that zoning inspectors don't go out on witch hunts looking for violators.

But if a neighbor complains because he suspects that someone is renting the basement of the house next door, the complaint will receive attention and the owner will be confronted by a man with a request to examine the property.

This could be a rude awakening and a sad day for the owner who was looking forward to receiving his monthly rent.

When a builder buys an old cracker box for the purpose of demolishing it and erecting a new house on the land, you can be sure that he will have done his homework to ensure that he can do just that. Or he will buy the property with a condition in the purchase agreement that will allow him to get permission to build or there will be no sale.

You be just as cautious. If you are going to buy a house with the idea of supplementing your income by renting part of it, I strongly urge you to do some homework.

Visit the municipal office and ask questions. Ask to see the by-laws concerning use of your intended purchase.

60

CONDOMINIUM OWNERSHIP

The first funds for condominium development in Canada were provided by Canada Mortgage and Housing Corporation in 1967 when it made $4.3 million available to finance the construction of 296 condominium units. In part, these were trial projects. But by 1971, private lending institutions and some provincial housing agencies were also putting their money into this kind of housing and CMHC was able to reduce its direct participation. So the condominium method of ownership has had the support of both the public and private sectors of the economy. All the provinces and territories of Canada have passed legislation to make condominium home-ownership possible.

Condominium enables a person to share in the ownership and operation of a housing development while having negotiable title to his own unit. Condominium describes a form of tenure or ownership that can apply to many kinds of housing including single-detached houses, town houses, garden homes and highrise apartment units.

Owing a condominium home includes a variety of important benefits:

1. The security of tenure of permanent home-ownership.
2. A better opportunity for those of average and modest income to buy rather than rent in areas where land costs are high.
3. The possibility of financial benefit to the owner in the event of a resale at a better price.
4. Opportunity to have a say in the management of the affairs of the condominium as well as serving fellow owners by being a member of the Condominium Board of Directors.
5. The opportunity to enjoy services and facilities normally only associated with rental projects.

6. The availability of economies often available only to those who can purchase various commodities as a group.
7. The advantage of homeowner grants that are provided by some provinces toward initial purchase as well as taxes for home ownership.

What Does Condominium Home-ownership Mean?

Condominium housing is an apartment or townhouse complex in which the residential units are owned by the individual owners and the rest (common elements), including land, is owned in common with the other owners. The condominium legislation of each province provides a broad framework for the proper administration and management of each project as a whole. The project documents, when registered, bring the project into being as the form of tenure known as condominium. This form of tenure is known as strata titles in British Columbia, and co-ownership of immoveables in Quebec. Condominium housing may be located on land which is held freehold, or on leasehold land which is subject to a long-term lease and the condominium corporation is tenant.

The Unit

In most provinces the part of the condominium which you will own outright is called the *unit.*

As a condominium owner you will have full and clear title to this unit which will be legally registered in your name. The definition of the elements and space you will own as a part of the unit may differ from project to project and a precise description will be provided in the documents prepared for each condominium.

Common Elements

The definition of *common elements* can be simply stated as "all the property except the units."

The common elements include lobbies, elevators, parking areas, roads and walkways, service equipment, recreation facilities, yards, plumbing, electrical systems and portions of walls, ceilings and floors and so on. Part, or parts, of the common elements may be designed for the exclusive use of one or more of the individual owners. These *limited common elements* may include balconies, patios, parking spaces and roof gardens, and the like.

The usual division of responsibility for maintenance and repair of elements in a condominium will be that owners maintain their own units, but that parts such as exterior walls, the basic structure of the building and plumbing, electrical and heating systems, will be maintained by the condominium.

Common Expenses

As a condominium owner, you will be required to share with the other owners the costs of maintenance, repairs, alterations and improvements to the common elements.

Such payments, usually referred to as *common expenses*, can vary over the life of a particular condominium project depending on the extent of maintenance decided on by the owners, the amount of any reserve fund to cover unforeseen condominium expenses, the type of insurance coverage for the condominium and the arrangements for the management of the condominium.

Project Documents

These documents deal with the outlining of the "government" or administration of a condominium project.

The documents that are registered with the land titles office to create a condominium are known as:

a) a *description* and *declaration* in Ontario, Nova Scotia, New Brunswick, Newfoundland and Prince Edward Island.
b) a *plan* and *declaration* in Manitoba, Yukon and Northwest Territories.
c) a *condominium plan* and *by-laws* in Alberta and Saskatchewan.
d) a *strata plan* and *by-laws* in British Columbia.
e) a "plan of the immoveables" and a *declaration of co-ownership* in Quebec.

The requirements for the creation and operation of a condominium are generally similar across the country. Although the provincial condominium acts refer to these documents by different terminology, the condominium documents may be expected to contain the following information:

1. A commitment of the property to the condominium form of ownership;
2. A description of the entire project (including plans and drawings) indicating the location and boundaries of each of the separate units and of the project as a whole;
3. A determination of the percentage of each "unit owner's interest" in the common elements;
4. A system of assessment for maintenance and operating expenses;
5. A statement of the fundamental rights and obligations of all parties involved; and
6. A description of the organization of the condominium owners.

The importance of the project documents is that they specify and regulate the constitution of each condominium and are intended to be of a lasting nature. A declaration, for example, can only be changed or amended by the unanimous consent of all the owners and mortgage holders, except in Quebec where a 75% affirmative vote of the owners can amend the Declaration of Co-ownership.

By-laws

To ensure the successful operation of a condominium, it is necessary to formulate and observe rules concerning the use of the common elements, the conduct of members of the condominium and provisions for changes to the project and its rules. The various provincial acts provide for the establishment of by-laws for this purpose.

By-laws can be amended or revised by a majority vote of the owners as specified in the project documents.

The use of the term by-laws does not have the same meaning in every province. Some provincial acts clearly define what may be included in the by-laws and others are quite permissive in that they only ask that the corporation establish by-laws to provide for the control, management, administration, use and enjoyment of the units and the common property. These rules are known as by-laws in the

Territories and all provinces except Quebec which does not have by-laws but uses the Declaration of Co-ownership instead.

Association of Owners

In order to carry on the necessary collective action involved in the operation of a condominium project, an organization of the owners is necessary. All provincial condominium acts require that an *association of owners* be formed to manage the property and affairs of the condominium.

The owners' association is known as: (a) a *corporation* in Ontario, Manitoba, Alberta, Saskatchewan, New Brunswick, Yukon, Northwest Territories, Newfoundland, Nova Scotia and Prince Edward Island; and (b) a *strata corporation* in British Columbia; and (c) the *co-proprietors* in Quebec.

The association of owners will have the power to carry out all the requirements of the provincial condominium act and the project documents. If the condominium is to be adequately maintained, the owners' association must have control over the parts of the condominium which are owned in common. In most condominium projects, the repairing and maintenance of buildings, the removal of snow, the maintenance of lawns and landscaping, driveways and walks, etc., will be managed by the association of owners.

The Board of Directors and Management of a Condominium

As a unit owner and member of the condominium you will have the responsibility of electing an executive or *board of directors* to direct the affairs of the condominium. The directors are elected primarily, but not exclusively, from among the members of the condominium and for the period of time outlined in the project documents. The board of directors will administer the *common funds* of the condominium and be responsible for project administration, regulation and maintenance.

The board of directors may employ any people and agencies it needs in connection with the control, management and administration of the common property and the exercise and performance of the powers and duties of the condominium association of owners.

Sometimes for the first year of operation or longer, the developer of the condominium project may enter into a management contract with the condominium corporation to provide the necessary management services. His experience with building management can be a valuable asset in the first years of a condominium's operation.

The condominium corporation may decide to hire the services of a professional management firm or it may decide to manage the project by itself and possibly invite the developer to act only in an advisory capacity on the board of directors. In a large condominium, because of the sophistication and complexity of the tasks involved, some form of professional management is almost essential.

The condominium management performs the services that ensure the orderly and efficient functioning of a condominium. It prepares the annual budget for the board of directors which, when adopted, becomes the program for the maintenance and upkeep of the project and the basis for the monthly common expenses. It also carries out the routine duties of invoicing and collecting common expenses, ordering repairs, making improvements and employing and training staff.

What Are the Costs Involved in Owning a Condominium Unit?

After the initial down payment has been made and the sale transaction has been closed, you will have two payments to make each month: mortgage payments (in Quebec, *hypothecary* payments) and common expenses.

Of course, if you pay cash for your unit, you will only have taxes and common expenses to pay.

Mortgage Payments

As a condominium owner, an individual mortgage will be arranged on your unit, and you alone, as purchaser, make your payments directly to the mortgage lender. The monthly payments will usually include charges for the principal, interest and taxes.

Because you have your own mortgage with the lender you are in a position to negotiate new terms for the repayment or refinancing of your unit.

Under a National Housing Act loan, your monthly payments to the lender will include an amount equal to one-twelfth of the estimated annual taxes on both your unit and the share of the common elements apportioned to your unit. The tax bill is then paid by the lender and your account debited.

Assessment for Common Expenses

Common expenses will cover the operating costs of the common elements and are subject to readjustment if expenses increase or decrease.

Your unit will be charged a certain percentage of the project's total operating costs. This is established in the condominium declaration and may be determined by the original purchase price for each unit in relation to the value of the total project. You and your solicitor or notary should ensure that all items of common expense to which each unit owner is to contribute are clearly spelled out in the project documents.

If the project is in operation, the directors or managers can quote you an exact figure for the common expenses. As a rule of thumb, one might estimate monthly common expenses to be between .125% and .25% of the purchase price of your unit. For example, if your unit cost $100,000 to purchase you might expect your common expenses to be in the order of $125.00 to $250.00 per month.

The payments for the common expenses are usually made to the condominium and should cover the following items:

Insurance: Find out what is covered by the policies of the condominium and arrange your own accordingly. The condominium normally carries public liability insurance, and fire insurance for the common elements and in most cases for all the units as they exist at the date of the first sales. The owner is usually responsible for insuring personal belongings and any improvements he makes to his unit after the registration of the condominium.

Maintenance and Repair of Common Elements: This covers costs for building repairs, maintenance and landscaping, recreational facilities and services equipment. Each owner is responsible for the cost of normal maintenance and repairs inside his unit.

Operating and Service Costs: The provision of heat, water, hydro and snow removal are some of the service costs which may be included in the common charges.

A Reserve Contingency Fund: Money out of this common fund will provide for the replacement or major repair of common elements that become obsolete or wear out.

Management Costs: These are payments made to professional management firms or private individuals hired to administer all or part of the day-to-day functions of the condominium.

When Will You Legally Own Your Unit?

To gain title to your unit, the condominium must be legally registered at the land titles or registry office with copies of the description of each unit, the description of the entire condominium and the legal documents relating to the management of the condominium and the rights and responsibilities of the owners.

If you are thinking of buying a condominium unit which has not yet been registered, find out when the condominium is scheduled to come into being and what conditions remain to be met before the *registration* takes place. You can get this information from the developer or lender. After this, talk the whole thing over with your lender or lawyer before signing an *offer to purchase.*

If you move into your unit before the condominium is registered, you may have to pay a sum in the form of rent to the developer. The rent may, or may not, be used to partially reduce the price of your unit. It is only when the project has been legally registered, and you receive title to your unit, that your payments are made to your mortgage lender and the condominium association.

What to Look for in the Design of a Condominium

As with the purchase of any home, there are several factors about design that you should consider.

The Location of the project should be reviewed in relation to distances to work, shopping, schools and transportation. Have a look at the present and projected development of the area surrounding the condominium.

Common Elements and Facilities, such as open space, recreational areas and equipment and the quality and durability of the landscaping are important both from the aspect of their suitability to your needs and their long-term maintenance costs.

Unit Design should be suitable for your present and future needs. The project documents, along with the condominium plan, will outline the boundaries of your unit and the areas to which you have exclusive use. Like the single family dwelling, you have the right to alter and maintain the parts of the unit you own outright but you would have to receive permission from the board of directors to alter any parts of the dwelling that are classified as common elements.

Privacy Arrangements are important, such as the distances between units, the fencing, planting and separation of your unit from walkways, roads and common areas. Adequate sound insulation of the surfaces between adjoining units is an important factor in multiple housing. Ask the developer about the provisions he has made to ensure proper sound insulation.

Parking Facilities for both yourself and visitors should be looked at closely. Will you have long uncovered distances to carry articles from your car to your home? Is there parking space available for a second car or for a boat or trailer?

Storage Spaces for articles such as bicycles, sleighs, unused furniture, etc., within and outside your unit are as important to consider as the garbage storage and collection procedures from your unit and the project.

Quality of Materials should be looked at carefully since you will be paying for the upkeep of your own unit and will have to share in the upkeep of the common elements through your common expenses.

Some Additional Suggestions

Most people realize that buying a new home is going to be one of the largest financial decisions they will ever make. Before signing any papers, before paying any money, make certain you have all the available documents applying to your particular condominium.

Discuss the condominium documents with your solicitor or notary. Let him consider them thoroughly. At the same time, see your mortgage lender and house insurance agent to discuss your other legal and financial obligations.

Once these preliminary checks have been made, you are ready to sign and "offer to purchase." At this point, with the help of your solicitor or notary, you will have determined the date of occupancy or of delays in occupancy and alternative arrangements in the event of delays in registration of the condominium.

Further information and advice may be obtained from other condominium owners, the developer, an approved lending agency or bank that has handled condominium projects, or the local office of Canada Mortgage and Housing Corporation.

61

CAVEAT FOR CONDO BUYERS

What's the best thing to do for yourself when considering a condominium unit as your next home?

Check the performance of the management firm. Nothing will displease a condominium owner more than paying for lousy service, or no service at all.

I personally know of an owner who has suffered from gas fumes leaking into the unit from an underground garage. This problem has been there for over a year, and it still exists. When the owner called the building management firm about it, the response was "that's your problem."

So the owner called the fire department. Some high-ranking men looked the situation over, but could offer no solution. I suggested that the owner should go right to the architect who designed the building and take it from there.

This horror story is not an isolated one.

A good way to ensure you won't get pushed around is to knock on several doors in the building and ask the owners if they are happy with the firm employed to manage the building.

Another thing I suggest is a walk through the building with a pair of critical eyes. See if the place has a nice fresh appearance about it, and that the condition and maintenance of the carpets, walls, elevators, doors, lights and locks is all okay.

Find out how many units in the building are for sale. If there seem to be too many, it could be a case of trying to abandon a sinking ship. And nothing can sink a good condominium building faster than lousy management.

And here's something I would personally urge you to do if it is a large building: visit the local fire hall and find out how many false alarms rang from the building during the past six months. Vandals like pulling such capers.

Each unit will have a fire alarm bell inside the unit, and to listen to that bell clang in your ears for one solid hour will drive you up the wall. If it happens more than once an evening, you could be a candidate for a nut house.

Take a good, hard look at the financing that is available. If the mortgage has about one year to run to maturity, can it be renewed? Remember, lenders are more restrictive with money in condominiums than houses. As a matter of fact, some lenders won't touch them.

If you are used to apartment living you will take to a condominium like a duck to water. But remember that when things go wrong inside the walls of the unit, the owner is the one who gets it fixed. No calling the superintendent.

When something goes wrong with such things as elevators, service, equipment, recreation facilities, lobbies, parking areas, etc., it will be looked after and paid for by the money you pay each month into the common expense fund. Be sure to check that no special assessment has been levied to offset some expensive unexpected repair.

Well, I've been negative enough, so what's good about condominium ownership?

- The security in knowing you have a permanent place to live.
- A better opportunity for those of modest means to buy rather than rent, in areas where costs keep rising (which is just about everywhere).
- The possibility of financial appreciation in the event of resale.
- The opportunity to have a say in the management of the affairs of the building by being a member of the board of directors.

Just remember to do your homework before buying one.

62

BUYING AND LEASING CROWN LAND

Once upon a time when money was a scarce commodity, one could buy a quarter-section of land out west for ten dollars from the government. That's 160 acres, or about 65 hectares.

Land is still being purchased and leased from provincial governments, but not as freely as it once was. Even the governments are beginning to realize that land is not manufactured, and they are protecting what they have left. Here is a brief synopsis of what one may expect in our provinces, and the addresses of government offices to which one may write for further information.

BRITISH COLUMBIA: Prior to 1970, it was possible to obtain land by pre-emption (homesteading). That's gone, and there are now no free lands in B.C.

Only Canadian citizens are allowed the right to purchase and obtain a Crown grant leading to title. Waterfront lands can be obtained only on a leasehold basis. A 31-page booklet concerning the disposition of Crown lands can be obtained by writing to the Director of Land Management, Parliament Buildings, Victoria, B.C. V8V 1X5

ALBERTA: To acquire a homestead sale, one must be a resident of Alberta for twelve months within the three years immediately prior to the date of making application.

Land is available, and Alberta will provide you with an interpretation of the *Public Lands Act* and a large, interesting map of Alberta clearly showing what is and what is not available. Write to: Public Lands Division , Alberta Energy and Natural Resources, 9915 - 108th Street, Edmonton, Alta. T5K 2C9.

SASKATCHEWAN: Applicant must be a Canadian citizen or landed immigrant. The *Saskatchewan Farm Ownership Act* limits nonresidents to having an interest in no more than 160 acres of agricultural land.

Sale policy provides only for the sale of cultivation leases to the lessee who has leased for a minimum of five years. Grazing leases are not eligible for sale. Write to: Lands Branch Dept. of Agriculture, Administration Building, Regina, Sask. S4S 0B1.

MANITOBA: Presently one may purchase Crown lands for primary residential use or for intensive commercial development, subject to Cabinet endorsement.

Crown lands are leased for a wide variety of purposes, and the Minister's authority to lease is restricted to 21-year terms. All requests are circulated to other governmental departments and agencies for clearance prior to commitment. Write to: Chief, Crown Lands, Manitoba Natural Resources, Lands Branch, Box 20,000, 123 Main Street W., Neepawa, Man. R0J 1H0.

ONTARIO: There are 343,092 square miles of land in Ontario, which is 88.5 million hectares, or about 220 million acres.

The province owns 87% of it, which is called Crown land. The federal government has 4% — also Crown land. The remaining 9% is in private hands.

This Crown land business goes back hundreds of years when monarchs owned all the land. They progressively gave some of it to loyal followers, principally of the warring kind, but most of our land is still held by the Crown.

When the federal government handed over control of the land to the provinces, what it kept for itself was land around harbors, for military installations, some parkland and Indian lands.

Land controlled by municipalities is not Crown land. It is owned by the cities, towns and villages — and metropolitan corporations.

This municipal land doesn't amount to much in area because it consists mainly of streets and parks. All the rest of the land in a municipal area is in private, or corporate, hands under all those buildings.

So, seeing as how Ontario owns all that land and we are the taxpayers who keep it in business, what can we do to get some of it for our own personal use?

Just a little bit, like maybe an acre or two on a nice clean lake. For a cottage.

The provincial government has pre-identified a number of cottage lots for release in northern Ontario. These lots are described and their approximate market values are published regularly. Contact the Forestry Department of the Ontario Ministry of Natural Resources for a complete list.

However, there is plenty of Crown land available to the private sector for other uses. You want a good location for a service station, motel, tourist resort, marina or perhaps a trailer camp? Land is available in most northern districts in 2.5- to 15-acre lots.

If you have bigger ideas and need enough land for a golf course, or an airstrip, you can also be accommodated.

Waterfront sites and highway locations are usually preselected by the government, but a site chosen by an applicant may be given favorable consideration. Of course, all sites and improvements will be subject to the approval of local health authorities and the municipality.

There is also plenty of agricultural and grazing land available, for sale or lease, but city slickers are discouraged from getting any. Naturally, it is expected the applicant will be an experienced farmer.

The price for agricultural land is based on its appraised market value. Ontario has no homesteading regulations, so Crown land is not available in free grants, or at reduced prices. Write to: Director, Lands Administration Branch, Ministry of Natural Resources, Queen's Park, Toronto, Ont.

QUEBEC: Leases: Long term, 10 years or more, used when the plot of land is surveyed and classified as a permanent resort development. Short term, more than 12 months and less than eight years, used when the plot of land is not surveyed.

Priority for renting granted to Quebec residents when a site is chosen, or when there is more than one applicant for the same land, and this, for a period of six months after date of receipt of the request.

Write to: Ministère des Terres et Forêts, Gouvernement du Québec, Québec, P.Q.

NEW BRUNSWICK: It is not the policy of the government to dispose of Crown lands, except in very exceptional cases. Homesteading is no longer provided for. Campsite leases are available, but do not convey exclusive hunting or fishing privileges. Write to: Lands Branch, Dept. of Natural Resources, Centennial Bldg. P.O. Box 6000, Fredericton, N.B. E3B 5H1.

NOVA SCOTIA: Crown land no longer available and, not only that, all non-resident land owners must file a disclosure statement on their holdings in Nova Scotia. Forms for disclosure can be obtained from: Registrar of Land Holdings, Dept. of Natural Resources, Halifax, N.S. B3J 2T9.

PRINCE EDWARD ISLAND: Provincial land resources are extremely limited, and there are non-residency restrictions. Brochures concerning the purchase and lease of agricultural lands available can be obtained. Write to: Director, Island Information Service, P.O. Box 2000, Charlottetown, P.E.I. C1A 7N8.

NEWFOUNDLAND: Land is available for agriculture, residence, commercial establishments, e.g. accommodation of tourists etc., summer cottage, fishing and hunting cabins and use by religious organizations.

Leases for up to 50 years, and most reasonable rent. Title can be obtained on some types of property. Write to: Director, Crown Lands Administration, Dept. of Forestry and Agriculture, P.O. Box 8700, St. John's, Nfld. A1B 4S6.

YUKON TERRITORY: A moratorium has temporarily suspended the alienation of Crown lands for agricultural or grazing purposes. Cottage lots are available in planned recreational subdivisions only. Policies change from time to time. Write to: Supervisor of Lands, Dept. of Indian and Northern Affairs, 200 Range Road, Whitehorse, Y.T. Y1A 3V1.

NORTHWEST TERRITORIES: In 1975 the disposition of lands for agricultural purposes was suspended, pending a new policy which is currently being formulated. Homesteading is not allowed.

Small parcels of land for recreational nonresidential purposes only are available, mostly in cottage lot subdivisions near major settlements. Write to: Regional Manager, Land Resources, Dept. of Indian and Northern Affairs, P.O. Box 1500, Yellowknife, N.W.T. X1A 2R3.

63

GOVERNMENT TAX SALES

For about the first two years of municipal tax arrears, the property owner will receive sharper and sharper reminders to get the bills paid. If all the reminders are ignored, the municipality naturally gets cheesed off with the delinquent taxpayer and gets tough.

Getting tough means eventual sale of the property to satisfy the municipal tax debt, but the municipality really bends over backwards and gives the property owner every reasonable opportunity to retain the property.

There is not enough room in this book to cover every provincial statute concerning penalties for property owners who have not paid their taxes, so I'll fully relate what can happen in just one province: Ontario.

A most important change in the law regarding municipal tax sales concerns the transfer of title. Previously, a successful bidder at a tax auction was required to wait one year before he knew if he really did get what he bargained for.

The one-year grace was to allow the delinquent tax-paying property owners to pay the arrears and redeem the property. If he did this, the successful bidder got his money back and that ended the matter.

Not any more!

Before I explain the new rules, some definitions are in order:

Real Property Taxes include the amount of taxes levied on property under the *Municipal Act, Education Act* and *Unconditional Grants Act* — also, any amounts owing under the *Drainage Act,* the *Shoreline Property Assistance Act*, and the *Local Improvement Act.* Any amounts such as hydro arrears or weed-cutting charges are not included.

Tax Arrears: Read this one carefully. They are real property taxes placed on or added to the collector's roll that remain unpaid on the first day of January in the year following that in which they were placed on, or added to the roll. For example, taxes levied on January 1, 1985, became arrears if any portion was outstanding on January 1, 1986.

Improved Land is land which is liable to be separately assessed, and which has a building on it. Land which is in actual agricultural use is also considered improved, whether or not it has any buildings on it.

Vacant Land is a parcel of land with no buildings on it which is separately assessed but which does not include any improved land. There is a reason for the two land definitions, as you shall see.

Cancellation Price: This can blow your tax bills to the moon, and must be paid by the taxpayer or successful bidder before clean title can be produced again.

It is an amount equal to all the tax arrears owing, plus all current real property taxes owing, penalties and interest, and all reasonable costs incurred by the municipality after the treasurer becomes entitled to register a tax arrears certificate.

It also includes costs such as those incurred in any initial title search undertaken in contemplation of proceeding under the *Municipal Tax Sales Act.* Plus, of course, legal fees and disbursements, the cost of the survey, the costs of preparing and registering an extension agreement and advertising expenses.

If all property owners were fully aware of the foregoing financial implications, there most certainly would be greater efforts made by many to ensure their taxes are paid up to date.

Now we shall examine the beginning of bad news for taxpayers.

Where any part of municipal taxes are outstanding on January 1, after a two-year period for vacant land and three years for improved land, the municipal treasurer may prepare a tax arrears certificate and register it against title to the land in the appropriate land registry office.

The certificate must contain an accurate description of the land suitable for registry office purposes.

Within 60 days of registering the tax arrears certificate, the treasurer must send a notice to the property owner (and all interested parties) advising of the registration *and potential sale of the property.*

When a tax delinquent has received notice of the tax arrears certificate registration, a period of *one year* is allowed, during which time tax (and costs) must be paid, or the process of selling the property moves into high gear.

However, it may be possible to enter into an agreement with the municipality extending the time in which payment must be made. But if one wishes to try this route, no time should be wasted because the agreement must be authorized by a by-law passed prior to the end of the one-year period.

The property owner is certainly kept informed and given every opportunity to rectify his tax problem. If the arrears and costs remain unpaid 280 days after the day of registration on the tax arrears certificate, the municipal treasurer will fire off a final notice.

This final notice again warns of a pending sale if the matter isn't settled before the expiration of the one-year redemption period. If the property owner has done nothing by this time, the treasurer *must advertise that the property will be sold.*

The advertisement will be placed once in the government's *Ontario Gazette*, and once a week for four weeks in a local newspaper. The sale will be by public auction or public tender, and the *minimum* acceptable offer on the property will be the cancellation price, which is the total of all outstanding taxes and various costs.

The municipality can also bid or tender on such property sales, but only if it has a municipal purpose for the property.

If there is a successful purchaser at a sale, the municipal treasurer must prepare and register a tax deed in the name of the purchaser or in another name directed by the purchaser. The deed is final and binding when registered.

As I have previously pointed out, there is no one-year period after a sale for the tax delinquent to pay up, as was formerly allowed.

If there is no successful purchaser who offers to pay as a minimum all tax arrears and costs, the municipality will receive title to the property.

It is interesting to note that when a municipality sells a property for tax purposes, it is not required to ensure that any persons living in a residence on the property at the time of sale are removed before the purchaser takes possession of his newly acquired property.

The money received from a sale is first applied to the municipal taxes and costs, then to any person other than the owner having an interest in the property according to the priority at law, and finally to the former owner.

64

OPTIONING PROPERTY

An option in real estate is an agreement whereby one has the right to purchase another's property at an agreed price, at some time in the future, with a time limit.

The purchaser (optionee) is not bound to purchase the property, but the vendor (optionor) is bound to sell if the purchaser "exercises" the option agreement into a binding agreement of purchase and sale.

It is customary for a purchaser to give some cash to the vendor when receiving the option, which is retained by the vendor regardless of whether the purchaser ends up buying the property or not. If the deal closes, this cash is often credited to the purchase price on closing, although not always.

A common example of the foregoing is for A to give B the right to purchase A's property for $100,000 within one year.

B gives A $1,000 cash, which A keeps.

B may exercise the option at any time within one year. If B fails to do this, A keeps the thousand dollars and the agreement is automatically cancelled, unless, of course, there are renewable clauses in the option.

At this point, I wish to point out a red-flagged warning sign to a vendor. In the option to purchase within one year, it will say that when notice is given to exercise the option, the deal will close within, say, 60 days from that date.

This is where many vendors become upset. The vendor may assume that he will have one year from signing the option to move, not realizing that he will have just 60 days to move from that date of exercising the option. If the purchaser wished to move quickly on the purchase, he could exercise his rights within 24 hours, and the deal would close 60 days from then. It is important to understand this clearly.

It is a common practice to use the services of real estate agents in obtaining options. On some agents' option forms there will be a commission agreement on the bottom whereby the vendor agrees to pay the agent for procuring so-and-so to become the optionee, and if the property is purchased the vendor pays the agent. I don't agree with this, because in 99% of such agreements, the agent is really working for the purchaser who pays the agent.

Some agents may take the attitude that it is six of one or half dozen of the other, so what does it matter who pays? Well, it can matter quite a lot, and for this reason: I have found through experience that when approaching a vendor for an option, the reception is more cordial if the vendor fully understands that he won't have to pay a commission to the agent. All the money in the deal is his, so to speak, with no deductions.

So, if you are going to use an agent to help obtain your options, make your own agreement with the agent to pay him for his services. The arithmetic in the whole thing may not make any difference in the end, but it will smooth the way for negotiations if the agent asks the vendor for nothing.

If you are interested in optioning just one property, you will get your answer soon enough, but if the interest is in obtaining options on a number of properties, then there are certain guidelines I would suggest.

The first is to remember that very few agents will be interested in spending a lot of time obtaining options for you without some "front money" — after all, you may end up dropping everything, and the agent knows this. He wants to be paid for work done.

So have a contract drawn up between you, the purchaser, and the agent. But before the contract, consider how you are going to proceed. A good example follows:

Assume there are 10 properties you wish to acquire. Before doing anything about them, check the ownership of each through your municipal offices. If it is found that more than one property is owned by the same party, it could be that someone else has his eye on eventual ownership of the 10, or at least eventually getting a bigger price than the others from some eventual buyer. Contact this multiple owner first and get his reaction to your plans — it could save you a lot of time.

If the 10 properties have 10 different owners, all living in the houses, you cannot assume that there will be clear sailing, because *somebody* is going to give you a hard time. So a testing of the market must be made. This is done with short term options with renewable clauses.

Instead of asking for one-year options, with a payment of about $1,000 to each vendor, ask for a 60-day option with a payment of about $200 to each vendor for the 60 days. In each option have renewable clauses, giving the purchaser the right to renew for six months at the end of the 60 days for $500 to each vendor, and a one year renewal at the end of the six months for $1,000. Here are the reasons for this:

You will save money. If you were successful in obtaining options for seven of the ten properties and found that the remaining three were holdouts for sums that would create financial problems for your plans, you could forget the whole thing and drop it. At a cost of $1,400. Going for yearly options for $1,000 each would cost you $7,000 if you drop your plans.

The basic idea of the 60-day option is to find out how many properties you can secure. If things look promising at the end of 60 days with only a couple to go, you could renew for $500 each for six months. This will be the period in which you must obtain the remainder. Of course, maybe you'll be lucky and get the 10 during 60 days, which would relieve you of any nervous strain in this part of the operation.

If this is the route to go, then the agreement with the agent could be to pay the agent about $200 each time he brings you an acceptable option. On closing, the agreement would stipulate a further payment from you to the agent, the figure being one you negotiate.

On one optioning job I did for a developer, he showed me the houses he wanted, and because of his "packaging" it for me, it was agreed he would pay me $1,500 on closing each one, less my front money. This was less than the usual 5% or so, but was certainly fair because the developer set it up.

If, on the other hand, I did all the ground work for a project and took it to a developer, I would not only look for higher fees, but a bonus on completion of the project assembly.

Time is a big factor in optioning. It must be done as quickly as possible to forestall the probability of holdouts. People have a habit of varnishing the truth, and if a property were optioned at a price of $60,000, word of mouth might balloon this to $85,000 by the time it reached the ears of some listener who just happened to own one of the houses needed for the project. An agent must therefore be found who will work full time on your behalf.

As an example of what the application of option money can be, I approached an owner to secure a one-year option at not more than $100,000. The owner sent me back to my client, the buyer, with a written agreement at $100,000 but stipulated he wanted an immediate $5,000, and furthermore, the $5,000 was *not* to be credited to the purchaser if he closed. It would therefore cost the purchaser $105,000.

The purchaser agreed because he *knew* he wanted the property, would close the deal in one year, and a $5,000 payment meant that he could "carry" the financing for a year for about 5%, which was better than buying now and carrying the financing at about 10%. Plus the fact that the buyer wouldn't have the responsibility of maintaining the property for a year.

Every option goes on its own merits and the best deal each party can get for himself. I remember obtaining yearly options for as low as $2.00 for the year, and I also remember that the buyer went through with the purchases, and the vendors were all satisfied with the price.

Big dollars have been made with options which involve small amounts of money on the part of the buyer — the rights to the options were sold to others for a profit. But most options are obtained by buyers who have some specific plans for redeveloping the area, or converting the property to other uses. The time period in the option gives the buyer time to put everything together in his planning and financing.

If you want a property, but need time to swing it, an option just might do it for you.

65

WHO NEEDS A LAWYER?

Who needs a lawyer in a real estate deal?

Well, despite the fact that one legal lecturer facetiously observed that "we all know of at least one real estate agent whose parents were married," it's unwise to do without a lawyer in my opinion.

And the time to see a lawyer is not after you have accepted an offer — see the lawyer before the acceptance is made.. If it's not possible to see the lawyer personally, at least read the offer to him or her over the telephone.

Consulting a lawyer before you sign is legal advice at its most useful, whether you're buying, selling, leasing or mortgaging. Here are some of the things a trained legal mind will think about — on your behalf — if you seek advice before signing an offer to purchase:

a) Is the description of the property clearly stated?
b) Is there a private drive or a mutual drive?
c) What are your rights and responsibilities over a mutual driveway?
d) Are there any easements to which your property will be subject?
e) Where do you stand financially when the mortgagees have to be paid off?
f) Are there any hidden charges?
g) Does the purchase involve the sale of your present property?
h) If it is a summer residence:
    i) Is it leasehold, or freehold?
    ii) Is there a right of way to a beach?
    iii) Is there an assured right of way to the cottage from the public highway?

The time to be thoroughly advised is before you sign the contract. Your lawyer is the best one to advise you. He or she will explain, and advise about the offer to purchase as part of the service of acting for you.

After your offer has been accepted by the vendor, your lawyer has a number of responsibilities:

a) To discuss with you legal aspects as to how you will have the property registered:
    i) In your name.
    ii) In your spouse's name.
    iii) To the two of you jointly, or as tenants in common. Here there can be complications, which your lawyer will explain
b) To search title. Are there any legal interests outstanding which will interfere with your full legal enjoyment of the property, or hold up a sale when the time comes? Title defects have a way of lying dormant for years only to come to light when selling the property.
c) To approve of the deed, affidavits, statutory declarations, and to prepare legal documents.
d) To attend to proper registrations of the various legal documents when the purchase is closed.
e) To give an opinion as to your title and a complete report to you of the transaction.

A lawyer's training qualifies him to serve you by giving your legal affairs and problems patient study. He will advise on the laws of real estate and mortgages, explain fine print, draft legal documents and, above all, think and act for you in working out the terms and the completion of an important legal contract.

Purchasing real property requires the professional judgment of a well-trained lawyer to advise and assist — from the beginning to the final registration. That help is no less important in selling or leasing.

Do yourself a favor — let your lawyer in on your plans from the beginning, before you sign.

How to Find a Lawyer

Finding a lawyer to handle a mortgage or real estate deal in Quebec and B.C. is a simple matter; just head for the nearest notary.

In Quebec, there are three categories of legal practitioners; the barrister, the solicitor and the notary.

Generally speaking, the barrister and solicitor both can give legal advice, prepare and draw up notices, motions, etc. for use in cases before the courts, but when the time comes to go to court, it is only the barrister who appears.

Don't call a barrister or solicitor to handle a real estate deal in Quebec. It is the Quebec Notary who is a very special person to anyone involved in real estate.

The notary is a legal practitioner whose chief duty is to draw up and execute deeds and contracts. No one in the province of Quebec, other than a practicing notary may, on behalf of another person, draw up deeds under private signature effecting real estate and requiring registration.

Well, you say, that's fine for Quebec and B.C., but what about the rest of Canada?

The legal profession has maintained a discreet silence in just what areas of law its people practice. It has not considered it proper for lawyers to advertise their special qualifications in law.

However, this is gradually changing. It has changed in parts of the U.S. with some results that are a bit shocking to the profession. Razzle dazzle and hoopla advertisements from lawyers, and on TV? Yep.

All this Yankee hoopla is not lost on the Canadian law societies, and probably is doing the societies a favor by providing them with no nos and restrictions on how far a lawyer can go when we eventually will see the rules changed here.

Right now we can go on personal experience, or personal recommendations. Real estate brokers are not supposed to recommend specific lawyers, but I certainly see nothing wrong in a broker's having a list of half a dozen lawyers in his area available for buyers and sellers; lawyers who the broker *knows* are specialists in real estate conveyancing. Just give a copy of the list to the consumer and say take your pick.

Of course, one can always walk into a large office building, check the directory, visit several legal offices and ask if they have real estate specialists available.

But, however one selects the lawyer, it is quite possible to save money by getting a quotation on costs for handling the real estate transaction. Don't be afraid to ask — it is your money, so save a bit if you can.

Shop around.

66

A CASE OF NEGLIGENCE

Remember what we were told when we were kids? "Ignorance of the law is no excuse."

Well, it seems that we may have been misinformed. A Mr. Justice Gerald Jewers of the Manitoba Court of Queen's Bench has said: "The law as I understand it is that a solicitor is not liable to his client for a mere error of judgment or even ignorance of some aspect of the law."

He went on to say, "But he is liable if his error of ignorance was such that an ordinarily competent solicitor would not have made or shown it."

The remarks are contained in a recent judgment where a lawyer was found negligent in a real estate deal.

I don't know exactly how one would define "an ordinarily competent solicitor," but I presume that it would refer to any average lawyer working in real estate.

If one can be excused for being ignorant of some aspect of the law after having years of legal training and being admitted to a provincial bar, where does that leave the layman?

Sounds a bit lopsided to me.

In this case, a builder sold some vacant property and contracted with the buyers to build a house on the land.

Unfortunately, the house was built on the wrong lot.

The lawyer acting for the buyers also acted for a mortgage lender who provided the money that made the project go.

Then the unforeseen happened.

The owners of the new house fell upon hard times and couldn't keep up with the mortgage payments. The lender instructed the lawyer to proceed with legal action to recover its loan.

To get things under way, the lawyer requisitioned a surveyor's certificate and, probably much to his horror, discovered that the house was not on the mortgaged land.

Fortunately, land under the house was owned by the father of the builder who was very cooperative in helping to straighten out the mess.

But it took time and money.

When everything was legally resolved about the land, the mortgage lender foreclosed and obtained title to the property.

The lender then sold the property, but the selling price fell short of the mortgage debt.

The lawyer then found himself in court, charged with negligence in the matter.

The lender said the lawyer did not take proper and reasonable steps to ascertain that the mortgage security was actually registered against the right parcel of land.

The enquiry then was: What steps would an ordinarily competent lawyer, in the position of the defendant, have taken to ensure that the house in question was actually situated on the land proposed to be mortgaged?

The lawyer did obtain from the builder a declaration that the house was being erected on the mortgaged land.

Not good enough, said the lender, who observed that the lawyer ought to have gone further and should have followed the "usual practice of a competent solicitor namely, to counsel his client to get a surveyor's certificate which would have put the location of the house virtually beyond doubt."

He did do this, but only when it was too late.

He paid for his mistake.

So listen carefully: Before you hand your money over to a lawyer, or anyone else for a mortgage investment, demand a survey of the property. Don't take no for an answer. And ensure that your lawyer's advice is comprehensive — ask questions and make sure the answers are clear.

67

DON'T BE AFRAID TO MAKE AN OFFER

In 1867 the United States Government offered Russia $7,200,000 worth of gold for Alaska, and it was accepted.

Later, it was discovered that Alaska could have been purchased for five million dollars. In retrospect, paying 44% more than an acceptable price for Alaska was still a bargain, but at the time it must surely have made the U.S. negotiators think that they should have been a little less hasty with the offer.

Unless the heart rules the head, there is a certain amount of thought and discipline required before signing.

There is basically one of four price tags on every parcel of privately owned land in Canada. The highest is on the land that is not for sale.

Walk in cold on a man with his dream house, where he is comfortable, compatible with his neighbors, has a nice garden, is settled in the community and is supremely happy with his home and lifestyle. If that man's home has a current market value of $75,000, how much would it take to get him out of there? Certainly a lot more than one would care to pay, and in some cases money would *never* move him.

The next price tag down the scale is that of an owner who is "thinking of selling" but hasn't reached the point of making a firm decision about it.

An offer *could* be made to this owner. His $75,000 home *might* be purchased for slightly more than its market value, but if one fails with such an offer, the result will be a "free appraisal" of the man's realty and inflation of his property ego.

Now we are approaching a more reasonable situation. The house that is for sale; on the market. (The overpriced listings can be flushed out with a bit of viewing, so we'll ignore them.)

How much does one offer for property on the market?

Do a little probing. Reasons for selling can have a great bearing on the price. Has the vendor bought another house? Is there a breakup in the family? Is the vendor leaving town?

Which leads us to the lowest price tag: distress selling. An example would be a vendor's desire to beat a final order of foreclosure on his property which he has not redeemed. At least something can usually be salvaged from his predicament by selling, if he can find a buyer in a hurry who will close quickly.

Once you know the circumstances surrounding the sale, you are ready to make an offer. How much?

This calls for some calculations on your part. If you bid too low, the vendor might react negatively or insist upon the full price, or perhaps reject the offer entirely which won't help with any attempted further offer.

A higher price might be grabbed immediately, and then you will be left wondering if you could have purchased the realty for a bit less. You will never be sure.

Armed with all the information you can get about the sale, and considering what you can afford, make an offer that is a little lower than what you sincerely believe to be fair under the circumstances.

It may not be accepted, but if it is not an insulting offer, you will undoubtedly find it counter-signed by the vendor with another price which you can accept, or negotiate further.

And if by some chance your offer *is* accepted, you can smile and consider yourself a shrewd buyer.

Of course, there are cases where you will rightfully offer a full price (or even more) for a property you absolutely *must* have, but remember that an offer is a most important step that requires very careful consideration and one that can hurt or please your bank account.

Think it out well in advance, make a realistic offer, and you probably will be pleased with the result.

68

PUT EVERYTHING IN THE OFFER

A buyer should be especially careful when instructing an agent to prepare an offer to buy a parcel of real estate, regardless of what it is.

A big safeguard one can take is to instruct the agent to include any special features important to the buyer.

I recommend this even if the features of the property are noted on the real estate listing and even if the agent's responses to one's questions are reassuring.

Here are two very good examples of why I say this:

In the first case, a real estate agent listed a parcel of land, was told by the seller that the property was an "apartment site," and the listing showed the property to be "apartment zoned."

The property was actually zoned for single family dwellings, though it was adjacent to land zoned for apartments.

The listing agent did not check the zoning with the municipal authorities and forwarded the listing through the MLS system to other agents — with the false zoning information included.

One of the sub-agents received a visit from a buyer who expressed a wish to purchase a lot which was apartment zoned, for building purposes.

The sub-agent recommended the listing, but before making an offer, the buyer asked the agent to check the zoning. This agent did, but not with city hall. He phoned the listing agent who said it was apartment zoned.

Thus assured, the buyer incurred expense by having the property surveyed, moving an existing house and clearing the lot.

Then the roof fell in. The true nature of the zoning was discovered and everybody ended up in court.

The judgment found the sellers liable to the plaintiff (buyer) for fraud and had this to say about the two real estate agents:

The listing agent was negligent in representing the property to be "apartment zoned," without ensuring it in fact, and he and his employer were liable to the plaintiffs.

The same considerations applied to the selling agent even though he was encouraged by the listing agent to believe the property to be zoned for apartment construction.

In another example, a couple bought a home which, according to the listing, said cable television was available.

After closing the deal, they were told by the cable company that it was not available in their area.

The buyers, after spending more than $900 to have a TV tower erected, sued the agents involved, but lost.

The judge said he accepted the agent's statement that the buyer made no mention of cable television as a priority and observed that the buyer could have protected himself by asking the agent to deliberately check the availability of the service, or have included it in the agreement of purchase and sale.

He also said there was no law cited to suggest there is any duty on a listing or selling agent to check the items listed and there was no guarantee by any of the defendants as to the accuracy of the listing.

I like that part about including it in the agreement. If the foregoing buyers had done this, a lot of time, money and grief could have been saved.

If you spot something on the listing you like, especially if it is partly instrumental in causing you to make an offer, put it in writing.

Make it a part of your agreement of purchase and sale.

You can't believe everything you hear, or see on a listing!

69

MOM AND POP STORES

Mom-and-pop variety stores and smoke shops are popular. They are all over the place, with buyers waiting in line to snap them up if the price is right.

What are they worth? How does one know that the real estate agent listed at a fair price? Do you have to buy all the old, stale stock that has been gathering dust on the shelves? How do you know you will enjoy operating such a business?

The first thing to look at is the term of the existing lease. If the shop owners' lease has just two or three years left, it would be a lousy investment if the lease couldn't be renewed.

The way to overcome this is to make your offer subject to obtaining a renewable leasing agreement from the lessor (building owner). Not a short agreement, but one that will have you as a tenant for at least 10 years from the day you take over.

Once the agent satisfies you something can be done about the lease, get down to business and start by asking for a statement of tangible assets and liabilities. Tangible assets are things you can see and touch such as stock, shelving, fixtures, freezers, etc. It all has dollar value but the question is, how much?

The most common way to decide this is not necessarily the best way. The seller will show you all his stock invoices and offer to sell the tangibles at what he considers to be a fair discount.

A better way is to have a firm of professional stock takers go right through the place and properly take stock, providing you with an estimate of value.

This will take about a day and will cost money, but it could save you much more than its cost. And you will know the price is right.

The owner will want some additional money for goodwill and the fact the business has been established in the neighborhood for a number of years. After all, the business is already there and all the buyer has to do is open the door and he's in business, so it certainly is worth *something*. Ask your accountant how this part of the purchase price can be recovered.

And just what is goodwill? A court has described it as the whole advantage, whatever it may be, of the reputation and connection of the firm which may have been built up by years of honest work or gained by lavish expenditures of money. If it's there, you'll pay for it.

If you invest your money somewhere else, what interest rate would you expect to receive? Use the same rate for your new business. It should provide a reasonable salary for you, the new working owner, plus the required return on your invested capital.

Have your accountant or lawyer go over as many annual financial statements as you can get from the one selling the business. If the present owner is reluctant to provide them, or can't, forget it and look somewhere else.

If you have never owned a variety store, remember it is no 9-to-5 operation with an hour off for lunch. You will be on your feet for long periods of time so you may as well have a medical check-up before you even consider it.

Before investing your hard-earned money in a venture that appeals to you, a good way to find out if you will be able to handle it is to actually work in a variety store for a month.

Such employment may be difficult to find, but if you lay your cards on the table to a shop owner and tell him just why you want to work for a month, even at the cost of donating your time, it could be done.

Spending a month gaining this experience would not only prepare you for your new venture, but also save you from making a big mistake if you discovered that it isn't exactly your cup of tea.

Location is naturally a big factor. Spending some time at different hours outside the shop watching the customer traffic can be time well spent. Be a people-watcher, and know what you're getting into.

70

BUYING AN OFFICE BUILDING

It can be said that the bigger and more impressive an office building, the easier it is to appraise.

Take a building in first-class condition in an excellent location, one that has been well designed and recently constructed, filled with tenants with first-class credit ratings who pay their rent on time, and where everything is running smoothly. Such a building will carry a high price tag. What is it worth? Well, just capitalize the net cash flow at the lowest market point (%) possible, and the result will be a fair estimate of its market value, viz:

$$\frac{\text{Cash flow: } \$100{,}000}{\text{Fair Point: } 8\%} \times 100 = \frac{\$1{,}250{,}000}{\text{Cash to Mortgage}}$$

The trick is to determine just what the fair market point, or capitalization rate, should be. It will be determined by a number of factors: the lowest point at which a buyer would be satisfied with the investment, the occupancy, length of leases and possibility of increases in revenue when the leases expire.

But what about the average, small, multi-tenanted office building with tenants in a variety of occupations, some with shaky credit ratings and some with no problems. What does one look for in this one?

A first consideration will be the physical condition of the building. Major repairs or renovations will not only cost a great deal of money, but will inconvenience the tenants and their clients or customers. So give the building itself a real going over. Get professional help and be prepared to pay for the advice, which will be in writing. If you are in a hurry to get your offer presented, you could make such an inspection a condition of your offer, with a time limit of course.

Check the municipality to ensure that the building satisfies current zoning regulations. It may be possible that the building is there under legal nonconforming use and, if such is the case, have your lawyer check to ensure that on transferring the deed, the new owner can carry on with the investment as it is, without having to make any alterations or provide more parking spaces.

Check with the fire department to ensure that the building is being operated in a manner satisfactory to this body.

Check with the hydro authority and get its blessing.

Check the rents being charged in comparable buildings in the area, if possible. If the rents in the building that interests you are above the area average, find out why. If there is no logical reason for it you could be in for a shock when leases expire, finding yourself with empty space on your hands.

Check the background of the tenants. If the building contains an over-supply of lessees who could be considered risky covenants, think twice about the whole thing. You don't want any problems worrying about the income.

Read Chapter 79 "Buying an Apartment Building," and follow its useful guidelines on financing, etc. Remember that the less attractive the investment, the more you are entitled to financially expect from it, and your capitalization rate will be higher.

When you are prepared to make an offer, ask the real estate agent, if there is one, to prepare the offer, and then *take it to your lawyer.* If no agent is involved, get your own lawyer to prepare the offer.

A well-located, well-tenanted office building is a nice investment, but take it easy and think it over very carefully before buying one.

70

BUYING AN INDUSTRIAL BUILDING

One of the plus features of owning a residential building is that people always have to live somewhere, regardless of the economic barometer. The multiple tenancy factor is another, which is a form of income insurance itself because the income is not dependent on one tenant.

It is for this reason that the importance of tenancy strength in an industrial building cannot be stressed too strongly. There are many fine industrial buildings, large and small, with just one tenant.

It is a common practice to lease an industrial building on what is called a "net net" basis; that is, the owner has a fixed net return on his investment, and the tenant pays for everything; the rent and all the charges connected to the building, including the municipal taxes. The reason it is called a "net net" basis is to emphasize the fact that it is on a "net" basis. How about that? I have even heard it referred to as a "net net net" lease. Maybe somebody was afraid nobody heard him when he said "net," so he said *net net net.* (Like banging the fist on the table three times instead of just once).

The reason for the net lease is very basic. If, for example, one purchased an industrial property for $100,000 cash to a $300,000 mortgage, a net, fixed, guaranteed return on the $100,000 would be required. Suppose the required return on this was 10%, or $10,000 a year.

Now, a tenant would have to be found who would be willing to pay a rental that would not only pay the $10,000 but also pay the mortgage. Here is what the annual rent would have to be:

Example:	Annual mortgage payment (including principal and interest)	$ 33,620.00
	10% interest on $100,000	$ 10,000.00
	Annual Rent	$ 43,620.00

In addition to this rent, the tenant also pays everything else, including the municipal taxes.

The owner has a fixed (net) return on his $100,000 investment, plus a bonus in repayment of the mortgage principal by the tenant. (The amortized mortgage payments include interest *and* principal). This bonus, on an 11%, 30-year mortgage, would amount to about $9,000 over the first five years.

The owner, of course, would pay tax not only on his net investment return of $10,000, but also on the mortgage principal payment received in rent.

It is possible sometimes to obtain a commitment in the lease requiring the rent to reflect an increase to match a rise in the cost of living, which would help to keep the dollars received up to date.

Well, if the foregoing looks like a cozy deal, it could turn into a nightmare if the tenancy turned sour, and leave the owner with a migraine.

Before accepting an offer to lease a single tenancy building, be very very careful about the covenant of the proposed tenant — its responsibility to care for the property and its ability to pay the rent, not only on time, but for the entire term of the lease. This is especially directed to the new owner of a small building, who may be so anxious to get it rented he will grab the first half-decent offer he sees.

Before buying an industrial building, ensure that you are fully conversant and aware of the going rent in comparable buildings. One might also stretch the closing as long as possible to give the new owner or agent as much time as possible to find a good tenant.

The best agent to approach when looking at industrial properties is one who *specializes* in them. Such an agency has plenty of know-how on the buildings and construction, and can answer a multitude of questions to your satisfaction.

A building with a net lease can be a very attractive investment, but it must be purchased with care, and leased with care. Your best guide is an industrial broker and your solicitor.

The lease, prepared by your solicitor, will run to about twenty pages in clear understandable language. Here are some basic covenants one can expect to see:

1. The tenant will, as additional rent, in each and every year during the term of the lease, pay and discharge when due all taxes, including local improvement rates, charges, duties, fees and assessments that may be levied against the property.
2. The tenant will pay all charges for public utilities, including water, gas, electric power or energy, steam or hot water, and for fittings, machinery, apparatus, meters or other things leased, and for all work or services performed in connection with such public utilities.
3. The tenant shall operate, maintain and keep the premises in good order and condition and promptly make all repairs and replacements. An exception to this would be reasonable wear and tear, and damage by fire, lightning, explosion, riot and civil insurrections, sprinkler leakage, smoke, airplane impact, hurricane and other insurable hazards.
4. The tenant will keep the premises well painted and clean, and at least once every four years paint the exterior of the building and the office area.
5. It will be lawful for the landlord to enter and inspect the premises at reasonable times, and if repairs are necessary that are the responsibility of the tenant, the tenant will have such repairs completed within 45 days of such notice.
6. If the tenant does not effect the foregoing repairs, the landlord may do it and charge the costs to the tenant as if the same were arrears in rent.
7. The tenant will comply with all federal and provincial statutes, laws, orders and regulations respecting the property, and comply with any lawful order of any governmental or municipal board or other competent body.
8. The tenant will not assign the lease or sublet the premises without the authority of the landlord, who is not to be unreasonable about it. Any assignment or subletting will not release the tenant of its liabilities under the lease.
9. The tenant will pay all premiums with respect to insurance placed by the landlord; such insurance will be spelled out and agreed to by both parties covering such things as "all risk" insurance, public liability, boiler, machinery etc., plate glass, and

any special coverage indicated by the nature of the tenant's type of business.

10. The proceeds of insurance will be paid to the landlord or to any mortgagee or encumbrancer. Insurance details can be lengthy.
11. There will be clauses concerning the conditions that will cause a forfeiture of the lease.
12. The landlord will not be held responsible for any accidents or damage.
13. If the tenant fails to maintain any payments on taxes, fees, insurance premiums, etc., the landlord may pay such items and charge the amount to the tenant as rent.
14. The monies provided to be paid by the tenant to the landlord shall be net to the landlord and clear of all charges, except the landlord's business and income taxes, payments of mortgage principal and interest and any expense for repairs which may be the landlord's responsibility under the lease.

72

BUYING A BUSINESS

This can be a complicated legal undertaking, requiring a good deal of financial advice from an accountant. What I can do is simply provide an overview of what may be involved here:

If the purchase of the business includes the purchase of land and buildings, the offer to the vendor will be made describing the land and buildings first, and then go on to say it includes the goodwill, trade name, chattels, fixtures and equipment of the business which will be listed on a schedule attached to the offer.

After running through the mortgage details, it will outline the financial adjustments to be made on closing for such things as the inventory of stock in trade, insurance, service contracts, taxes, water, hydro, any local improvement commitments and mortgage interest.

Then, and here is where it can be dicey, an appraisal must be made apportioning the purchase price to land, buildings, fixtures, chattels, equipment, stock, goodwill and the trade name. See the help one needs?

How many appraisers are needed? What assurance is there that the income tax department will agree to the breakdown in the total purchase price?

Competent appraising is needed because, for example, the building will require a cost base for capital cost allowances over the coming tax years. Not only that, it will be important to establish a fair price for the "good will" of the business.

Prior to 1972, goodwill was not recognized as being deductible from income either as an expense or by way of capital cost allowances. It is now recognized as an eligible expenditure.

Taxpayers are now allowed to establish an account comparable to a capital cost allowance class for goodwill. One half of the fairly established cost of the goodwill will be included in this account, and the taxpayer may then deduct 10% of the balance of the account on a reducing balance basis.

And just what is goodwill? Here are two quotations of how courts have referred to definitions of goodwill:

a) Goodwill is the whole advantage, whatever it may be, of the reputation and connection of the firm which may have been built up by years of honest work or gained by lavish expenditures of money.
b) It is "the privilege, granted by the seller of a business to the purchaser, of trading as his recognized successor; the possession of a ready-formed "connexion" of customers, considered as an element in the saleable value of a business, additional to the value of the plant, stock-in-trade, book debts, etc."

Goodwill cannot be divorced from the business itself. It follows the business, and may be sold with the business, but it cannot be sold separately. Generally speaking, goodwill arises as a recognizable asset only when a business is acquired at a price in excess of the going or in-use value of its net tangible assets.

So you see, you will need expert advice in these areas. Your lawyer and your accountant will be your best guide. I do not recommend taking a vendor's advice about cost apportionment, without having it completely verified.

On the date of completion an inventory will be taken of the stock at the invoice prices to the vendor, less any trade discounts.

It is customary for the vendor to make his peace with his suppliers and pay all his trade bills before closing, and to covenant to be responsible for other accounts rendered for payment for assets purchased from the vendor. You can be sure your lawyer will particularly take a good hard look at the financial details of stock and fixtures, and what's paid for and what isn't.

As for the accounts receivable in the business, it is customary for the one buying the business to purchase them from the vendor at an agreed discount. The list of receivables purchased should not include any receivables outstanding over 90 days, unless there are mitigating circumstances, with the buyer's satisfactory assurance that they will be paid.

The vendor will reveal all details of guarantees and service contracts that affect the business, and also assign rights to all franchises, if any.

It has been said that the best location for any business is right across the street from a competitor. However true this may be, the business buyer certainly doesn't want his vendor becoming his competitor lest he take all his former customers with him, so it is usual to have the vendor agree not to become the proprietor of a competing business, or be employed by one. This agreement will have a time limit, and specify an area, or distance from the business he is selling.

Don't put all your beans in one pot, which means keep some reserve cash at least for the early months of operating your new business venture. Unexpected expenses have a way of cropping up like weeds, and you will want to have the ability to establish a good business name for yourself in your new location.

73

BUYING A FARM

Federal and provincial governments are anxious to keep people on the land. Farm attrition, coupled with Canada's ever-increasing population, results in the governments' full cooperation in assisting one to get the plow moving and the cows milked as quickly as possible.

The best sources of information about farms that are for sale or rent are *farm* real estate agents, advertisements in *farm* magazines, *farm* newspapers, and rural journals.

The logical farm real estate agents will be ones in rural communities and towns. Drive around the country, pick your location, and visit nearby agents. Also, pick up a copy of the area's weekly newspaper.

If you become seriously interested in an area, or a particular farm, talk to neighboring farmers about the land. Contact the local provincial government agricultural agent, and talk to him about the land. You must know about the land, unless of course you are just looking for a huge building lot in the country.

Take advantage of the many services provided by provincial and federal agricultural departments.

The federal Department of Agriculture carries on research into the physical and economic problems of agriculture. Experimental farms and research laboratories are located in many parts of Canada. The results of this work are made available to farmers by means of bulletins, posters, articles in newspapers and farm magazines, and radio and television programs. Information on markets and prices for agriculture products is distributed in daily and weekly reports on radio and television, in farm magazines, and some newspapers.

Each province has an agricultural extension service with a representative located in each county or district. These agents interpret research data for farmers, provide assistance and advice in resolving problems, distribute extension bulletins, and give short courses on various aspects of farm management and other subjects. In addition, the extension services usually have a staff of consultants in specialized fields who may be asked for advice. Some of the extension services have home economists on staff who provide extension education services.

Many agricultural marketing and supply firms have staff to advise farmers. For example, feed companies give advice on rations for livestock and poultry; building supply firms on building construction; chemical companies on the use of pesticides and herbicides; fertilizer companies on fertilizers and cultural practices; grain marketing companies on grain varieties and markets. Also, many colleges and vocational schools have special short courses designed for farmers.

Financial Aspects of the Farm

The amount of capital needed to start farming on a full-time basis depends on the type of farm, the productivity of the soil, the proximity of the farm to markets, and whether the farmer buys or rents.

A farmer specializing in the production of hogs or poultry requires a small acreage of land compared with a wheat farmer, but has a large investment in buildings and livestock. A cattle rancher, in common with the wheat producer, needs a large acreage of land but ranchland usually costs much less per acre than cropland. Lands near large urban centers naturally cost more than lands farther away.

The capital requirements of a beginning farm operator can be lessened if he rents land and equipment. However, competition from established operators greatly reduces the opportunities for him to obtain enough land for an efficient operation by renting. Purchasing used machinery, and hiring, borrowing or exchanging large machines are other means of reducing the initial investment, but starting with less machinery and equipment than is necessary for an efficient operation makes it difficult for a beginning farmer to compete with his established neighbors.

Volume of business is one of the chief things to consider when starting to farm. Reducing capital requirements by obtaining a smaller acreage of land or fewer livestock than is necessary for an efficient farm unit results in a small business. Unfortunately, the operator of a small farm usually finds it difficult to increase the size of his operation.

Financing the Purchase

The one selling the farm sometimes accepts a mortgage for a substantial part of the purchase price, which simplifies the financing. If this cannot be done, go after the government.

Several government agencies lend money to farmers to finance the purchase. The Farm Credit Corporation of the federal government is the main source of this type of credit, and some provinces have agencies for lending provincial government funds for buying farms.

To be eligible for a government loan a borrower must be a bona fide farmer, and under provincial schemes a borrower must be a resident of the province.

An objective of all government farm credit agencies is to help a farmer establish his farm as a sound economic farm unit. The maximum loan allowed to a farmer is set by legislation and varies from province to province. Legislation of the federal government and some provincial governments provides for more credit and easier collateral to young farmers, but the farm operations are subject to supervision by the lending agency until the loan is reduced to a certain level.

Financing the Operation

Farmers may obtain short and long term credit for production, farm improvement and development from several sources.

The Federal Government: The Farm Credit Corporation was established to help Canadian farmers and those wishing to become farmers, purchase, develop and maintain sound farm businesses. Assistance is provided in the form of long-term mortgage credit.

Applicants must be principally occupied in farming or about to become full-time farmers at the time of the loan. Young persons under 35 years of age may retain off-farm employment while developing an economic farm business, providing farming becomes their principal occupation within five years.

A number of factors must be considered by the applicant and the Farm Credit Corporation before a loan is approved and before the actual amount of any loan is agreed upon. The applicant must demonstrate that the farm business under his or her management will generate enough income to meet all financial obligations and to allow for a reasonable standard of living. Also, the applicant's management ability and experience are taken into consideration.

Borrowers must be either Canadian citizens or landed immigrants.

Loan funds may be used to:

- purchase farm land
- make permanent improvements
- purchase breeding stock and equipment
- pay debts, or for any purpose that will facilitate the efficient operation of the farm.

Repayment terms are most generous: A borrower may take up to a maximum of 30 years to repay a loan, and the loan may be prepaid at any time without notice.

Loans are secured by a mortgage on real estate and, where necessary, on farm livestock and equipment.

Provincial appeal boards, made up of practical farmers of proven ability and judgment, are established to hear appeals from applicants who are not satisfied with the Corporation's decision on any loan application.

An application for a loan should be made at the local Farm Credit Corporation office. The address of the one nearest you may be obtained by writing to: The Farm Credit Corporation, 434 Queen Street, P.O. Box 2314, Postal Station D, Ottawa, Ontario, K1P 6J9.

Provincial Governments: Most provide credit to individual farmers for purchases of farm machinery, livestock, land clearance and drainage.

Commercial Banks: For operating capital and other transactions requiring short-term credit. Banks may be the same in what they do for a living, but they are certainly not the same in how they go about laying out the carpet for borrowers. Don't ever take no for an answer if one bank manager says nay — go to another bank. They are still the best source of general borrowing, and the large growth of Canadian banks is proof that they like to lend as much money as they can.

It is also possible to obtain money from banks for farm improvement loans backed by government.

Credit Unions: Members of a credit union usually may obtain short and intermediate term credit for almost any purpose, and in the face of current rates and terms are very reasonable places to do business.

Merchants, dealers and finance companies: Credit may be obtained directly or indirectly from dealers wishing to sell their products. Finance company rates are usually higher than banks, but their loans are often easier to obtain.

Processing and supply firms: May extend credit as part of what is termed "contract farming." There are various types of contracts, ranging from simple credit deals to profit-sharing arrangements. Sometimes company supervision of farm operations is involved; protecting the investment, so to speak.

Urban smog, dirt, noise, pollution, contamination and corruption is enough to drive anyone into the country. If it's your bag, I hope you make it.

74

HOW ABOUT A PIECE OF LAND?

Hindsight is great fun. If only we had done this or that, how our lives would be different today!

In 1942, I was a flight sergeant stationed at an RCAF Air Observers' School in Malton, Ontario. I didn't know it but at the time a man purchased a farm about a mile south of us for $12,000 with $2,000 down. When I met him years later, he told me his friends thought he was nuts for paying so much for the land.

A few years ago I approached him on behalf of a builder to see if he would sell the place for $1 million. He turned me down flat, pointing out that he had three sons and wanted to keep them on the farm. Any persuasion of mine about him going out of town with the money and buying farms for each of the boys did no good.

Well, he finally sold — for $1.3 million.

Now my hindsight sees me back in 1942. I would have bought a corner property on the airport strip for peanuts, hung onto the land for 40 years, and sold. I would now be planning for an extended trip around the world.

So this writing today is for all you young people who have spare cash in the bank drawing modest interest. Get some of it out of there and put it into a piece of land. Buy it and keep it. Don't sell it for 30 years.

During the 30 years, rent the land on a net basis, whereby the tenants also pay for your taxes. You just go on about your business, and put the land on the back burner until you approach retirement age.

You don't think you would have the willpower to hang onto the land for 30 years without selling? No problem. Lease it and put the land in escrow in such a way that it can't be sold for 30 years. There, I've just set you up for retirement.

I am not talking about land in the city. It's out in the country, millions of acres of it.

In 1968, I sold 100 acres near Orangeville, Ontario, for $13,500.

The buyer sold the 80-year-old barn off the place for $4,000 to a man who decorates rec rooms and restaurants with old barn lumber.

The land was immediately rented to a local farmer for $600 a year. His net cost was $9,500 so that gave him an active return on his investment of about 6%. Which wasn't bad in 1968. And as long as he owns the land, it keeps going up in value.

There is no simple magic formula for deciding what land to buy. You have to get out and start looking.

Learn something about land. Local farmers are your best bet.

Get to know some country brokers in those small towns. Some of them have been at it so long they know every farmer in the country by his first name. They know where the good stuff is, who might sell, and who might help with the financing.

If you don't want to lease your land, use it yourself. Get some friends and parcel it out in garden plots. Everybody will enjoy the weekend outings and have enough food left over for the in-laws.

Or plant something like Christmas trees. If there are a few acres of bush on the land, get a chain saw and enjoy making money selling fireplace logs. Do you know what they cost these days?

As Harry Golden said: "Enjoy, enjoy." And make it pay.

75

BUYING A HOTEL

Now, I'm not talking about a Royal York or a Hotel Vancouver, or the Chateau Laurier; this is about buying a small hotel, one that you would find in the downtown area of any community in Canada, or in the countryside. These hotels usually have rooms; however, because of the general age of the properties, they cater to weekly and monthly tenants, and not to the travelling public as do the motels and modern motor hotels. The main source of revenue in these hotels is derived from their food and beverage operations.

Unlike other forms of real estate transactions, few hotels are sold privately; they are generally sold through hotel brokers. The reasons are basic — because of an owner's desire not to upset his staff or customers, he will want the transaction handled discreetly. This is practically impossible on a direct sale basis which depends on the knowledge of the sale being transmitted by word of mouth by persons connected with the industry. Another reason why the hotel broker plays a necessary role in the sale of hotel properties is that potential buyers on their own do not have the opportunity to compare similar properties which are available on the market and, unlike residential properties, the hotels available may be separated by great distances, and without comparisons, prospective purchasers cannot determine if the asking price is realistic.

You will notice that I said "hotel broker." There are few brokerage firms that specifically deal in the sale of hotels; however, those that do can be found by contacting the Hotel Association of the province that interests you. The association will provide you with the names of companies specializing in this form of real estate.

When you have made contact with a hotel broker, discuss your requirements with him. Be sure to outline fully your background experience, financial resources, and requirements as to location preferred, living accommodation required, etc. This information is necessary to enable the real estate agent to qualify which properties he has for sale which may appeal to you.

When you have seen the financial reports of the prospective properties that meet your requirements and you have chosen the ones that appeal to you, it is time to go and physically inspect them. It is important to have the agent accompany you. It allows him to assess your reaction first hand, to see how well he has qualified your requirements. Remember, you are contemplating making a very large purchase, and it may take time — very rarely will a purchaser buy the first property he has viewed — and often your requirements may change after seeing a couple of properties, as the prerequisites you had can change very quickly as you go through your inspections. Another reason why it is important to have an agent accompany you is that with his general knowledge of the industry he is most likely to ask questions and obtain answers that you would not think of at the time.

When you have found a hotel that appears to meet all your requirements, spend some time there at different times of the day observing the physical operation of the business, but remember, be discreet. Some hotels may be quiet enough in the daytime, but when the sun goes down things can change.

Some hotel businesses have a very noisy clientele and alcoholic beverages can bring out the worst in some people's character. However, if you have questions about the reputation of a particular establishment, the best way to get answers is to visit the local police station. It will certainly know if a hotel has a bad reputation or not.

Have your solicitor check the municipal zoning; ensure the property conforms to all municipal zoning regulations, and make sure there is sufficient land to allow expansion. The latter may detract from the value of the property if expansion is not allowed.

The following is an overview of what one might expect to find in an agreement of purchase and sale:

The offer will describe exactly who is purchasing the property, yourself personally or a limited company of which you may be a director. Often companies are formed to purchase businesses for tax reasons, and it can be costly. Consult your lawyer and accountant as to the advantages and disadvantages of buying personally or with a limited company.

The offer will state the purchase price and the amount of down payment being offered. Remember, in hotel purchases a deposit of 5 to 10% of the down payment (your cash equity) is usually required with any offer.

The purchase price will be allocated to a stated number of dollars for (1) land, (2) building, (3) chattels and equipment and (4) goodwill. For goodwill, review the chapter, "Buying a Business."

The allocation to land, building, etc. is as important as the purchase price itself as it determines what depreciation (capital cost allowance) can be claimed, and will affect your tax payable on the profits of the business. For an understanding of this, read chapter 79, "Buying an Apartment Building."

Hotels are very rarely sold for cash, and usually involve the vendor's taking back a mortgage for part of the purchase price. Interest rates on these purchase mortgages are usually lower than rates quoted from lending institutions. The interest rate charged on vendor's mortgages has a great bearing on the value of the hotel, because prices can be adjusted according to the interest rate being charged.

Most land and building mortgages taken back by vendors will be collaterally secured by a chattel mortgage on the furniture and equipment of the hotel. The chattel mortgage will contain clauses allowing you to dispose of or replace any chattel so long as it is replaced with an item of comparable value. It will also contain a clause allowing the chattel mortgage to be transferred to a future purchaser without the approval of the mortgagee, or the acceleration of payments. This is very important, as it will allow you to transfer the mortgage without paying a bonus when deciding to sell.

The list of chattels in the chattel mortgage is compiled by the taking of an inventory. This is usually completed by the purchaser and the vendor soon after an agreement of purchase and sale is executed by both parties, and because of the difficulty in preparing this list, it is usually done on the first day the hotel is not open for business, following the signing. However, any chattels or equipment on loan, lease or commission basis must be referred to in the offer to purchase, as they are not included in the purchase price. For example, electronic games, laundry, linen, signs, ice cream cabinets, cigarette machines, and sometimes TV, in bedrooms may be rented.

On closing of the transaction, just as in the closing of a house sale, there will be adjustments to be made. Such things as insurance premiums, taxes, prepaid rental contracts, security deposits, fuel oil, water, etc. In addition to these adjustments a purchaser will be required to pay for the merchantable stock which is on the premises in addition to the purchase price. The value of this stock is determined by the invoice price paid by the vendor. It is important to take into consideration these adjustments when calculating the amount one will offer for a particular property.

The foregoing is a simplified overview of some things to look for when buying a hotel. Your lawyer will certainly have more to add and say to all this.

76

BUYING A MOTEL

Operating a motel, even a small one, in today's competitive market is not a job for retired persons or even for the semi-retired.

It is a full-time job which frequently demands considerable physical stamina. It demands poise in the face of pressure. It requires an aggressive, business-like approach to profitmaking. To be sure, there is a reasonably good future ahead for the motel business, and for many of those in other branches of the time-honored calling of innkeeper. But the right starting time is not the year in which one quits work and retires.

The motel industry offers considerable opportunities to persons who are willing to invest adequate sums of money, to discipline themselves, and to adhere faithfully to proved standards of business practice.

On the other hand, anyone entering this business must bear in mind that, regardless of how hard and skillfully he works, it is possible to fail anyway, because of an oversupply of motel rooms in some areas (leading to price cutting) or because of business conditions, local or national. In other words, if in your particular area there are too many motel rooms for the number of travellers, whatever the cause, one or more of the motels is going to be forced out of business.

The Basics

Your primary business as a motel operator will be renting rooms to guests, but there are other allied sources of income you may also want to explore.

Motels which have a restaurant on the premises, or nearby, generally are more popular than those which do not. As a motel owner, you may build and operate a restaurant yourself; you may erect the restaurant and lease it to an experienced restaurateur; or you may have no investment whatever in the restaurant, but refer your guests to one that is close by.

Some motels make money on gift shops, or on service stations. Vending machines add to income. So can auto or boat rentals. And there are other possible profit-producing services. Any extra income, however, is usually peanuts compared with the take from the primary source — room sales. Unless room occupancy keeps above the break-even level, the motel itself will decline, regardless of minor secondary sources of on-premises income.

The motel industry has grown dramatically, and in many areas the competition is fierce, and yet there are other areas begging, through chambers of commerce and other development agencies, for operators to come in and build sorely-needed motels.

Pitfalls

A rude awakening for many novice motel operators occurs when they realize that they have taken on a 24-hour job with no days off.

As a host, you must see to the comfort and happiness of your guests, and as a businessperson you must show a profit. These two responsibilities will keep you on the job for long hours and the work is often hard.

You not only must be a good and hospitable desk clerk, you also must be a fair plumber, electrician, advertising person, mechanic, accountant, and interior decorator. Of course, only a very few exceptionally gifted persons can be good at all these jobs, but as a motel manager, you must hire personnel competent to perform these tasks, or you frequently will find you must do the best you can in situations for which you may not have been trained.

Physical stamina is essential, which makes motel management a poor choice as a retirement job. This does not mean that some middle-aged couples have not taken up motel owner-managership successfully. But it does mean that retirement is not found in the motel business.

As the operator of a small motel, you may be on your feet all morning as you go about supervising and assisting in the cleaning of rooms, repairing equipment and fixtures, and tending to highway signs. During the afternoon, you may have to get the bookeeping up to date, purchase supplies, and prepare direct-mail advertising. Meanwhile, you will have to keep smiling, and in the afternoon and evening, greet guests and see that each party is comfortable. During the night, there may be late arrivals or complaints from persons already roomed that the air conditioning has failed, that plumbing has broken down, or that guests in the next room are too noisy.

If you own and manage your motel, you may find yourself tied to it with seldom a chance for a day off. Rooms must be rented every night, and finding a person who is competent enough to manage the motel, and willing to work only on the occasions when you would like a holiday could be difficult.

Your family must be able to adjust to the confining routine. As a matter of fact, in the owner-managed hotel the entire family usually works at various motel chores, and the temperament and training of each member must be considered.

There will be other pitfalls over which you may have little or no control. You may have an excellent location and do a good business — but others are aware of it and may build a bigger, better motel near yours. You may think the future looks cozy, but your provincial highway department may decide it is necessary to by-pass your community or build a super-highway which will take away your direct access to traffic lanes.

Hazards

In fires, storms, and other natural disasters, you may find your insurance doesn't fully cover you, particularly if you count the business you lose due to the disaster. Also, the death of a guest on your premises could result in a lawsuit which could hurtle you into bankruptcy, if your negligence is proved, and your insurance is inadequate. Or a dishonest employee may slowly rob you into insolvency through almost invisible techniques of embezzlement.

Your biggest danger is also your greatest asset: *You.* It is your managerial abilities which will make or break your motel. It is your ability to act as a good host and a good salesman, day in and day out. It is your success in building and maintaining a high room occupancy rate at adequate price levels which will determine whether your motel will make money or lose it.

Your attitude toward your business, your dealings with your guests, with your fellow motel operators, with your suppliers, and with all other persons with whom you come in contact in the course of your business will have direct bearing on your success or failure.

Qualities You Need

Ask yourself how well you are prepared for the essentials of motel management:

1. Ability to work long, hard hours.
2. Willingness to accept the confinement to the job (the smaller the motel, the less freedom for the operator).
3. Ability to deal tactfully with people, many of whom may have been travelling under difficult conditions all day, and are not in the friendliest mood.
4. Knack of being a good host, making guests feel wanted, and anticipating their needs.
5. Constant awareness and practice of public relations.
6. Willingness to cope with all kinds of problems, which may range from a coin jammed in a soft drink machine to a guest who suffers a heart attack at 3 a.m.
7. Some knowledge of business management, personnel handling, accounting, and sales promotion, plus being a general handyman for do-it-yourself repairs and maintenance.
8. An appreciation of how important it is for you to take an active role in affairs affecting the entire motel industry, acting through joint efforts with others like yourself in local, provincial and national motel trade associations.
9. Ambition to prove your own standards as a motel manager by studying books and journals on the subject; attending short schools, seminars and expositions; keeping abreast of current industry developments; and otherwise training yourself and your helpers.
10. Executive ability, at least to the extent that you can and will be able to delegate authority.

Judging a Motel's Location

Actually, only the record of the motel's profitability over a long period can be the final test of whether its location is good. The fact that you are beside a busy highway isn't enough, for a thousand passing automobiles are not worth the single car that stops and discharges guests who rent rooms.

In searching for a good motel location, keep these fundamental principles in mind:

1. The trading area must have an adequate potential. Look beyond the motel industry itself. If retail business generally is declining, if the region is losing population and otherwise slipping downward, a motel also may face a struggle for existence.

   Of course, on the other hand, the area you are considering may show no immediate evidence of current progress, but still have some good potential for the near future. Perhaps you will find out that a sizeable new factory is being started, or that other industries will be expanded. Possibly you will learn that two super-highways will be completed with an intersection at an nearby point. Or perhaps your survey will disclose the fact that the proposed location is in a good spot between the two growing urban areas and that highway changes between the two centers could conceivably generate business for the motel.
2. Guests should be able to get to the motel easily, and with a minimum of confusion.

   If access to your place is difficult and if the directional signs are bewildering, strangers may give up after one try at finding you, and will go on and stop somewhere else.
3. You should pick your location with a view to whether it is a convenient stopping place for travellers. Locations which are an average day's drive from major centers are likely to be good. Even a motel in an inconspicuous location can succeed if it is just about the right distance from a big city. Usually, however, more business can be intercepted at well-travelled highway interchange points, and, of course, near airports.
4. A group of motels often can help each other. In fact, each one seems to do better when several of them are not far apart. This is

partly because many travellers like to shop around before they reach a decision and sign the register. Travellers who know there are several motels at a given location will drive to that point.

Additional business develops also when there are large meetings that cannot be handled by a single motel. The delegates will occupy several in the same area.

5. Compatibility with other nearby businesses is desirable. Some types of enterprises help to build motel volume, while others drive potential guests away. Restaurants, drug stores, service stations, and similar businesses serving needs of the travelling public are assets to the location. Junk yards, railroad yards, slums, and noisy or dirty neighborhoods do not invite the traveller.
6. Although, as noted, competing motels can sometimes work together to mutual advantage, the prospective operator nevertheless should try to find out whether there will be too much competition for the business available. He should find out how many rooms there are in motels and other tourist accommodations in the area, and what percentage of them are occupied on an average night.
7. The prospective owner-manager should learn as much as he can about other possible hazards. For example, will the zoning by-laws of the municipality permit a livestock yard to be built next door? (A little extreme, but you get the point.) Are there any plans for highway relocation which would result in the motel being by-passed by the bulk of the traffic?

   The location will be a key factor in determining the type of motel you eventually build or buy. It will determine whether you will have a small one or a large one, whether you will offer nothing but room rentals, and whether you will need a swimming pool, restaurant, gift shop, barber shop, bellman, rooms with kitchenettes and a lot of other extra services. It will determine whether your customers will be mostly vacationers, or parents visiting children in college, or salesmen.

Remember the three most vital factors are location, location, location.

The Established Motel

There are certain advantages in buying an established motel. New motels require from 6 to 18 months to go through a shake-down period during which daily operations are smoothed out and a regular clientele is developed. However, a successful, existing motel will have already been through this shake-down. Personnel will be trained and on the job. The advertising and public relations programs will have attained some momentum. The motel perhaps will have acquired a solid reputation.

You also should be aware of the disadvantages of buying an established motel:

1. What changes would you expect to make in the property and in its established ways of doing business?
2. How much extra money would be required to correct deficiencies and shortcomings in the motel's construction and methods of doing business?
3. Is the motel in danger of losing its recommendation by an Association or referral agency? Why?
4. Has the motel acquired an unwholesome local reputation which may take years to overcome?
5. Are the established rates in line with others in the area? Does the motel enjoy favorable comparison with others in the area?

The Purchase Price

In evaluating the price, keep in mind these helpful points:

1. Appearance is perhaps the most important single factor in attracting business to a motel, but it might be a secondary matter in buying one. This is because external appearance can be changed, if you're willing to spend the money to do it. However, before you buy, you must get the facts about the structural quality of the buildings themselves. Are the foundations adequate? Notice whether the builder cut corners to save costs.
2. Don't be misled by gracious living quarters for the owner or by spacious and attractive lawns, a big lobby or by wide curving sidewalks. These are nice, but they won't directly produce reve-

nue for you. They mean the present owner has put a lot of money into these extras, and the price he will try to get you to pay will include the cost of these things.

3. Inspect the books. Pay no heed to claims of unrecorded income or to estimates of income. If the books are not made available to you, just forget that particular deal. Once you have the full financial records, you'll want to divide the gross annual revenue by the number of rooms to get the actual "per room per year" figure, one of the most accurate measurements of motel achievement. Let your accountant see the books, too!
4. Consider factors related to the books. The current owner may have had to operate under conditions you will not have to face (for example, a long period of severe weather or of highway reconstruction). Also, consider whether you'll have to spend additional money for expansion or upgrading. Place a realistic value on the motel's earned reputation, for good or ill.
5. You are accepting the new burden, so buy for yourself, not the seller. Try to find out and take into account his reasons for selling. If the price looks too low, the proposed deal should be scrutinized carefully. Remember that successful operations do not have to be sold at salvage prices. Pay for fair value. Also, be sure to obtain a satisfactory agreement that will prevent the seller from re-entering the motel business in the same area, thus becoming your competitor.

Firms which sell products may miss a sale today but sell it tomorrow for the same profit. Revenue from a motel room not rented tonight, however, never can be regained — it is lost forever. Fixed expenses continue, nevertheless.

In view of the size of the investment and the risk, one should give plenty of time and thought to reach a decision about going into this business. Do not be rushed.

77

BUYING A COTTAGE

There are two basic but false assumptions in buying that retreat to get away from it all. The first is that "the beach in front of the cottage is mine," and the second is that since a cottage is not too far away from the water, there must be access to the water.

Ever heard of Crown riparian rights? This is a strip of land owned by the government along the shores of lakes and rivers, and it is public property. The public usually assumes that because the cottage is on the beach, the beach must be the property of the cottage owner. Here are some general observations to deter this thinking:

In the Yukon Territory and the Northwest Territories, the *Territorial Lands Act* makes it quite clear that, unless otherwise ordered by the Governor in Council, a strip of land 100 feet in width (about 30 metres) measured from ordinary high-water mark or from the boundary line, as the case may be, shall be deemed to be reserved to the Crown out of every grant of territorial lands, where the land extends: (a) to the sea or an inlet thereof; (b) to the shore of any navigable water or an inlet thereof.

In Manitoba, since 1930, the Crown reserves out of every disposition of Crown land "a strip of land one and one-half chains in width (99 feet, or again about 30 metres) measured from ordinary high-water mark. And all subdivisions abutting on navigable water must provide for a public reserve along the shore, which is vested in the responsible municipality.

In Saskatchewan, title to shorelands of a body of water is normally retained by the Crown to permit public access to and use of the water body.

In Alberta, with certain limited exceptions, the title to the shores of all rivers, streams, watercourses, lakes and other bodies of water is vested in the Crown.

In Ontario it is a very complex subject. Some appear to own the shoreline, and some don't.

In Newfoundland, under the *Crown Lands Act (1970)*, a strip of Crown lands not less than 33 feet wide (about 10 metres) around and adjoining all lakes and ponds and along each bank of all rivers, shall be reserved in all grants, leases and licences issued under the Act.

The point is, a buyer of a waterfront lot cannot assume that ownership of the shoreline goes with the lot. The odds are against it.

If the cottage lot is not on the shore, it is advisable to ensure that at least the owner of the lot has access to the shore itself. Make this a condition of your offer in buying the lot.

When considering the purchase of a cottage, you will save yourself many hours, and a great deal of frustration, if you list your major requirements. A big consideration is whether the cottage is to be used simply as a summer retreat, or will there be plans in the future for year-round use or a home for retirement? The municipal by-laws may have something to say about this.

In deciding on a general location in your search, you will soon realize that some compromise will occur, and price will be the big leveler. Prices are generally dictated by distance from major urban centers, and it is understandable that the closer you are, the more you pay.

The size of the lake or river, and quality of the water has a great bearing on price. Generally, the larger the body of water, the higher the price. River frontage prices usually go at about the same price as smaller lakes. Type of terrain and summer or year-round road affect price.

When you find a property that appears to suit your needs, and pocketbook, here are a few things to think about in making the offer:

Access to water will be your prime consideration.

Check the basic structure, foundation, and particularly the joists, for dry rot.

It is important to ensure the roof will stand up under a heavy winter's snowfall. There will be no one there to clean it off for you and this can cause concern. Perhaps a local resident may be employed to clean the snow off the roof periodically, but remember it.

Ensure that the septic system meets municipal requirements, and that your supply of drinking water is potable and meets the requirements of the local health authorities.

If it is on a private road, who pays for its upkeep — and how much?

If the cottage is advertised as winterized, is the water system installed for winter use? A most important point.

If it is a lot only, determine from the municipality just what you can build on it, and what the septic requirements are.

If it is your intention to use the property for future year-round use, check the zoning and ensure it is not zoned for seasonal recreational use.

Before making the offer, think it over carefully, and make your offer subject to any of your doubts. The worst that can happen is that you won't get the property, but who wants to buy a dream and end up with a nightmare?

78

RIPARIAN RIGHTS

The word "riparian" pertains to the bank of a watercourse. Riparian rights of landowners have produced much litigation in our courts, and, after reviewing 21 judgments on the subject, here are some highlights from our provinces.

- A riparian owner is entitled to an injunction without proof of actual damage, where the waters of the stream along which his property lies are polluted, as by the discharge into them of raw, untreated sewage.
- A riparian owner of the banks and bed of a river who constructs a dam which destroys or materially reduces the current (but without destroying passage as such) is not liable to a log-owner who had theretofore floated his logs downstream in the current.
- Title is acquired to such property only as is actually described in the registered conveyance and where the conveyances described one side of certain property as being bounded by a riverbank, without more, than ownership is limited on that side to such riverbank and does not extend to the middle of the riverbed.
- The owner of land abutting on a nontidal river has the exclusive right of fishing opposite his land according to the extent to which his land abuts on the river. The fact that there may be a public right of passage along the river does not impair the exclusive right of fishery.
- A riparian owner bordering a lake is entitled to an injunction restraining a municipal corporation from holding a speed-boat regatta on the lake when there is reasonable apprehension that the regatta would result in diminution of the purity, wholesomeness and potability of the water in the lake.
- In Ontario, at common law the boundary between land and water

was established by placing it at the water's lowest mark. Then the *Beds of Navigable Waters Act* was amended in 1940, establishing the *high*-water mark as the boundary. But an amendment in 1951 reestablished the common law position, so that today the boundary between land and water is at the *lowest*-water mark.

Accordingly, a description in a deed in 1907, carrying the boundary line to the lower-water mark, determined when the low mark was by law the boundary between land and water.

Now, along came someone claiming possessory title to part of the land in this 1907 deed. He committed sporadic acts of possession such as the hunting of ducks on marsh land between high- and low-water marks, the pasturing of cattle thereon, and the erection of a diving board at the water's edge.

The judgment said such acts are neither continuous nor exclusive of the true owner and so are not sufficient to establish possessory title.

- Here's an expression I found in one judgment that got me looking in big books for an answer: the "solum of the foreshore." Now, what do you suppose that means?

  Why, when you are walking along a beach and step into the water, you are on the solum of the foreshore. Impress your friends with that one!
- The rights of an owner to unimpeded flow of water can be substantial. A plaintiff diverted a brook to create a reservoir for cattle and a pond for swimming. The defendant, a lower riparian owner, then diverted water from the brook above the plaintiff's land. The trial judge granted injunctions to both, after finding they each had impeded the flow of water. Both losers. How about that?

79

BUYING AN APARTMENT BUILDING

There are buyers all over the country with $100,000 or more who are itching to invest it in an apartment building to produce the following results:

a) Require the tenants of the property to pay all the expenses, including the interest and principal repayments on the mortgages.
b) Provide a return of about 10% on the original investment.
c) Provide a profit on the property in the event of a sale.

In 1965, I made my first sale to such a buyer, for $150,000. A well-placed, solid, well-tenanted 17 suite building. The buyer got it for a $40,000 down payment to a $110,000 mortgage fully amortized over 20 years.

Well, 20 years have passed. The mortgage, interest and principal, was repaid by the income from tenants. The income also paid all the operating expenses and municipal taxes, and provided the owner with a good net annual return on his investment. All paid for now, and what was the market value of this property in 1985? Oh, I would think about $800,000. How about that?

Deals like this are being made every day across Canada, but only by people who are not afraid to get their financial feet wet, and possibly take a bit of risk. If it required little or no effort, with 100% guaranteed security, everybody would be doing it. They would not necessarily have the $100,000, or downstroke as it is called, but they would insist on getting involved through some sort of share basis. After all, 10% is much better than a lot of other investments we can think of, especially when one considers the fringe benefits and a possible whopping increase in value at the end of the line.

All these people who turn up with about $100,000 don't have it all in their own bank account. Many of them have partners: one, two, three, possibly as many as a dozen. They all have one common goal. Get involved. Make money.

Every building in Canada is owned by someone. Some people undoubtedly wish they had never become involved in owning investment real estate, for personal reasons, or a bad buy, but the majority of owners are whistling all the way to the bank. How did they get started? What makes one man a wealthy property owner, and another, who had the same opportunities, just another average Joe?

Some got their start in building trades. They started out as laborers on a house construction job, kept their eyes and ears open, saved their money and, when the opportunity arose to purchase a couple of building lots, they took the plunge, either alone or with a partner. The demand for houses was constant, they worked hard and stuck to business and eventually ended up being one of the big ones, or at least moderately successful.

Others did it through education. Becoming a lawyer, for example, is one of the surest ways to financial success. It not only gives one a great education into legal aspects of how other people make money, but it puts one close to these people and great opportunities to get involved.

Some people simply inherit estates. Others are talked into buying by salesmen; stumble onto a good thing; lend someone money and foreclose; marry property; obtain it by accepting real estate to settle a debt; or find themselves sitting on a gold mine due to re-zoning, and, realizing the potential, go right out and buy more. But the majority of investment properties are owned by people who went head on into it after a lot of thought, and plunged the bankroll into the financial whirlpool that is the greatest money-maker of all time — real estate.

If you have worked hard for years, watched the pennies and saved diligently, it is not always an easy thing to bring yourself to write out a cheque that will seemingly wipe out your life savings. You watched that bank book balance grow over the years, and sometimes it is a bit of a shock to look at it after all these years and find it so depleted, regardless of the knowledge that it left the bank and ended up as bricks and mortar.

If you have felt the urge to get involved, and have a timid heart, or nagging doubts about going it alone, don't. Get a partner. Someone you have known for some time. Someone you feel is a very solid type, with a good clear head on his shoulders, but especially one who has the kind of money you are considering as your investment. You can always be a minor or major shareholder, but don't set the scales too far off balance. If your allowance for this venture is modest, get two or three partners. After you do buy the property, you can always sell your share to your partners under your agreement if it doesn't work out.

Before you consider buying *any* property, you naturally have to know something about it, and you should know as much about it as possible.

Have the investment listing form shown on the following page copied. It will enable you to have a clear picture and record of every property you inspect. It is basically intended for listing apartment buildings, but can effectively be used for any type of investment property.

Five points: location; condition of building; income; expenses; and proper financing.

The ideal location for an apartment building is close to main traffic arteries. Not right on them; close to them. Traffic creates noise, and regardless of what you have heard about "getting used to it," it can still create problems with tenants, who didn't realize what they were getting into. Being near the main artery provides your tenants with transportation. It is nice to take a four-block walk to the bus on a sunny spring day, but in the winter? Proper location will provide you with a better chance of keeping the building fully occupied.

If you have had no experience with the ins and outs of building construction, and you find a property that seriously interests you to the point of submitting a respectable offer, get some expert advice. Buildings that have been mortgaged through an approved lender of Canada Mortgage and Housing Corporation are built to its standards, so you won't have to be very concerned about the quality of construction. Sloppy maintenance and appearance of the property can be

INVESTMENT LISTING FORM

Bldg. Name ______
& Address ______
PRICE $ ______
CASH $ ______

1st Mortgagee ______
Amount $ ______ At ______ % Due ______
Payable $ ______

2nd Mortgagee ______
Amount $ ______ At ______ % Due ______
Payable $ ______

GROSS ANNUAL INCOME ______

OPERATING EXPENSES

Taxes ______
Insurance ______
Heating ______
Light ______
Water ______
Maintenance ______
Supplies ______
Elevator ______
Superintendent ______
Misc. & Audit ______
Management ______
Vacancy Allce ______

Income Before Debt Charges $ ______

MORTGAGE PAYMENTS
1st mortgage ______
2nd mortgage ______

Net Cash Surplus (%) $ ______

PRINCIPAL PAYMENTS
(Average ______ years)
On 1st mortgage ______
On 2nd mortgage ______

GROSS RETURN (%) $ ______

Estimated Capital Cost
Allowance 1st Year $ ______

SUITES ( )	**MONTHLY**	**ANNUALLY**
______ Bachelor		
______ 1 Bedroom		
______ 2 Bedroom		
______ 3 Bedroom		
______ 4 Bedroom		
______ Garages		
______ Spaces		
______ Laundry		
Sundry Income:		
GROSS ANNUAL INCOME		

Assessment Land: ______
Building: ______
Construction ______

Fireproof ______	Age ______
Lot ______	Laundry ______
No. Storeys ______	Refrig. ______
Brick ______	Stoves ______
Incinerator ______	Inter-Com. ______
Heating ______	Lobby ______
Floor Suite ______	Rec. Pl. G. ______
Floor Hall ______	Air-Cond. ______
Elevator ______	Balconies ______

REMARKS

blamed on poor management, a careless superintendent or inconsiderate tenants. This can be corrected. A badly constructed building is another matter.

Don't be dazzled by an income figure that seems great. It may be too high. You should check rental figures in the immediate area for comparable accommodation. If the figures are too high in your comparison, you could be in trouble at a later date. Work on the averages.

Despite the "audited statement" of expenses you may see, you should again speak to someone familiar with the expenses of operating comparable buildings. The average figures will give you an indication of what you may expect after ownership, regardless of what the owner tells you. Of course, there are many ways to cut down the expenses, and you should look critically at each item. Heat control is a good example. Some superintendents just blast away with the heat to forestall any possible telephone calls from a tenant with a complaint. The lack of storm windows is another thing to watch for in the heating bills. Is the hot water heated off the furnace or does it have its own unit? Are the garage doors properly controlled to remain closed? There isn't much point in having your financing well considered if the expenses are going to knock you right into a nil balance or debit.

When you have satisfied yourself as to the gross income and operating expenses (including taxes, which are easy to check), you have two other items to consider, which will come under operating expenses.

Vacancy Allowance: It was customary a few years ago to charge a minimum of 5% of the gross income as an allowance for vacancies. Recently, this figure has been reduced because of low vacancy factors. You must decide what this figure should be in view of present and foreseeable expectancy in vacancies. An argument you will undoubtedly receive today from vendors is, why should there be *any* vacancy allowance when the building is filled and with possibly a waiting list of tenants?

Management: Larger buildings will usually be managed by contract at anything from a flat fee to 3–5% of the gross income. Some owners spend their own time actively managing their own properties, and the owners of small buildings invariably manage their own. No matter who manages the building, the time is worth money, and should not be forgotten in the debit side of the ledger.

Now, deducting all these expenses and allowances from the gross income, you arrive at the net income before financing. This is where the importance in mortgaging enters the picture. The more you save, or the less your outlay in mortgage payments, the more money you will have in your pocket as your net cash flow. As I have pointed out, your expense will include the principal payment as well as the interest.

There are just three ways to stretch the mortgage and make this item of expense thinner: lower interest rate, lengthy amortization, and smaller or no principal payments.

If you are going to assume an existing mortgage, there is nothing you can do about the rate of interest. If you are going to arrange a conventional mortgage, there is little you can do to lower the going, or current rate of interest. The only possible saving you might have is in the event of equitable financing on the part of the vendor. If the vendor will agree to accept a mortgage from you as part of your purchase price, you might be able to get a lower than conventional rate of interest from him. However, sometimes the only inducement for this as far as the vendor is concerned is a higher top price. So don't count on the possibility of saving money on the mortgage rate of interest.

The longer the period of mortgage amortization, the smaller the payments. The smaller the payments, the more cash in your pocket. The following will illustrate this; carrying charges per thousand dollars per month:

10 1/2% mortgage, interest compounded twice-yearly

Years	*Amount*
5	$21.39
10	13.37
15	10.92
20	9.84
25	9.29
30	8.99
35	8.81

Of course, the longer the amortization, the longer it will take to reduce the debt to zero. Some people aren't too concerned about long-term debt for two reasons: it produces a higher cash flow and gives the borrower a higher tax deduction due to the interest charges. Another reason is that future payments are made with cheaper dollars.

The difference between a 20- and a 30-year amortization plan in the above example amounts to $10.20 per year per thousand dollars. This means a plus or minus in your net cash surplus of $10.20 per year for every thousand dollars you have mortgaged. For example, on a $100,000 mortgage this amounts to a difference up or down of $1,020 per year to you in your hand.

The more money you owe, the more interest you pay, and the more interest you pay, the higher the figure you will show on your income tax return as a deductible item.

One thing you must remember to watch for very carefully is the *term* of the mortgage, or the length of time you have to reduce the debt using somebody else's money.

If your mortgagee is *amortized* for 30 years, with a *term* of five years, what happens in five years? The balance of the debt is due forthwith. If the mortgagee doesn't feel inclined to renew the mortgage, you have to arrange to borrow funds somewhere else. This can be costly. It involves discharging one mortgage and paying the tariff for the new one. Get the longest term you can, or at least an agreement to renew the loan at the end of the five years.

The third means of reducing the mortgage payment expense, and thereby leaving you with more cash in your hand, is by having small, or no payments to make on the principal sum. This, of course, will mean that some day you will have a day of reckoning when the principal sum becomes due at the end of the term, but in the meantime it will provide you with more cash.

Financing is the big thing. You want to obtain a reasonable return on your investment, so you will naturally want to be clear on the four steps of investments:

1. The money you have left after deducting the operating expenses and vacancy allowance from the gross income is the *net return before financing*, or income before debt charges.

2. The money you have left after deducting the mortgage interest and principal payments from this figure is the *net return*, or *cash flow*, or *net cash surplus.*
3. The figure shown after you *add* the mortgage principal payment to the net return, is the *gross return.*
4. From this figure you deduct your capital cost allowance (depreciation) if it is necessary, or desirable, to take it, and the figure you have left is what you will show on your income tax return as taxable income.

We have gone through the stage of arriving at the net return before financing, and we have discussed the mortgaging. Therefore, all the operating expenses of the building *and* the total yearly mortgage payments (interest and principal) deducted from the gross income will take us to the end of the second step, and leave a figure that represents the net return, or cash in your hand.

When the mortgage payments were made they included the principal payment, and, insofar as your net cash flow is concerned, they represent an item of expense. However, the government doesn't take the same attitude, and as far as Ottawa is concerned, the only expense you have in connection with a mortgage, for income tax purposes, is the interest you have paid. So now you have reached the end of the year with about 10% cash return on your investment, and the government says you made more than that as far as they are concerned, so you have to add the mortgage principal payments you made to the 10%, or net cash flow you have, to arrive at your *gross* return on your investment for income tax purposes.

The only way you can reduce this figure is by taking as much capital cost allowance, or depreciation yearly as the law allows, and deducting it from your gross, income tax return, figure. This final figure will be what you will use as your taxable figure on the operation for income tax purposes.

The Capital Cost Allowance

A *Building* is a term of wide range covering any structure with walls and a roof affording protection and shelter. The courts have held that the word structure includes anything of substantial size which is built up from component parts and intended to remain permanently on a permanent foundation. Portable shelters such as housing, office and other service units are also regarded as buildings if they are installed and intended to remain in a particular location.

The *Capital Cost of Property* means the full cost to the buyer and in addition to the cost of the real property includes such things as legal, accounting, engineering or other fees where they are incurred in order to acquire the property.

When purchasing an investment property, the capital cost of the building is separated from the capital cost of the land. The reason for this is very simple — land cannot be depreciated for income tax purposes — just the building.

One popular method of doing this has been to take the ratio of municipal assessment for the property and apply it as a guide. However, the income tax department will not always accept this, so it would be advisable to obtain expert advice in placing the value on the building. Also, some provinces are now using a "blended" assessment, which unfortunately does not show the separated value of land and building.

Assuming you purchased a small building and land for a total of $100,000 with a fair separated value of (1) land, $20,000, and (2) building, $80,000, the $80,000 would be your capital cost for income tax purposes, in determining your capital cost allowance, or "depreciation."

Depreciation allowances are not all the same. Some are greater than others. A common class is a "class 1" building, which is brick, blocks, etc., and has a 4% rate. Frame buildings have a 10% rate*.

In each taxable year, you are allowed, for example, in "class 1" to take an income tax deduction of a maximum of 4% of the undepreciated balance of the capital cost of the building.

The first year's allowable depreciation on the $80,000 would be $3,200. The second year, 4% of the undepreciated balance of $80,000 minus $3,200 ($76,800) and so on.

* Government rules change on the subject of depreciation, so I suggest that you check this carefully. There may be something new that would be to your advantage. This information is general in nature. If purchases were made prior to certain dates, different rules may apply and definitions may have changed. Check with your accountant for specific guidance.

If, for example, the first year showed a net return to you of $3,000 on the operation of a building, you would not take the $3,200 because you would not need it. This would leave an undepreciated balance for the second year of $77,000.

You and the government keep track of all the depreciation you have taken and on which you have not paid any income tax, because when you sell the building your day of reckoning arrives and you pay tax on it.

The tax is payable at your choice of either (1) all at once in the tax year of selling, or (2) adjusting your past returns over five years.

Depreciation cannot be taken to reduce other areas of income, as it was in the past, and it cannot be transferred to another acquired building to avoid the tax bite.

Selling the Building

The "sale price of property" means the *net* sale price after deductions of all fees and commissions paid in connection with the sale.

When you sell a depreciable property, and, subsequently, part or all of an amount owing to you in respect of the asset is reduced pursuant to a negotiated adjustment of the sale price, or pursuant to a legal obligation under a guarantee, warranty, etc., in the agreement of sale, such reduction should be taken into account in the year of sale for the purpose of calculating the amount to be included in income, or for the purpose of calculating the undepreciated capital cost of the property.

When you sell depreciable property and the proceeds of disposition include an agreement for sale, or a mortgage on land which agreement or mortgage is subsequently sold by you at a discount from its principal amount, the amount of the discount will, if the sale of the agreement or mortgage takes place in the year of disposition of the depreciable property, reduce the proceeds of disposition.

If the sale of the agreement, or mortgage, takes place subsequent to the year of disposition of the property, the discount will be deductible in computing your income for that year to the extent that the amount of the discount exceeds any capital gain (excess of proceeds over capital cost) calculated at the time of disposition.

Remember the three areas of income tax in selling an investment property:

1. The profit on the operation of the investment for all or that part of your taxable year in which you own the property.
2. The "recaptured" tax on the capital cost allowance (depreciation) taken during your ownership.
3. The capital gain tax.

When you have a situation where the land is worth more than the present use of the property as land and buildings, and it is your intention to abandon the buildings (or demolish them) in order to avoid paying a recaptured tax on depreciation, ensure that you check with the Income Tax Department first. The rules of the game here have changed.

The Purchase Agreement

When you instruct an agent to prepare an agreement of purchase and sale, the following are points in your offer that should not be overlooked. The initial part of the offer will cover the financing: deposit with offer, mortgage details, cash on closing (subject to adjustments), and any other financial consideration. Then you get into the property itself, and should note the importance of the following:

> The purchase price shall include all plant, machinery, attachments, fixtures and installations and equipment of every nature and kind, now on the subject property and which are not the exclusive property of the existing tenants, and, without limiting the generality of the foregoing, shall also include the master television antenna and all electrical and other appliances, fixtures and chattels.
>
> The vendor warrants and represents that the apartment building on the subject property comprises (   ) apartments suites and that there are no outstanding orders issued by the Fire, Police, or Health Department of the City of (   ) and/or the Municipality of (   ) requiring change in or addition or alterations to the subject property.
>
> The vendor warrants and represents that it has complied and will continue to comply with all building, zoning and other by-laws of the City of ( ) up to and including the date of closing hereinafter referred to, and that it has not committed or created a nuisance on the subject property.

The vendor warrants and represents that now and at closing, all mechanical equipment including heating, plumbing, drainage and electrical wiring systems, and elevator equipment and facilities in the subject property, will be in good working order and condition, and that the roofs of all buildings, structures and appurtenances are water-tight and that the basement is dry.

The vendor warrants and represents that Schedule "A" attached hereto sets out all pertinent information for all the tenancies in effect in respect of the subject property, and covenants and agrees that on closing, it will deliver to the purchaser the following: a proper assignment of all leases herein, all copies of all leases herein and directions to each of the tenants herein authorizing payment of rentals thereafter to the purchaser as he may direct.

The vendor covenants and agrees that on closing it will deliver to the purchaser a Statutory Declaration made by one of its officers which will contain the following and other reasonable clauses that may be required by the purchaser:

1. That the leases referred to in Schedule "A" to the agreement of purchase and sale herein dated ( ) are valid, binding and enforceable in accordance with the terms thereof:
2. That there are no disputes between the vendor, as landlord, and the said tenants with respect to any matter arising out of the tenancies.
3. That all rent has been paid to the ( ) day of ( ) and that there are no prepayments or rent beyond the current monthly rental. (Note: if there are, this will be settled in the adjustments on closing and credited to the purchaser).
4. That none of the said leases have been assigned nor have any of the tenants sublet the premises leased to them:
5. That the leases have not been amended, changed or varied in any way whatsoever, and
6. That there are no other tenancy arrangements affecting the subject property other than those set out in the said Schedule "A" to the Agreement of Purchase and Sale dated ( ).

The vendor shall within fifteen (15) days after acceptance supply to the purchaser all plans, specifications, sketches, drawings and up-to-date surveys of the subject property.

On closing, the vendor shall assign to the purchaser all contracts and the benefit thereof, made by it in respect of the subject property, and the vendor shall further deliver all licenses, agreements, books, records and accounts and, without limiting the generality of the foregoing, all other documents, information and papers in the possession of the vendor relating to the subject property.

The vendor warrants and represents that the gross income received by it for the fiscal year ending ( ) was ( ).

The within offer and the obligation of the purchaser to complete the within transaction is entirely conditional upon verification by the vendor to the purchaser of the fulfillment of all conditions, warranties and representations herein set out.

Provided the title is good and free from all encumbrances except as aforesaid: The purchaser is not to call for the production of any title deed, abstract or other evidence of title except as are in the possession of the vendor. The purchaser is to be allowed until closing to investigate the title at his own expense. If within that time any valid objection to title is made in writing to the vendor which the vendor shall be unable or unwilling to remove and which the purchaser will not waive, this agreement shall, notwithstanding any intermediate acts or negotiations in respect of such objections, be null and void and the deposit shall be returned to the purchaser without interest or deductions. Save as to any valid objection so made within such time, the purchaser shall be conclusively deemed to have accepted the title of the vendor to the subject property.

The sale of the subject property shall be made in accordance with the *Bulk Sales Act* (Province) and the *Retail Sales Act* (Province) and the vendor hereby, covenants, undertakes and agrees to comply with all the provisions thereof and to pay all taxes and costs in connection therewith.

This offer is to be accepted by ( ) otherwise void: and sale is to be completed on or before the ( ) on which date possession is to be given to the purchaser subject to the tenancies herein set out, and the purchase to be entitled to the receipt of the rents and profits thereafter.

This offer, when accepted, shall constitute a binding contract of purchase and sale and time in all respects shall be the essence of this agreement.

Until completion of sale, all buildings and equipment on the subject property shall be and remain at the risk of the vendor until closing and the vendor will hold all policies of insurance affected on the subject property and the proceeds thereof in trust for the parties hereto, as their interests may appear. In the event of damage to the subject buildings and equipment before the completion of this transaction, the purchaser shall have the right to elect to take such proceeds and complete the purchase, or cancel this agreement whereupon the purchaser shall be entitled to return without interest of all monies theretofore paid on account of this purchase without deductions.

Unearned fire insurance premiums, mortgage interest, rentals, taxes, fuel, water rates and heating to be apportioned and allowed to date of completion of sale.

Deed or transfer and assignment of leases to be prepared at the expense of the vendor, and mortgage at the expense of the purchaser.

Any tender of documents or money hereunder may be made upon the vendor at (address) and upon the purchaser at (address) or any party acting for him or it and money may be tendered by negotiable cheque certified by a chartered bank or trust company in the City of ( ).

The offer and its acceptance to be read with all changes of gender or number required by the context.

Dated at ( ) this ( ).

Witness:

....

Purchaser

Good luck!

80

THE BUSINESS FRANCHISE (AND RISKS)

Franchising ads are currently appearing in large numbers throughout the country. While most of them offer legitimate business opportunities, some of them do not.

Be wary of advertisements which promise "get rich quick" schemes, with little effort and no risk — they can frequently lead to disappointment and sometimes to financial disaster.

A good explanation of "franchise" is: A system used by a company (franchisor) which grants to others (franchisees) the right and license (franchise) to market a product or service and engage in a business developed by it under the franchisor's trade names, trademarks, service marks, know-how and method of doing business.

One of the reasons for the recent enormous growth in franchising is that it has caught the imagination of the small investor and provides him the opportunity to become self-employed. For instance, the risk of failure is reduced when the franchisee starts in business under a successful corporate name and trademark and when he receives helpful training and management assistance form experience personnel of the franchisor.

However, franchising arrangements do not always produce happy results. Franchising does not guarantee success as some promoters would have you believe. Franchising arrangements can produce severe financial loss, and on occasion have caused franchisees to lose their life savings.

Some of these franchisees have experienced disappointment and frustration by falling victim to a deceptive franchising scheme. The rapid growth of franchising has attracted a number of unprincipled operators who seek to take advantage of anyone they can. Their methods of operation and techniques are too varied to detail here but their objectives are the same, i.e., to take your money and give little or nothing in return. After the unscrupulous promoter receives payment he doesn't care whether you succeed or fail. In fact, contrary to what he tells you, you may never see him again.

This letter illustrates an investor's frustration after being bilked by one of these arrangements:

"My husband and I invested $15,000 of borrowed money in a restaurant franchise — my husband is working 14 hours a day, seven days a week for $50 per week. I work eight hours a day for no salary. There is not enough money for my salary. The spot just doesn't bring in enough people. The franchisor refuses to take the business back and wants a royalty which makes it hard to sell the business to anyone else. He has you invest $6,000 to $10,500 as an initial investment which he pockets."

In this instance, in addition to grossly understating the earning potential of the franchise, the franchisor misrepresented nearly every other aspect of the franchise agreement. The cost of the franchise was much higher than represented and discount supplies were not available. Moreover, the franchise was not a nationally known chain and the franchisor did not provide planned promotions or helpful training and supervision that he promised. This is a sample of the type of franchise deceptions in existence today.

Because the decision to become a franchisee may involve the investment of a lifetime of savings and effort, it is recommended that prospective franchisees carefully examine all aspects of a franchise agreement before becoming legally involved. By taking this precaution, the likelihood of financial disaster can be greatly reduced. To help evaluate a franchise opportunity it is suggested that you view the proposal in the light of the following points:

Who Is the Franchisor?

If the franchisor is well-known, has a good reputation, and has a successful franchising operation, you can naturally proceed with greater confidence than if little is known about him. You should find out everything you can about the operation including:

1. Number of years it has been in existence.
2. Whether the franchisor has all the successful franchisees he claims.
3. Whether he has a reputation for honesty and fair dealing with his franchise holders.

Personal contact with franchisees is an excellent way to learn about the franchisor. Obtain the names and addresses of a representative number of franchisees in the particular area in which you are interested, travel to see them, and learn about all aspects of the operation.

In addition to gaining valuable information about the franchisor, it will provide you with an opportunity to view samples of the franchise products or services, equipment, advertising material, etc., and to obtain profit data and other pertinent information about the operation.

Beware of the franchisor who will not freely give you the names and addresses of his franchisees. The financial standing and business reputation of the franchisor should be of utmost interest to you. Consult the Better Business Bureau and Dun and Bradstreet.

Sometimes, a dishonest promoter will use a franchise name and trademark deceptively similar to that of a well-known franchisor. Be certain you deal with the particular franchise organization you are interested in and that the individual representing this franchise has authority to act on his behalf.

Be skeptical of franchisors whose major activity is the sales of franchises and whose profit is primarily derived from these sales or from the sale of franchise equipment or services. This may be the tip-off to an unscrupulous operator.

Remember, the more you learn about the franchisor and his operation, before making a firm decision, the less likely you will become involved in a situation that you might later regret.

The Franchise Commodity

You should determine the length of time the commodity or service has been marketed and if it is a successful promotion. Is it a proven product or service, and not a gimmick?

Decide whether you are genuinely interested in selling the commodity or service. Be skeptical of items which are untested in the marketplace and are fads. For future market potential decide whether the commodity or service is a staple, luxury, or fad item.

If a product or service is involved, be certain it is safe, that it meets existing quality standards, and there are no restrictions upon its use. Is the product or service protected by a patent or has it liability insurance? Will the same protection be afforded to you as the franchisee?

If the product is to be manufactured by someone other than yourself, identify the manufacturer and learn how your cost for the item will be established. If a guarantee is involved, determine your responsibilities and obligations as the franchisee.

Under the franchise agreement, will you be compelled to sell any new products or services which may be introduced by the franchisor after you have opened the business? Will you be permitted under the agreement to sell products and services other than the franchise commodities at some future date?

The Franchise Cost

Find out the total cost of the franchise. The franchise promotion may only refer to the cash outlay needed to purchase the franchise, with no mention made that it is only a down payment and other charges and assessments may be levied against you to operate the franchise.

If other monies are involved, how is the balance to be financed? (Interest rates will be important to you.) Clearly establish what the down payment is purchasing. Is it a franchise fee? Or does it purchase any other equity such as the building, etc.?

Where do you purchase equipment and fixtures necessary for opening the business? If these are purchased through the franchisor, are his prices comparable with competitive prices on the open market?

Franchisors often attempt to secure income on a continuing basis through the sale of supplies to their franchisees. If this is part of the proposed agreement, how will the price of these supplies be established? What assurance do you have that the prices will be reasonable or competitive? Does the franchise agreement prohibit you from purchasing these supplies from a source at a lower price?

Another method franchisors use to charge franchisees on a continuing basis is the assessment of royalties based upon a percentage of gross sales. Be sure these royalties are not out of line with the sales volume and expected net profits for the franchise. Don't overlook the possibility that franchisors often assess franchisees an additional percentage of gross sales to cover the franchisee's share of advertising cost.

Think about franchise costs in the light of your financial position. Consider the additional funds and operating capital you will need to get the business underway and to sustain it during the months when profits will be small and expenses high.

What Profits Can Be Expected?

Many franchise arrangements provide excellent income-producing opportunities. Not all franchises, however, yield the fantastic profit sometimes promised. Many produce less profits than represented by franchise promoters. When deceptive promotions are involved, debts rather than profits are the usual rule.

Since "profits" are the overriding motive for entering a franchise business, don't take the promoter's word for granted. Verify the profits for accuracy. Ask to see certified profit figures of franchisees who operate on a level of activity that you expect to operate. Use personal contact with franchisees, quiz them regarding their financial rewards and evaluate the profit figures and comments of these individuals in the light of the territory and size of operation you have under consideration.

Training and Management Assistance

Most franchisors claim to train their franchisees. The type and extent of training varies from one day's indoctrination to a more lengthy training program. When good training is provided the franchisee enjoys better prospects for survival and prosperity.

Inexperience and lack of training can produce disappointing results. Clearly understand the specific nature of the training.

1. Will the training include more than a manual of instructions or hearing a few lectures?

2. What is the length of the training and where do you go to receive it?
3. Who will pay the expenses during the training period?
4. Will the training include an opportunity to observe and work with a successful franchisee for a period of time?
5. Do you believe that after taking the training you will be capable to operate the franchise successfully?

Will the franchisor furnish management assistance after the business is established? Spell this out specifically in your contract. If advertising aid is promised, will it be in the form of handbills, brochures, signs, radio, TV, or newspaper advertising, etc.? If you are required to furnish money for a franchisor-sponsored advertising program what specific advertising benefits can you anticipate and at what dollar cost?

Some franchisors promise management assistance with periodic visits by the supervisory personnel of the franchisor. Find out the specific nature of assistance, the frequency of the visits, and whether they will be available in times of crisis or when unusual problems arise.

The Franchise Territory

This is a critical factor to consider in evaluating a prospective venture. Here are some good questions to ask:

1. What specific territory is being offered?
2. Is it clearly defined?
3. What is its potential?
4. Do you have a choice of territories?
5. What competition will you meet in marketing the commodity today? How about five years from now?
6. Has a market survey been made of the proposed area?
7. If so, who prepared it? Ask for a copy and read it carefully.
8. What assurance do you have that your territory is an exclusive one?
9. Would you be protected from the possibility of the franchisor selling additional franchises in your territory at a later date?

10. Does the contract prevent you from opening additional outlets in your territory, or even another territory, at a future date?
11. Has the specific business site within the territory been selected? If not, how will this be decided?

Termination, Transfer and Renewal of the Franchise Agreement

Because some termination provisions can cause unexpected and sometimes severe financial loss to a franchisee, give careful consideration to this aspect of the agreement.

Some franchise agreements provide that at the end of or during the contract term if, in the opinion of the franchisor, certain conditions have not been met, the franchisor has the absolute right to terminate the agreement.

The contract generally provides the franchisor with an option to repurchase the franchise. If the franchisor should terminate the agreement under these circumstances and if the contract does not provide a means whereby a fair market price for the franchise can be established, the franchisor could repurchase the business at a low and unfair price.

On occasion, franchisors include a provision in the agreement that the repurchase price will not exceed the original franchise fee. This means that a franchisee could spend considerable effort and money building the business and be faced with selling it back to the franchisor at the price he paid for it.

Understand the conditions under which the agreement could be terminated and your rights in the event of termination. Does the contract extend to the franchisor the right of cancellation for almost any reason or must there be "good cause?" Beware of contracts which, under the threat of cancellation, impose unreasonable obligations such as minimum monthly purchase of goods or services from the franchisor or unrealistic sales quotas.

Keep these points in mind:

1. How would the value of the franchise be determined in the event of termination?
2. Under what circumstances could you terminate the agreement and what would it cost you?
3. Does the contract contain a restrictive covenant which would

prohibit you from engaging in a competitive business in the franchise territory in the event termination occurs?

4. Have a clear understanding of contract provisions dealing with your ability to transfer, sell, or renew the franchise. What would happen to the franchise in the event of your death?

Some reputable franchisors have established fair and permanent relationships with their franchisees and have provided for an arbitration clause which allows for a fair evaluation of the franchisee's contribution in the event of termination. Under this agreement the franchisee would recoup his initial investment as well as a profit on whatever business he generated.

Franchise with a "Name" Personality

When a "name" personality is connected with a franchise, consider the degree of participation the "name" gives to the business. Is he a figurehead with no capital investment in the enterprise? Will he make contributions of time and effort to promote the business? What guarantees do you have that he will make appearances at your business? Does the personality have a name of lasting value in identifying your franchise with the consuming public? How sound is the franchise operation without the prominent name?

Promoters Selling Distributorships

Be wary of promoters who primarily sell distributorships for some "new wonder product." Exaggerated income promises are common in these promotions. According to the promotion plan, the distributors solicit sub-distributors and salesmen to sell the product door-to-door. The idea is that a large portion of the distributor's profits will be received from a percentage of his sub-distributor's sales. Unfortunately, some distributors and sub-distributors find, to their mutual distress after making sizable investments of money, time and effort, that there is little profit and they are holding a large stock of unsaleable products.

Route Servicing Promotion

Be alert for deceptive route servicing promotions. These promotions are characterized by misleading representations (frequently appearing in newspaper want ads) concerning exaggerated profits and the availability of quality routes.

If equipment, such as vending machines, is to be purchased in connection with the promotion, find out if it is poorly made and highly priced. Compare the equipment and prices with those of reputable manufacturers. Carefully check out the validity of all statements made in these promotions, and remember that promoters promising assistance in locating quality routes after the contract is signed seldom deliver.

Qualifications as a Franchisee

Before you sign any franchise agreement, determine if your personal traits qualify you to be a franchisee.

Are you genuinely enthusiastic about the franchise plan? Are you physically and emotionally equipped to do the work necessary to develop a successful enterprise?

Franchisees can only expect to succeed by hard work and full-time effort. Franchise plans based on part-time work generally produce only modest results for the franchisee.

Summary

Don't be rushed into signing a contract or any other documents relating to a franchise promotion. Be wary of pressure for an immediate contract closing. Don't make any deposits or down payments unless you are absolutely certain you are going ahead with the franchise agreement. Remember, reputable firms don't engage in high-pressure tactics.

Find out all you can about the franchise. Resolve all areas of uncertainty before making a decision. Ask the franchisor for names and addresses of his franchisees. No reputable franchisor will object to giving you this information. Personally contact a number of the franchisees and discuss all aspects of the operation with them. Has the franchisor fulfilled all his promises and met his contractual obligations with them?

Check with your Better Business Bureau. Ask for a business responsibility report on the franchisor-promoter.

Be certain that all terms of the agreement are set forth in a written contract which is not a handicap on you and not weighted unfairly in favor of the franchisor.

Consult a lawyer and have him review all aspects of the agreement before you sign the contract or any papers relating to the franchise. It may turn out to be a very sound investment!

81

SPECULATION

A good real estate speculator is one who knows how to make money in real estate. This is the broadest and simplest definition. A dictionary defines a speculator as one who makes an investment or is engaged in a commercial operation that involves risk of loss with an implication of rashness. The key ideas here are the risk of loss and the implication of rashness.

The public perceives a real estate speculator as one who takes an unfair advantage of a situation or of someone, in order to make a fast dollar. To me it describes an opportunistic scamster rather than a true speculator. The same dictionary defines the world *speculate.* It means to form a theory or conjectural opinion bout something.

The true real estate speculator is one who has a theory or a conjecture regarding a piece of property. He will risk his capital, or gamble if you will, that his theory is correct and that the uncertainties of the venture will fall in his favor. If he is correct he stands to gain a handsome profit; if he is wrong, he stands to lose a sizable capital investment.

For example, a speculator will buy a piece of land theorizing that if he can successfully change the zoning from agricultural to industrial uses, the value of the land will more than double. He spends his money and tries to rezone, but finds that with the present town council there is no hope of such a change for at least 25 years. His speculation has failed but he still owns agricultural land. On the other hand, after two years he may succeed in getting the area rezoned, and he can then sell the property at a substantial profit; his effort and theory have been rewarded.

Another example is the speculator who buys a house that has been poorly maintained. His theory is that if he can fix it up, the improvements will substantially increase the value of the property. He risks his capital and spends money to improve the house. When he is ready, the house goes on the market. But the interest rate has just gone up and the market is dead. He can't sell his house for a profit. His theory and the risk of uncertainty make him a loser. On the other hand, if the interest rate dropped and house prices started to soar, he would make a profit and his speculation would be successful.

The first requisite in joining the ranks of these successful money-makers is a thorough knowledge of market conditions in a particular aspect of real estate. A land speculator usually sticks with land, buying and selling it, because he knows all about it. It is the same in speculating with housing, commercial properties and leases.

Review chapter 13, "Leverage," fully understand it, and then specialize. Not only that, but specialize in one particular urban area or county. This will require a good deal of homework on your part, because you will want to be very, very familiar with the market. Nobody is going to hand you handsome real estate profits on a plate.

A sound way to start is in housing, and not only that, but a particular type of house. Take a six-room brick detached bungalow for example. In the area selected, drive along every street and make a physical note of every six-room bungalow with a "for sale" sign on it. Inspect them. Compare them. Obtain facts on recent selling prices. You will soon discover that you are somewhat of an expert on the market value of six-room bungalows.

You will learn to spot the plus and minus features, and what they are worth. The attached double or single garage or carport, the extra bathrooms and washrooms, the finishing in the basements, the fireplaces, the condition of the buildings and the grounds, and a very important aspect, the reason for selling.

You will spot good, bad, tough and easy financing.

When you have spent a good solid month or so doing your homework, you will be ready to make your first offer. Before doing this, review chapter 67, "Don't Be Afraid to Make an Offer."

It is important to establish good rapport with a local lawyer *before* you are ready to proceed. Tell him of your plans. You will undoubtedly find that he will have some good advice for you, and perhaps he may even have access to a bit of cash for that extra few thousand you may need for an extra mortgage to swing a deal. Ensure that he sees all your offers *before* you sign them; he may show you how you can improve the offers to your advantage, and will certainly legally protect you.

It is also important to have a good rapport with an aggressive real estate salesman. Tell him also of your plans. You will find that some salesmen will not pay much attention to you when they discover you are speculating because they simply won't want to bother presenting "cheap offers," but don't let this deter you. By persistent viewing and meeting salesmen, you will find one who won't mind working to flush out the good buys for you. Once you have made the first purchase through an agent, you can be sure he will stick with you like glue, because he will want more. Especially if there is a chance that he will get a piece of the action in selling your hot buy.

In searching for a profit-making property, the first advice I would offer is to *check the zoning!* This cannot be stressed too strongly.

Do not assume, for example, that because there happens to be an occupied basement apartment in a house that it is a legal undertaking. It may be contrary to local municipal zoning by-laws and this type of zoning trap can be found in many residential areas. A homeowner could be receiving rent from an illegal basement apartment for years, even unaware that it is not right, and be bothered by no one. No one, that is, until a snoopy neighbor blows the whistle on the operation with a resulting visit from a zoning inspector. Game over. Income stopped. If you spot it, and are interested in the house, quietly check the zoning for the street — you could save yourself money and a headache.

It is possible to sometimes obtain a bonus by knowing the zoning. A house on a street zoned commercial, for instance. All sorts of possibilities here. Or one with a lot large enough that when joined with a next-door property might produce three or four building lots.

Always remember that when house speculating, the house will be empty when you offer it for sale. This means that the flooring must be inspected carefully. Some houses have carpeting laid over plywood flooring, and if the vendor would decide to take the carpeting, legally or not, you will be left with the prospect of replacing it because a plywood floor is just not attractive to buyers. If the floor is hardwood and bare, it would be advisable to have it sanded and varnished.

The house you are selling must be made to look as attractive as possible to prospective buyers, which will require a very careful inspection of its interior. Remember to view it mindful of the fact that you will be selling it empty. Furniture can cover many flaws and unattractive features that will appear as soon as the vendor moves out.

An attractive setting is also an asset. Trees are priceless, especially if well placed.

The front door and verandah must be made to look attractive to buyers, because this is the first impression they will receive of the building when approaching it for inspection.

It has been said that there are three things to look for in speculation; Location, location, location. Near transportation and schools, for example, and know where they are when showing your house.

Don't bother looking at houses that have been all spruced up. Someone else has done this, and they have upped the price. This is what you are supposed to do. Pretty soon you will know what is and what isn't a good buy.

Don't try to become wealthy overnight with your first purchase. This one will be your trial run, getting your feet wet. Look for a modest profit. When successfully completing your trial run, review everything about the operation and improve your performance for the next deal. After half a dozen you will be amazed at how much you know about house speculation.

More Details

Some people view a speculator as one who hovers like a vulture over a poor old widow ready to pounce on her with a pittance for her cherished nest of memories and force her into the old folk's home.

I suppose it has happened, but in my memory the only "poor old widow" I wanted to move ended up getting a lot more than her house was worth.

The dear old soul was the last hold-out on the street, and my principals had to cough up because they had to have the place. I think she's still laughing all the way to the bank.

Aside from viewing a speculator as a money-grabber of the first order, there are speculators who do a municipality a big favor. These are the ones who buy run-down homes, renovate them and put them back on the market.

If you see this happening on your street, go out there and thank the guy for improving your neighborhood. The municipality should also thank him, because his work will produce higher taxes from the house for perhaps the next 50 years. And the lucky municipality did nothing to earn this increased revenue.

How does a speculator find all his hot buys? Very simple; he constantly reads newspaper ads, constantly calls dozens of real estate agents, constantly looks and looks at houses, and makes offers.

My, how he makes offers. He figures that if he makes enough of them, even at his price, some of them have to be accepted. And they are.

I knew an agent who had a stack of signed, blank offers in his briefcase. He knew his buyer so well that he would just fill in the blanks and present the offers. Most of the time he got thrown out of the house but he nailed one or two a month, and I might add that he was one hell of a hard worker.

If you think you would like to try your hand at this game, make improvements to a run-down neighborhood and make money doing it, here are some guidelines.

a) If you are not a Mr. Fixit yourself, you should get a partner who is. One who knows what the inside of a hardware store looks like and knows his way around a lumberyard. And one who also has the kind of money you have.
b) Pick out a part of town that has a good variety of modest homes, and inspect listings for at least a month. Become an expert in property values before you even consider making your first offer.
c) Four things must be looked at first. The plumbing, heating plant, wiring and the roof. If you are lucky and find a modest house with all these in good shape, you may be able to improve the place considerably with nothing more than a cosmetic facelift.
d) Become an expert in the different methods of financing. Get to know a couple of mortgage brokers and pick their brains. Having a vendor help by taking back a mortgage or two would be even better.

e) Don't put more cash into a house than 15% of the purchase price.
f) Don't spend more than 5% of the purchase price fixing it up. If you have to, it is too shot to bother with, so go on to another one.
g) Sell it for a modest and fair profit. Remember, if you do this just three times a year at a profit of $5,000 each, you will add $15,000 to your yearly income. And you just might find yourself on the road to something bigger.

When you have the title deed, move quickly to smarten the place up, sell it, and go on to the next one. Turnover is what it's all about, so don't waste any time.

On the other hand, I knew a speculator who didn't like turning them over and ended up owning 42 houses. But he was something else!

New Homes

It has been said speculators are lining up to make a mint out of the new home business.

The idea is to find a reasonably priced new-home subdivision, buy a house before it is built and sell the purchase agreement to another buyer for a fat profit. Sounds easy, huh? Well, just slow down and consider a few things before getting all fired up to make your pile. There are a few guidelines I can offer that may save a few headaches.

The first thing I would consider is the reputation of the builder. Now we all know some builders, whatever their good intentions, have been known to cause heartaches for buyers through non-completion of the home, or a misunderstanding of the mortgage terms.

A builder's track record is easy to check. Just find out where he has built during the last couple of years and ask some of his buyers if they were satisfied with the deals. Did he complete the house on time? Good workmanship? Mortgage and other financial commitments okay?

Fine, the builder is one of the good ones. Now you have to do some homework to justify the selling price with the location; this is most important. Did a comparable new house recently sell for the same price 10 miles closer to the subway? You are looking for real value that can increase in price in six months and still look like a good deal to someone else.

How much deposit is required with the deal, and how long is your money going to be tied up until the closing date? And you had better ensure the closing date is stretched just about as far as it can go because you have to find a buyer.

As long as there are unsold homes in your area, no one is going to pay you more for your paper than the builder can offer. So you sweat it out hoping the whole subdivision is sold quickly. Then your chances rise.

If you agree to purchase the house in your name personally, cannot find the buyer to provide your profit and decide to forget the whole thing, you could be in for a mess of trouble. Don't assume the builder will just keep your deposit and say, "sure, Jack, that's okay." It's not okay.

The builder could sue you under your contract and haul you into court. If the judge decides it is a binding contract and the builder gets a judgment against you forcing you to close, you will close.

However, before the builder takes such action, he will probably check you out very carefully to ensure you do have the means to close. There would not be much sense bothering about it if your only tangible assets aside from your down payment proved to be next to nil.

So you see, there is a bit of responsibility attached to all this. It has been financially successful for some, and a disaster for others.

Commercial Building Speculation

Here are five reasons why a buyer may speculate in commercial property:

1. Present income on the property is obviously too low, the leases are about ready to expire, and the situation could be drastically improved.
2. The building is in terrible condition though structurally sound, and could be renovated to attract higher income. But before you get into a deal like this, have an expert give you an estimate of renovating costs. When you have added this to the proposed

purchase price of the building, have a rental appraisal done to see if it is profitable.

3. The land under the building is obviously worth more than the entire parcel. You will need expert advice on this and be prepared to pay for it. Sometimes you're not as clever as you think you are.
4. There is a good chance the area zoning could be changed to create an inflated price on the land.
5. It can be purchased for a song. There are several reasons for a seller wanting a deal in a hurry. Pending foreclosure or power of sale, partnership disagreement, moving out of town, closing another deal, getting rid of creditors. Always ask why the owner is selling.

As for the commercial building itself, there is a limit to the income it will realize and this is the true determining factor in the value of any such property. If its use is to remain constant. *Income less expenses leaves you what?* That's the question.

Don't be afraid to make an offer if you know it will be on the low side.

The agent will do all the legwork for you and if he fails you have lost nothing. If he succeeds you are a winner, and believe me when I say I have seen some incredible offers accepted!

Putting one's extra dollars to work speculating in real estate can be very rewarding, but remember that I said "extra" dollars.

Don't speculate with money you can't afford to lose — it hurts!

Land Speculation

How much income can one realize from a vacant parcel of land? Other than leasing it to a local farmer, not much. Keep this in mind when looking at the prospects of making it with land. Mortgage payments will have to be maintained and municipal taxes paid.

One good method of land speculation is to obtain an option on the property for a minimum period of one year. The cash consideration given to the owner of the land will be about 1 percent of the agreed price in the option. Then the would-be purchaser scrambles around during the option period trying to find a buyer at a higher price, or arrange for rezoning of property to greater density use, creating a higher value. If successful, money is made, and in some cases, a great deal of it. If not successful, but close to something promising, it may be possible to obtain an extension of the option for a further cash consideration. If all fails, a small loss is sustained and a lesson learned.

If the speculator has a property optioned for $100,000 and put up $1,000 cash, he is really out of pocket just the $1,000 plus the interest earning power of the thousand dollars. This is much better than sinking a large chunk of money into such a scheme by buying the property outright.

The truly big winners in land appreciation are the farmers on the fringes of the urban areas, the men who live on the old homestead and work the land. If you or I obtained a piece of land for $30,000 and someone came along and offered us $40,000 for it soon afterward, we would probably take it. This purchaser in turn would probably behave in the same manner, so that over the years the value of the land could appreciate tremendously, with the profits spread through several hands. The farmer, on the other hand, living and working with the land, possibly with his sons, resists initial bids on the land, but as time goes by and his land value soars, possibly when he is ready to retire, he would realize the entire appreciation built up over the years.

If you intend to speculate with land, be very careful not to get in too deep and do it preferably on an option basis. Review chapter 64, "Optioning Property."

In searching for land, get to the *local* brokers, preferably ones who have been working your chosen area for a few years. They know local market values, trends, and can offer helpful advice. Also, subscribe to local weekly newspapers and read the ads carefully.

Lease Speculation

Very basic. Obtain a lease in a good location for less than the going rate, and sublet the property for a higher figure.

This one requires particular caution. Be sure you fully understand all the clauses in the lease, especially restrictive clauses. When assured that your lease (and zoning) allows you to sublet, be sure it will allow you to sublet to the type of tenant you have in mind. And be sure you have the tenant, or you will be paying the rent for nothing.

Also, talk this over with a good insurance agent to be quite clear about who pays what, and ensure your sub-tenant is properly insured. Remember, in a lease, in the event of fire or damage, the rent goes on and must be paid. You are the one who pays it to the lessor regardless of whether you get it from your sub-tenant or not, so ensure the sub-tenant is a reliable one.

Little or Nothing Down

There has been a lot of talk about making money in real estate with little or no money down. Getting something for nothing sounds good to me, but in reality it rarely, if ever, happens.

I remember seeing ads in the paper — come to our seminar and we will teach you how to get rich fast in real estate with no money down. Soon afterwards real estate offices started getting calls. One man I spoke to had never owned a home, had no equity, had no job, and wanted to buy a home with no money down because the guy from California who gave the free introductory seminar said it was easy and it made him rich. The free seminar was the bait and hook, but if you wanted the secret you had to pay $600. His ideas didn't work in California, so he thought perhaps Canadians, being intelligent as they are, would see that it was easy to get something for nothing.

In reality there is no secret about how such things are financially engineered. In practice, however, it would be an amazing thing to find an astute vendor willing to sponsor such a scheme.

The most popular way to do it is use a property owner's money to buy his property. In other words, find an owner willing to take back a mortgage for a good slice of the purchase price.

If an owner wants $100,000 for his property, offer him $110,000. Agree to put up a couple of thousand, arrange a first for $50,000 and have him hold the balance of the second mortgage.

You point out he gets the $50,000 plus your deposit, and has an income from his mortgage. And, after all, he is receiving a bonus of $10,000 in the deal.

The buyer would have to be very well connected in the mortgage business to get a lender to put up 50 grand knowing the borrower has only two thousand in the deal. But no doubt it has been done.

Ideally, you are supposed to find an income property with enough income to pay all the expenses, including full mortgaging. Try to find it — that's the problem. Otherwise, you have to come up with monthly carrying charges yourself.

Another way is to get an option on property for a nominal sum. This is simply an agreement that gives a buyer the right to purchase the property with a time limit at an agreed price. The property owner keeps the front money whether the buyer goes through with the deal or not.

Then the buyer shops around for another buyer who will buy the property at a higher price. The one with the option simply sells his rights to the option and buyer number two closes the deal.

The first buyer does it this way to avoid paying land-transfer taxes and all those closing costs. If he doesn't find buyer number two, he drops the whole thing and kisses his option money goodbye. This also has been done successfully.

Syndication

A real estate syndicate is a group of individuals financially committed to pulling off a big deal and making, it hopes, plenty of money.

However, there is one member of the syndicate who usually stands to make more out of the deal than the others. An example would be a real estate broker who has an apartment building or perhaps an office building listed for sale.

If the selling commission is to be, say, $50,000, the broker will invite investors to form a corporate body with him and buy the building. The broker puts up no cash in the deal. His share is figured to be worth $50,000, the selling commission, which is thrown into the deal. Other investors go into the deal with $50,000, and everybody has an equal share.

The broker then has an agreement with the syndicate whereby he will be authorized to do two things: manage the building, and when an agreed-upon time comes to sell, he is to be the listing and selling agent.

Managing the building provides an assured, steady, year-round income for the broker's separate corporate entity he has set up to manage property. Listing and selling the property, of course, gives the broker another fifty grand or more. And he gets his share of the building's profit. A nice piece of business!

There is also plenty of room out there for an enterprising individual to form a syndicate and make a pile. To do it, one must be as sharp as a tack about the value of rental properties — preferably commercial buildings, because they don't come under any government rent control legislation.

Months will be spent poring over brokers' listings and inspecting properties. When the wheeler-dealer is ready to set himself up for his windfall, he knows as much, or more, about commercial rental values than the brokers who have been educating him.

To other investors, the No. 1 man argues successfully that his expertise is worth plenty, so he often gets in for nothing. His knowledge and management ability is arguably worth an equal share in the venture. Then, when the property is acquired, he sets himself up as the business manager for the syndicate. For a fee naturally.

Once the first venture is well under way and everything and everybody is in place, our man goes on to another one.

No money down for him, and more business management fees pouring in. In a couple of years he could be a really big operator with a first-class reputation. Which makes it easier to raise investment capital and keep the whole thing rolling.

There are other ways for a syndicate to make money in real estate. Assembling land, for example, with similar basic rules for the front man in the operation. It has been argued that demolishing homes to make room for other buildings takes housing out of the marketplace. My own experience can dispute this with a loud roar.

There is a park in Toronto across Yonge Street from the Rosedale subway station. Overlooking that park, years ago, were 52 homes of all types. Semis, detached, small apartment buildings . . . there was even a row of 17 attached frame homes built on a wooden street supported by piles called Northview Terrace.

They are all gone. I negotiated the purchase and sale of every one of them.

And what is there replacing those 52 homes? Two towers containing hundreds of residential suites, that's what. Not a bad ratio.

The City of Toronto sure got its money's worth in that deal!

If you should aspire to becoming wealthy through real estate syndication, stop dreaming, put your feet on the ground and locate the following:

a) Half a dozen people with similar ideas you can trust. One with your kind of money.
b) Determine just what type of investment property would be most suitable for *all* of you. Not just you.
c) Carefully select your areas for searching and inspecting properties. This is going to take time, separating the wheat from the chaff, as they say. Stumble in your first venture and nobody will talk to you again.
d) A friend and ally can be a knowledgeable real estate agent working in your selected areas. Stick with him. The agent will know that if you are pleased with your first deal, he will stand a good chance of reaping steady income from your group.
e) And don't forget a sharp real estate lawyer. One who knows your game. Shop around, you'll find one.

Oh yes, and you will need an accountant with a sharp pencil!

General

When buying and selling, always try to find the property where the vendor will help with the purchase by lending you part of the purchase price by way of a mortgage. Private mortgages can often be secured at lower than going rates, and repayment privileges can be more generous, such as repaying the mortgage before maturity without bonus or penalty. Sometimes mortgages can get in the way — a purchaser might want to buy for cash, and it is nice to know that any mortgages can be discharged without additional costs.

Don't be greedy. Anticipate a reasonable return on your investment.

Ensure there are no outstanding hydro or municipal work orders registered against property that interests you.

Take a good hard look at the property. What has to be done to improve it? Why are they selling? Who would buy it from you? Structure the financing to make it as easy as possible for a buyer to swing the deal.

Speculating is an interesting, educational and profitable way to spend your time and money, but it requires a very thorough knowledge of property, areas, zoning, financing and the *market.*

Speculate with your "extra dollars," not the ones needed for necessities or bills that must be paid.

82

EXTRA COSTS IN OWNING A HOME

The way some people talk, hoping to own your own house nowadays is like hoping to win the Irish Sweepstakes or break the bank at Monte Carlo.

Which leads me to the question: "Just how much does one need to buy a house?"

Once you get past the down payment and closing costs, you come to the most important part of it — carrying costs.

The first thing to look at is the monthly cost of the mortgage. But don't stop there.

We have municipal taxes. This cost is often added to the mortgage payment, and it is a good thing to do it this way. Otherwise an owner might procrastinate about paying taxes and find himself facing a large, demanding bill he may not be able to pay.

Money has a way of dribbling out of your hands, so if your mortgage payment does not include taxes, open a special bank account to be used only for household expenses. The tax bill is just for openers.

The place has to be heated, so ensure the furnace is in good shape when buying. Nothing worse than to have to pay for a new furnace a few months after moving in.

Hydro takes a bit, and won't wait for its money like a tax office. You don't pay, you get cut off.

So just off the top, in addition to the mortgage you figure you can carry, you are faced with taxes, heat and hydro. Be sure you know what these items will cost.

A fair yearly example would be: Taxes, $2,500; Heat, $800; Hydro, $700. Total, $4000, which means $333 each month on top of your mortgage. Still with me?

How about the roof? One day you are walking around the house after a storm and you see a couple of shingles lying on the ground. This could mean the start of a $1,200 bill for a new roof. So check it and its guarantee.

And remember, roofers are not prone to wait for payment either. They want it now.

Plumbing. Oh boy, this can be grief. Take a good look at it. Ditto for wiring. Any idea what plumbers and electricians charge today?

To ensure you won't get stuck with a financial problem in the basement, remember that a good time to view houses is after a helluva rainfall. If it won't leak then, it probably won't leak. Not always possible of course, but it is worth remembering.

One popular way to get behind in the mortgage and other expenses is one's desire to have the home nicely decorated and furnished. If you can't keep up with the Joneses don't try.

I have seen fine homes with absolutely no furniture in the living and dining rooms. The families eat in the kitchens and I take my hat off to them. The breadwinner is a responsible person more concerned about a secure home than impressing others with expensive furnishings. They can come later.

What you must do is be realistic and honest with yourself. Don't sink every nickel you have into your dream home with no thought for the future and its carrying costs or you may end up with a nightmare.

Don't let anyone pressure you into buying by saying the mortgage will carry for just so much. You must be prepared for other costs. And while you're at it, see if you can have a reserve fund for contingencies — payment for those unknown breakdowns that do happen and must be taken care of.

Home ownership is nice. It's tax free when selling, but while you are watching the value of your property increase, it must be carried.

By you.

83

MOVING DAY

You have found your dream home, and everything is ready for closing the deal. Your lawyer is meeting the seller's lawyer in the registry office and you will soon be the elated owner of something special.

The lawyers are to close at about 1 p.m. so you figure on getting the key a couple of hours later. That will give you lots of time for a move in the afternoon.

The moving van, which is costing you plenty with three men, is picking up all your worldly possessions at 2 p.m., and three hours later you will be supervising the move into your new digs.

That's the way it's supposed to go, but in this case the seller hasn't moved out of the house and doesn't expect to be out until about 11 p.m. or so.

Now what are you going to do?

Your moving van with those three workers is parked on the street at 5 p.m. and it looks like it may be sitting there for another six hours before you can get a stick of furniture into the house.

Naturally, you are absolutely furious.

It is a common assumption for buyers to expect they will be entitled to vacant possession the moment the deal has closed.

After all, the buyer's lawyer has handed over the money and other covenants to the seller's lawyer, so shouldn't that be enough to get prompt possession?

Many will be surprised to discover that it is not necessarily so.

The Ontario Supreme Court has decreed that sellers of real property have until the end of the day of closing to give buyers possession, unless the contract is more specific about it.

The court ruled that a seller having bona fide intentions to leave on the day of closing and leaving before midnight on that day constituted vacant possession.

This is well worth remembering. It would only require a couple of extra lines in your agreement of purchase and sale to be definite about when you expect to be able to move into your newly acquired property.

The extra cost of a delayed move into a house could be as much as $500. So think about it.

84

DO YOUR GRANDCHILDREN A FAVOR

We are going back to 1910 . . .

The North Toronto Land Company Limited was incorporated to deal in and with real estate, proposing to make a specialty of north Toronto lands. Here are some of the things it had to say about it:

> Toronto is destined to become one of the most important cities in the world. One hundred years ago the whole site of Toronto was not worth the present value of 100 feet of Yonge St., between King and Queen Sts.
>
> More money has been made by the holders of real estate in Toronto than in any other way.
>
> There have been periods of speculation craze and land inflation, yet Toronto land is worth today more than at any time in its history and it is predicted Toronto suburban property in the next 10 years will make the fortunes of many.
>
> No locality appears to have a greater future than the Town of North Toronto.
>
> Its proximity to the center of the city, the value of its soil for garden purposes, the lowness of the assessment and tax rates, the remarkable healthiness of the location (being high and dry) and above all the ridiculously low price at which building lots may be purchased, all denote coming prosperity.
>
> Those who invest there today, those who settle there today, will reap the harvest.

The foregoing bang-on prophecy was made a long time ago.

The only possible changes I can see are in many of today's assessments and tax rates, which certainly are not the "lowness" type.

And what kind of deals was the North Toronto Land Company offering?

Here are a couple of examples:

For a total cost of $1,400, a buyer could get a brand-new house on a 100-foot lot, fully financed at 6%, plus municipal taxes of $16. That means a monthly carrying cost of $8.33 per month.

If one couldn't afford that, a new house on a 50-foot lot was available for $650. This deal carried for $3.92 per month!

And, as an additional inducement to go so heavily into debt, the company would attend to the transfer of the land, which meant no legal fees for closing.

All this sounded too good to be true, even in those days. So I checked the "homes for sale" in a 1910 daily paper. Wow!

A good supply of brand-new brick homes available under $2,000. With stone foundations, gas furnaces, the works. A 100-foot lot in an exclusive part of town could be had for $75.

So why am I telling you all this? I want all you tenants who can afford it to get out of there and buy a house.

Do you realize there are tens of thousands of young people today who are (or should be) most grateful that their grandpa bought one of these houses I have been talking about? Where the hell would half of them be without that home today?

A lot of them would be squawking about greedy landlords and their grubby fingers milking them dry.

So what have you got against your grandchildren-to-be?

What's today's home going to be worth in 30 or 40 years?

85

JUDGMENT-PROOF YOURSELF

This chapter concerns residents of Ontario, although it may apply, with variance, to all our provinces. For anyone with the slightest interest in real property, it could be a subject well worth remembering. Especially those considering buying property with little cash.

I received a call from a man who had just had a substantial judgment registered against him; he was extremely worried and wanted to know what "they" could do to him and his assets.

Registering a judgment in the sheriff's office means a writ of "seizure and sale" can be served on the debtor. This means just what it says. A sheriff's officer can seize assets and sell them to satisfy a judgment debt. Legally conducted by the sheriff, of course, with a credit balance going to the debtor after the sale.

But before this happens, it is customary to discover just what assets a debtor has.

This is done by ordering a debtor to appear before a judge, where an agent for the creditor can question the debtor about his ability to pay the debt.

If the order to appear is ignored, the judge can issue an arrest warrant to ensure appearance.

Perhaps a more common way to find assets is to order the debtor to appear for an "examination" which will be done under oath, but not in a courtroom. In the examination, the creditor's solicitor will question the debtor about such things as what assets he has, where he banks and where he works. The one doing the questioning is there for one purpose only, and that is to determine what the debtor has that may be legally seized. After the examination, a first step may be to garnishee wages, the maximum of which can be 20% of a debtor's gross income, regardless of how many judgments there are.

Other things, such as bank balances, cars, bonds, stocks and boats can also be seized. So you can see, a judgment can mean headaches — big ones.

If these assets were legally in a spouse's or other trusting person's name before the debt was incurred, it is unlikely they could be seized. Unless, of course, a bit of fraudulent intent was involved.

And how would a judgment affect one's home? Horrendously!

When the sheriff's office receives a copy of a judgment, the land registry and land titles office makes a record of it. If any real estate registered in the debtor's name is sold, this will surface when the buyer's lawyer searches the title. So the judgment(s) will have to be taken care of before a transfer of title can take place; subject, of course, to a spouse's right under the *Family Law Act*.

And any refinancing of the debtor's real estate could create similar problems.

But the real biggy can crush one buying real estate with little or no money down.

This is why I say it is most advisable to be judgment-proof. Consider the following:

Don't believe it if you are told there are no properties that can be bought with small down payments; it goes on all the time. But the downstroke is one thing and the *financing* is another.

When one buys real estate this way, financing the purchase with two or three mortgages, it is most important to look down the road to the end of the mortgage terms.

If mortgages can't be renewed, or the property refinanced, or sold to at least cover the mortgage debt, the borrower may be hit with a lender's power of sale. Problems. Problems.

If a reasonable mortgagee's sale cannot produce enough money to pay off the mortgages, the lender can sue the borrower for the shortage.

I don't have to draw you a picture, do I?

86

BEWARE THE LAND SWINDLER

How can one be protected against a land swindler?

You may recall reading about the conviction and sentencing of three men who cheated buyers in real estate scams. Unfortunately, innocent victims of the $1-million swindle did many things that should not be done when buying land.

Buyers were shown country land that was not the property they eventually committed themselves to buy. There is no reassuring municipal number on a house when looking at vacant land, so a legal description of the land must be obtained from the seller.

If the "seller" is a crook, the very act of asking for this information will make him suspect that you are going to do a search (which you should) to verify ownership, and may cause him to back off — which will save you a lot of grief.

But even if the seller gives you a legal description, it could be what he is really hoping to sell you, and not what you are looking at. How can one properly pinpoint land in the country?

Registry office clerks are most helpful.

Make a note of the nearest concession road corners and your approximate location. If there is an occupied farmhouse nearby, ask the occupant for a brief description of his land. Show all this to a clerk in the county office and he will put you at ease.

Despite all this, a crook is still a crook, and devious methods to cheat you will be used.

So if you are really interested — to the point of making an offer — go to the nearest town and retain a local lawyer to protect you. I say this because if you go back to the city and get a lawyer, he will probably end up using the services of one of the local lawyers anyway — which will cost you more.

Victims of the scam were often encouraged to use an "inhouse" lawyer, recommended by the seller.

One of the biggest no-nos in real estate is to use a lawyer who acts for both a buyer and seller; one cannot serve two masters, and there could be a severe conflict of interest in it.

Another thing to check very carefully is a claim that there is easy road access to the property. Ask for proof, then verify it at the county office.

Also, if there is water nearby, see what legal access there is to it. You may discover you'll have to trespass over private property to avoid a two-mile hike for a swim.

When looking at land and visualizing what your summer retreat would look like when you get it built, stop dreaming and visit the local planning or zoning office. Building may be prohibited due to land unsuitable for septic tanks or other reasons. One may even be restricted in the use of tents.

And now we come to a most important part of all this — money.

The fraud artists insisted buyers put up deposits, which went right down the crook's drain. *Never, ever* hand over money in a real estate deal unless it is done through a lawyer, or a real estate broker.

And when you do, mark the cheque "in trust" and have the land purchase for which it is intended clearly shown on the cheque.

If a seller insists on having a cheque made payable to him, think very, very, carefully about it.

87

TWO STIFF WARNINGS

I have a couple of go-slow signs for you, so read them carefully. The first is about municipal "work orders" and how they can affect a real estate deal. Boy oh boy, sometimes nothing but grief!

These are orders that cover all sorts of things to ensure municipal standards are maintained.

A happy vendor was ready to close the sale of his house, and was all set to leave on a trip to Europe the day after closing. Everything was rosy, just great, until someone from city hall lowered a boom on him.

An inspector walked in with a list of things that had to be done to the house and they had to be done before title could be conveyed to the buyer because the buyer's lawyer was clever enough to protect his client.

In an agreement of purchase and sale of older property, it is an accepted practice to insert a condition that says there are to be no municipal work orders outstanding against the property.

Fair enough, but the timing of this clause is most important.

If the agreement says there will be no orders on the "date of acceptance" of the offer, the vendor is off the hook and is not responsible for any placed against the property from that date until the date set for closing.

The purchaser would be ill-advised to allow the condition to be dated this way, and it could prove to be very expensive.

If the closing date were 60 days from an acceptance of the agreement, any work on the property ordered to be done under a municipal work order registered against the property within the 60 days would be at the expense of the purchaser.

What the clause should say is that there will be no work orders on the *date of closing*. Then, if any are registered against the property, the vendor must either have the work done or possibly compensate the purchaser so he could have it done later.

On the other hand, the vendor of an old house should not be happy about using the closing date for freedom of conditions, and here's why:

A sharp purchaser could arrange to have a municipal or other inspection made of the property before closing and come up with some expensive work. Which would have to be done, or paid for by the vendor.

So it depends on who you are. Vendor or purchaser.

The other warning sign is for a purchaser to be absolutely sure the vendor is a legal Canadian resident. If the vendor is not, steps must be taken to protect the purchaser and possibly save thousands of dollars.

Section 116 of the *Income Tax Act* provides for the collecting of a tax when a non-resident disposes of taxable Canadian real estate, and there is plenty of that around.

If the vendor, being a non-resident, fails to comply with the act, the purchaser may become liable to pay tax on behalf of the vendor. How do you like that?

The amount of tax payable by a vendor is a flat rate of 25% of the excess of the proceeds of disposition over the adjusted cost base of the property. In other words, 25% of net financial gain.

And if Mr. Smarty thinks he can put one over on the tax man by selling the property to Cousin Joe for a figure that will show no gain, think again. If the deal looks fishy, the sale will be assessed at fair market value and tax will be paid.

Here's the sad part. If tax clearance from the government is not received, the purchaser is obliged to pay tax on behalf of the vendor as high as 15% of the cost of the property.

There are ways to get around this, and quite legally. Just ensure the lawyer you retain knows what conveyancing is all about.

PART FOUR

SELLING

88

SELLING YOUR HOUSE

If one has lived in the same house for years and has watched the activity of real estate brokers in the neighborhood, it is likely that one firm will stand out in its aggressiveness by its number of Sold signs. You will notice that I did not say For Sale signs — there is an obvious difference.

However, most homeowners don't give this much thought until faced with a move, or the prospect of one.

Here are the basic moves. Yours will be one of them.

1. In a hurry to sell.
2. To sell and move by a specific date.
3. In no hurry to sell.
4. To sell before buying another property.
5. To sell after buying another property.

If the move has to be done as quickly as possible, it will require an all-out effort, which means listing the property on the local real estate board's multiple listing service (MLS). This opens it to all members of the board who are provided with details of the listing, including a photograph of the property.

It will also require the property to be listed at the *right price*. An overpriced property is a wasted exercise — it discourages agents from showing the property. Active agents *know* the local market, and they will not waste time trying to get someone an over-the-market price.

When you have decided on the firm that you would like to handle the sale, give the firm a listing agreement and get on with it. A listing agreement at a fair market price means that you are well on your way to a successful sale.

The MLS listing will be with one realtor, and all appointments for inspection will be made through this agent. A vendor can, of course, advise the agent that other brokers may phone directly to the vendor for appointments, but it is better to do this through the listing agent to avoid confusion, and ensure that the agent is aware of all viewings. It is necessary for the listing agent to retain a tight rein on the progress of the brokerage and to keep well informed of all progress.

Ensure that your MLS agent holds an "open house" date for inspections by other realtors. This is most important. On one open house I held, no fewer than 57 agents inspected the house, and it was sold very quickly. Most agents inspect properties *every day* to keep abreast of the market and have personal knowledge of the properties.

One of the distinct advantages of listing on MLS is that one of the agents may have the waiting buyer for your property, and when your listing comes to his attention it could be sold very quickly. So MLS is your best listing when in a hurry to sell.

To sell and move by a specific date can provide a bit of concern for a vendor. If an acceptable offer comes along but the moving date doesn't suit you, be careful about any thoughts of rejecting it because of this. Remember that in selling anything, it is always a good idea to "make it easy for the buyer," and if everything in the agreement suits you but the moving date, you could jeopardize the deal by simply rejecting it and telling the buyer he will move when you want him to move.

Instead of touching the offer on this point, have your agent discuss it over the telephone with the buyer. This is important, because if you change the date (or anything else) on the offer the agreement is dead unless the purchaser agrees with the change. If your buyer is adamant about the moving date, then you may be faced with interim financing, which brings up another concern.

If the buyer wishes to close his purchase of your property later than you do, there are two things you must immediately consider:

The first is the amount of the deposit money placed in trust on your behalf. If the buyer has deposited $1,000 against a long closing, it then becomes your concern about whether this $1,000 would be enough compensation for you in the event that he did not go through with the deal, leaving you with an empty house on your hands.

The second is your own financing. If you have to close the purchase of another property before the closing date on the sale of your own, it will require funds to effect this. Some real estate brokers, especially the larger ones, have such interim funds available for vendors on whose behalf they have acted. Other than that, your bank may help, or perhaps your own lawyer. The foregoing points are to be carefully weighed, and the advice of your lawyer can be of great help and assurance to you.

But remember, try and avoid missing a good deal if the only thing standing between you and the purchaser is a closing date.

As described in chapter 46, "The Local Real Estate Board," the MLS system evolved from the concepts of open listings and exclusive listings. Although these methods are still available they have to some extent become obsolete. Agents are not willing to work on an open listing basis because it doesn't pay in most cases and the agent ends up working for nothing. People selling privately will often pay a commission to an agent with a buyer. If the agent happens to have a client for that type of home he might be willing to make the effort and show the property and earn the selling portion of a commission. On the other hand, it is unlikely that he will spend money and effort promoting your home in the hopes of finding a buyer for it.

An open listing is useful in screening unscrupulous agents — those who say they have clients waiting to buy your home and you must list with them today. They are the agents that want to exploit your lack of understanding of the MLS system. They promise bus loads of Hong Kong buyers or other offshore investors. Or perhaps you have received an agent's flyer in the mail claiming that because of his or her superhuman effort in selling a neighbor's home they have several leftover buyers wanting yours. Put these agents to the test with an open listing. Tell them to bring an offer; if it is acceptable, you will pay them a selling commission. Otherwise, they will have to wait until your favored agent lists the property on MLS, when they will be more than welcome to bring all those buyers, provided that they line up at the door in an orderly fashion. Don't be surprised if you never see these agents again. But if one actually does have a buyer, it's your opportunity to save some commission dollars.

By selling your home through an exclusive listing, you are really saying to the public that your home is for sale but it's a secret so don't tell anyone. If your house is for sale you want everyone to spread the word. The more people aware of it the better are your chances of successfully selling. What possible reason would a vendor have in limiting the exposure to one agent or to one brokerage firm? In a city the size of Toronto, would you ask one person or one brokerage firm to find a buyer when you could have asked for 25,000 agents to help you find a buyer?

Some agents selling specialized industrial, commercial or investment properties may not even be members of a local real estate board but may maintain an effective private network of buyers, sellers, and cooperating brokers. They tend to be very specialized and their market very narrow and specific. But for the housing market such an approach just doesn't make sense unless there is a very specific reason. Perhaps the agent has a buyer for your home and needs 48 hours to arrange an appointment — in such a case an exclusive listing would be justified and the agent would charge less commission than normally. For the short period of a week or less, an exclusive listing may be acceptable; otherwise get serious and list your home on MLS.

To sell before buying another property is a move I would condone only if the sale has a long closing, such as 90 days or more. Providing, of course, it is your intention to buy another property. An exception to this would be a deal that is just so sweet and impossible to turn down that you would move into short term accommodation to effect the sale.

Once you have sold before buying, you will need not only time to look at other properties and find one you would like, and can buy, but you will need closing time. The vendor of the one you want to buy might want a bit of time to move himself.

So, you could spend a good four weeks finding your property, only to find that the vendor won't close for eight weeks. Total time 12 weeks. If you have sold before buying with a closing of 10 weeks, you have created a sticky wicket for yourself.

If you sell after buying, again you are faced with closing time, so give yourself a good span in closing what you buy, so you can be flexible in selling.

In buying before selling, it is often advisable, but not always possible, to have it a part of your agreement that the purchase is conditional upon selling your own home. An advantage in selling after buying is that you know you have another home to move into.

On the other hand, an advantage of selling *before* buying is that you know exactly how much money you will have available for buying.

If you have thrown up your hands after all the foregoing, don't despair. A good agent can be very comforting.

Now, when you have listed your property for sale, and thereby retained the services of a broker, remember that you have agreed to let *him* effect the sale. You can help a great deal by not only making your property as attractive as possible to potential buyers, but also by doing your best to be as inconspicuous as possible during your agent's showings. Don't volunteer any information; it may be something the buyer doesn't want to hear. Make yourself available for answering questions, nothing more. Leave the negotiating to the agent, and when you receive offers, then *you* start negotiating.

Make every bit of information about the property available to the broker. Mortgages, site plans, surveys, municipal tax bills, heating bills, receipts for major repairs, roof and other guarantees and contracts, and leases. It would be a nice gesture to provide your own list of preferred neighborhood shops, servicemen, and suppliers. And don't forget to mention the location of all church denominations, and schools, both public and private.

Give the agent your fullest cooperation. By this I mean such things as bending over backwards to accept appointments at hours that may not be convenient for you. Keep the property as attractive as possible at all times for showings. Doll the place up with a few flowers, and give it the old fresh air scent spray treatment before showings. Nothing turns a buyer off quicker than a house that reeks of unsavory odors.

First impressions are lasting impressions. So ensure that your front door, verandah and the immediate area here is attractive. When the agent is waiting for you to open the door, the buyer is standing there with nothing to do but look at that part of your house. This is most important.

Get all the junk out of the house and store it in the garage. Or better still, have a garage sale and get rid of it.

It might be difficult, but try and have the children playing outside when showing the property, or at least have them doing something *quietly*. This means leaving the TV set turned *off*.

There are many means of financing the sale. The most common one vendors shoot for is cash to mortgage(s). You get cash for your equity, and the buyer carries on with the mortgage payments.

If the buyer "agrees to assume" the mortgage, it simply means that he agrees to maintain the payments. But if you signed the mortgage deed, you are still responsible for the debt. So you might discuss this aspect of the sale with your lawyer before you even have the property listed. He will advise you on the means available to avoid this, although if there is a large amount of cash going into the property for the purchaser's equity, there would be little concern about covenant for the mortgage.

If the price is a top price, but the purchaser needs a little help with the financing, you can always consider holding a mortgage as part of the purchase price. But if you do this, try and keep the interest rate comparable to current market rates, and the term down to about three years. The reason for this is very basic; you want to sell the mortgage, and the lower the rate and the longer the term, the less you will get for it.

If your property is clear of debt, there is usually no problem in getting all cash. Mortgaging today can be obtained with a high ratio to the selling price. You get the mortgage money on closing, plus the cash going into the deal. Or maybe you will hold that small second.

If your property has a mortgage or two against it and you receive an all cash offer, find out just how much it will cost you to remove the mortgage(s). The buyer doesn't want any encumbrance and he will expect you to pay the cost of removal. Better still, find out before you even list the property — the cost could be sizeable.

Well now, you have an acceptable offer in front of you. *Call your lawyer.* If you can't see him personally, at least read the offer to him or her over the telephone. You are retaining a lawyer to close the sale, so let him protect you all the way. Lawyers have sharp eyes for sharp clauses.

89

IMPROVING THE OFFER

Not many vendors are cool about waiting for their listing agent to present an offer. The property has been placed on the market and now the vendor wants some action.

First, there will probably be inspections of the property made by other agents, and then the showings to the househunters will begin. The grumpy one giving your home the once over could be the ultimate buyer, and the pleasant, enthusiastic couple could be nothing more than a couple of snoopers. One can never tell about buyers or who they will be in housing.

Then the phone rings. Your agent has an offer. The agent will want to present it as soon as possible, and you are naturally anxious to see it. When the agent arrives, ensure that you have a quiet and private place to inspect the offer. This could be anywhere, of course, but turn off the TV and shoo the kids out of the room.

The first thing you will look for and look at is the price in the offer, and this is when you can become a little upset or even uptight. After all, your agent listed it at $85,000 and here is an offer of $80,500. Such nerve, you think. How could the buyer be so greedy to expect you to drop the price by almost five grand?

But remember, this is an *offer.* Before rejecting the offer because of the price, go through the whole thing with the agent, item by item, clause by clause. After all, the agent is only doing what the law tells him to do, and that is bringing the offer to your attention.

When you have gone over the offer with the agent, ensure that the arithmetic is quite clear to you. Seeing an offer of $80,500 with a $2,000 deposit, assume a $55,000 first, pay a further $16,000 on closing, vendor take back a second, etc. You will only be confused unless it is put down in order, viz:

Deposit	$ 2,000
Closing	16,000
First Mtg.	55,000
Second Mtge.	7,500
Offer	$80,500

Now it is clearer. You can see that your part of it will be a total of $18,000 cash plus a $7,500 second mortgage the purchaser is asking you to hold. Here are some financial points in this offer to consider:

The buyer is prepared to put up $18,000 cash. He could very well have another $20,000 in the bank but doesn't want to put up any more, as evidenced by his asking for the second mortgage. So you ask the agent a few probing questions. A good agent will have found out all he can about the buyer, and may have some interesting answers for you.

If you do want to hold that second mortgage, you will want it turned into cash, so remember that the shorter the term and the higher the interest rate, the more cash you will get when selling it. Ask your agent to phone his broker and see if he will give you a commitment to buy the mortgage. Get a cash figure from him, or someone, perhaps your own lawyer. If, for example, you know you can get $6,500 cash for the second mortgage, the discount of $1,000 off the mortgage now must be taken off the price from the buyer. Now we effectively have an offer of $79,500 cash to your registered mortgage.

What about a bit more cash from the buyer and a smaller second? The discount off the smaller second mortgage may bring the price up to $80,000.

If you think a second mortgage would be okay, determine just how long you would want your money invested here. And carefully consider its rate of interest. This second mortgage could be the answer in getting yourself a sale that is to your satisfaction.

Now about that price of $80,500. If you think your asking price has been shaved too much, remember that you are just $4,500 apart, which is a little more than 5% off the asking price — which certainly is at least a reasonable starting point. If you sign the offer back at the full price, there is a good chance you will kill the deal. Negotiate.

In cases like this, splitting the difference has created many sales. If you sign it back at another $2,250, that is being reasonable, and there may be a good chance your buyer would take it. If the agent, in presenting your counter-offer to the buyer, discovered that the buyer doesn't have the $2,250, perhaps he will come back to you with an offer to add the $2,250 to the second mortgage. Then you will have to sharpen your pencil again.

If there is a mortgage on your property and you receive an all cash offer with the buyer requiring you to remove all financial encumbrances, you will have to take the cost of discharging your mortgage into consideration. This probability should be taken care of at the time of listing the property. Ask your mortgagee what the interest penalty would be in such an event.

If the mortgage term has three or four years to run, and the lender wants a six months' interest penalty to discharge it, this could mean a large sum of money which *you* would have to pay. The amount would have to be deducted from the selling price of the property, so don't be hasty in agreeing to discharge your mortgage for the cash buyer. See chapter 37, "The Conventional Mortgage." You may be able to increase your mortgage, blend the interest rate and transfer it to another property, depending on the policies of the lender.

When counter-signing an offer, be very particular about the time limit you give the other party to make up his mind about accepting it, and *ensure* that this is taken care of. Remember, when you have counter-signed, you can't accept any other offers until this one is disposed of.

A most important point about a reasonably good offer is to keep it alive. Back and forth between buyer and seller if necessary, but keep it going until all is exhausted, the offer is a sale, or it is dead and you wait for another one. One of the puzzling things about real estate is that quite often the first offer is the best offer!

Give it a chance.

90

SELECTING YOUR AGENT

How does competition between real estate brokers affect the cost of housing?

A broker is in business for the same reason others are in business — to make money. If a broker has no listings — no "stock" on the shelf — he probably won't stay in business very long unless his revenue comes from areas other than selling.

A homeowner who has paid attention to real estate activity in his neighborhood will usually have a rough idea of the potential market of his own property. To close the gap in his thinking, the services and advice of a real estate agent active in the area are required.

The first agent called is often the one who does not list the property for sale. The homeowner can have an inflated idea of the value of his property, and when agent No. 1 expresses an opinion of market value, it may not suit the owner. So a second agent is called.

The owner may tell agent No. 2 of the opinion and advice given by No. 1 and here is where a real estate broker can be at odds with himself.

If No. 2 agrees with the opinion of No. 1 and informs the owner of this, it is possible No. 1 will get the listing. But if he quotes a higher price, he stands a good chance of defeating No. 1 in his attempt to get the listing.

When this happens, and the property is exposed for a period of time and no offers are presented to justify the listing price, the broker can always blame it on a number of factors and possibly end up with a sale more in line with the property value expressed by agent No. 1.

However, if the property is sold at the higher price, or close to it, who is to say what the value really was, or should have been?

Was the first agent wrong? Not necessarily. An agent who has been actively working in a given area for two or three years knows from experience what a property can be reasonably expected to bring if listed for sale. The exception to this, of course, is the house that was custom built and does not conform to standard plans.

If sold at the higher price, the sale becomes common knowledge among local brokers (and property owners in the area) and a new price structure may begin; new listings on other similar properties will be adjusted upwards.

A property owner when selling naturally wants to realize as much as possible in the sale. If two comparable brokers are competing for the listing, the one with another couple of thousand dollars or more in mind is the one who will probably list the property.

In an active neighborhood, if a "for sale" sign remains on a property more than three weeks, it is mainly because the property is listed at an inflated price or the financing is difficult. Or, unfortunately, it's got formaldehyde foam.

The cash requirement can often be overcome by discounting a vendor's mortgage but inflated price is a barrier.

The method of discounting the mortgage which the vendor agrees to take back is very simple. When the listing agent presents an offer he will have in his possession a firm commitment to purchase the mortgage at a discount. The selling price of the house will be shaved a bit, but the vendor gets all cash.

Have you received one of those offers of a "free evaluation of your home?" They are mailed in bulk, in good faith, by real estate brokers who obviously have listings in mind.

There are many hard-working agents out there, plugging away, following up on responses to the offerings.

But if you are going to sell, should you stop at hearing what just one agent has to say about the value of your house?

Here are my recommendations for selecting a listing agent:

I'm a strong advocate of loyalty, personal commitment, and outstanding service. Call an agent whom you know personally, a professional whom you feel comfortable with and trust. You can be sure your loyalty will be appreciated, and he or she will most likely give you a realistic valuation and good advice.

If you have no personal contacts, ask your friends for a recommendation. If they had a bad experience with an agent you can be sure you will soon know about it.

If you still have no agent, drive around your area covering about two square miles. You need this wide area because you are looking for signs. Brokers' signs. Preferably "sold" signs. Note the names of the three most active brokers; they are the ones you are going to call.

Ask each office to put someone on the phone who has been actively working in the area for about the past two years. You are looking for experienced agents who know what they are talking about in your neck of the woods.

Tell the three agents you are thinking of selling, and would appreciate a visit. One at a time, naturally — Monday, Tuesday, Wednesday.

A good agent will show you comparable sales figures in your area and describe features of houses that have been sold. An agent active in one area inspects every house on the market in that area, so you can be sure the ones you have called will know their business.

Unfortunately, some agents have been known to inflate a listing price in the hopes of grabbing a fast listing and perhaps try to bring the price down later after the owner has tied up his property for a couple of months.

If this should happen to you, with one agent giving you a figure highly out of proportion to the other two, eliminate the agent and call another office to replace him.

When you have received the verbal appraisals of the three agents, average their suggested listing prices. This will indicate what the listing price should be, because agents working the same area will be pretty close in their estimates.

The most popular method of listing is the widely accepted MLS service of real estate boards, which exposes photos and details of your property to all interested members.

In a hot market, money can be saved by listing the property exclusively with one agent. All other agents in this area will call your listing agent anyway; they usually cooperate with each other. The saving is usually 1% of the selling price.

I recommend listing your property with the agent who handled your call in the most businesslike manner. That's the one who gave you the most direct opinions and answers to your questions. The one who took time to inspect your plumbing, wiring, furnace and roof; the one who suggested alternate means of financing your property for a buyer; the one who probed with sensitive questions and didn't appear to be over anxious to get a signature on a listing.

The one who gives your home the once over lightly, enjoys a cup of coffee while trying to decide what your reaction is going to be to his price, would be a no-no for me.

Buying and selling houses is big business, with big commissions right out of owners' pockets.

Handing over this kind of money means owners deserve the best they can get.

The Agent's Commission

Do real estate brokers charge too much for their services? Some property sellers view the broker with suspicion. They see a "for sale" sign appear on a neighbor's lawn and two or three days later, it turns into a "sold" sign.

The neighbor confides that he got $150,000 cash for his house and right away the wheels start spinning. Let's see now, 5% of $150,000 is $7,500.

What! $7,500 for hammering a sign on a lawn and in a couple of days yet! Holy mackerel, how do I get into this racket?

Well, just cool it. Moving real estate is no sinecure, as thousands of dropouts will tell you.

Most exclusive listings are at 5% or 6% so we'll work with that. In the first place, taking it from the top, here is how the commission is broken down and shared by all:

Total commission on $150,000 at 5%	$7,500
Listing Broker	3,750
Selling Broker	3,750

Sounds simple. Fifty/fifty. But when the split is received by each broker, he breaks it down further and a part of it goes to the listing broker's sales agent and a part to the selling broker's sales agent. Commission breakdowns vary and are set only by the broker, we won't concern ourselves with the fine details.

The homeowner must realize the sales pay for the no-sales. Of all the homes listed for sale, about 40% sell during the first two months in a normal market. That means 60% don't. And who pays for all the advertising, leg work, time and overhead spent in trying to move the 60% that didn't sell? The 40%, of course.

Placing this in perspective, if 40% sell, then the overall commission income from all listings is not 5% but 40% of 5%, which averages 2%.

Now we are getting it straight. The average broker's gross income from all those $150,000 listings is $3,000 — not $7,500.

The basic reasons so many houses don't sell is that they are overpriced.

Real estate boards used to tell brokers what they can charge, but not anymore. It's up to the broker. With the competition for listings today, you can shop around and save money. One percent of $150,000 is $1,500 — which will help you move.

91

THE AGENT'S DUTIES

When you list your property with a real estate broker, it will interest you to know what his basic duties to you must be. There are seven of them.

1. The first thing he must do after getting the listing agreement signed is give a copy to each person who signed it.

   It is not good enough to provide one copy for Mr. and Mrs. Jones if Mr. and Mrs. Jones signed the listing. Each must get one. This is required by law and if this is not done the agent could very well jeopardize his commission for the simple reason that each co-owner signing a listing agreement would assume liability for paying the commission. So each should certainly get a copy.
2. The broker must give the owner an honest effort in brokerage and promote and protect the principal's interest by proper guidance in matters of price, law (with limited application) and shall render conscientious service.

   In the matter of price, when presenting an offer lower than the listed price, valid, comparable and market reasons should be given to enable the vendor to arrive at a sensible decision.

   A broker is not a lawyer and therefore cannot give you any legal advice, but can advise you on matters in which he has been trained. For example, when a broker presents you with an offer to purchase your property, you will not have a lawyer sitting beside you at the kitchen table. So he will certainly protect you in important matters such as correctly limiting the time you allow the purchaser to consider acceptance of your counter-offer.

   This is a most important example because if the purchaser gave the vendor 48 hours to consider the offer, and the vendor accepted it subject to some changes, the vendor should have his own time limit for acceptance by the purchaser.

Why? Because if this is not done, it may be interpreted as giving the purchaser until the date of closing in the offer to make up his mind about the counter-offer which could be a long way down the road.

3. The broker is to offer the property at one price and one price only — the listed price. If an agent says, "It's listed at $120,000 but I'm sure we can shave quite a bit off that," he is certainly not thinking as much of your pocket as his own. I have known of vendors asking a friend to make pointed inquiries about price, sometimes placing the agent in quicksand.

   This duty means what it says. If a prospect wants to make a lower offer, that's his business, but the agent certainly owes it to the vendor to get him as close to the listed price as possible. After all, the agent is being paid by the vendor, not by the buyer.
4. The broker will accept the agreed listing commission from his principal. This means that if the agent is fortunate enough to get a juicy deal for the vendor, he must not look for any bonus for being a hotshot.
5. The broker will inform the vendor of any and all offers to purchase the property. This does not restrict the agent to presenting signed offers. If a prospect says he would be interested in making an offer which the agent considers to be unacceptable, the agent should at least pass this along verbally to the vendor. The vendor must be fully informed of everything concerning any interest in buying his property.
6. The broker must declare any personal interest in the transaction. For example, if a pal of the broker is buying the property with the agent as his silent partner, hoping to turn it over at a profit, the agent had better reveal this. Woe to the agent who gets caught.
7. The broker shall be honest, loyal to his principal and shall not be negligent. Amen.

92

THE 10% COMMISSION

When I write giving advice to property owners about saving money when dealing with an agent, I get calls charging me with being a fink, rat, and worse. All from agents, of course.

Well, here I go again.

A few years ago, an acquaintance bought a few acres of land overlooking water, about 100 miles from Toronto. His intention was to build on it when he retires.

An agent arrives at his home one day, out of the blue, with an offer in hand. When they were discussing it, the agent said: "You will have to pay 10% commission, because it is raw land."

Well, let me tell you about the 10% business.

It started many years ago when a city agent listed a cottage about 150 miles from home base. He pointed out that to show the place to prospects, he would have a 300-mile drive with no guarantee of a sale, so he should be paid more.

This sounded reasonable to the owner, so they made a deal — the commission would be 10%.

Then city brokers began recruiting agents in the country, who worked out of their homes. Many of them were within two or three miles of vacant land and cottage listings, but the 10% business stuck.

In 1890, the U.S. Congress passed the Sherman Act, which protects trade and commerce against unlawful restraints and monopolies.

A few years ago, the U.S. government decided a real estate board in Maryland was doing the wrong thing by setting a schedule of realtor fees, and started a civil action, citing the Sherman Act.

In 1969, as a result of that, the real estate board was forbidden to fix, establish or maintain any commission for the sale, lease or management of real estate. It also was forbidden to enforce any percentage division of commissions between selling and listing brokers.

This judgment drastically changed the habit of fixed commissions. Real estate boards in Canada also have dropped the practice of fixing commission rates, and now all charges are negotiated between a broker and his principal. No other way.

The question of paying a 10% commission should be weighed in the light of how much extra time, effort and expense a broker may spend to move the property. A real estate standard of business practice says an agent shall charge for his services such fees as are fair and reasonable. If it means a lot of driving at today's prices, it could be justified, but if the property is just a mile or two away from the agent's office?

You work your own deal with the agent, but don't let one tell you what you must pay, because a fixed fee is a thing of the past.

My acquaintance also mentioned that the agent told him he must pay for a survey. Now, the question of who pays for what in a real estate deal is something to be negotiated between buyer and seller. It is not something a seller must do.

However, if you get an attractive offer in which the buyer has required you to pay for a survey, think seriously about it. If you argue on this point and change that lovely offer, the deal could die on the vine.

The strangest things can kill a real estate sale. I remember one lost because the buyer wanted three beautifully painted garbage cans owned by the seller. They had nothing to do with real property, but animosity set in — and that was that.

Don't lose a deal because of some relatively minor consideration.

93

LOW REAL ESTATE FEES

I see a real estate broker has emerged with an offer for homeowners to save money by listing with him at a reduced rate.

No law says he can't do it; nothing ventured, nothing gained as they say. I tried it once and it didn't work.

Twelve years ago I offered homeowners a choice. I would act as a consultant for the owner wishing to sell his property privately, thereby saving the commission, or I would act as the broker and do everything for a reduced fee.

In the offer to act as a consultant, the owner would pay me the sum of $300 for which he would receive the following:

1. The services of a highly qualified broker to assist with appraisal of the property.
2. The necessary documentation in listing property details for prospects.
3. Professionally painted, attractive "for sale" signs with wording to suit the owner.
4. Advice on how to prepare and show the property, and advice about safeguards to take when showing.
5. The agreement of purchase and sale when a verbal agreement was reached with a buyer. I would also ensure that it would be properly executed.

Nobody took me up on it, despite the fact that the offer was well advertised in the press. All my dreams of being the homeowner's savior were shattered.

I was prepared to act as the broker all for a flat fee of $1,000 regardless of the selling price of the home.

I would be responsible for advertising, showing the property, negotiating the sale and documentation. Just one owner took me up on this, which was a great disappointment to me.

Over the years various money-saving plans have come onto the market, only to fade and disappear. One did last for a few years, providing "private sale" signs and other helpful aids, but it too has gone.

This has always puzzled me. Why wouldn't a homeowner take a broker up on an offer that could save the owner thousands of dollars? At the end of a short listing of about 30 days, if it didn't work out the owner could always switch to another broker.

At the other end of the scale we have "Previews Inc.," a worldwide organization that publishes a book of dream houses. In it you will find the most interesting and exotic properties in all the world, some of them in Canada, with full details and asking prices.

The properties get in the book when owners pay in advance a listing fee of about 2% of the listed price. The book is then distributed to brokers all over the world who can work on the listings. When a property is sold, the selling broker gets his own fee from the owner.

Try asking the average Canadian homeowner for some money up front and you will starve to death. Regardless of what it costs, "sell it first and then I'll pay" is the procedure here, and come hell or high water Canadians won't change.

We have well-oiled machines at our disposal from coast to coast, the real estate boards of Canada. The combined knowledge of their members is staggering and it is this that steers sellers into the mainstream of real estate.

A real estate broker can lower his sights all he wants, but homeowners in Canada will make it difficult for him to succeed because they feel comfortable with things the way they are. That's the message I got when my plan fell flat on its face.

94

PLAY FAIR WITH YOUR AGENT

There are three basic types of listings in real estate. The MLS listing is one where the property is listed with a member of a real estate board. The listing is processed by the board and a photograph and all details of the property are sent to members of the board who can then work on it.

The exclusive listing is one where the property is listed exclusively with one agent, who may or may not allow other agents to work on the listing. However, if the listing broker decides to bar other agents, he cannot prevent any prospective buyers produced by other agents from inspecting the property. Whether or not he agrees to part with some of the selling commission to such a broker is another matter.

The third is an "open" listing, where a property owner will allow an agent to show the property to prospects, but it does not preclude the owner from selling the property without benefit of an agent.

Then there is no listing at all. Can an agent collect a selling commission if he didn't produce an offer, and if there was no listing agreement?

You better believe it. As a matter of fact, sometimes an agent can collect a commission from a vendor when the property was sold to a buyer the agent never met! How do you like that?

If you should ever get any bright ideas about being clever by circumventing a real estate agent, I suggest you digest the following:

An agent called a lady about the possibility of selling her house and during the conversation mentioned the commission charged for effecting a sale.

The lady said she might sell if she could "get her price," and shortly thereafter the agent called and arranged for a showing to a prospective buyer.

There was no listing agreement and the agent did not produce an offer.

Later, the lady contacted the prospect directly and sold her house to him without involving the agent. The agent then sued for a selling commission.

This matter went right to a supreme court, which decided in favor of the agent and ordered the lady to pay a full commission to him based on the selling price of the house.

The court pointed out that the owner was fully aware of the basis on which the agent was working, i.e., that he would be paid if the vendor made use of his work, which resulted in a sale.

It ruled that the sale was the direct, if not the immediate, result of the agent's efforts.

The principle appears to be that if an agent starts a chain of events which leads to a sale somewhere down the line, the agent will be well advised to look to the vendor for payment, even if the agent didn't produce an offer.

If an agent shows property to a prospect who in turn tells someone else about the property and that someone else buys it directly from the owner, the agent may be able to collect because he started the unbroken chain which led to the sale.

An agent, of course, would be well advised to ensure that the property owner is made fully aware of just who the prospect is and make a note of the showing in his diary. Judges like to see a bit of evidence in settling disputes.

Another example I give is where an agent had an offer accepted which contained a condition which was not fulfilled. The deal fell apart because of this, but later the vendor got together with the buyer and they cooked up a little deal of their own, the vendor claiming it was a brand new deal.

The agent got wind of it, and he collected a commission through court.

If an agent shows your property to a prospect, which results in no offer, and you later receive an acceptable offer from the same prospect but through another agent, then what?

If both agents are members of a real estate board, the matter will be settled internally. If they are not, a court may well rule that you will pay a commission to the first agent, the one who never got the offer. He started that little old chain of events

The commission clause in a standard MLS Listing agreement, which, of course, is a contract, says the seller will pay the realtor an agreed commission on any sale or exchange from any source. The holdover clause further states that commission must be paid if within 90 days after the agreement expires the property is purchased by a buyer who was introduced to the seller by the agent during the listing period.

A seller who takes the foregoing with a grain of salt and blithely cheats a realtor out of an earned commission could sadly regret it.

The realtor works hard on the listing, advertising the property and showing it to several prospective buyers.

The listing expires without a sale and the seller won't renew.

Why? Because he has worked a deal to sell with one of the prospects who inspected the property with the realtor.

I have just finished reading a court judgment on the subject, in favor of a realtor in Ontario, where the seller defendant was ordered to pay the commission, plus interest, plus costs, which would be plenty.

95

SELLING WITHOUT AN AGENT

You can pay a fee to learn how to sell your home successfully, or you can read it right here.

Your first consideration will be price. How much? You can be a cheapskate and invite a couple of local realtors over and ask them the listing price. I don't recommend it. After all, you're trying to save thousands of dollars on sales commission — so don't lower yourself by stealing someone's expert advice.

Check the neighborhood for the most active real estate signs. That will indicate a firm that knows the market in your area. Call the housing manager and tell him you want a written appraisal. It will cost about $250.

This won't be a full-blown lengthy document. It will be a letter informing you of the agent's expert opinion of value and it will be done properly, with consideration. By signing the letter the agent puts the firm's reputation on the line. It will justify your asking price.

Your next step: Take the appraisal letter to your lawyer, explain your plans and ask him or her to suggest alternate means of financing the sale. Remember, the best way to sell anything is to make it easy for the buyer. Your lawyer will have some first-class suggestions.

Your lawyer will explain the pros and cons of alternate financing, pitfalls to avoid and the most advantageous methods of doing it. After all, you're going to retain him to close your sale, so get him involved from the beginning.

Measure all your rooms, list all the details of the property, the extras that go with the sale — not forgetting to list all the local schools, churches, public transport facilities, shopping areas, etc. Have several copies of this detailed list available for prospective buyers.

Have a sign painter provide you with a professional-looking sign.

Your For Sale sign will have your telephone number with the notation "by appointment only."

When making appointments, make them at a time when a man will be in the house. If someone should knock on your door, give him a copy of your information sheet and politely but firmly ask him to telephone for an appointment. Or, make an appointment right there — for another time, when a man will be home. Do not open your door to strangers.

Advertise in local papers under the heading "Private Sale".

It goes without saying that you must clean the house. Clear out all the junk. Store it in the garage or a corner of the basement.

A most important point to remember is to brighten up the entrance area. First impressions are important. As a potential buyer stands on your verandah, waiting for you to answer the door, he has nothing to do but look around.

When showing the house, ensure the buyers are accompanied throughout the showing. It would be most disconcerting to notice a missing Royal Doulton after two strangers have departed.

If more than one couple arrives at the same time (which you shouldn't allow), ask one couple to wait in the living room. Don't let people crowd you.

Make the home look as attractive as possible for the showings. No harsh lights, music down low, children out of the way, dogs outside.

When a prospect wishes to make an offer, ask the buyer to have his lawyer prepare the offer. Then take it to your own lawyer.

96

SLICK BUYERS

The speculator and the developer are in business for the same reasons — to make money. As much as possible and as cheaply as possible. But there is a difference.

A developer is one who proceeds with a well-defined plan to expand the value of existing land use, principally through rezoning. It is time consuming and costly but very rewarding if successful.

However, one developer's plan to rebuild an entire city block in Toronto failed because just one homeowner absolutely refused to sell at any price. The developer ended up disposing of dozens of houses acquired over many months by hard negotiating — so you can see it's not exactly a gravy train.

The speculator, on the other hand, is one who hopes to get between a homeowner and a developer.

He couldn't care less about orderly development of a city block, except for the possibility of making a fast buck at the expense and exasperation of others.

Here is how he operates:

The two basic means of successful speculating are the conditional offer and the option. A real estate agent is usually used as a go-between, often finding he will do a lot of work for nothing. No closing, no payday.

The conditional offer can be very insidious. Conditions are many and varied — phrased to appear reasonable to an unsuspecting homeowner but designed to benefit no one but the speculator. Some of the common ones are:

"The sale being subject to the buyer acquiring other property in the area" (when the buyer has no intention of so doing).

"The buyer obtaining rezoning approval from a municipality." (I have seen such conditions with a two-year expiry date, which means that the homeowner's property will be tied up during all that time.)

"The buyer obtaining suitable financing." Suitable only to himself, of course.

The conditional offer will have a small cheque attached to it. If the homeowner goes along with the deal, the cheque will be held in trust by the real estate agent. If the deal doesn't go through, the deposit will be returned to the speculator, who won't lose a nickel on it.

The offer will state that all conditions will be strictly for the benefit of the buyer, who will have the right to waive any or all of them at any time.

The reason for this is most important to him:

The speculator really doesn't want to close the sale, which would require financing and paying land transfer taxes, to say nothing of lawyer's fees. He just wants to sell his rights to the paper in the transaction, hopefully to a developer. A conditional offer can make it possible.

The option is an agreement by the homeowner to sell his property at an agreed price in the future, with a time limit. It will usually require the buyer to pay a sum of nonreturnable money, and I have seen options with as little as a $1 payment and others with thousands.

There is one aspect of an option to be particularly aware of. During its time limit, the buyer may exercise his rights at any time, and close, which may be very disruptive to the seller, who could find himself out on the street.

What you do with your property is your business. But to maximize your benefits in an unsolicited offer, remember that the agent is working for the buyer, so don't agree to pay him any money. Let the agent get it from his principal, the buyer.

97

THE OKLAHOMA OFFER

One of the meanest financial flim-flans devised and used by money-grabbers is the "Oklahoma Offer."

It is slick, professional, and to the untrained eye hard to spot. It enables one to purchase property with nothing down and make a substantial and immediate cash profit.

Unfortunately, it leaves a vendor (property seller) stuck with a mortgage, most of which is not worth the paper it is written on. If you are selling property, watch for it — here is an example of how it works:

The following are briefly the financial contents of an offer to purchase property:

1. Purchase Price: $47,000
2. Deposit with Offer: $2,000
3. Purchaser agrees to pay vendor $30,000 on closing.
4. Vendor agrees to hold second mortgage for $15,000.
5. Purchaser agrees to arrange, at his own expense, a first mortgage of not less than $30,000.

The innocent vendor adds it up:

Deposit:	$ 2,000
Cash:	30,000
Mortgage:	15,000
TOTAL:	$47,000

If the offer is accepted, the purchaser can go to work and arrange a first mortgage of not $30,000 but $40,000. Remember, it was agreed that the first mortgage will be *not less than* $30,000.

Out of this $40,000 first mortgage, the purchaser will pay the vendor the agreed $30,000, give himself $2,000 to get back the deposit, and put $8,000 in his pocket.

Proof?

First Mortgage:	$40,000
Second Mortgage:	15,000
	$55,000
Purchase Price:	47,000
Profit to Buyer:	$ 8,000

The vendor, having agreed to hold a second mortgage of $15,000, is now in the unenviable position of having $8,000 of the $15,000 mortgage *exceed* the purchase price of the property.

If the purchaser is a corporate shell with no assets, it could then walk away with the $8,000 profit and forget the property.

If the vendor (now the second mortgagee) ended up owning the property again, he would owe $40,000 to a first mortgagee. Here is the spot he would be in:

Property worth:	$47,000
Owing:	40,000
Equity worth:	7,000
Cash received:	32,000
	$39,000
Selling price:	47,000
Net loss to vendor:	(8,000)
(plus headaches and legal fees)	

What this means, of course, is that it will cost the vendor (mortgagee) $8,000 out of his own pocket to regain possession of the property.

This money-making scheme is triggered by a clause in the agreement that will allow the purchaser (mortgagor) to increase the principal amount of the first mortgage "without necessarily applying the increase to reduce the principal amount of the second mortgage," which allows the purchaser to arrange and secure the $40,000 mortgage.

If questioned on this point, a glib person will say something to the effect that money obtained from such an increase will be required to improve the property, resulting in greater security for the second mortgagee (vendor). Which is hogwash! Watch it!!

Also, the purchaser may ask to assign the agreement to a third, unnamed party. This may release the purchaser from his covenant, and the assignee could be a corporate shell with no assets.

And, in any agreement of purchase and sale, here are two warning signs:

Be careful about accepting an offer from a buyer who shows the words "in trust" after his name.

"In trust" could be a corporate shell with no money, and when the time comes to close it would be useless to attempt to legally force a closing if the purchaser decided not to close.

It is tantamount to giving the purchaser an option on the property. Therefore, a serious consideration must be the amount of the deposit made with the offer and the length of time to close the sale. If the purchaser defaults, the vendor could retain the deposit money, which should be an amount considered to be fair compensation for the length of time the property was tied up . . .

When selling an older property, be careful about agreeing to warrant that there will be no municipal or other legal work orders registered against the property on the date of closing.

A sharp purchaser, under such an agreement, could have the property inspected by the municipal fire and building departments resulting in unheard of orders to repair and/or improve the property. The vendor would be stuck with the bill.

Agree only to there being no work orders registered against the property on the date of acceptance of the agreement.

Caveat emptor? Let the buyer beware?

Let the *seller* beware!

98

PROBLEMS WITH A SMALL DEPOSIT

Can there be such a thing as a contract to buy or sell real estate with no money paid as a deposit?

In an agreement of purchase and sale of real estate, the seller is promising to sell and the buyer is promising to buy. It is this exchange of promises that makes the contract. However, to make this contract legally binding, some form of consideration of value must be exchanged. It could be a dollar or a couple of beans or a seashell. Without it, you have a contract but it is not necessarily enforceable or binding.

The reason why money is involved is two-fold:

The seller certainly isn't going to rely on nothing but a promise from someone he never met before. He wants something tangible, like money. The more the better.

And the real estate agent likes to see at least enough deposit money to cover his commission. When the deal closes, this amount will be moved from his trust account to his general account, and he gets paid.

If the deposit doesn't cover all the commission, he could have a problem collecting the balance from the seller. How does one collect if the seller picks up his cheque on the day of closing and promptly takes off for points unknown? There are a lot of horror stories out there about such things.

Well, how much deposit should there be?

The agent will try for that magic figure — enough to cover the commission — and this seems to be the norm.

But the buyer, who is putting up thousands of dollars, certainly should ensure he will receive interest on the money while it is held in trust. His lawyer can see that a clause covering this is in the agreement.

The dangers to the seller in accepting a modest deposit are many. If the buyer should change his mind and walk away from the deal, the seller is left with little more than a headache to fall back on. It's all very well to say the buyer can be sued, but this can be costly and time-consuming.

To sue the buyer for specific performance and make him go through with the deal can be especially time-consuming. And before you consider such action, it should be established that he has the money or assets available to do so — because if he hasn't it's all for nothing.

What generally happens in the event of a buyer defaulting is that the property is put on the market again. If the proceeds from the second sale are less than the first would have been, then the seller has grounds to sue for the difference — plus other little items his lawyer will come up with.

If these damages exceed the amount of the deposit and the buyer has no money and declares bankruptcy, then all that you have won is an argument. There is no money to be had. If, on the other hand, you had a substantially higher deposit locked in the trust account, then that money would be available to you in a successful lawsuit whether or not the buyer had additional money or was bankrupt.

And what about that deposit money the real estate agent is holding in his trust account? It will stay where it is until a judge decides who gets it, unless both buyer and seller sign a voluntary release to decide this themselves.

If the seller gets the deposit and releases the buyer from his obligation, the agent may wonder about getting some of the money for the work he has done. He may have a problem here, because he didn't produce a buyer who was ready, willing and able to close.

Sometimes an agent will insert a clause in the commission agreement with the seller that says if the buyer defaults, the agent and the seller will split any deposit forfeited — with the agent's share to be no more than his commission would have been. Sounds fair to me.

But usually the property is listed again, with everyone keeping their fingers crossed hoping that nothing goes wrong the second time around.

So, if you are selling, get as much as possible in the deposit.

99

DANGERS OF BUYER ASSUMING MORTGAGE

What does it mean when you sell your house and the buyer agrees to "assume" the existing mortgage?

It's important for the house seller to be fully aware of his own responsibilities to a lender when this is done.

How would you like to be served with a writ charging you with a few thousand dollars in mortgage arrears two years after you sold your house?

Don't think it can't happen!

The one who signed the mortgage deed is responsible for the debt until it is paid. Period.

You put your house on the market. A buyer likes the mortgage registered against the property, so he agrees to pay "cash to mortgage" and further agrees to assume the mortgage.

Now, stop right here and remember this.

What the buyer is really saying is that he will continue making the payments on the mortgage.

But a very important point to remember is that the lender in the mortgage deed, the mortgagee, does not legally agree with this.

When you obtained the loan, the lender checked your credit rating and your ability to repay the money. The agreement under the mortgage is with you and the lender. No one else.

So after you have sold the property and conveyed your equity and title deed to the buyer, you are still responsible for the mortgage debt.

If the buyer continues to make the payments on time, there is no problem.

But if the buyer purchased the property with a modest down

payment, and defaulted under the mortgage, the lender could go after the property — and you — under a power of sale.

If, by some freak in the market, the sale didn't cover the mortgage debt, the lender could go after you for the balance owing.

If your buyer sold the property and his buyer agreed to maintain the mortgage payments, your buyer is off the hook and the second buyer is now in the picture.

And so are you. You are always there until the mortgage is paid off, or until the lender agrees to accept someone else's covenant for security. Then you're home free.

When there is a substantial amount of cash involved in the sale, don't worry about it. No buyer is going to walk away from a chunky down payment.

But sometimes properties are sold that have mortgage debts which come close to the sale price. It's here one may be forgiven for keeping fingers crossed praying nothing goes wrong.

If you help with the sale by taking back a second mortgage from the buyer, think carefully about the size of the loan. If the buyer gets the property with about 5% down, a quick recession could wipe out its market equity.

Then, if your buyer sold the property, possibly because of circumstances beyond his control, you may have a problem. The first mortgage and your second just cover the market value of the real estate.

When lending a buyer money this way, check the buyer's credit rating, his ability to repay the loan, stability of work record and character. If you are satisfied about all this, you can breathe easier about it.

It is common practice today to find two clauses in mortgage deeds. One says if the property is conveyed, or sold to another, the mortgage must be paid off.

The other is that if the lender approves of the property buyer, the mortgage may be assumed by the buyer if he passes a credit check. Also, the lender may require the new guy to pay an adjusted market rate of interest.

But only if the interest is currently higher than that in the mortgage deed. Naturally.

Those lenders are getting smarter every day. . . .

100

THE CONDITION PRECEDENT

Someone asked what is meant by "vendor has bought," an expression found on MLS listings.

Right off the bat one may say it is self-explanatory; the seller has bought another home. But hold on there. . . .

The intent of the expression is basically that the owner is very serious about selling. It says he has bought.

But has he really?

Perhaps he has bought, but in his purchase agreement there might be a clause saying the deal will only go through if he sells his own house.

So he has bought conditionally — which doesn't necessarily mean he is going to be pushed into accepting an offer that doesn't please him, because he does not have to sell. If he doesn't accept an offer, he just won't close the other deal. And that's that.

What's the difference whether a listing owner has bought conditionally, or not bought at all?

Simply it is in the owner's favor if he has bought conditionally, because he knows where he is going if an acceptable offer comes along. If the selling owner has bought with no conditions, then a buyer might have a chance to get a good little deal. Time might be running out on the seller's closing date on the house he bought.

Sometimes an agent will point out that the "vendor has bought" and suggest there is good reason to believe a buyer can get a red-hot deal.

After all, the buyer has to move!

Maybe. But I would be inclined to take such thinking with a grain of salt and try the agent's mettle.

If the house suited me, I'd given him a lowball offer to work on. Then we would see if there is any panic about moving.

To those who are selling, be very careful about accepting an offer, especially one containing conditions precedent — commonly called a conditional offer.

Real estate agents conduct their business in a para-legal manner. For example, drafting an agreement of purchase and sale to be signed by buyer and seller is something not all agents are well qualified to do.

When the agreement is signed by both parties, they have legally bound themselves to a very serious contract involving a substantial sum of money. Such drafting is not to be taken lightly, especially the ones containing conditions.

The two basic conditions are ones such as those which depend on an act of the buyer or seller and those depending on an act of a third party. A common use of a condition is one that makes an agreement of purchase and sale subject to the buyer obtaining a rezoning of the property within say, a year from the date of acceptance of the offer.

If such rezoning can't be obtained, the buyer may be of the opinion he may waive the condition and close the deal.

If the seller did not agree to close, the buyer would be out of luck because the condition depended upon the action and will of a third party, the municipality.

Another common condition would be having an agreement subject to the purchaser being able to arrange and obtain mortgage financing and still another is probably the one most used, the condition about the buyer's own home being sold.

Conditions can be drafted as a condition precedent or as a condition subsequent. There is a subtle, but important, difference.

A condition precedent is structured to say that there is no firm and binding agreement until a specific event takes place. Once the event takes place, the other party is notified, the condition is waived, and the parties confirm that a binding agreement exists.

A condition subsequent, on the other hand, is drafted to imply that the parties have a firm and binding agreement in hand. However, if a specific event does not take place within the allotted time frame, the other party is notified to that effect and the parties confirm that their agreement is terminated.

For example:

"This offer is conditional upon the purchaser being able to sell his property at 101 ABC St., Toronto, on or before March 31, 1992." Note that in this example, the event being the sale of the purchaser's property, there is no binding agreement until the specified property has been sold. This is drafted as a condition precedent.

"The purchaser has the option to terminate this agreement in the event that he is unable to sell his property at 101 ABC St., Toronto, before March 31, 1992." In this case the event is being unable to sell the purchaser's property. There already exists an agreement, and it will continue to exist unless the vendor is notified that the event did not take place during the time frame. This is drafted as a condition subsequent.

In condition precedent the vendor assumes that if there is no notification, there is no agreement. In condition subsequent the vendor assumes that in the absence of notification he has a firm and binding agreement.

If there is a condition in an offer presented to you, for heaven's sake do not consider accepting it, unless you have shown the agreement to your lawyer, or at least read it to him or her over the phone.

101

BE WARY OF CONDITIONAL OFFERS

Caveat Emptor: Let the buyer beware!

Well, I have some news for you. Let the *vendor* beware.

It's quite common for a seller and purchaser to agree to a contract which allows the purchaser to cancel the contract if he is unable to sell his own home. When such an agreement is made, there's usually an escape clause which says the vendor can go on entertaining offers to buy the house. If an acceptable offer is received, the vendor tells the first buyer. He will have an agreed time limit to remove all conditions in his agreement. Otherwise the property will be sold to the second buyer.

Now the foregoing can be a costly deal for the vendor, as you will see.

Part of the condition usually states "the vendor may notify the purchaser in writing of such an offer, and the purchaser shall have — hours from the receipt of such notice to waive his right of termination, otherwise this contract shall be null and void and the deposit shall be repaid to the purchaser."

In other words, the first purchaser may remove the condition and close the deal.

Well, what about the vendor and the offer he received from the second buyer? What if this second buyer offered substantially more for the property?

Too bad. If the first removes his conditions, he gets the property at his agreed price, regardless of the better second offer.

The way for the vendor to protect himself is to instruct his lawyer to change the wording of the condition. Instead of giving the buyer the right to remove the condition and close the deal at the first price, a second clause could be added.

For instance, "the vendor may notify the purchaser in writing of the terms of such offer, and the purchaser shall have — hours from the receipt of such notice to agree in writing that the terms of his offer be amended to meet the terms of the new offer without the right of termination, otherwise this contract shall be null and void and the deposit shall be repaid to the purchaser."

Get it? In the common condition, the vendor can't get any more money if the buyer removes his condition. Adding the second clause will still enable the first buyer to get the property — but at the improved price.

The agent who obtained the offer from the first buyer will do his utmost to expedite a sale of the buyer's property to ensure himself of pay cheques in two closings. He may not be too happy adding the second clause — if the vendor gets a better offer from a second purchaser and his buyer doesn't wish to match, he loses the sale.

When listing your property for sale, discuss this important point with your lawyer.

There are other things a vendor should watch for in an offer. One of them is a "work order" clause. Hydro and municipal authorities can order a property owner to improve the property in many ways and, when such orders are issued, the work must be done.

A clever buyer might make it a condition that there are no work orders registered against the property on the date of closing. A naive vendor could agree with this and find himself stuck with thousands of dollars in needed repairs.

What happens between the time of accepting the offer and the date of closing? It could be three or four months, during which time work orders could be slapped against the property. The vendor will pay — not the buyer.

If you spot one of these little clauses in the buyer's office, ensure that it is changed to read "there are no work orders registered against the property on the date of acceptance herein."

This isn't legal advice. Just notes I've made from agreements I've seen — and I've seen plenty.

PART FIVE

LEASING

102

INTRODUCTION TO LEASING

An agreement for a lease, or an accepted offer to lease, is not a lease. The agreement provides for the execution of a document — the lease.

The agreement contains the basic terms of the lease, the lessor and the lessee, a description of the property to which exclusive possession is to be given, the stipulated rent, and when payable, the term, and commencement date. From these essentials, the lessor and lessee carry on with their particular terms and fine print for the lease.

There are basically three types of leases:

Net Lease: The *lessor's* responsibility embraces all the municipal changes and property operating expenses.

Gross Lease: The *lessor's* responsibility embraces all the municipal charges and property operating expenses, but this is quite often watered down in the lease by requiring the lessee to pay for one or more of the operating expenses, such as heating, janitor, cleaning, hydro, and hot water.

Percentage Lease: The lessor receives, as rent, an agreed upon percentage of the lessee's gross business sales.

There are two common methods in practice:

a) The lessee agrees to pay a fixed rent *or* an agreed percentage of his gross sales to the lessor, whichever is greater.
b) The lessee agrees to pay a fixed rent, *plus* an agreed percentage of his gross sales over and above an agreed annual sales figure, to the lessor.

If the rent resulting from a percentage lease is greater than the basic rent, the additional rent paid is called "overage." This can sometimes produce startling and pleasant returns to the lessor, at the same time possibly giving him an inflated idea of the value of his property, but a sophisticated investor will recognize this "overage," not as a fixed return to be used as a basis of true valuation, but something subject to the vagaries of the buying public and the economy of the municipality, and certainly not guaranteed. Buying property leased on this basis, and allowing the "overage" to be used as a basis for additional property valuation, is quite often a calculated risk, and possible gamble.

If you are going to rent an apartment, you will usually be required to deposit a sum of money with an application equal to one month's rent. The lessor then checks your application to ensure that you will be reasonably able to maintain regular payments of rent. If he approves of you as a tenant, he will invariably shove a document under your nose and say "sign here." *Don't do it.* Take the document to a lawyer and ask him what it is you are required to sign, and ask him to outline the rights of lessor and lessee in terms of the document. A responsible landlord can have no valid objection to waiting one or two days while you determine what you are doing.

A Form of Apartment Rent Control that Can Work

If one mentions rent control to a landlord, the suggestion will undoubtedly draw a look of abhorrence. On the other hand, if the landlord mentions an increase in rent, he will probably have the look returned.

There could be a solution, and a fair one to both landlord and tenant in apartment buildings.

The owner of a building, having a financial investment at stake, is being reasonable in his assumption that he should receive a fair return on his money.

One of the problems in renting an apartment, especially when it involves a lease, is the landlord's knowledge that his maintenance costs and municipal taxes are surely going to rise during the tenancy, and this is an unknown factor to him.

A commercial lease, which is usually executed for a longer period of time than an apartment lease, will likely contain agreements covering future increase in maintenance and taxes. These agreements are called escalation clauses.

This clause guarantees that the lessor (landlord) will suffer no financial loss by these future increases. If the lessee occupies 10% of the area of the building, he will agree to pay, under the clauses, an increase in rent equal to 10% of any increase in maintenance and taxes charged to the lessor during the term of the lease.

This enables the lessor to give a long-term lease to his tenant, by ensuring that the lessor will be reasonably assured of a fixed return on his investment. If he had to bear increased taxes and maintenance over five to ten years without receiving any increase in rent, he would be in a precarious financial position.

So it is with the apartment building owner. When he initially gives one a two-year lease, he bases the rent on a projection that will give him a fair return. At the end of the two years, taxes and maintenance costs will have invariably increased, and he is forced to increase his rent to compensate for it.

An apartment tenant can only see the monthly increase. Moving means a new address, which is very disruptive, and inconvenient, and the tenant knows that his costs of moving will often amount to about the same as one year's increase in rent. This results in a feeling that the lessor is taking advantage of him; that the lessor is making too much money. The lessor justifies his demanded rent increases on the strength of increased taxes and maintenance costs, the current yield on money, and little else; unless, of course, he has an insatiable appetite for money.

The rent control that can work is one that the apartment owner imposes on himself and his tenants, by applying the escalation clauses to his apartment leases.

There is no secret about what any increase in taxes will be once the mill rate has been set by the municipality. It is a matter of public record.

In the happy event that a reduction of taxes might occur, the clause could also cover this, thereby slightly reducing the rent, but such a reduction would probably be offset by an increase in maintenance costs.

It could produce interesting results. The yearly statement provided by the lessor to his tenants would clearly outline the tax and maintenance costs for the initial year of the lease (when the tenants' rent is unchanged) and show adjustments to justify any increase in rent.

How could a tenant possibly have any objection to the rent structure under such an agreement; and what objections could a landlord have?

Why, they might even smile at each other!

The Offer to Lease

The balance of this chapter is basically written for lessees other than apartment dwellers. The first document you will sign is an agreement, or "offer to lease." Although the lease will be signed by both parties at a later date, it is well to keep a few points in your mind in your offer to lease. If they are not covered initially, you could be disappointed at a later date after you have made plans to move.

Ownership: it is essential that you determine at the outset just who is the lessor, and verify his authority to lease the property to you. A lease is a conveyance of an estate, and therefore title should be searched by your solicitor in the same manner and extent as though you were purchasing the property. To ensure that you are leasing from proper authority, the identical wording as in an offer to purchase could be used: "Provided the title is good and free from all encumbrances except as aforesaid and except as to any registered restrictions or covenants that run with the land providing that such are complied with."

The reason for establishing title can be obvious if your offer to lease contains the proviso for an option to purchase the property, or your right of first refusal in the event of a prospective sale. Searching title may bring to light registered easements that you may not wish to contend with; and you will most certainly wish to be reassured of your right to possession.

Description of Property: You must first fully determine just what it is you wish to lease. Exactly. Be specific.

For single properties such as a house or small building you wish to lease intact, the municipal address will usually suffice.

Description of a duplex, or triplex, etc., should include your rights for parking, use of the grounds (you may like outdoor barbecues), laundry facilities, and basement area. You might even define your right of ingress and egress.

Commercial space should include a floor plan of the exact space to be leased, and attached to the offer. It is sometimes advisable to include a survey to properly identify the building and parking spaces, etc.

In *any* offer to lease a *part* of a building, ensure that a proper plan outlining the area, floor number, etc. is included and attached to your offer.

The Rent: Paying the rent is one thing, and knowing what your financial responsibilities encompass is another.

It is advisable to outline exactly what municipal and building operating charges you will pay for, and exactly what your lessor will pay for. Be specific about these charges, *including taxes.*

Check the assessment on the property. If your lease is to contain a tax escalation clause which will require you to pay any *increase* in taxes on your assessed part of the premises, you could be in for a stiff financial jolt if the premises had been renovated and/or improved, and not re-assessed.

Your offer to lease should be checked by a lawyer for your protection and reassurance. He is going to be responsible for ensuring the cognizance of your rights and obligations in the actual lease, so do yourself a favor and let him help you from the beginning. You can be sure that the lessor is going to have a lawyer protect *his* interests!

You and the Landlord

The landlord's basic obligations are (a) covenant for quiet enjoyment, and (b) non-derogation from his grant.

Thousands of pages have been written on the subject of quiet enjoyment, many quoting judgments of higher courts in specific examples.

Basically, it is intended that you, the tenant, should be able to have undisturbed possession and enjoyment of the premises, without being *substantially* interfered with by the lessor. There would be no point in your running to a lawyer and claiming foul because of some minor irritations.

A breach of covenant for quiet enjoyment is almost always the result of some physical interference with the enjoyment of the premises.

While the covenant for quiet enjoyment is applied to a physical interference, the lessor's covenant not to derogate from his grant would be consideration at law for remedy where the covenant for quiet enjoyment would not apply.

The lessee's basic covenants are usually (a) to pay the rent, with the right of the lessor for re-entry if in default; and (b) to maintain the premises in good repair. It is well for the lessee to be quite clear about who will pay the taxes, as this may be considered to be a "usual covenant." Spell it out.

On the question of *buying* property, you will find some good advice in chapter 47, "Caveat Emptor." When leasing property, take the same attitude. Let the lessee beware! Know what you are leasing. Look the situation over from every angle. Don't take anything for granted, because once the lease is signed, it is signed, and you could find yourself on a sticky wicket.

Remember that a lease has the same effect as a sale of the demised premises for a specified term; in effect, you own the property for the term of the lease. Having the express right of quiet enjoyment, the lessor keeps out unless you agree to allow him access to your leased property, but remember that this places responsibility on your own shoulders, the responsibility that would be yours if you owned the property. The safest attitude to take is that you are in responsible possession; provide yourself with every safeguard — fire and liability insurance, proper maintenance and repair, etc., unless of course it is expressed otherwise in the lease. It is very distressing for a lessee to find that when the leased premises burn down, his business loss not only creates a severe hardship on him, but he is forced to go on paying the rent. The Chinese traders who invented insurance learned their lessons the hard way. All you have to do to protect yourself is call your insurance agent.

Nowhere in real estate is it more important to retain the services of a lawyer than in leasing. This cannot be stressed too strongly.

103

LEASING OFFICE SPACE

People have been known to walk in, take a quick look around the premises and say "I'll take it." And people have been known to regret this, believe me. Don't let it happen to you.

The following is a comprehensive check list for leasing office premises, prepared by former senior leasing negotiator of A.E. LePage (Ontario), John Hudson, F.R.I., F.R.I.C.S. Before starting your search for suitable space, review this and make a note of the points that will be of special interest to you.

THE LOCATION — CHECK:

1. Public transportation (buses, subways, trains, airport).
2. Accessibility to expressway or freeway.
3. Traffic congestion at rush hours.
4. Parking.
5. Restaurants, hotel and convention facilities.
6. Banks, post offices, shopping.
7. Type of neighborhood. Is it improving, stable or deteriorating?
8. Location of residences of present staff and potential employees.
9. Accessibility for clients, customers and suppliers.

THE SPACE — CHECK:

1. Age, quality and image of building.
2. Ownership and reputation of management (are existing tenants satisfied?)
3. Roster of tenants.
4. How long has space been vacant? Is other space vacant? Why?
5. Number and size of floors, number of tenants (with eye to future expansion, theirs and yours).
6. What is the rental rate per square foot or per square metre? Is the

given floor area accurate? What is the basis used for measurement? Does the measurement include a percentage of the common areas?

7. Think in terms of cost per m^2 per annum. An efficient floor layout may well bring a better building within your budget.
8. Check the width of the window module which will dictate the size of private offices. Note the size and spacing of the columns. If lessee's space is measured to the glass line, how much, if any, is lost by wall projections and heat/air conditioning induction units?
9. Allow 150 to 200 square feet per person depending on manager-to-worker ratio.
10. Where the terms Gross and Net are used determine exactly what the lessor's definition is in each building as they relate to (a) floor area; (b) services included.
11. To compare building rentals, try to determine the "effective rental rate" in each case. This may be necessary due to the variety of ways in which different owners calculate and quote their rents, escalations and allowances.
12. Does the lease contain a realty tax escalator clause, an escalator clause for operating expenses, or both? What is the "Base Year" for each or is the lessor using the alternative "Base Cost" approach? In new buildings check how the base year relates to extent of completion and percentage of occupancy. The later the base year the greater the advantage to the lessee.
13. Does the lessor do the following work or give any of these allowances:
    a) a "turnkey deal" — defined as all lessee's interior work completed to building standards at the owner's cost;
    b) a partitioning or "leasehold improvement allowance" towards lessee's interior work. Demising walls and standard entrance doors are normally provided at owner's cost;
    c) electrical, mechanical and lighting changes;
    d) a tiled floor, a broadloomed floor or an allowance for broadloom;
    e) a number of power and telephone outlets.

14. Does the lessee pay for hydro charges, fluorescent tube replacement, ballasts and starters? This is usually the case.
15. Type of heating and air conditioning system — does the lessor pay for its maintenance and hydro costs? Will air circulation be effective when partitions are erected?
16. Are the following included — if so, are they satisfactory? — heat, water, air conditioning, janitor service, window cleaning inside and out, snow removal, landscaping, fluorescent lighting (check candle power), washrooms, drinking fountains, elevators, windows (double or single glazed?), window coverings (drapes or blinds?), wiring, soundproofing, floor loading, underfloor ducts, services in ceiling, staff coffee and eating facilities.
17. In offices previously occupied, specify all items to remain for your use, e.g., partitions, counters, shelving, broadloom, drapes or blinds, air conditioning units.
18. Parking — how many spaces and are they reserved? Are they a part of the lease, or can the present monthly cost be increased? Is there additional parking in the area?
19. What is the most desirable lease term? Will longer lease protect against future rent increase or expansion by a larger tenant? Is this type of space in demand so that if necessary could readily be sublet? Has the lessee the right to sublet? Can the lessee keep any profit rental obtained in so doing?
20. Is there an option to renew? If so, at what rental? Is the space under option to another tenant at a later date?
21. Can the lessee be given notice to vacate if the building is sold or demolished? If so, is there any compensation for lessee's improvements?
22. Check if lessee is required to restore premises to their original state on termination of lease or if improvements are to remain and become lessor's property.
23. Date of possession — check this with the telephone company, contractors, movers, furniture suppliers and allow for delays. Give notice to present lessor. Make sure lessee has the right of prior entry rent free to prepare the new premises for his use.
24. What are the provisions for signs or identification?

25. What is the position regarding shipping and deliveries? Note if there are charges for use of elevators for furniture, materials or delivery of parcels.
26. Check availability and cost of storage space.
27. How is the security? Has the building 24 hour access? What time are the doors locked? What hours or seasons are heat, air conditioning, elevator service curtailed?
28. Note if the lessor levies a fee for the supervision of the installation of lessee's leasehold improvements.

104

LEASE-BACKS

This common expression is derived from two separate and simultaneous transactions, the sale by the owner/occupant of a building to a purchaser who immediately leases it to the seller, who stays right where he is.

A benefit to the seller is that the sale provides additional cash for the business operation. This additional cash also can provide more cash, because a bank loves to see chunky bank balances, which usually makes it easier to borrow.

A loss to the seller is the loss of its real estate. All future increases in the market value now belong to the new owner.

An ideal lease-back would be one where the seller has the right to regain the real estate at a future date by purchasing it for about 20% of its selling price. This would provide the buyer with a good return on its investment through the lease, plus a 20% bonus at the end of the lease. An agreement could be incorporated in the original transaction allowing the seller to buy-back at earlier dates at specific prices. However, the majority of buyers in a lease-back won't want any part of this; they buy it to own it, period. If there is an agreement to turn it back to the seller, it would probably be at an appraised price at the time of selling.

The cash-short owner considering a lease-back will naturally explore all other avenues of raising money before getting serious about the lease-back. Mortgaging a property to 75% of lending value in a $400,000 parcel may leave the owner with a yearning for the $100,000 balance, which is tied up in equity, and which could be turned loose for expansion and other purposes. It is the converting of this equity into cash that is the prime reason for the lease-back.

There are two factors that will water down the yearning for the $100,000. If the owner had taken a capital cost allowance over a number of years in its annual tax returns, a "recaptured tax" will have to be paid on such deductions, if the property were sold at a price in excess of its depreciated value, which today is certainly most likely.

Another slap at the $100,000 may be a capital gain tax on disposition. So these two factors will be carefully weighed in selling to determine if it really would be a wise move.

If the owner decided to proceed, here is an example of what the agreement would entail:

If the building is new, and was constructed by a reputable builder, the costs of land acquisition and building will be the figure used to proceed with formal negotiations. If the building is a few years old, a professional appraisal will be made to arrive at its reasonable current market value, and this figure will be used.

a) The property would be leased immediately to the now former owner on a net basis (it would pay *all* charges against the property) for an agreed period.
b) The rent paid would be established by the strength of the lessee's covenant (the stronger it is, the less it pays) and by the term of the lease.
c) The lessor (new owner) would treat the investment as a sort of annuity, and it would be amortized completely, including principal and interest, over the period of time under the term of the lease, which would be what the lessee would pay as rent. The interest rate in such amortization is generally slightly higher than current, conventional mortgage rates, the reason for which is that 100% of valuation financing is effected.
d) The long-term net lease may contain a cost-of-living index, to ensure that the owner's dollar return will not be shattered by inflation during the term of the lease.

The seller will attempt to obtain two favorable considerations in the agreement: (1) a buy-back right on attractive terms; and (2) a renewal right in the lease at a sharply reduced rent, the reason being that the investing body will have recovered its capital cost.

The lessee, being on a net lease, and therefore required to pay all municipal taxes, local improvements, utilities, insurance, etc., will covenant to pay these charges as "additional rent," which will enable the lessor to have the same recourse for breach of this covenant as he will have for nonpayment of the basic rent.

In the event of loss by fire or other cause, it will be the lessee's responsibility to rebuild, which makes it necessary to detail at length the insurance clause in the lease. It will be required to cover itself, the lessor, and possibly a mortgagee fully with a wide range of coverage. Smaller, agreed-upon claims will be settled by the lessee alone, larger amounts being settled through the lessor.

A most extensive part of the lease will be that which concerns the rights and/or obligations of the lessee to repair, renovate, remodel, add to, or even completely replace the building. This will cover such aspects as performance bonds, restrictions under municipal building by-laws, etc., and the building, regardless of the approved changes, will of course remain the property of the lessor.

In case of loss or damage when the lessee will be required to promptly remedy this at its own expense, it will be bound to continue paying the rent during such period, unless otherwise provided for by moratorium in the lease.

The stiffness of the requirements of the lessee will soften as the lease approaches expiration, when it will probably have option agreements covering loss during this latter period. For instance, if the lease contains an option to purchase the property at the end of the lease, and the buildings were damaged or destroyed during this period, the lessee would normally have a clause giving it the option to rebuild, or terminate the lease by purchasing the property from the lessor, plus indemnifying the lessor for its unrecovered capital cost plus interest.

The seller deals with one body for the full treatment. No middleman looking for commissions in the transaction, which could amount to sizeable sums. The seller gets the money, and can do what it wants with it. The rent will be a tax deductible item.

If the seller had financed by conventional mortgaging, the only tax deductible part of it would be the interest on the mortgage. The rent is, in effect, a mortgage, but the principal repayment is considered a part of the rent, and is therefore also tax deductible.

However, caution must be exercised if the deal is to contain a buy-back right, because the income tax department may take the position that all the seller was doing was using the property effectively as security for raising capital. Also, in lease-back projects, the subject of the true market value of the property may be raised.

One would be well advised to seek expert accounting and tax advice in entering into any sale-lease-back contract, both buyer/lessor, and seller/lessee.

105

FINDING A GOOD TENANT

I like the living on a two-way street in life. You scratch my back and I'll scratch yours.

We are told we cannot rent a house by being nitpickers, but must rent it to the first applicant with the rent money in hand. Who dreamed up that nutty idea?

Have you ever seen the inside of a rented house after some bum who hasn't paid the rent for a few months finally skips out?

Paint splashed all over the place, toilets plugged, light fixtures ripped out, holes in the wall. Owners who have rented houses know whereof I speak.

Who is to protect the landlord from people like that?

I heard from one such owner who declined to rent a house to some people because he didn't think much of their lifestyle, and they promptly threatened to go to the Human Rights Commission.

This thing can work both ways.

If people inspect a house and decline to rent it because it didn't suit them, why shouldn't the owner of the house be able to complain to the Commission because they wouldn't rent his house?

What I mean by the two-way street is that if you are good tenants, I'll be a good landlord.

But how can we tell that about each other?

Well, a good landlord is one who will offer his premises in spotless condition, all the equipment in good working order and the exterior and grounds presentable.

And a good tenant, of course, is one who will respect the other's property — not abuse it — and live throughout the tenancy with a good sense of responsibility.

How do we find each other?

It's easy for the tenant to find a good landlord; just go and inspect the house. If it is as I have described it, you can be sure that he will want to keep it that way.

But a good tenant? All landlords like good tenants, but not all landlords get them. Here is one sensible suggestion made to me:

After showing the house to a prospect, and if you are satisfied he can pay the rent and utility charges, tell him you will let him know the next day. That evening, knock on his door unannounced, and take a look at the way he is maintaining his present digs.

I remember making this suggestion to a well-known newspaper and TV personality, and I was promptly reminded that "perhaps that would be discrimination."

Really? My house, and I'm supposed to rent it to some slob?

Many houses are leased to tenants the owner never sees — mostly through the services of real estate agents. What assurance has an owner got that he is getting one of the good ones? If the agent knows nothing about the prospective tenant or his lifestyle, the owner may as well keep his fingers crossed if he accepts the offer.

I just don't believe an owner should be required to rent his house simply because someone arrives with the first and last month's rent.

There must be a better way — and 90% of it is to know as much as possible about the person.

106

TENANTS HAVE STRONG RIGHTS

Peaceful enjoyment in one's apartment or condominium is not something to be taken for granted.

Recently, the owner of one of those downtown Toronto high-rises hauled a tenant to court in an attempt to end a lease and gain vacant possession of the apartment.

The occupant living directly below this tenant complained of the tenant walking around with shoes on bare flooring, dragging furniture, and loud thumping in the early hours of the morning.

The complainant said the noises awakened him from sleep and detailed each in writing.

This caused the landlord to eventually serve a notice of termination on the noise-maker.

The judge said there was no reason to dispute the complainant's evidence that he was disturbed in his sleep and accepted the evidence that the upper tenant made such noises. But he noted that the question is two-fold: (1) Whether or not the conduct of the respondent substantially interfered with the complainant's enjoyment of the premises; and (2) If this conduct is so found, whether or not the respondent has failed to rectify the conduct.

For there to be a substantial interference with other tenants' enjoyment — in breach of the *Landlord and Tenant Act* — the noise caused by the tenants cannot be noise that arises in the usual course of occupation of residential premises.

The judge gave examples of this from other court judgments:

One said: "Although the crying of a baby was noise that interfered with the enjoyment of a complainant, it was a normal inconvenience of daily living and a tenant with this child should not be evicted because another tenant is unable to put up with such noise."

On the other hand, this judgment found that a dog continuously barking constituted substantial interference of a tenant's enjoyment and held that it was not a normal inconvenience of daily living. "In facts at hand, there can be no doubt that ongoing interference with the sleep of another tenant constitutes anti-social behavior."

Which obviously is the reason dogs are not very welcome in apartment buildings. They can create substantial problems for landlords.

Here is another one: "A repeated disturbance of the same nature becomes, by process of repetition itself, almost untenable." And the trial judge observed that not only must the behavior be anti-social, but the disturbance must be ongoing.

And another: "The use by a tenant of a CB aerial substantially interfered with the other tenants' stereo and radio and television equipment. The interference was not an isolated incident but was ongoing."

The trial judge summarized that a landlord must show the following to prove substantial interference:

- The behavior complained of is anti-social;
- The behavior is ongoing;
- The use interfered with is reasonable use.

The *Landlord and Tenant Act* says where a notice of termination has become null and void by reason of the tenant complying with the terms of the notice within seven days and the tenant within six months again contravenes the Act, the landlord may again serve notice of termination on the tenant.

The judge dismissed our subject action because the problem had been corrected and the complainant said he hadn't heard anything lately.

So it's round one for the tenant — but don't do it again!

107

GETTING A TENANT OUT OF YOUR HOUSE

A landlord's worst fears must surely be a bum cheque! This is a signal that there could be trouble ahead — a tenant who can't, or won't, pay the rent. We all know how difficult it can be to have a tenant removed: a landlord holding a bum cheque in his hand can be forgiven for reaching for the bottle.

So what to do?

When things sour financially, a man will often vent his anger at the easier targets, like the wife and kids, who cannot defend themselves. Just for openers.

In the midst of all this ranging frustration, a note arrives from the landlord. Pay up, or legal action will commence to have vacant possession.

Oh boy. This can really send some guys right to the moon. The tenant figures he has enough problems without his landlord picking on him, so what can happen?

The tenant knows he will eventually be removed if he doesn't pay the rent and, sadly, this sometimes leads to some pretty nasty stuff.

The tenant's anger may now be aimed at the landlord, with varying degrees of mayhem.

By the time the landlord has the irate tenant removed, the house could look like something I really don't want to itemize, from excrement on the walls to plugged toilets.

Such a mess can cost thousands of dollars to put right. And there would be little point in suing the former tenant; he hasn't got any money.

The foregoing is not fiction; it is fact. But here is an answer to the problem, which comes from vendors selling houses occupied by tenants.

In today's market, some very delightful things can happen to house owners — such as unheard-of and unhoped-for cash offers.

With the prospect of not getting a barrel full of money because the tenant just won't budge, the logical course of action is make it worth his while to move.

Which means money. The amount of money involved in such an offer will, of course, depend on the type, size and location of property, to say nothing of the tenant's attitude.

I can see justifying a payment of from $5,000 up to make a good sale possible.

This method of vacant possession can also be applied to a landlord with a dubious tenant, but to a lesser financial degree.

The minute a landlord suspects his tenant has fallen on hard times, it could be wise for the landlord to take direct and immediate action to gain vacant possession. And I don't mean by the long, legal route.

Be friendly about it. Go armed with a sympathetic understanding of the tenant's problems, *and money.*

Offer to help him move. Forget the unpaid back rent. Provide the moving truck, supervise the loading, give the tenant some cash and wish him well.

Isn't that better than having the prospect of a wrecked house to worry about? Let the next landlord do the worrying.

Remember, during all those weeks and months it can take to remove a nonpaying tenant, he may stay in possession of your house until a judge orders him out.

By the time he is gone, you have lost a bundle. The house could have been rented to another, with everything in place.

108

A COMMON RENTAL SCAM

If you intend to make an offer to lease a house, it would be a good idea to do a title search of the property to be sure about not only who owns the house, but also who owns any mortgages registered against the property.

When you have done this, find out if the mortgage payments are up to date.

Now, you might ask, why go to all this trouble? After all, the man did show you through the house, so he must be the owner. Maybe not; maybe he is renting it from somebody else. Ever think of that?

There is nothing wrong with legally subletting a house, but the foregoing remarks about checking on the mortgage payments' being up to date can have serious consequences for you if they are not.

You move into the house with a two-year lease. Nice neighborhood; you are looking forward to having your children attend school just a couple of blocks away and your wife likes that shopping plaza nearby. All your friends attend the housewarming and you settle down with your family, feeling secure about the whole thing.

Then, wham, a couple of months later you receive a notice to vacate. And *I mean* vacate: Get out!

How can this happen? Let me make it quite clear about which has priority, a mortgage or a lease.

If the mortgage was registered before the lease was signed, the mortgage lender's rights come first, and he can take possession of the property if the borrower defaults in the mortgage.

If the lease was signed and the tenant was in possession of the house before the mortgage was registered, the tenant can stay until the end of the term in the lease, whether the mortgage lender likes it or not.

Now it gets interesting. If a tenant is forced out of the house due to an action by the mortgage lender, the tenant can sue the homeowner if the lease was signed by the homeowner.

So there is legal recourse for the disruption, but small comfort if the homeowner has fallen on hard times and has no money. It wouldn't do much good to sue, would it?

But here is the really sad part. If your lease is a sublease, one where you rented the house from one who already has a lease with the rightful owner, you can't sue the owner of the property. Tough luck.

So maybe you had better do a little checking before renting that house. Here are some things to keep in mind.

The landlord cannot demand a security deposit beyond one month's rent, which he is to apply as payment for the last month's rent in the term of the lease.

In Ontario, he must pay interest on this deposit to the tenant at the rate of 6% per annum. This is why you will find real estate agents drafting an offer to lease that contains two months free rent: The first and the last month of the lease.

The tenant has the responsibility of taking the rent payment to the landlord. He cannot expect the landlord to come and pick it up, although many do just that.

It is the responsibility of the landlord to pay the municipal taxes on the house, although a lease may require the tenant to pay for this through the landlord. Some leases also contain tax escalation clauses; that is, future increases in taxes will be borne by the tenant regardless of who pays the current year's taxes.

And here's something to especially remember. Any building erected by a tenant on leased land must be left there for the benefit of the landlord, and if the tenant has planted and nurtured some expensive plants, they also stay where they are.

PART SIX

LAST WORDS

109

PROPERTY INSURANCE

Insurance secures protection against property loss in consideration of a payment proportional to the risk involved.

Property insurance includes real property, buildings and contents, machinery, merchandise, household furnishings, valuables, automobiles, boats, aircraft, ships and cargoes, and in fact any insurable object in which a person has an insurable interest.

When you are going to have property insurance placed, don't call your cousin Joe and ask him for advice, unless he happens to be in the profession of placing property insurance. Consult a properly qualified insurance agent.

In the process of obtaining property insurance, you bump headlong into the matter of good faith between you and your agent. If you know something materially affecting the acceptability of the risk, and do not tell the insurer something that is not in accordance with the facts, that is "misrepresentation." Your non-disclosure or misrepresentation of material facts when the insurance is applied for makes the contract voidable, at the election of the insurer, upon his discovering the situation.

You must have an *insurable interest* in property, without which your insurance contract is void. An insurable interest in property is when you stand in such a legal relationship to it that you may be prejudiced by its loss or damage and stand to benefit by its continued existence. If you simply took out a policy on property belonging to somebody else in which you have no financial interest, you are merely making a bet with the insurer that the property will not be lost during the policy period, and such a contract would be void.

You do not, of course, have to be the owner of property to have an insurable interest in it. For example, those who have possession of the property of others, such as bailees, pledgees, pawnbrokers, warehousemen, carriers, jewellers, furriers, tenants, etc., have an insurable interest. Their interest arises out of their potential liability to make good loss or damage to the property in their care. Others with an insurable interest are executors, administrators and other trustees, mortgagees, lienholders, vendors under conditional sales agreements; and lessees and other users of property which they employ for gain and who may therefore suffer business loss if it is damaged or lost.

Your indemnity, up to the limit of the policy, is to be fully indemnified for what you have actually lost in money value, but you can make no profit out of the occurrence in case of loss. Your loss is the cost of restoration or repair in the event of partial loss, with due allowance for betterment, and, in the case of total loss, it is the depreciated actual cash value of the property at the time of loss — the insurer pays the true *pecuniary* loss, no more, no less.

A *valued policy* is one covering loss or damage to chattels under which, on *total* loss of the insured property, a fixed sum is payable which has been agreed upon between you and the insurer at the inception of the contract. Generally speaking, and subject of course to gross or fraudulent overvaluation, the stated amount is payable by the insurer without reference to your actual monetary loss. Generally, your insurer requires you to obtain an independent valuation of the property before entering into such a contract.

The first form of insurance was marine insurance on ships and cargo. Next came fire insurance, and today fire insurance accounts for about 20% of all insurance business written in Canada.

A fire insurance policy will cover you in the event of your property being destroyed or damaged by fire or lightning, or an explosion of natural, coal or manufactured gas, without allowance for any increased cost of repair or reconstruction by reason of any ordinance or law regulating construction or repair, to an amount not exceeding, *whichever is the least* of:

a) The actual cash value of the property at the time of destruction or damage.
b) The interest of the insured in the property.
c) The sum set opposite an applicable item in the policy, and subject to any pro rata provisions.

The policy does not cover:

a) Loss, destruction or damage to goods occasioned by or happening through their undergoing any process involving the application of heat.
b) Loss, destruction or damage caused by riot, civil commotion, war, invasion, act of foreign enemy, hostilities (whether war be declared or not), civil war, rebellion, revolution, insurrection or military power.
c) Loss, destruction or damage to electrical devices or appliances caused by lightning or other electrical currents unless fire ensues and then only for such loss, destruction or damage as results from such fire.
d) Loss, destruction or damage caused by contamination by radioactive material.
e) Money, books of account, securities for money, evidences of debt or title; automobiles, tractors, and other motor vehicles; aircraft; watercraft.
f) Loss, destruction or damage to a building or its contents during alteration of or addition to the building and in consequence thereof, unless written permission therefor has been previously granted. Normal repairs are allowed without permission.
g) While the building insured or containing the property insured is to the knowledge of the Insured vacant or unoccupied for more than 30 consecutive days or, being a manufacturing establishment, ceases to be operated and continues out of operation for more than 30 consecutive days.
h) While to the knowledge of the Insured there is situated or used in the building insured or containing the property insured gasoline, benzine, naphtha or other substance of an equal or lower flashpoint, in total quantity greater than one gallon in addition to that contained in tanks of vehicles.
i) Loss directly or indirectly, proximately or remotely, arising in consequence of or contributed to the enforcement of any by-law, regulation, ordinance or law regulating zoning or the demolition, repair or construction of buildings or structures, which by-law, regulation, ordinance or law makes it impossible to

repair or reinstate the property as it was immediately prior to the loss.

The cardinal principle being that the contract of property insurance is a contract of indemnity, you will not recover more than the actual value of your property at the time of the loss.

A provision of your fire policy is that in no event shall the insurer's liability exceed what it would cost you to repair, or replace, the property with material *of the same kind and like quality.* This is not the proper measure of damages which you may invoke, but, rather a limitation on the insurer's liability.

The term "value" is difficult to define with exactness, and as a result several interpretations have developed. Establishing value is, to some degree, a matter of opinion, but several concepts are useful in arriving at the true meaning of value as used in insurance contracts. One of the basic concepts of value is "actual cash value," which is defined as replacement cost less depreciation. This concept is useful in that it establishes a value which is designed to restore you to the same financial condition you were in prior to the loss.

A problem arises here because you usually must replace the damaged or destroyed property at full cost, and so must pay the cost of the depreciation at that time. On certain types of property it is often possible to avoid this situation by insuring on a *replacement cost basis* so that the value will be determined on the actual amount required to restore your property without having to take into consideration the item of depreciation.

Interrelated to actual cash value and replacement cost are the concepts of : (1) value in use, and (2) value in exchange. Value in use refers to the benefits you derive from property in the form of shelter, income, health, or pleasure. Value in exchange is a measure of goods which can be valued in terms of the price at which the property would have sold, not exceeding the cost of replacement.

There are two primary and fundamental obligations which you must assume if a fire insurance contract is to be effective and binding upon the insurer. You are responsible for the determination of the amount of insurance for which the policy is written, and for proving a claim in case of loss. Unless you meet these obligations, the effectiveness of the policy is jeopardized and its purpose is materially affected.

Misunderstanding by you as to your responsibility for these two points would probably be partly due to the fact that insurance is future indemnity, purchased today against loss, which may or not be realized. Loose thinking could also be a factor. The amount of a fire policy relates to the value of the property to be insured. You should insure for the full value of the property in order to get the best protection. At the time the contract is purchased a properly qualified appraiser should enter the picture.

Remember that your insurance policy will cover you to the extent of the actual cash value of your property at the time of loss, but not exceeding the amount which it would cost to repair or replace the property with materials of the like kind and quality, and not exceeding the amount of the insurance you have effected. You must realize that premium cost for the protection is based not only on the value you put on your property, but also upon its type and character. Indemnity payable at time of loss is based upon a specified type of value at that time.

Judges and lawyers have expounded on the meaning of actual cash value, but are still confronted with new and exception interpretations of it. It is not book value, historical cost, purchase cost, trended costs, nor the result of cube or square foot computation, although this information when properly applied can assist in its determination. Remember that the intention of the contract is to place you in the same position after the loss as you were before.

In many instances when an insured business suffers a severe loss from fire and additional perils that may be covered, the insurance settlement falls short of the loss. Primarily the reason for claim settlements coming into this picture are (a) insufficient coverage against the background of the present day values, and (b) the insurer's misunderstanding of the basic fundamentals of a standard fire contract.

There are several advantages in securing an appraisal beyond the point of satisfying an insurer's inquiry as to whether insurance to value has been written. Primarily, appraisals for fire insurance are invaluable for the following reasons (a) to insure proper coverage without over or under insurance; (b) to provide immediate proof of loss in the event of fire, as required by the conditions of the fire policy, and (c) to facilitate settlement of claims through availability of a written record covering inventory of destroyed property with itemized values. Appraisals will also help you in the following:

a) Sale or purchase — to assure the seller that he is receiving a reasonable price under current market conditions, and to provide the purchaser with an analysis of the value of the property, both from the standpoint of current market and long term investment value.
b) Financing — to provide the lending institution with an unbiased statement of value which could be accepted to expedite a loan.
c) Expropriation — to ensure adequate compensation for actual value of property taken in whole or in part for public improvement, or expropriation.
d) Reorganization or merger — to establish, through the opinion of a disinterested appraiser, a fair value of the assets, thus assuring equitable distribution of the assets to the interested parties.
e) Litigation — to provide an expert opinion as to the value of the property to assist the court in ascertaining value, and the assurance of the availability of expert testimony if required in the process of litigation.
f) Liquidation — to provide accurate estimate of the sum that may be realized from liquidation of assets.
g) Accounting — to provide an estimate of the cost of replacing assets under current conditions, and to establish present worth of assets.

The appraisal will be paid for by you, and if you don't have it done, you are being "penny wise and pound foolish." Without it, in the event of partial or total destruction of your property, you will undoubtedly find that to furnish a proof of loss, stating the exact value of the property to the satisfaction of the adjusters, may present a serious problem.

You should review your insurance coverage periodically. *All of it.* It is something we are sometimes guilty of ignoring until it is too late. Place a bookmark in this page to remind you to call your insurance agent. Or, better still, never mind the bookmark. Call him now!

110

PROPERTY PROTECTION

The first thing you must do to start protective measures for your home is make a note of your police department number. Keep it near the telephone, clearly visible. In an emergency dial 911 and ask for police, and immediately give them your name and address.

Protection of the home begins with you. In the home. It cannot be effectively carried out without your assistance and cooperation.

No home, whether apartment or house, can be burglar-proof. However, the security of every home can be improved to the point that a burglar will not risk the chance of detection which is ever-present in a well protected home.

1. Have your doors mounted so that the hinge bolts are not exposed on the outside.
2. Have your locks properly mounted, of good quality, and able to be dead-locked.
3. Have your doors equipped with a chain-type doorstop, to prevent the door being pushed open suddenly when unlocked.
4. You should know where all the keys for your locks are distributed, and don't distribute them indiscriminately.
5. Don't leave a key under the welcome mat at your front door; a stranger might take it literally. Don't "hide" it outside the door. It won't be hidden from a burglar.
6. It is not a good idea to have car and house keys in the same key case, if your name and address is in the case. In case of loss, and discovery, someone knows where they can gain easy access to a home.
7. If you have lost or mislaid keys, you should have your lock changed.

8. Have your window locks and catches in good working order, and be sure to use them.
9. Windows that provide easy access to your home should be protected with extra locks.
10. When inspecting your home for weak points, keep in mind that burglars will use ladders, garbage pails, trellises and low roofs to reach windows and doors that are not normally accessible.
11. Consider also these other openings into your home:
    a) The milk chute which may allow someone to enter by crawling through, or which may provide access to the door lock.
    b) The coal or wood chute, again a way of entering.
    c) Openings which contain air-conditioning units or exhaust fans which can be pushed in to gain entry.
12. Your garage should be kept locked to prevent burglars using your tools and equipment to break into your home, and to prevent theft.
13. When going out for the evening, leave lights on in one or two areas in your home, *and a radio playing.*
14. When going away for extended periods of time, you should:
    a) Arrange with your neighbors to watch your home, and notify the police department if they see anything suspicious.
    b) Arrange to have all deliveries stopped, such as newspapers, *and have a neighbor pick up handbills and circulars.*
    c) Have some type of equipment, such as an automatic timing device, to turn lights on and off at designated times.
    d) Arrange to have the grass cut regularly.
    e) Leave instructions with a neighbor or your building superintendent where you can be reached in an emergency.

    In other words, when you are going away, leave your home so it has that "lived-in appearance" which helps to frighten off the burglar.
15. If you are an apartment dweller, you should:
    a) Refer unknown persons seeking entrance to your building to the superintendent and never let them in with *your* key.
    b) Let your superintendent know at all times when your apartment is usually vacant.

c) Report the presence of suspicious persons to the superintendent or to the police department.

16. If you live in a house:
    a) Ask a neighbor who knows when your home is usually vacant to report to the police any suspicious person around it.
    b) You should report the presence of suspicious persons or automobiles in the neighborhood to the police department.
17. If your doors are solidly constructed, have a peep-hole device which will enable you to identify a caller without opening the door.
18. Your valuables and extra cash should be kept in a safety deposit box at your bank or trust company.
19. You should keep a record of serial numbers and other identifying marks on your valuables in the event they are stolen.
20. Do not trust your memory with such things as license numbers. Write them down.
21. Always verify the identity of hydro, gas and other servicemen who seek entry to your home.

Now that you have read this chapter, there are two things you can do right now.

a) Place the emergency services number on your telephone, clearly visible.
b) Read this chapter again, and check the points one by one to see how much safer you can make *your* home for you and for your family.

Most Important: if you employ a babysitter, have your *address* clearly posted near the telephone. In case of emergency, a babysitter could panic and not remember the address. When I say address, I mean the address where your children and the babysitter are located.

111

FIRE PROTECTION

Read this chapter carefully, and when you have read it, read it again. It could save your life, and the lives of your loved ones.

In Case of Fire

Shout "Fire": to arouse persons nearby if you see fire, or smell smoke or gas. If you believe the fire to be in a room, a cupboard or in a basement section, keep the doors closed. Quickly shut any doors and windows that will help confine the fire, cut down the draft and prevent spread of deadly gases. This will give everyone more time to escape.

Out You Go: Save lives by getting everyone out of the building as quickly as possible. Don't wait to dress yourself or children — wrap them in blankets.

If you have to go upstairs or away from exits to rescue children and you are unable to return to the ground floor, or if you are otherwise trapped, get to a room with a window, quickly shut the door between you and the fire, and shout for help. Don't jump from upper-story windows except as a last resort — wait for help.

Remember, the air is usually better near the floor in a smoke-filled building.

Summon the Fire Department: by telephone *only* after all are out.

Never go back into a burning building. It can be totally immolated in seconds.

Try to hold the fire in check with equipment at hand while the fire department is responding. Fight the fire only if you are not endangered.

Don't waste time or your life.

Plan in Advance: Have your plan of escape from fire worked out in advance. Everyone should know the plan, and the reasons for each part of it.

Alternate escape routes are a *must* because one or more of the ways out may be blocked off by fire.

Escaping from one-story buildings is relatively simple — there are alternate routes through any of the windows to the outside. But remember, storm and screen windows may be difficult to get through. Make sure there is something such as a chair available to smash them out.

Two-story buildings require more planning because the stairway may be blocked off by fire, smoke or hot gases. Be prepared to use upper windows, perhaps to the roof of an adjacent building, by having ladders strategically located, or by means of a rope with knots at every two feet anchored to the inside of windows.

Remember, in the event of a fire during sleeping hours, a closed bedroom door may save your life.

If conditions permit, gather everyone together into one room before attempting to escape. Children are easily lost in the confusion.

When escaping *never* open the window before the door is closed behind you. This cuts down the draft which would help to spread the fire into your area of escape.

Fire drills should be carried out often enough so that everyone's role becomes automatic.

Methods of evacuating children and sick or aged persons should be studied particularly.

Everyone, including children, should know how to telephone the fire department and the number to call.

If in doubt, have your local fire chief check over your escape plan with you.

How to Fight Home Fires: When you blow out a match you extinguish a fire. It is easy to do at this stage. However, small fires can grow and join to destroy an entire city. The first five minutes are vital. Keep calm, don't panic! Remember, each fire is different.

Clothing Fires: Don't run, it fans the flame. Act quickly to smother the fire. Make victims lie down, then roll them up in a rug, coat, or blanket with the head outside. Gently beat the fire out. Give burn or shock first aid.

Cooking Fires: (involving fat, grease or oils): Turn off the stove or appliance and cover the pan, or close the oven, or pour baking soda on the fire, or use an approved type of fire extinguisher. Never use water! It will spread the flame.

Electrical Fires: (motors, wiring, etc): Unplug the appliance if possible. Use an approved type of fire extinguisher, or throw on baking soda. Never use water on live wiring, or you may get an electrical shock.

Fires in Ordinary Combustibles: Keep near the door so that you can escape if necessary. Stay low out of heat and smoke. Aim a stream at the base of the fire. For floor fires sweep from the edge in, for wall fires sweep from the bottom up. Stay outside closets, attics, etc., and shoot the stream in. Ventilate the area only after the fire is out. Remember, if the fire is large, get out and close the doors behind you.

Home-type fire-fighting tools are very effective against small fires. Brooms, or mops soaked in water, blankets, rugs, buckets and garden hoses are good examples. A threaded hose connection on each floor of the house (in bathroom, kitchen and basement) and a good length of garden hose properly coiled is a good fire protection.

There are numerous fire extinguishers on the market suitable for home use. Make sure that you use a type listed and labelled by a nationally recognized fire testing laboratory, such as the Underwriters' laboratory. Otherwise you cannot be sure it is reliable.

Home fire-fighting equipment will not be of any help unless you know how to use it. You will not have time to learn how after a fire breaks out. Read the instructions on the fire extinguisher *now* and be sure that everyone in the house knows how to use it and the other equipment as well.

The equipment is of no use unless it is in good working order. Check with the dealer or your local fire department regarding maintenance of your type of extinguisher.

Do not risk your life unless it is to save another life. The house can always be rebuilt, and unless it is a small fire you probably cannot extinguish it by yourself anyway.

Instruct Your Babysitter: During your absence the babysitter is responsible for safety of your children and your property. Impress upon her that in the event of fire, the first and most important thing to do is to get the children out quickly and stay with them. Tell her to wrap them in blankets, not take time to dress them. The following rules will assist you in advising her:

Show her through your house so that she will be familiar with each part of it, and leave *your* address, the place where the babysitting takes place, by the telephone.

Be sure she knows the quickest way out for the children.

Show her the alternate escape routes in case the regular route, such as the stairway, is blocked off by fire.

Give her the telephone number of a nearby friend who can come to her assistance quickly, and if possible, a number where you may be reached.

She must call the fire department as soon as possible from a neighbor's house.

A Fire Safety Test

Can you answer "yes" to all these questions? Questions which receive a "no" answer indicate potential danger spots which need prompt attention and correction. Inspect your home yourself — today!

In Case of Fire: Is the number of the nearest fire department or a reminder to call 911 posted near the telephone?

Have you instructed your family in a plan of action if fire breaks out?

Has your family been instructed and drilled on the location of exits from the house and how to close all windows and doors in case of fire?

Do you keep exit routes clear — especially of such things as room heaters and stoves which might start a fire and block your escape?

Are bedroom windows large enough and sufficiently unobstructed to serve as emergency exits?

Care of Children: Do you make it the rule never to leave small children alone or unattended?

Do you show your babysitter the escape routes from your home, and give instructions on the right way to call the fire department?

Do your babysitters (and you) know the first rule of safety in fire emergencies: get everybody out fast, and don't go back in?

Are your children trained to keep a safe distance from flame and spark sources?

Electrical: Has wiring been checked by a qualified person since installation?

When new appliances were added to the load, was wiring inspected and any necessary new wiring installed by a qualified electrician?

Do you check your fuse box regularly to see that only specified sizes are being used?

Are all electric motors kept oiled, clean and free from dirt accumulation?

Lightning Protection: Has your radio or television antenna been equipped with a properly grounded lightning arrestor?

Heating Equipment: Have your stoves, furnace, chimney and smoke pipes been checked and cleaned where necessary within the past year?

Are furnaces and stoves at least 18 inches from any exposed woodwork?

Do any stove pipes run through attics or concealed spaces?

Are smoke pipes, when running through combustible partitions, protected by a double ventilating metal thimble?

Do you prohibit the use of gasoline or kerosene for starting or quickening fires in your home?

Does your fireplace have a metal screen in front of it to prevent sparks from flying onto the carpet or furniture?

Are all portable heaters of a type listed by the Canadian Standards Association?

Is your portable oil heater always placed on a level floor to ensure proper operation?

Do you always refill the fuel tanks of portable heaters out of doors and in the daylight?

If you use a wick-type portable oil heater, do you trim the wick and clean it regularly?

Do you always turn your portable oil heater out upon retiring at night or when moving it from one part of the house to another?

Flammable Liquids: Are small quantities of gasoline stored in safety cans?

Have you made it a rule never to use flammable liquids like gasoline or kerosene for cleaning clothes or starting fires?

Are oil-saturated or paint rags properly disposed of or stored in metal containers?

Smoking Habits: Are approved-design ashtrays provided?

Is smoking in bed strictly against the rule in your home?

Do you make a bedtime check for smouldering butts lodged in chesterfields and also upholstered furniture?

Are you careful how you dispose of cigarettes, cigars and pipe ashes?

Are matches and lighters kept out of the reach of children?

General: If you use L.P. gas, are the cylinders outside the building on a solid foundation and located away from windows and basement doors?

Do you keep rubbish cleaned out of the attic, basement, closets, garage and yard?

Do you use extreme care when using lighter fuel to ignite your barbecue?

Do you spray your hair only away from open flames or lighted cigarettes?

Fire Protection: Have your fire extinguishers been checked and recharged if necessary within the past year?

Do you have approved fire extinguishers?

Do you have as many approved smoke detectors as your home's square-footage requires, and in the recommended locations?

Do you have enough garden hose supplying water?

Like many of the tragedies in life, fire, or at least its worst effects, can be avoided if we only think about it beforehand, and act wisely. Remember — if you learn the rules, and never need them, you lose nothing: If you never learn them and need them, when fire occurs, you may lose everything — including your life.

Hundreds lose their lives each year in Canada as the result of fire — most of them children.

112

METRIC REAL ESTATE

As the majority of Canadian residents know, conversion of weights and measures to the metric system of measurement in Canada is, of course, approved federal government policy, endorsed and implemented by all provinces.

Consumers already have been at least partially conditioned to recognizing and working with the metric system. Products such as film, cameras and related photographic equipment, skis, other sporting goods, drugs and medicines have been available solely in metric sizes for decades. Since 1975, temperature and weather forecasts have been reported in metric values.

Metric dimensions are now on articles of clothing and hardware items. Food products are now packaged and marketed in metric containers. Canadians have been driving their automobiles at speeds and distances measured in kilometres.

In the real estate industry, conversion to the metric system of measure requires all construction and all real estate transactions to be expressed in metric units and terms. This includes, but is not limited to, the appraisal, leasing, purchasing and selling of real property.

The real estate industry has perhaps a special or almost unique problem when adapting to the metric system of measure. For many industries conversion is a one-time proposition. Individuals active in the real estate industry, however, will be working with land titles, surveys and other historical documents which originated and date back over periods from one to hundreds of years. Unless and until these documents are amended to show dimensions in metric equivalents, the industry must, of course, convert the existing dimensional references to metric.

Accordingly, since real estate brokers and salespersons are working directly with the public, it is a never-ending process of educating — or at least assisting — vendors and purchasers in becoming knowledgeable and comprehending dimensions with regards to their real estate transactions.

It has been suggested that perhaps the largest challenge to metric conversion in the real estate industry and indeed all industries, is not the metric education or commitment by industry and business. Instead, the challenge and opportunity is the education and acceptance of the metric system by the public at large.

Real estate personnel must, and will, be in the "metric public familiarization business" long after they themselves have accepted and become familiar with metric units and terms.

Canada's commitment to changing to the metric system of measurement is no longer a debatable issue. It is a rational and required modern contemporary fact of life. For the real estate industry, it is an ongoing challenge and an opportunity to assist the public to learn and work with metric units.

The real estate industry has historically adapted to change. Real estate practitioners will continue this tradition by adapting to the metric system as it has adapted to various other changes affecting the industry in the past.

There are literally thousands of volumes of metric related publications, conversion tables and charts available for individuals wishing to obtain reference and resource information. Following is a portion of the material appearing in the "Metric Guide for Real Estate" brochure, published by the Canadian Real Estate Association, endorsed and approved by Metric Commission Canada. This material, reproduced with the express permission of the Canadian Real Estate Association, is intended to serve as a guideline only.

Specific application of metric measurements and metric terms to real estate advertising and all real estate related documents, will be as required by local custom and existing regulations.

Measurement Units

LENGTH

Metre(m) — is the basic unit of length in the metric system and is used for most real estate measurements. The metre replaces the foot and yard. It can be described as equal to a long pace. An average door is approximately two metres (2 m) high.

Kilometre (km) — equals one thousand metres (1000 m) and is used for most distance measurements, replacing the mile. Sixteen kilometres (16 km) is approximately 10 miles.

AREA

Square metre (m^2) — is the basic metric unit for area measurement and is used to measure the area of individual rooms, entire buildings and building lots. The square metre replaces the square foot and square yard.

Note: Never express an area as being so many metres square. There is a difference of 90 square metres between 10 square metres and 10 metres square.

Hectare (ha) — is used to express the area of larger parcels of land, for example subdivisions, farm and recreational properties. A hectare is equal to a square measuring 100 metres by 100 metres or, stated another way, 10,000 m^2. The hectare replaces the acre.

Square kilometre (km^2) — is used to measure only very large areas of

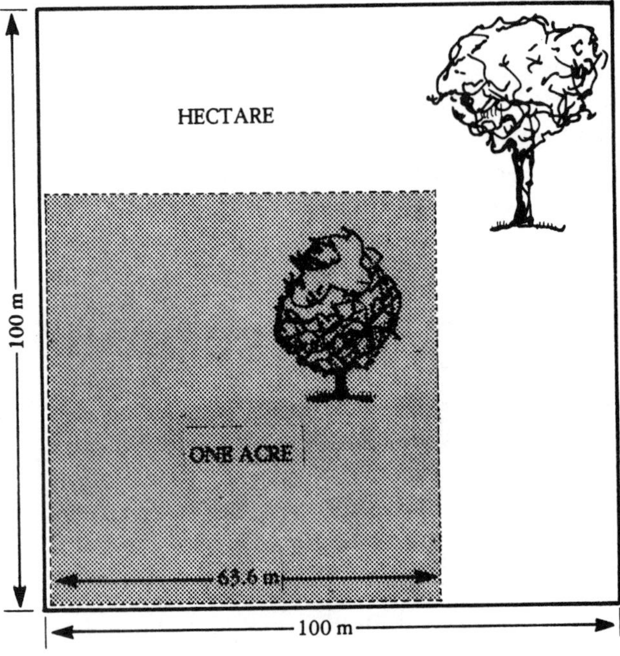

land, such as a district or entire county. The square kilometre replaces the square mile and is equal to 100 ha.

VOLUME

Litre (l) — replaces gallons. The litre is used to express volume of hot water supply and fuel tanks.

Cubic metre (m^3) — replaces cubic feet, cubic yards, and is used to measure storage and warehouse volumes.

Application and Accuracy of Metric Units

In other metric countries, metric measurements related to real estate advertising have been rounded off and applied on the following basis. This custom is being followed in Canada.

Residential:

Lot size and room dimensions — expressed in metre to the nearest 0.1 m. Areas — given in square metres to the nearest 5 m^2.

Commercial:

Dimensions — metres to the nearest 0.1 m.

Areas — square metres to the nearest 1 m^2.

Industrial:

Dimensions — metres to the nearest 0.5 m.

Areas — square metres to the nearest 10 m^2.

Volume — cubic metre to the nearest 100 m^3.

Land:

Dimensions — metres to the nearest 1 m.

Areas — square metres to the nearest 5 m^2.

Larger properties:

Areas between:

1 hectare and 10 hectares — to the nearest 0.1 ha.

10 hectares and 100 hectares — to the nearest 0.5 ha.

100 hectares and 1,000 hectares — to the nearest 1 ha.

1,000 hectares and 10,000 hectares — to the nearest 10 ha.

Areas over 10,000 ha (100 km^2) — to the nearest 1 km^2.

Rounding of Numbers

In the metric system, the rounding of measurements follows the same principle as previously used in the Canadian system.

For example:

8.2503 m becomes 8.3 m to one decimal place
8.3492 m becomes 8.35 m to two decimal places
8.3257 m becomes 8.326 m to three decimal places.

Note: The rounding of a number should be made in one step. For example, 9.1948 m correctly rounded in one step becomes 9.19 m. If the same number (9.1948) is rounded in two steps, an error occurs. 9.195 m (first step) and 9.20 m (second step).

As area or volume measurements are calculated by multiplying, rounding is always applied *after* the calculation is completed.

Writing Metric

There is a unique and easily recognized symbol for each metric unit. These symbols remain constant in all languages and for each application. A few of the basic rules for the use of symbols are:

- Use symbols instead of writing out full unit names. (3 m, *not* 3 metres — 9 ha, *not* 9 hectares)
- Never pluralize symbols (1 m, 5 m, *not* 5 ms).
- Always insert a full space between the quantity and the symbol. (3 m, *not* 3m — 9 ha, *not* 9 ha).
- Always use decimals when writing metric — *NOT* fractions (9.5 m *NOT* 9 1/2 m — 0.5 km^2 *NOT* 1/2 km^2)
- Separate long lines of digits into more easily read blocks of three digits, with regard to the decimal point. (96 343.581 583, *not* 96343.581583). A space is optional with a four digit number. (4567.1234 or 4 567.123 4)
- Do not use a period after a symbol, unless the symbol occurs at the end of a sentence.

Simplified Conversion Tables

Until such time as all real estate surveys, deeds and legal records have been converted into metric units, conversion of Canadian system units to (and from) metric system units will be unavoidable. The following table provides conversion factors for most Canadian units used previously to express measurements relating to real estate.

Note: When converting existing Canadian units to metric units, do not use numbers which imply a greater accuracy than was acceptable in the past. Dimensions should be expressed in metric units to the minimum number of significant figures — consistent with the need to express them with sufficient accuracy to serve their purpose.

Length

1 m = 39.370 inches
1 m = 3.28084 feet
1 m = 1.09361 yard
1 inch = 0.0254 m
1 foot = 0.3048 m
1 yard = 0.9144 m
1 km = 0.621371 mile
1 mile = 1.609344 km

Conversion factors for other Canadian units of length.

1 pole or rod = 5.0292 m
1 chain = 20.1168 m
1 arpent = 0.2012 km
1 furlong = 0.2012 km

Area

1 m^2 = 10.7639 square feet
1 m^2 = 1,1960 square yards
1 ha = 2.47105 acres
1 km^2 = 0.386102 square mile
1 square foot = 0.092903 m^2
1 square yard = 0.836127 m^2
1 acre = 0.404686 ha
1 square mile = 2.589988 km^2
= 258.998 ha

Conversion factors for other Canadian units of area.

1 rood = 1011.714 m^2
1 arpent = 0.3419 ha
1 quarter section = 64.752 ha
1 half section = 129.504 ha
1 section = 258.998 ha

Volume

1 m^3 = 35.3147 cubic feet
= 1.30795 cubic yards
1 cubic foot = 0.028317 m^3

1 cubic yard = 0.764555 m^3
1 litre = 0.21997 gallon
1 gallon = 4.54609 litres

Price Conversion/Comparisons

$100 per m^2 = $9.29 per square foot
$10 per square foot = $107.64 per m^2
$1,000 per ha = $404.69 per acre
$100 per acre = $247.10 per ha
$1,000 per km^2 = $2,590. per square mile
$1,000 per square mile = $386.10 per km^2

113

QUICK APPRAISALS

An appraisal is an opinion of value, and it logically follows that the better-qualified the appraiser, the higher the rating of the appraisal. A good arbiter of an appraisal is the buyer, the one who agrees with an appraisal to the point of paying the price.

The most recognized appraiser in Canada is the one with the designation "A.A.C.I." (Accredited Appraiser, Canadian Institute). If one were to seek a real estate degree of qualification that carries with it an assured professional income, this is the one to shoot for. It is a degree recognized by our courts, requiring years of application to obtain.

There are professional appraisers from coast to coast, and if you require a highly regarded opinion of value, call one. But there are times when all you want is a rough idea of the value of your property, which is where this chapter can help.

In appraising *any* property, the first thing one must establish is its legal use. Check the zoning. There would be no point, for example, in trying to establish the value of a house as a rooming house operation if the zoning stated that the area is strictly designated for single family dwellings.

The three generally accepted areas of appraisal are (a) comparable sales; (b) replacement value; and (c) capitalization of a cash flow.

Housing

Comparable sale values are most commonly used in housing, and are reasonably reliable. If three houses of a similar plan and condition to yours sold recently for about $175,000, there is little point in expecting that you could get a few thousand more for yours, although some try. Usually an overpriced house is easy to spot — the "for sale" sign has been there for more than three weeks or so. In an active market there is a buyer for every house, if it is priced right, and a house that is priced right certainly won't take any more than three weeks to move.

An excellent opinion of the market value of your home can be obtained from a real estate agent who has been active in your neighborhood for two or three years. The agent is on top of local values and has a full knowledge of what every house for blocks around sold for.

Many brokers will provide a verbal opinion of value without charge, obviously because they think that sooner or later they will get your listing. The easiest way to get it is to simply call an active local broker and say you would like to talk about the possibility of selling. He, or one of his salesmen, will be there lickety split, believe me.

This is your free "appraisal," but if you want the price with a view to selling, it is better to obtain a figure from about three different agencies and average the results.

The homeowner who has done quite a bit of renovating, such as finishing a recreation room, installing a bar, laying top-grade broadloom, decorating with expensive wallcoverings, etc. may be of the opinion that all these costs can be recovered in selling. Forget it; they can't. Even if one is fortunate enough to find a buyer who thinks all these extras suit him just fine, the buyer won't feel like paying any more than about half the costs of the work. So keep this in mind when pricing your home.

If the house is in an overall average price range for your area, a quick stab at pricing can be to work on average price increases over a number of years. Average increases, even to local areas in a municipality, can often be obtained from a member of a real estate board.

If the home is something out of the ordinary, not a standard plan, it will take something more than sales comparisons to establish value, because there won't be any comparisons to use. This is where replacement value can come into play, and requires a heavier inspection and examination than one of a standard plan. Which will cost money, because it will call for the work of a fee appraiser, who certainly won't work for nothing.

Commercial Buildings

Capitalizing the cash flow is a common method of appraisal here. Study chapter 12 "Capitalization," and then go to work on it.

Annual gross income:	$100,000
Annual operating expenses:	50,000
Income before debt charge:	$ 50,000

The operating expenses will include everything, including municipal taxes. The $50,000 is the cash return for the year. If the property is clear of mortgage debt, this figure could be capitalized at the local going rate. If it is 8%, then one could say the property is worth $625,000. But the buyer probably won't agree with this because he won't be buying for cash. He will finance the purchase with a mortgage or two, and the mortgage payment will have a large bearing on what he will pay.

If current mortgage rates are 12% on such a building, and the buyer reasoned he could get a $400,000 mortgage through his connections, here is what the financing will show. The mortgage is amortized over 25 years.

Annual gross income:	$100,000
Annual operating expenses:	50,000
Income before debt charge:	50,000
Annual mortgage payment:	49,531
Cash flow:	$ 469

See the problem? Nothing left but petty cash. The mortgage lender would take a look at this and probably say no way. Too close to the vest. If a vacancy occurred in the building, there would be a debit cash flow. Zilch.

So the buyer takes a look at a $350,000 mortgage. Same rate and amortization.

Income before debt charge:	$50,000
Annual mortgage payment:	43,339
Cash flow:	$ 6,661

Now the buyer will capitalize the cash flow at 8%, which will produce a figure of $83,262.

This $83,262 will be added to the principal amount of the mortgage ($350,000) and the result is what a buyer will say the property is worth: $433,262, or round it out at about $435,000.

So you can see that the costs of financing will be the criterion in establishing market value of the property.

If the property has a mortgage on it at a lower rate, say 9%, then the price will go up, with reservation. I say this because if the 9% mortgage has just two or three years to run, then the buyer will be faced with renewal or refinancing, and of course he couldn't be sure that he would do it at 9%. A long term, of course, is a different matter.

Other factors in this appraisal could be the possibility of increasing the income if the majority of leases were to expire soon. The value of the land itself, without the building, may also be an overriding factor.

Industrial Buildings

A good appraisal here can be done by determining the *rental value* of the property on a *net* basis. Study the chapter "Buying an Industrial Building."

After a little probing, if it can be reasonably assumed that the building could be leased at $1.25 per square foot per year, and the building has a net rentable area of 10,000 square feet, the net annual rental income would be $12,500.

Now, I ask you to first review chapter 12, "Capitalization."

The strength of the tenancy can have a bearing on the price; it is reasonable to assume that the stronger the covenant, the less the rent. For an example, let us assume that with a good tenant, one who we know will pay the rent promptly and behave in a responsible manner in caring for the property, a satisfactory rate of return would be 9%.

Capitalize the projected net return of $12,500 at 9%:

$$\frac{12{,}500}{.09} = \$138{,}888$$

So a reasonable assessed market value of the property will be $138,888.

However, remember that not many buyers will purchase a vacant industrial building unless they are getting what they consider to be a very good deal. The arithmetic of the buyer of the vacant building will be worked in a similar manner to the foregoing, but he may be a little tougher because the building is vacant.

With a building tenanted to a good covenant, the value is comparatively easy to establish.

Vacant Land

Again, we look at the zoning. What can the land be used for? Its maximum use. By that I mean that if the zoning will allow a 20,000-square-foot building to be erected, complete with parking facilities etc., then it will be appraised on that basis, and not on anything less.

However, remember that to realize the appraised price, a buyer will have to be found who would be willing to buy it on that basis. The eventual selling price of anything is the proof of the appraisal. If a buyer cannot be found for maximum use, we have to hang in there until we find one, or lower our sights and look for offers.

Take a piece of land that is zoned for construction of a nice little three-story building with 10,000 rentable square feet on each floor. Complete with parking.

Step one: Estimate a reasonable rental figure. A gross figure — one where the owner pays the building expenses. Do a little probing of other buildings in the area. If it is determined that the gross rental would be $10 per square foot then the gross income would be $300,000 (plus a bonus in the rental income of the parking spaces).

Step two: Take about 50% of the gross income and allow that figure ($150,000) for operating expenses, including taxes.

Step three: Determine the construction costs for such a building. This figure can be obtained possibly from your local real estate board, or from a firm of quantity surveyors. Assume the costs average $30 per square foot.

Step four: The building should show a net return of about 10% as an investment, so we will capitalize the net return of $150,000 at 10% and this will be the allowable cost for the project, including land ($1,500,000). Remember, this is a quick appraisal, so we won't go into the mechanics of mortgaging. You can doodle with that later.

Step five: Deduct the construction costs from the allowable cost:

Allowable:	$1,500,000
30,000 s.f. @ $30	900,000
	$ 600,000

The $600,000 is the quick appraisal of the land value. When you have all this worked out, call a commercial and industrial real estate broker and ask him what adjustments should be made in your figures. The foregoing is only an example of the mechanics of the appraisal — the location of the land will have a lot to say about it, which is where the advice of the local broker can be invaluable.

With vacant land zoned industrial, use the same principle, but assess the rental on a net basis, as mentioned before.

With other vacant land, building lots, farms, bush, swamp, etc., call a *local* broker and seek his advice. Always call the local brokers. They know what they're talking about (most of the time).

114

SELLING REAL ESTATE AS A CAREER

Most real estate is bought and sold through the efforts and/or assistance of real estate salespeople. They are employed by real estate brokers who, in effect, operate a clearinghouse for the salespeople's business.

Some brokers are tied to their sales staff and would perish without them. They are excellent administrators, but weak salesmen.

Other brokers are top-drawer salespeople and if their sales staff deserted them they could press on and make a remarkable living on their own.

Do not assume that because a real estate salesman has had his licence for years, he is an encyclopedia on the subject.

Some are lazy and do not care to exert themselves to learn anything about the business that does not touch their particular field. Others are just the opposite. They are the ones who, aside from selling ability, are constantly confronted with questions and problems they cannot answer immediately, but who just as constantly find the answers. And remember them.

An amazing thing about the business is that no one can really spot a potentially hot-shot salesperson. Brokers can give applicants all the available tests, but my experience over the years is that tests won't always determine winners.

The greatest salesman I ever met couldn't spell "cat." And I mean it.

The first time I noticed him was when he brought a couple through an open house I was sitting on. The couple liked the house and asked him to make a note of a few things for an offer they were going to sign. Instead of writing them down, he handed the prospects a pen and paper and said it would be better if *they* wrote things down, so there wouldn't be any misunderstanding.

Later, I saw his draft of the offer. As an exercise in English, it was a disaster. But the office secretary knew what he was saying. He got his deal and I had to go sit on another house.

It is difficult to give a balanced view of the real estate industry to a person seeking a career in sales. I received a government publication in the mail listing future expected employment needs in our country. Talented engineers were predicted to be in short supply, as were real estate agents. As a real estate salesperson myself, I found that difficult to understand. After more thought I concluded it depends on your perspective.

If you were to ask your local real estate board about a career in real estate sales, you would probably be given a pen to sign up for the next available course. The more members the board can enlist, the more fees it can collect and the better services it can provide. The board's first obligation is to the needs of the broker.

Ask a real estate broker if he would have a job opening in real estate sales coming up in the near future and he will probably lead you to a desk and say, "This desk is reserved for you." If the office was already full he would start rearranging the furniture or put a desk in the hall if he had to just so he could accommodate one more agent. If he has only one agent who produces 50 deals a year it is the same as having 50 agents making one deal a year. Fifty deals is fifty deals. More agents means more deals. It also means more headaches, but that's secondary.

Governments argue that with more agents there is more competition. More competition is good because it forces commissions down and gives consumers a better break.

And what about the salespeople? What do they feel? Agents say there are too many agents. Agents from the same office compete with one another and with agents from other brokers. They complain that there are too many part-timers. Part-timers complain that because there are so many agents, they can't earn a living full-time and need to supplement their income with another job or a pension. Overcrowding the industry does not reduce commissions; it creates resistance to lowering commissions because an agent can no longer afford a reasonable life and demands more from each deal. To an agent a 1% cut in total commission means an unacceptable 30% cut in gross pay.

Here are some real numbers. In Toronto there are 25,000 agents, and the Toronto real estate board reports on average about 2,500 sales a month. If you assume one selling agent and one listing agent per deal then only 5,000 agents out of 25,000 have a deal each month. Likewise 20,000 agents are starving without a deal every month. That represents only one deal a year per agent. In a good market there might be 6,000 deals a month or 12,000 agents with a deal each month. Still, more than 50% of the agents are without a deal every month. There are 80,000 agents in Canada. That means one agent for every 125 houses. Perhaps three agents on every block.

Between 1980 and 1992 we experienced two recessions. Those years — 1981–82, 1990–92 — have been disastrous for real estate salespeople. The recovery years from 1983 to 1986 showed average sales, and the remaining years were excellent. Out of 12 years, five were disastrous, four were all right and three were excellent.

Here are the incomes earned by real estate salespersons in Canada in 1988, a good year. These are gross commission earnings. Most agents have sales expenses between \$10,000 and \$30,000 per year, some as high as \$50,000 or \$60,000. Keep in mind that 52% of agents had a university degree.

Gross Earnings (× \$1000)	
Less than 10	16%
10 – 20	12%
20 – 30	11%
30 – 40	10%
40 – 50	10%
50 – 60	8%
60 – 80	12%
80 – 120	10%
120 +	11%

The median for gross earnings was \$52,800. During the recession of 1990–92 it was common among agents to earn 50–60% less than in the preceding years. Between 25% and 30% of the agents did not survive the recession and have not renewed their licenses.

To earn a better-than-average income in real estate sales you must be prepared to put in 60 to 80 hours a week. You must be highly self-motivated, and willing to give up evenings and weekends. You must be able to focus on the routine of prospecting daily while having a cow bell around your neck — that is, you must be available to take calls at any time of day or night.

The lure of big commission dollars and the minimal education requirements may make the real estate career appear to be a dream from heaven, but many are not successful. There is a very high dropout rate during the first eight months in the business. And after some years in the business, an agent may well ask, "Why am I doing this to myself?" There are months so bad that you are ready to quit the business altogether. The next month could be the best month ever. Ups and downs, frustrations and disappointment are a way of life. If you can't deal with discouragement on a daily basis this business is not for you.

Success does not depend on formal education but on your hard work, a bit of luck, some good contacts and a head that won't crack when you bang it against a brick wall. These are the realities of the real estate business.

Good luck!

115

INTEREST RATES

Remember, the more frequent the compounding, the greater the yield to the *lender*. The tables on the following pages will provide helpful information in determining interest calculations for a number of mortgage loans:

1) Interest only loans
2) A fixed principal payment, plus interest
3) A blended payment (interest and principal)

The last column on each page shows the effective annual yield to the lender.

However, before calculating interest, ensure that you are familiar with the Federal Interest Act, and its effect on mortgages. If you cannot obtain a copy locally, write to the Queen's Printer, Ottawa, Ontario, and get one.

Interest only loans: simply use the rate applicable to the compounding frequency and the period of payment.

Fixed principal payment, plus interest: On the first payment, use the appropriate rate for the entire amount of the loan. On subsequent payments, use the appropriate rate and apply it to the outstanding principal balance of the loan.

Blended payment (interest and principal): Calculate the interest using the appropriate rate. The payment will include interest and principal, so the balance of the payment will be the amount of principal to be deducted from the principal balance owing.

For example, take a $10,000 loan, at 10%, compounded half-yearly, repayable at $100 monthly. The first month's interest will be $81.64 on the $10,000 so the balance of the payment ($18.36) will be applied to the principal. Deduct this $18.36 from the $10,000 when estimating the second payment, so the interest on the second payment will be \$9,981.64 × 0.816485, or \$81.50. The balance of this month's payment of \$100 will be \$18.50, which will be applied to principal. Repeat this throughout the loan.

COMPOUNDED MONTHLY

	Payable Monthly	*Payable Quarterly*	*Payable Semi-Annually*	*Payable Annually*
10	0.833333	2.520891	5.105331	10.471307
10¼	0.845167	2.584450	5.235695	10.745514
10½	0.875000	2.648036	5.366192	11.020345
10¾	0.895833	2.711647	5.496825	11.295801
11	0.916667	2.775285	5.627592	11.571884
11¼	0.937500	2.838950	5.758496	11.848594
11½	0.958333	2.902640	5.889533	12.125933
11¾	0.979167	2.966357	6.020706	12.403901
12	1.000000	3.030100	6.152015	12.682503
12¼	1.020833	3.093869	6.283459	12.961736
12½	1.041667	3.157665	6.415039	13.241605
12¾	1.062500	3.221487	6.546754	13.522108
13	1.083333	3.285335	6.678605	13.803248
13¼	1.104167	3.349210	6.810592	14.085026
13½	1.125000	3.413111	6.942715	14.367444
13¾	1.145833	3.477038	7.074975	14.650502
14	1.166667	3.540992	7.207371	14.934203
14¼	1.187500	3.604972	7.339902	15.218546
14½	1.208333	3.668978	7.472571	15.503535
14¾	1.229167	3.733011	7.605375	15.789169
15	1.250000	3.797070	7.738318	16.075452
15¼	1.270833	3.861156	7.871397	16.362382
15½	1.291667	3.925267	8.004612	16.649962
15¾	1.312500	3.989406	8.137965	16.938195
16	1.333333	4.053570	8.271454	17.227078

COMPOUNDED QUARTERLY

	Payable Monthly	*Payable Quarterly*	*Payable Semi-Annually*	*Payable Annually*
10	0.826484	2.500000	5.062500	10.381289
10¼	0.846973	2.562500	5.190664	10.650758
10½	0.867453	2.625000	5.318906	10.920720
10¾	0.887930	2.687500	5.444723	11.191176
11	0.908390	2.750000	5.575625	11.462126
11¼	0.928846	2.812500	5.704102	11.733571
11½	0.949293	2.875000	5.832656	12.005511
11¾	0.969732	2.937500	5.961289	12.277947
12	0.990163	3.000000	6.090000	12.550881
12¼	1.010586	3.062500	6.218789	12.824311
12½	1.031001	3.125000	6.347656	13.098240
12¾	1.051407	3.187500	6.476602	13.372667
13	1.071805	3.250000	6.605625	13.647593
13¼	1.092194	3.312500	6.734727	13.923019
13½	1.112576	3.375000	6.863906	14.198945
13¾	1.132949	3.437500	6.993164	14.475372
14	1.153314	3.500000	7.122500	14.752300
14¼	1.176927	3.562500	7.272628	15.074166
14½	1.194020	3.625000	7.381406	15.307664
14¾	1.214360	3.687500	7.510976	15.586101
15	1.234693	3.750000	7.640625	15.865042
15¼	1.255017	3.812500	7.770351	16.144487
15½	1.275333	3.875000	7.900156	16.424437
15¾	1.295641	3.937500	8.030039	16.704893
16	1.315940	4.000000	8.160000	16.985856

COMPOUNDED HALF-YEARLY

	Payable Monthly	*Payable Quarterly*	*Payable Semi-Annually*	*Payable Annually*
10	0.816485	2.469508	5.000000	10.250000
10¼	0.836478	2.530483	5.125000	10.512656
10½	0.856452	2.591423	5.250000	10.775625
10¾	0.876405	2.652326	5.375000	11.038906
11	0.896338	2.713193	5.500000	11.302500
11¼	0.916254	2.774024	5.625000	11.566406
11½	0.936149	2.834819	5.750000	11.830625
11¾	0.956024	2.895578	5.875000	12.095156
12	0.975879	2.956301	6.000000	12.360000
12¼	0.995715	3.016989	6.125000	12.625156
12½	1.015532	3.077641	6.250000	12.890625
12¾	1.035329	3.138257	6.375000	13.156406
13	1.055107	3.198837	6.500000	13.422500
13¼	1.074866	3.259382	6.625000	13.688906
13½	1.094605	3.319892	6.750000	13.955625
13¾	1.114325	3.380366	6.875000	14.222656
14	1.134026	3.440804	7.000000	14.490000
14¼	1.153708	3.501208	7.125000	14.757656
14½	1.173370	3.561576	7.250000	15.025625
14¾	1.193013	3.621909	7.375000	15.293906
15	1.212679	3.682207	7.500000	15.562500
15¼	1.232243	3.742470	7.625000	15.831406
15½	1.251830	3.802697	7.750000	16.100625
15¾	1.271397	3.862890	7.875000	16.370156
16	1.290946	3.923048	8.000000	16.640000

COMPOUNDED ANNUALLY

	Payable Monthly	*Payable Quarterly*	*Payable Semi-Annually*	*Payable Annually*
10	0.797414	2.411369	4.880885	10.000000
10¼	0.816485	2.469508	5.000000	10.250000
10½	0.835516	2.527548	5.118980	10.500000
10¾	0.854507	2.585489	5.237826	10.750000
11	0.873459	2.643333	5.356538	11.000000
11¼	0.892372	2.701079	5.475115	11.250000
11½	0.911247	2.758727	5.593560	11.500000
11¾	0.930082	2.816279	5.711873	11.750000
12	0.948879	2.873734	5.830052	12.000000
12¼	0.967638	2.931094	5.948101	12.250000
12½	0.986358	2.988357	6.066017	12.500000
12¾	1.005040	3.045525	6.183803	12.750000
13	1.023684	3.102598	6.301458	13.000000
13¼	1.042291	3.159577	6.418983	13.250000
13½	1.060860	3.216461	6.536379	13.500000
13¾	1.079391	3.273252	6.653645	13.750000
14	1.097885	3.329948	6.770783	14.000000
14¼	1.116342	3.386552	6.887792	14.250000
14½	1.134762	3.443063	7.004673	14.500000
14¾	1.153145	3.499481	7.121426	14.750000
15	1.171492	3.555808	7.238053	15.000000
15¼	1.189801	3.612042	7.354553	15.250000
15½	1.208075	3.668185	7.470926	15.500000
15¾	1.226313	3.724237	7.587174	15.750000
16	1.244514	3.780199	7.703296	16.000000

116

DEPRECIATION ALLOWANCE TABLES

This is a 30-year table covering the maximum capital loss allowance (depreciation) permitted for income tax purposes on a class 1 (brick) building — 4% reducing on $1 million for example.

It is easy to use for your own purposes. For example, if you wish to do some advance figuring on the maximum depreciation allowable over the first 15 years, you will find that your undepreciated balance is 54.2086% of the original capital cost of the building. Looking at it another way, you will have depreciated your building by 45.7914% of its original cost.

Year No.	Maximum Allowance	End-of-Year Undepreciated Balance
1	$40,000.00	$960,000.00
2	38,400.00	921,600.00
3	36,864.00	884,736.00
4	35,389.00	849,346.56
5	33,973.86	815,372.69
6	32,614.90	782,757.79
7	31,310.31	751,447.48
8	30,057.89	721,389.58
9	28,855.58	692,533.99
10	27,701.35	664,832.63
11	26,593.30	638,239.33
12	25,529.57	612,709.76
13	24,508.39	588,201.37
14	23,528.05	564,673.31

15	22,586.93	542,086.38
16	21,683.45	520,402.93
17	20,816.11	499,580.81
18	19,983.47	479,603.34
19	19,184.13	460,419.20
20	18,416.76	442,002.44
21	17,680.09	424,320.34
22	16,972.89	407,349.45
23	16,293.97	391,055.47
24	15,642.21	375,413.25
25	15,016.53	360,396.72
26	14,415.86	345,980.85
27	13,839.23	332,141.62
28	13,285.66	318,855.95
29	12,754.23	306,101.72
30	12,244.06	293,857.65

117

CAPITAL GAINS TAX APPRAISALS

Most Canadians are not affected by capital gains tax on their real estate. A gain on the sale of your residence will not be taxed as long as you use it only as your principal residence.

Generally speaking, real estate, other than one's principal residence, when sold will be subject to a capital gain or a capital loss. The gain would normally be when the property is sold for more than it cost. The net gain, after all deductions, will be subject to our capital gains tax.

When a net capital gain is established, 25% of the gain will be free of tax, and the other 75% will be added to your income tax return filed for the year of disposition. The capital gains tax payable will therefore be determined by your tax bracket for the year.

For example, if a net gain is $5,000 and your tax bracket is 40% after adding your gain, here is what will be *tax free* of the $5,000:

25% of $5,000	$1,250
60% of $3,750	$2,250
Tax Free:	$3,500

Capital losses can be deducted from capital gains. Excess loss can be carried back three years and forward indefinitely against past or future capital gains as the case may be.

If you are in a loss situation, contact your local income tax office for the detailed application of this to your total capital loss.

A capital gain or capital loss occurs when you dispose of your real estate (other than your principal residence). A capital disposition, however, is not limited to a sale. Other transactions or events may also give rise to a capital disposition, such as: a) The exchange of real estate; b) Giving some real estate to another; c) Expropriation of your real estate.

While as a rule a capital gain or loss occurs whenever there is a change in the ownership of a property, there are other situations in which a capital gain or loss occurs even though there is no actual change in ownership. These *deemed dispositions* may occur when (1) The owner of property becomes a non-resident of Canada; (2) The owner of property changes its use (for example, he starts to rent a house in which he lived); (3) A person dies (he is "deemed" to have disposed of all his capital property immediately before his death).

Valuation Day

The inclusion of half of capital gains in income began on January 1, 1972, necessitating a method for ensuring that no tax would be assessed, or losses allowed, for any capital gain or loss which arose before that date. This was accomplished by establishing a starting point, *Valuation Day*, for calculating capital gains and losses.

Valuation Day will affect those who on December 31, 1971, owned real estate (other than a principal residence) such as cottages, land and rental property.

When a taxpayer disposes of real estate held on December 31, 1971, its value on that day is used to determine the capital gain or loss since that date.

Valuation Day is important only for property acquired before January 1, 1972. There are no Valuation Day implications for property acquired on or after that day.

To determine any capital gain or loss when you dispose of these properties, you must know its fair market value at Valuation Day. You do not have to establish or report the Valuation Day value of your property to Revenue Canada, Taxation, until you dispose of it, nor will any value be considered or accepted beforehand.

Although you may not be planning to dispose of your property for several years, it is to your advantage to determine the Valuation Day fair market value of the property now; if you wait, the value becomes increasingly difficult to establish.

You should keep in mind that all property will eventually be disposed of for income tax purposes. Even if it is never sold or otherwise disposed of, disposal will be deemed to have occurred on the death of the owner.

It is your responsibility to establish the Valuation Day market value of your property. Determining the value may be a simple matter, which you may wish to do yourself, or the size and type of the property may make it sufficiently difficult that you require a professional appraiser.

Note, however, that the cost of appraisal fees is not deductible from your income and cannot be deducted from any capital gain on eventual disposition of the property.

There are two methods for determining the fair market value of real estate on Valuation Day:

1. Obtain from a professional appraiser a fully documented appraisal with supporting data which adequately explains the investigation carried out. It should include a detailed explanation of the basis used to arrive at the estimated value. Remember that these figures may not be required for several years, when the appraiser may no longer be around to explain his method.
2. Establish the value yourself. Collect information on sales of similar properties in the same area around December 31, 1971. This will help you to arrive at the fair market value of your own property. To support your valuation, you should retain documents containing the following information:
   a) A brief description of the property, including location, lot, building size, and date and type of construction.
   b) The cost and date of purchase.
   c) The cost of any additions or improvements.
   d) The property assessment for municipal tax purposes.
   e) Insurance coverage.

Keep receipts for the cost of labor or materials for any improvements, and tax assessment notices. These documents will help to support your estimate of the value. Additional information may be required for certain types of property. For example:

Farm Property	a) The type of land (arable, bush, scrub). b) The type of farming done.
Rental Property	a) The gross annual rental income. b) The net annual income before depreciation (capital cost allowance).
Commercial/ Industrial	a) The type of business for which the property is used. b) The gross annual income derived from it. c) The new annual income before depreciation (capital cost allowance).

Remember, any capital gain on the sale of your home is not normally subject to tax. Thus your home need not be valued, provided you use it only as your principal residence. Any type of structure you own and ordinarily inhabit may qualify as principal residence. Shares of capital stock of a cooperative housing corporation may also qualify.

If you use your home partly for producing income, capital gains may be taxable when there is a change in use of part of the property or when the property is sold. This rule applies where part of the home is used as the residence of the owner and the remainder is rented or used for carrying on a business. In this case, a valuation of the home would be required and the valuation must be apportioned between the part used to produce income and the part occupied as a principal residence.

If your principal residence is part of a farm, you should establish the value of the principal residence separately in addition to the value of the farm as a whole. An option is available in computing any capital gain on the sale of a farm, which requires a Valuation Day value for the home as distinct from the value of the remainder of the farm property. Contact your local tax office for details of farm disposition options.

The income tax department has set up a Real Estate Data Bank containing information to assist in verifying Valuation Day value reported in income tax returns. This bank contains records of real estate transactions which took place in 1971 and 1972, and information in it has been computerized and kept in district tax offices.

Taxpayers who are disposing of property may obtain information from the Data Bank.

The disposition of real estate other than your principal residence will usually result in a capital gain and may require a Valuation Day value. Cottages, summer homes, second residences, residential rental property, farms, commercial and industrial land and buildings are included in this type of real estate.

If you own property purchased before Valuation Day, you would be well advised to get its Valuation Day value established now.

NOTE: Please see also chapter 9, "Capital Gain Tax Rules."

118

REAL PROPERTY DEFINITIONS

Abstract	A written, condensed history of title to a parcel of real property, recorded in a land registry office.
Abuttals	The bounding of a parcel of land by other land, street, river, etc. A boundary.
Acceleration Clause	On mortgage payment default, the entire balance of the loan is due and immediately payable.
Administrator	One who has charge of the estate of a deceased person who died without a will, or one who did not appoint an executor. Appointed by court order.
Adverse Possession	When someone, other than the owner, takes physical possession of property, without the owner's consent.
Agent	One who legally represents an individual or corporate body.
Agreement of Sale	Written agreement whereby one agrees to buy, and another agrees to sell, according to the terms of the agreement.
Agreement to Lease	Written agreement whereby one agrees to lease real property to another, according to the terms of the agreement.
Amortization	To extinguish a loan by means of a sinking fund.
Appraisal	A written estimate of the market value of real property, made by a qualified expert.
Appreciation	Increased market value of real property.

Appurtenances	Additional rights that are an adjunction to real property.
Assessed Value	Value of real property set by a municipality for taxation purposes.
Assessor	Person employed by a municipality or other government body empowered to place valuation on property for taxation purposes.
Assignment	Legal transfer of interest in real property or a mortgage from one person to another.
Assumption Agreement	An agreement whereby a person other than the mortgagor covenants to perform the obligations in the mortgage deed.
Attornment of Rent	Taking of rents by Mortgagee in Possession to protect his rights in case of default by mortgagor.
Blanket Mortgage	Single mortgage registered to cover more than one parcel of real property.
Bond	A binding agreement to strengthen the covenant of performance.
Broker	A person who legally trades in real estate for another, for compensation.
Certificate of Charge	Provincial government acknowledgment of registration of mortgage in a land titles office.
Certificate of Title	Provincial government acknowledgment of registration of title deed in a land titles office.
Chattels	Moveable possessions, such as furniture, personal possessions, etc. A furnace, before it is installed, is a moveable possession. Once installed it is not.
Chattel Mortgage	A mortgage on moveable possessions, personal property.

Closing The time at which a real estate transaction is concluded legally in a registry office.

Cloud on Title An impairment to title of real property, such as executed judgment, mortgage, lien, etc., registered legally against the property.

CMHC Canada Mortgage and Housing Corporation, a Crown agency administering Canada's National Housing Act.

Commission Financial remuneration paid to an agent for selling or leasing property, based on an agreed percentage of the amount involved.

Consideration Something of value for compensation.

Contract An agreement upon lawful consideration which binds the parties to a performance.

Conveyance Transmitting title of real property from one to another.

Covenant Solemn agreement.

Convenantee Lender in a (mortgage) deed.

Covenantor Borrower in a (mortgage) deed.

Date of Maturity In mortgages, the last day of the term of the mortgage.

Deed A document containing an agreement that has been signed, sealed, and containing proof of its delivery; effective only on the date of delivery. (Mortgage deed, title deed, etc.)

Demise To transfer or convey an estate for a term of years, or life.

Deposit Money or other consideration of value given as pledge for fulfillment of a contract or agreement.

Depreciation Reduction in market value of property. Also used to indicate capital cost allowance.

Derivative Mortgage	Mortgage on mortgage. Mortgagee assigns his mortgage to lender to secure loan.
Dower	Rights of wife or widow in freehold property owned by her husband.
Easement	A right acquired to use another's land or buildings, generally for access to some other adjoining property.
Encroachment	Undue or unlawful trespass on another's property, usually caused by a building, or part of a building, or obstruction.
Encumbrance	Any legal claim registered against property.
Escheat	Conveyance of property to the Crown (Government) due to intestate person dying and leaving no heirs.
Escrow	A deed or contract delivered to a third party to be held until the payment or fulfillment of the agreement by the grantee.
Estate	One's interest in lands and any other subject of property.
Equity	The financial interest of a property owner in excess of any encumbrances, limited by its market value.
Executor	Person legally appointed by testator to carry out the terms of his will.
Exclusive Listing	An agreement granting sole and exclusive rights to an agent to sell property.
Fee Simple	Absolute ownership of property.
Fee Tail	Property ownership, limited to some particular heirs.
First Mortgage	One that takes precedence over all others. (Mortgage seniority established by date and time of registration.)

Fixture Permanent improvements to property that remain with it.

Foreclosure A legally enforced transfer of real property ordered by a court to satisfy unpaid debts. The most common is a foreclosure by a mortgagee.

Freehold Property held in fee simple (untrammelled tenure) or fee tail (for the term of the owner's life.)

Frontage Property line facing street.

Gale Date The date on which interest is charged.

Grant An instrument of conveyance transferring property from one to another.

Grantee Person to whom a conveyance is made; one who receives legal transfer of property from another; the buyer.

Grantor Person who makes a conveyance; one who transfers property to another; the seller.

Hereditament Property that may be inherited.

Hypothèque Lien on real estate (Quebec).

Hypothecary Creditor Mortgagee (Quebec).

Hypothecary Debtor Mortgagor (Quebec).

Indenture An agreement between two or more parties. Originally, indentures were duplicates placed together and cut in a wavy line, so that the two papers could be identified as being authentic by corresponding to each other.

Instrument A writing instructing one in regard to something that has been agreed on.

Intestate	Not having a will.
Joint Tenancy	Ownership of real property by two or more persons; when one dies, his share automatically passes to the survivor(s).
Judgment	Binding decision of the court.
Landed Property	Having an interest in and pertaining to the land.
Landlord	A lessor. One who allows another to occupy his land or building for a consideration.
Lease	Binding contract between a landlord (lessor) and tenant (lessee) for the occupation of premises or land for a specified period of time, and a financial or other consideration.
Leasehold	Property held by lease.
Leaseholder	Tenant under a lease
Lessee	The tenant. One who pays rent.
Lessor	The person granting use of property to another.
Lien	A legal claim affecting property.
Lis pendens	Notice of commencement of court action, recorded against title of property.
Market Value	The courts have defined this as being the highest price estimated in terms of money which a property will bring, if exposed for sale in the open market, allowing a reasonable time to find a purchaser who buys with knowledge of all the uses to which it may be put, and for which it is capable of being used.
Mechanic's Lien	A lien filed and registered against property by a person or corporate body, for labor and/or materials supplied for the improvement of the property.

Moratorium	Provincial statute deferment of mortgage principal payments during depression. Nonexistent now.
Mortgage	Read chapter 14 in this book, "The Mortgage Deed."
Mortgage Bonds	Bond holders are represented by trustee, who is the mortgagee. Bonds can be traded, making them more flexible than individual mortgages.
Mortgaged Out	Situation whereby total mortgage debt on property equals or exceeds market value of property.
Mortgagee	The lender in a mortgage deed. The one receiving the mortgage.
Mortgagor	The borrower in a mortgage deed. The one giving the mortgage.
NHA	National Housing Act.
Option	An agreement whereby one has the exclusive right to purchase another's property at a specified price, with a time limit.
Personalty	Personal property, chattels.
Postponement Clause	In mortgaging, the agreement of an equitable mortgagee to allow the mortgagor to renew or replace a senior mortgage that becomes due before such equitable mortgage.
Power of Attorney	Legal authority for one to act on behalf of another.
Prepayment Clause	In a mortgage, an agreement giving the mortgagor the privilege of paying additional sums off the principal balance over and above the agreed payments.
Principal	A person or corporate body employing an agent.
Principal Balance	In a mortgage, the outstanding dollar amount owing on the debt.

Quit Claim Deed	A full release of one's interest in property to another, usually executed between mortgagees and mortgagors.
Real Estate	Landed property (land).
Real Property	Land and buildings thereon, and rights thereof.
Realtor	Certification mark being the property of the Canadian Real Estate Association. Designates broker-member of Association
Realty	Real Property.
Rest	The date upon which the amount between the parties to a mortgage is altered. It is not necessarily the date upon which payment is made, unless so agreed in the mortgage deed.
Sales Agreement	Purchase of property without obtaining title deed until a specified further sum of money is paid to the vendor.
Socage	A tenure of land held by the tenant in performance of specified services or by payment of rent, and not requiring military service (history).
Straight Loan	In mortgaging, a mortgage with no principal payments. Interest only.
Survey	Surveyor's report of mathematical boundaries of land, showing location of buildings, physical features and quantity of land.
Tenancy in Common	Ownership of real property by two or more persons, whereby on the death of one, his share is credited to his own estate.
Tenant	The one who pays the rent for the right to occupy land or buildings.
Tenant in Tail	Holder of an estate limited to the heirs of his body. The line of heirs is called entail.

Tenement	Property held by tenant.
Tenure	The right of holding property.
Title Deed	Proof of legal ownership of property.
Title Search	Research of records in registry or land titles office to determine history and chain or ownership of property.
Usury	An unconscionable and exorbitant rate of interest.
Zoning	Specified limitation on the use of land, the construction and use of buildings, in a defined section of a municipality.

119

BUILDING DEFINITIONS

Canada Mortgage and Housing Corporation has provided us with a comprehensive list of building terms in construction, including the areas of electricity, heating, plumbing and the roof.

Construction Types

Adobe Construction	A type of construction in which the exterior walls are built of blocks that are made of soil mixed with straw and hardened in the sun.
Block Construction	A type of construction in which the exterior walls are bearing walls made of concrete block or structural clay tile.
Brick Construction	A type of construction in which the exterior walls are bearing walls made of brick or a combination of brick and other unit masonry.
Brick-Veneer Construction	A type of construction in which the wood frame or steel structural frame has an exterior surface of brick applied as cladding.
Dry-Wall Construction	Interior cladding with panels of gypsum board, fibre board, plywood or gypsum plaster, a dry operation as opposed to wet plaster.
Fire Resistive Construction	Floors, walls, roof, etc., constructed of slow-burning or noncombustible materials recognized as such by building codes or local regulations applicable to the type of building proposed.

Monolithic Concrete Construction A type of construction or process in which the concrete for the wall, floor, beams, etc. are poured in one continuous operation.

Plank Frame Construction A type of construction in which the structural framework is composed of solid wood plank uprights and horizontally placed planks laid on edge, with or without sheathing.

Post and Beam Construction A type of construction made with load-bearing posts and beams in which the enclosing walls are designed to support no loads other than their own weight.

Prefabricated Construction A type of construction so designed as to involve a minimum of assembly at the site, usually comprising a series of large wood panels or precast concrete units manufactured in a plant.

Reinforced Concrete Construction A type of construction in which the principal structural members such as floors, columns and beams are made of concrete poured around isolated steel bars or steel meshwork in such a manner that the two materials act together in resisting force.

Skeleton Construction A type of construction in which all external and internal loads and stresses are transmitted to the foundations by a rigidly connected framework of metal or reinforced concrete. The enclosing walls are supported by the frame at designated intervals, usually at each story.

Steel Frame Construction A type of construction in which the structural parts are of steel or dependent on a steel frame for support.

Wood Frame or Frame Construction A type of construction in which the structural parts are wood or dependent upon a wood frame for support. In codes, if brick or other incombustible material is applied to exterior walls, the classification of this type of construction is usually unchanged.

Electrical Terms

Alternating Current	A flow of current which constantly changes direction at a fixed rate.
Ampere	A measure of electric current.
Cable:Armored Cable	Insulated wire having additional flexible metallic protective sheathing — often referred to as BX cable.
Ceiling Outlet	An outlet for ceiling lighting fixtures.
Circuit	Continuous conducting path through which current flows.
Circuit Breaker	An automatic mechanical device which serves the same purpose as a fuse, i.e., to prevent overheating in a circuit through overloading.
Conduit, Electrical	A protective, pipelike covering for electrical wiring.
Convenience Outlet	An outlet into which may be plugged portable equipment such as lamps or electrically operated equipment.
Current	A flow of electricity.
Direct Current	A flow of current constantly in one direction.
Fuse	A device for interrupting an electric circuit under conditions of overloading or short circuiting, comprising an element which fuses at predetermined excess loads so as to open the circuit.
Insulation, Electrical	Nonconducting covering applied to wire or equipment to prevent the flow of current to contiguous materials.
Kilowatt Hour	A unit of measurement of the consumption of electric energy at a fixed rate for 1 hour; specifically, the use of 1,000 watts for 1 hour.

Meter	A device used for measuring the amount of electric energy consumed.
Outlet	A point on an electric circuit designed for the direct connection of lighting fixtures, appliances and equipment.
Panelboard	A center for controlling a number of circuits by means of fuses or circuit breakers, usually contained in a metal cabinet. Switches are sometimes added to control each circuit.
Power Circuit	A circuit transmitting electric energy to a motor or to a heating unit too large to be served by an ordinary circuit.
Radio Outlet	An outlet having connected thereto an aerial and ground for the use of a radio.
Special Purpose Outlet	An outlet used for purposes other than ordinary lighting and power.
Switch	A device to open and close a circuit.
3-Way Switch	A switch designed to operate in conjunction with a similar switch to control one outlet from two points.
Transformer	A device for transforming the voltage characteristics of a current supply.
Voltage	A measure of electric pressure between any two wires of an electric circuit.
Watt	A unit of measurement of electric power.
Wiring: Knob-and-Tube Wiring	A method of exposed wiring using knobs and tubes of nonconducting materials to insulate the wiring from the surfaces on which or through which it is installed.

Heading

Heating

Air Conditioning	The process of bringing air to a required state of temperature and humidity, and removing dust, pollen and other foreign matter.
Baseboard Heaters	A radiator shaped like a regular, decorative baseboard, but having openings at top and bottom through through which air circulates. Provides convected and radiant heat.
Conduction	The transfer or travel of heat through a body by molecular action.
Convector	Having removable front. Air enters through the arched opening near the floor, is heated as it passes through the heating element and enters room through the upper grill.
Hot Water Heating	The circulation of hot water through a system of pipes and radiators either by gravity or a circulating pump.
Indirect Heating	A system of heating by convection.
Panel Heating	Coils or ducts installed in wall, floor, or ceiling panels to provide a large surface of low intensity heat supply.
Panel Radiator	A heating unit placed on or flush with a flat wall surface, and intended to function essentially as a radiator.
Radiant Heating	A heating system in which only the heat radiated from panels is effective in providing the heating requirements.
Radiation	The transfer of heat from a substance by the emission of heat waves.
Radiator	The part of the system, exposed or concealed, from which heat is radiated to a room or other space within the building; heat transferring device.

Space Heating	The methods of heating individual rooms or living units by equipment located entirely within these rooms or living units, such equipment consisting of single unit without ducts, piping, or other mechanical means of heat distribution exterior to the room in which situated.
Steam Heating	The circulation of steam through a system of pipes and radiators by any of the numerous methods employed.
Two-Pipe System	A heating system in which one pipe is used for the supply of the heating medium to the heating unit and another for the return of the heating medium to the source of heat supply. The essential feature of a two-pipe system is that each heating unit receives a direct supply of the heating medium which cannot have served a preceding heating unit.
Warm-Air Heating System	A warm air heating plant consists of a heating unit (fuel-burning furnace) enclosed in a casing, from which the heated air is distributed to various rooms of the building through ducts.
Warm Air Heating System, Forced	A warm air heating system in which circulation of air is effected by a fan. Such a system includes air cleaning devices.
Warm Air Heating System, Gravity	A warm air heating system in which the motive heat producing flow depends on the difference in weight between the heated air leaving the casing and the cooler air entering the bottom of the casing.
Warm Air Heating System, Perimeter	A warm air heating system of the combination panel and convection type. Warm air ducts embedded in the concrete slab of a basementless house, around the perimeter, receive heated air from a furnace and deliver it to the heated space through registers placed in or near the floor. Air is returned to the furnace from registers near the ceiling.

Plumbing Terms

Backflow	The flow of water into a water supply system from any source except its regular one. Back siphonage is one type of backflow.
Building Drainage System	All piping provided for carrying waste water, sewage or other drainage, from the building to the street sewer or place of disposal.
Building (House) Subdrain	That portion of a drainage system which cannot drain by gravity into the building sewer.
Building Main	The water supply pipe, including fittings and accessories, from the water (street) main or other source of supply to the first branch of the water distributing system.
Catch Basin	A small underground structure for surface drainage in which sediment may settle before water reaches the drain lines.
Cesspool	A covered pit with open-jointed linings into which raw sewage is discharged, the liquid portion of which is disposed of by seepage or leaching into the surrounding porous soil, the solids or sludge being retained in the pit.
Downspout	A pipe which carries water from the roof or gutter to the ground or to any part of the drainage system (synonymous with the conductor, leader, rainspout).
Dry Well	A covered pit with open-joined linings through which drainage roofs, basement floors, or areaways may seep or leach into the surrounding porous soil.
Dual Main System of Water Supply	The use of two underground conduits, pipes or lines, each to supply one side of a street.
Main	The principal artery of the system to which branches may be connected.

Plumbing Fixtures Receptacles which receive and discharge water, liquid or water-borne wastes into a drainage system with which they are connected.

Plumbing Stack A general term for the vertical main of a system of soil, waste, or vent piping.

Plumbing System A system of pipes including the water service line and building drainage lines from their several connections within the building to their connections with the public mains or individual water supply and sewage disposal systems, together with fixtures, traps, vents and other devices connected thereto. Storm water drainage pipes may be considered a part of the plumbing system when connected to a public sewage system.

Roughing-In The work of installing all pipes in the drainage and venting systems and all water pipes to the point where connections are made with the plumbing fixtures.

Septic Tank A sewage settling tank intended to retain the sludge in immediate contact with the sewage flowing through the tank, for a sufficient period to secure satisfactory decomposition of organic sludge solids by bacterial action.

Sewage The liquid or water-borne wastes carried away from buildings with or without such ground or surface water as may be present.

Sewer A conduit, usually closed, designed or used for carrying sewage from buildings and/or ground and surface water to sewage disposal plants or to natural bodies of water.

Sewer System A system comprising all sewers (sanitary, storm, and combined), culverts, and subsurface drains needed to conduct sanitary sewage and storm water from a site.

Sewer Types

Building (House) Sewer That part of the horizontal piping of a building drainage system extending from the building drain to the street sewer or other place of disposal (a cesspool, septic tank, or other type of sewage-treatment device or devices) and conveying the drainage of but one building site.

Sanitary Sewer A sewer designed or used only for conveying liquid or water-borne waste from plumbing fixtures.

Storm Sewer A sewer used for conveying rain or subsurface water.

Sewerage The composite parts of a sewer system including conduits, pumping stations, treatment works, and such other works as may be employed in the collection, treatment or disposal of sewage.

Soil Pipe Any pipe which conveys the discharges of water-closets, or fixtures having similar functions, with or without the discharges from other fixtures.

Tile Field The system of open-joint drain tiles laid to distribute septic tank effluent over its absorption area. A tile system laid to provide subsoil drainage for wet areas.

Trap A fitting or device so designed and constructed as to provide a liquid trap seal which will prevent the passage of air through it.

Vent A pipe installed to provide a flow of air to or from a drainage system or to provide a circulation of air within such system to protect trap seals from siphonage and back pressure.

Vent Types

Back Vent A branch vent installed primarily for the purpose of protecting fixture traps from self-siphonage.

Vent Stack A vertical vent pipe installed primarily for the purpose of providing circulation of air to and from any part of the building drainage system.

Water Closet A plumbing fixture consisting of a bowl for the reception of fecal discharge and equipment for flushing the bowl with water. A minor enclosed space in a building equipped with such plumbing fixture.

Water Distribution System All water mains and service lines, outside of building lines (or to a point near the building line), needed for domestic water supply and fire protection.

Water Supply System of a Building All the water service pipes, the water distributing pipes, and the necessary connecting pipes fittings and control valves.

Roof Types

Curb (or Curbed) Roof A roof in which the slope is broken on two or more sides; so called because a horizontal curb is built at the plane where the slope changes.

Deck Roof Having sloping sides below and a flat deck on top.

Flat Roof A roof which is flat or one which is pitched only enough to provide drainage.

Flat-Pitch Roof A roof with only a moderately sloping surface.

Gabled Roof A ridge roof which terminates in a gable.

Gambrel Roof A gable roof each slope of which is broken into two planes.

Hip Roof In general, a roof which has one or more hips. A roof which has four sloping sides that meet at four hips and a ridge.

Lean-To Roof A roof which has a single sloping surface that is supported at the top by a wall that is higher than the roof. A roof which has a single sloping surface.

Mansard Roof A type of curb roof in which the pitch of the upper portion of a sloping side is slight and that of the lower portion steep. The lower portion is usually interrupted by dormer windows.

Monitor Roof A type of gable roof commonly used on industrial buildings, which has a raised portion along the ridge with openings for light and/or air.

Pavilion Roof A roof which in plan forms a figure of more than four straight sides.

Pent Roof A roof, other than a lean-to roof, which has a single sloping surface.

Pitched Roof A roof which has one or more sloping surfaces pitched at angles greater than necessary for drainage.

Polygonal Roof A roof which in plan forms a figure bounded by more than four straight lines.

Pyramid Roof A hip roof which has four sloping surfaces, usually of equal pitch, that meet at a peak.

Ridge Roof A roof which has one or more ridges.

Shed Roof A roof with only one set of rafters, falling from a higher to a lower wall, like an aisle roof.

120

COMPLAINING ABOUT A BAD DEAL

The majority of real estate complaints are related to (1) the purchase of new dwelling units, (2) building additions for existing dwelling units, and (3) repairs to existing dwelling units.

For the unhappy consumer with complaints regarding the foregoing, here are the addresses of provincial government consumer protection bureaus that will give you a sympathetic ear. However, if you write a complaining letter to a government office, remember that the office can only act within statute authority.

Office de la Protection du Consommateur,
Ministère des Consommateurs,
700 est, boul St. -Cyrille, 15e étage
Édifice Place Hauteville, Québec, P.Q.
G1R 5A9

Consumer Bureau,
Dept. of Provincial Secretary,
P.O. Box 6000, Fredericton, N.B.
E3B 5H1

Director, Consumer and Commercial Relations
Dept. of Consumer Affairs,
P.O. Box 998, Halifax, N.S.
B3J 2X3

Consumer Services Division,
Dept. of Provincial Secretary
P.O. Box 2000, Charlottetown, P.E.I.
C1A 7N8

Dept. of Environment and Lands
Confederation Bldg., Box 8700
St. John's, NFLD.
A1B 4J6

Director, Consumer Information Center,
Ministry of Consumer and Commercial Relations,
555 Yonge St., Toronto, ONT.
M7A 2H6

Director, Communications, and Consumer Education
Manitoba Dept. of Consumer Affairs,
1025-405 Broadway Ave.
Winnipeg, MAN.
R3C 3L8

Director, Consumer Affairs Resource Center,
Dept. of Consumer Affairs,
11th Floor, SPC Building
2025 Victoria, Ave., Regina, SASK.
S4P 0R9

Director, Resource Center
Alberta Dept. of Consumer and Corporate Affairs
10025 Jasper Avenue
10th Floor, Edmonton, ALTA
T5J 3Z5

Director, Consumer Resource Centre,
Ministry of Consumer and Corporate Affairs,
838 Fort Street, Victoria, B.C.
V8W 1H8

Complaints against a real estate agent can often be satisfied by confronting the agent and/or his employer. Nobody wants any flak in his business, so start here.

If this route fails, take the matter to your local real estate board, if the offending agent is a member. Real estate boards are very conscious of the ethical responsibility of their members, and tolerate no nonsense.

If the agent is not a member of a real estate board, or if he is, and you are not happy about the result of your complaint, here are the addresses of provincial government officials responsible for the licensing of agents. Your complaint will be handled with dispatch.

Superintendent,
Service du Courtage Immobilier du Quebéc,
Ministère des Consommateurs Coopératives
et Insitutions Financières,
Hôtel du Gouvernement, Québec, P.Q.

Corporate Services Office,
Dept. of the Provincial Secretary,
P.O. Box 6000, Fredericton, N.B.
E3B 5H1

Director, Consumer Services Bureau,
Dept. of Consumer Affairs,
P.O. Box 998, Halifax, N.S.
B3J 2X3

Director, Division of Consumer Services,
Dept. of Provincial Secretary,
P.O. Box 2000, Charlottetown, P.E.I.
C1A 7N8

Superintendent of Real Estate
Dept. of Environment and Lands
P.O. Box 999, St. John's, NFLD.

Registrar, Business Practices Division
Ministry of Consumer and Commercial Relations,
555 Yonge Street, Toronto, ONT.
M7A 2H6

Registrar, Real Estate Brokers Act,
Manitoba Securities Commission,
1128-405 Broadway Ave., Winnipeg, MAN.
R3C 3L8

Director, Licensing and Investigations,
Dept. of Provincial Secretary,
Room 308, Towne Square, 1919 Rose St.
Regina, SASK.
S4S 0B3

Deputy Superintendent of Real Estate,
Consumer and Corporate Affairs,
9th Floor, Capitol Square
10025 Jasper Av. Edmonton, ALTA
T5J 3Z5

Director, Real Estate Council of B.C.
Ste. 900 — 750 West Pender Street,
Vancouver, B.C.
V6C 2T8

121

BITS AND PIECES

Why are there 640 acres to a section? And why is a square mile a section?

An Order-in-Council dated September 23, 1869, containing instructions to a Colonel Denis for the survey of townships in the west, states that the townships "were to consist of 64 squares of 800 acres each".

This standard of measurement was altered by virtue of Order-in-Council 874 dated April 25, 1871, which stated that henceforth, "Townships shall consist of 36 sections of one square mile each."

The Statutes of Canada, 1872, Chapter XXIII entitled *An Act Respecting the Public Lands of the Dominion* Section 15, states that in legal descriptions of land, "either a section or 640 acres may be used."

All sections, however, are not 640 acres. In Ontario, for example, sections also consisted of 1,000, 1,800 and 2,400 acres.

Much of the original surveying in Canada was done with the aid of "Gunter's Chain." This chain, so named after its inventor, Edmund Gunter (early 17th century), was generally used by the land surveyors. It is 66 feet in length, containing 100 links each measuring 7.92 inches. It was very convenient when required to calculate areas in acres and decimals of an acre, since 10 square chains equal 1 acre; also when linear dimensions were required in miles and furlongs, since 10 chains equal 1 furlong, and 80 chains equal 1 mile.

The chain was a faulty instrument that suffered greatly in accuracy in use, since there were 198 points of wear in its links, the wearing of which lengthened the instrument. However, it was the only efficient long measuring instrument until technology made possible the manufacture of the steel tape, and later the invar tape. All of these have been supplemented by electronic measuring instruments.

Looked at any fences lately?

There are provincial statutes regulating the responsibility of maintenance and repair of fences marking the boundary between owners of adjoining lands.

For example, The *Line Fences Act* of Ontario applies "mutatis mutandis" to unoccupied land as well as to occupied land in any township in a county or district if the council of the township passes a by-law declaring that the Act so applies, and provides that:

a) The owners of adjoining occupied lands shall make, keep up and repair a just proportion of the fence that marks the boundary between them, or, if there is no fence, they shall make and keep up and repair the same proportion of a fence to mark such boundary.
b) Owners of unoccupied land that adjoins occupied land, upon the unoccupied land becoming occupied, are liable to keep up and repair such proportion, and in that respect are in the same position as if their land had been occupied at the time of the original fencing.

Where an owner of land desires fence-viewers to view and arbitrate as to what portion of such fence each owner shall make, keep up and repair, or as to the condition of an existing line fence and as to repairs being done to it:

a) Either owner may notify the other that he will cause three fence-viewers of the locality to arbitrate in the premises.
b) The notices shall be in writing, and shall specify the time and place of meeting for the arbitration.
c) An owner notified may object to any or all of the fence-viewers notified, and in such case, a judge shall name the fence-viewers.

It is a very serious business. If, for example, an occupant who is not the owner of the property in question receives such notice of naming fence-viewers for arbitration and does not immediately notify the owner of the land, he shall be liable for all damages caused the owner.

The Act even tells about the responsibility of a tree falling across another's property. The owner of the land upon which the tree stood is responsible for making good any damage caused.

If such tree owner neglects or refuses to remove the tree within 48 hours after notice in writing to do so, one may remove the tree, fix the fence, keep the remains of the tree for remuneration, and recover any further amount of damages beyond the value of the tree from the person liable to pay it.

Write Canada Communications Group, Publishing, in your province and obtain a copy of the fence-viewers act. It makes interesting reading.

Interested in highways? The King's Highway, Controlled-Access Highway, Secondary Highway, Tertiary Road, Resources Road, Industrial Road, Development Road, Forces or Trespass Road, Quarter Sessions Road, Statute Labour Road, Provincial-Federal Resources Road, Mining Access Road, Connecting Link Road, Colonization Road, Streets on Subdivision Plans, Municipal By-Law Road, Road Allowances and 5 percent Reservation for Roads.

If you want to know what they all mean, writing to your provincial department of highways for definitions. And while you're at it, ask for a free road map.

A few centuries ago, an acre was considered to be the amount of land a man with a yoke of oxen could plow in a day.

The *British Weights and Measures Act* of 1878 defined it as containing 4,840 square yards (43,560 s.f.) and this "statute" acre was adopted by Canada and the United States. However, it is interesting to note that Scotland, Ireland, Wales and some English counties disagreed with it, and older land measurements of the acre are still to be found in these areas, and used.

The English, Canadian and U.S. statute acres don't mean a thing in the rest of the world, as evidenced by the following land area measurements in a few examples:

Country	*Unit*	*Size in Statute Acre*
Argentina	Manzana	2.47 acres
Austria	Joch	1.42 acres
Belgium	Hectare	2.47 acres
Brazil	Cuarta	0.92 acres
Cyprus	Donum	0.33 acres
Denmark	Tonder land	1.36 acres
Egypt	Feddan	1.04 acres
Ireland	Acre	1.62 acres
Russia	Dessiatine	2.70 acres
Scotland	Acre	1.27 acres
Wales	Erw	0.89 acres
Wales	Stang	0.67 acres

It has often been claimed that the esplanade of Edinburgh Castle in Scotland is a part of Nova Scotia, but what happened is this:

The institution of the degree of Baronet of Scotland, contemplated by King James, was carried out by his successor Charles I, the object being to aid Sir William Alexander's scheme for the colonization of Nova Scotia (New Scotland).

Sir William was granted a Signature under the Great Seal for a charter of the lands lying between New England and Newfoundland for a furthering of his proposed Plantation on 10 September, 1621. With respect to the Order of Knights Baronets of Nova Scotia, all of Nova Scotia was for the one purpose of seisin (the act of taking possession) incorporated in the Kingdom of Scotland; apparently the earth and stone required for the ancient feudal ceremony could have been taken from any part of the Kingdom. It was taken from Castlehill because Edinburgh was the capital and the castle the most eminent place in the Kingdom.

Some years ago the Province of Nova Scotia affixed a plaque to Edinburgh Castle to commemorate the historic connection between Old Scotland and New Scotland.

Andrew Carnegie said that "ninety percent of all millionaires became so through owning real estate. More money has been made in real estate than in all industrial investments combined. The wise young man or wage earner of today invests his money in real estate."

You know, I think he's right. Go get yourself some real estate.

So you think a perch is a fish? Not in this book. A perch is a rod, 16 1/2 feet, which was the length of the pole that was used to prod oxen. It is 1/4 of a chain, and a chain is 66 feet; 80 chains to a mile. One square chain is one tenth of an acre. It's enough to drive you up the wall.

What is meant by a bank's "prime lending rate" and who qualifies for it?

To determine this, the following question was put to Canadian bank presidents, with the resulting answer:

Question: "I have never been quite clear as to the meaning of 'best customer' where it relates to the bank's prime lending rate of interest.

"For example, it would be reasonable to assume that a best customer would be the Federal Government of Canada. *National Housing Act* mortgages are guaranteed by the Federal Government. If a borrower asked for a current, prime rate loan with the Federal Government as co-signer, what would the bank's attitude be?"

Answer: "Generally speaking, the bank minimum lending rate is accorded to national concerns of undoubted credit standing where the degree of servicing is minimal and where the loan can be clearly identified as a current operating loan. A current or operating loan is usually considered to be one which is subject to annual renewal, which liquidates at periodic intervals and is accompanied by sufficient credit balances at least to provide for the cost in respect to the chequing and other activity in the account.

"To the extent that a loan guaranteed by the Federal Government were to comply with these standards, that loan would normally be accorded at a rate no higher than the minimum lending rate. However, in the case of *National Housing Act* mortgages, these in no sense could be regarded as current loans. By definition, they are a type of long-term loan and are subject to the interest rates in the marketplace for this type of loan. The banks are merely one of the institutional sources of mortgage funds and can never be too far out of line with the rates prevailing in the market place." End of quote.

Bank managers, take note.

Why are 99-year leases so common? Why not 89, or 104?

As early as the 16th century (in England), leases were commonly found to be of 21, 40, 90 and even 500 years! The British *Settled Land Act* (1925), allowed building leases to extend for 999 years.

Research has shown that the 99-year lease originated many years ago when the term was often for three lives, the lessee, his wife, and son. It was considered that 99 years was a long enough period to cover the likely expectation of life of the parties concerned.

Read your property listing agreement carefully. One broker had "inside information" that a highway was to be widened. He sent agents out to list as many properties as possible along the route, the listing price apparently being unimportant.

Why? Because the agreement signed by property owners stipulated that in the event of expropriation, the owner was to pay the broker a commission based on the expropriated price.

As an old smoothie once said, "Keep your powder dry!"

Write to the Department of National Revenue, Ottawa, and ask to have your name placed on its mailing list for future copies of the "Interpretation Bulletins." Fascinating reading, and once in a while good stuff about real estate.

It appears to be an actuarial fact that over a period of any 20 years, 16 mortgagors (borrowers) in 100 will not live to complete the mortgage payments. The homeowner naturally would like to ensure that if the breadwinner is gone, his family will be left with a debt-free roof over its head.

Life insurance companies are ready to oblige, by providing term insurance (the cheapest life insurance one can buy) to cover the outstanding dollar balance owing on the mortgages. As the principal balance owing is reduced, the insurance coverage is reduced, the object being to have them both go down to a nil balance together.

Think about it, and do your best to fit its cost into your budget.

For a mortgage lender, title insurance is added protection to insure against loss that may be suffered because of concealed title defects that cannot possibly be discovered by lawyers who examine the titles for real estate loans, such as:

- Forged deed, releases, and so forth, in the chains of title to the properties on which money is loaned.
- False impersonations of former owners of the land.
- Instruments executed under fabricated or expired power of attorney.
- Undisclosed or missing heirs.
- Deeds not legally delivered in the lifetime of the grantor.
- Wills not probated.
- Deeds by minors or persons of unsound mind.
- Deeds by persons supposedly single, but secretly married.
- Marital rights of spouse supposedly, but not legally, divorced.
- Birth or adoption of children after date of will.
- Falsification of title records.

Title insurance is a definite insurance contract indemnifying the mortgagee, according to its terms, against financial or damage due to title defects.

123

THE LAST WORD

Years ago a man purchased the first edition of this book. He studied it, got interested in the subject, and got involved.

Today that man's *equity* in his real estate holdings is worth nearly $1 million. And that's a fact. An outstanding example of what one man did.

On the dust jacket of that first edition my advice was to get into the country and buy one hundred acres of land for one's future financial well-being. Well, we all know what happened to the price of 100 acres of land. Oops, I mean 40.469 hectares.

In 1969 I provided a chart for some university students on the cost of real estate. The chart started at the lower left-hand corner at 1939 and went up to the upper right-hand corner to 1969. All the way up there was a wavy line, dipping and climbing, but mostly climbing. And how it climbed.

I advised the students to make their own chart, with 1969 at the lower left-hand corner, and 1999 in the upper right.

That chart is still climbing. A bit wavy at times, but climbing, and I can't see any reason in the foreseeable future for it to stop climbing.

My last word is like my first word:

GET INVOLVED
BUY SOME REAL ESTATE

Don't dream. Don't procrastinate. Get a piece of the action — even a little piece. And for the 80,000 or so real estate agents in Canada who spend most of their time creating financial real estate success for others, while living on hopeful commissions, I have this piece of advice:

If you want to make it over the long haul, you'll seldom do it on your commissions. You must get involved.

As we all know, the federal government has provided a very generous pension plan that is tied to the cost of living. It must surely be the world's great pension.

Well, in the likely event that you will not retire on a federal government pension, what are you doing about your old age? The young generally don't like to think about 30 or so years ahead, it's just too far off. But with good health it will come just as surely as death and taxes.

Here is my suggestion: After you buy your house, go into the country, find a nice piece of concession-corner land you can buy with about $3,000 down, mortgage the balance for what you can carry without hurting yourself too much (which will dictate the purchase price) and then . . .

Forget it until you are 55 or so. Sell it, and live off the interest. That's your assured pension.

Don't think for one minute that land in this world is going to get cheaper. It won't. Not because I say so, but because of what the late Will Rogers reminds us all — "Buy land, they're not making any more of it."

If you follow this advice, and a couple of years later someone offers you double your equity, *don't sell*. Resist the temptation to take the profit and buy that new car or take that vacation. This is *your pension* that buyer is tampering with!

Go on, get a little piece of land. Enjoy it. Grow some vegetables on your pension. Rent it to a farmer. Stand on it and look around, you're a landowner!

Hang on to your pension.

The foregoing piece of advice may not go down too well with some economists, but what I am attempting to do here is have you take some of that money you will be pouring down your drains of frivolity and bury it in land.

My happy childhood was spent in a place called Westboro, now a part of Ottawa. Right across the road was a chicken farm. A big one. When the wind blew the wrong way on a hot day, we all knew it was one big chicken farm.

The old lady who owned the chicken farm didn't know it, but one day a man would come along and give her a big pile of money for that little spread and replace it with a street full of houses.

I bet she cackled all the way to the bank.

But you don't have to own a chicken farm to make money in real estate.

In the 1960s, we could buy a house in downtown Toronto for about $17,000. A thousand down and one mortgage for the balance.

The first buyer to come along and show us a $500 clear profit got the property and we thought we were pretty sharp operators.

History now says these buyers were the big winners — the wise ones — and we were the dummies. Shoulda known better.

One of the buyers ended up owning no less than 42 houses in Toronto this way.

I sold a beautiful 100-acre farm for $14,000. The buyer sold the old barn for $4,500 to a dealer who doubled his money selling the old boards to the builders, who in turn made a mint using it decorating recreation rooms.

The one I regret the most was selling 97 acres of bush near Peterborough, Ontario, on a paved road, for $3,000. What's a cord of firewood worth today?

Real estate agents are often so close to the forest they can't see the trees, as the saying goes. Don't you be as dumb as we were. You hang on to your real estate, even if it hurts.